HARVARD EAST ASIAN SERIES 20

China's Wartime Finance and Inflation, 1937-1945

The East Asian Research Center at Harvard University administers research projects designed to further scholarly understanding of China, Korea, Japan, and adjacent areas.

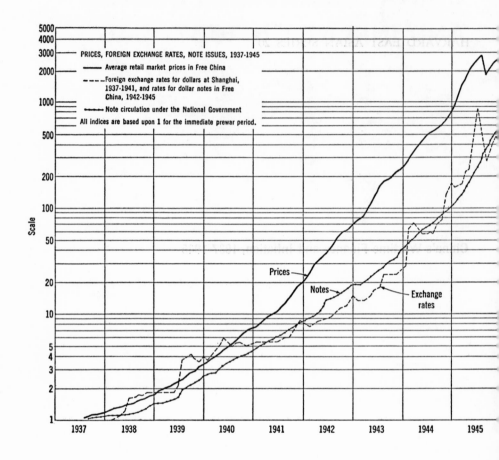

PRICES, FOREIGN EXCHANGE RATES, NOTE ISSUES, 1937-1945
—— Average retail market prices in Free China
– – –Foreign exchange rates for dollars at Shanghai, 1937-1941, and rates for dollar notes in Free China, 1942-1945
•–•–•Note circulation under the National Government
All indices are based upon 1 for the immediate prewar period.

Prices

Notes

Exchange rates

Scale

CHINA'S WARTIME FINANCE
AND INFLATION, 1937-1945

ARTHUR N. YOUNG   Financial Adviser to China, 1929-1947

HARVARD UNIVERSITY PRESS

Cambridge, Massachusetts | 1965

FOREWORD

China's finances have long puzzled experts as well as laymen, and reliable and comprehensive data have been meager and not easily available. Yet, from the Revolution of 1911 to the fall of the National Government on the mainland in 1949, the state of the finances profoundly influenced the course of events.

Mr. Young here describes, analyzes, and appraises China's financial experience in the war period, 1937–1945 — the time when China's fate for the following decades was being so largely determined. Of special importance is his treatment of the accelerating inflation, the policies followed, and the consequences. The data he presents have the merit of having been preserved by him from the flow of daily governmental business in which he was involved, and he uses them with the consent of the National Government. They thus represent materials upon which action had to be based. His account of the financial problems and how the government dealt with them is a unique inside study.

Mr. Young is one of the long line of Western administrators and specialists who have helped China's modernization. When Japan's invasion hit China in 1937 he had already spent eight years in China's service as Financial Adviser. His preparation was by no means confined to China: he held a doctorate in economics from Princeton and a law degree from George Washington University, and had been a financial adviser in Mexico and Honduras and, from 1922 to 1928, the Economic Adviser to the Department of State in Washington.

This volume is a companion to Mr. Young's recently published account of wartime aid, *China and the Helping Hand, 1937–1945*, published by Harvard University Press in 1963.

East Asian Research Center
Harvard University

PREFACE

This book deals with China's revenue and expenditure, internal borrowing, foreign financial aid, and currency management and inflation during the war years, 1937–1945.

China and the Helping Hand, 1937–1945, published by Harvard University Press in 1963, centers attention upon what China did for herself and what other countries did for China in that period; it also deals with what China and other countries did not do. That book necessarily contains much material on financial affairs. This one, however, centers attention upon the financial record. For the sake of completeness, a certain amount of duplication in treating here a number of subjects with which the other book deals is unavoidable. Chapter XIX, on gold, which is similar to a statement presented to a Senate subcommittee in 1956 in connection with my testimony, is practically the same as chapter XVII of *China and the Helping Hand*. Elsewhere, however, topics that are discussed in both books are treated more extensively in the more pertinent volume. Obviously it is not appropriate to include here a full treatment of the internal, international, and military events which provided the setting in which China conducted her wartime financial affairs. For such an account, I refer the reader to the other volume.

In this book the main reliance is upon the contemporary material which I collected as Financial Adviser. The Chinese government has consented to my use of this material, some of which, because of the loss of many official records during and after the war, is more complete than what exists elsewhere. The statistics herein cited and the statements made, unless otherwise indicated, are mostly derived from the papers which I collected during my service for China. Looking back, I could have collected more data then current, and thus avoided occasional gaps that now appear in the factual record. But it was a period of war, and my primary responsibility related to operations rather than research. In presenting the fiscal data, I have also made use of the *Public Finance Yearbook*, issued in 1948 by the Finance Ministry of China. Use of the statistical data of governmental operations presents at times some problems. In 1937 the fiscal and statistical organs of China were improving, but many of the personnel lacked training and experience. After the fighting began, full and accurate records could hardly be kept, with enemy forces overrunning much of China, bombing heavily behind the lines, and disrupting the government administration. Many Chinese statisticians and accountants worked loyally and well under enormously hard conditions. But they could not overcome the difficulties caused by wartime confusion and the imperfections of some original data. The data herein presented are in my opinion the best available, and I point out the qualifications *passim*. Because of reworking the statistical materials for this volume some figures differ from those in *China and the Helping Hand, 1937–1945*, but the differences are not of substantial importance.*

Also I have had access to a considerable part of the Morgenthau Diaries, in the records of the Internal Security Subcommittee of the Senate Judiciary Committee, which made them available to me without restriction when I testified before them in 1956. That material seems to cover the most important part of the American Treasury's dealings with China in 1940–1945. I could not gain access to the rest of these Diaries relating to the war period, because they are closed except to Mr. Morgenthau or his agent until after 1965.† Meanwhile, after this book was in type, the Subcommittee published lengthy extracts from the Diaries relating mostly to China, and in particular to the activities of Harry Dexter White of the Treasury.‡ These extracts contain a word-by-word record of conferences in which Mr. Morgenthau participated, together with many documents. The extracts include much of the material which I saw in the Subcommittee files, and more. The additional material amplifies but does not substantially add to or alter what I say in this book. With my book in type it was not feasible to insert references to these extracts. Since they are presented in the sequence of Mr. Morgenthau's "books," numbered from 189 to 863 (although not a complete series), a reader who so desires may find in this publication most of my references and certain additional material without undue trouble.

Besides use of the material from the Morgenthau Diaries, I was given access to the unpublished records of the Department of State covering the war period. I have used also pertinent published official and private materials, and have talked with many participants, Chinese, Americans, and Japanese.

Two studies centering upon China's inflation during and after the war have recently been published. These are Kia-ngau Chang's *The Inflationary Spiral: the Experience of China, 1939–1950* (New York, 1958); and Shun-hsin Chou's *The Chinese Inflation, 1937–1950* (New York, 1963), which latter appeared after my manuscript was substantially ready for publication. Dr. Chang, besides serving as Minister of Communications

---

* Figures in tables throughout this volume may not add to totals because of rounding. A billion is here used to mean 1,000 million.

† The Diaries are to be made available to qualified scholars 25 years after the close of successive Roosevelt terms. See J. M. Blum, *From the Morgenthau Diaries: Years of Crisis, 1928–1938* (Boston, 1959), p. x.

‡ Subcommittee to Investigate the Administration of the Internal Security Act and Other Internal Security Laws, of the Committee on the Judiciary, United States Senate, 89th Congress, 1st Session: *Morgenthau Diaries (China)*, two volumes, 1,699 pages, February 5, 1965. Foreword by Anthony Kubek.

during the war, was head of the Bank of China for many years before the war, and in 1947–1948 was Governor of the Central Bank of China. Dr. Chou was a staff member of the Central Bank in the postwar period. The general conclusions of both writers as to the nature and causes of the wartime inflation substantially agree with mine.

I have tried not to duplicate in any avoidable and material way these scholarly works. First, this volume deals only with the war period. Also, relying in part upon data not generally available, it sets forth in greater detail the main fiscal and monetary statistics, analyzing significant differences when they exist between these data and other presentations. Further, it describes and discusses from the inside viewpoint of a day-to-day participant the problems as they developed, the pressures felt by the responsible officers, the alternatives available, the factors influencing decisions, and the course of fiscal and monetary policy. There is advantage in having the feel of events while they are happening, but at the same time there is the problem of being objective. Whether I have succeeded in being fair in statements and judgments will be for the reader to say.

For permission to quote from publications, I am grateful to the following: The M.I.T. Press and John Wiley & Sons, Inc., joint publishers of Kia-ngau Chang's aforementioned book, copyrighted by the Massachusetts Institute of Technology; Union Research Institute, Hong Kong, Cho-yuan Cheng, *Monetary Affairs of Communist China;* and George E. Taylor, *The Struggle for North China.*

For critically reading parts of the manuscript I am indebted also to J. Lossing Buck, formerly of the University of Nanking; to J. B. Condliffe and Choh-ming Li of the University of California at Berkeley; to Owen L. Dawson, formerly Agricultural Attaché of the American Embassy in China; to Stanley K. Hornbeck, formerly Director of the Office of Far Eastern Affairs and Political Adviser to the Secretary of State; to L. K. Little, formerly Inspector General of the Chinese Customs; to Oliver C. Lockhart, formerly Financial Adviser and Associate Director of the Salt Revenue Administration of China; and to Tsuyee Pei, formerly of the Bank of China and Governor of the Central Bank of China. For help in a number of ways I am indebted to Kia-ngau Chang, former Minister of Railways and Minister of Communications; to R. W. French of the Export-Import Bank; to E. Kann, veteran authority on Chinese finance; to Y. C. Koo, formerly Vice-Minister of Finance of China; to P. K. Mok of Occidental College; and to Mrs. P. K. Mok, Librarian of Orientalia of the University of California at Los Angeles. G. Bernard Noble, Chief of the Historical Division, Department of State, and E. Taylor Parks of that office aided me with the use of American governmental materials. The staff of the Subcommittee to Investigate the Administration of the Internal Security Act, of the Senate Committee on the Judiciary, aided me with access to parts of the Morgenthau

Diaries. My sister, Sarah Adele Young, carefully prepared the manuscript. My wife, Nellie May Young, provided throughout invaluable help and encouragement.

My special thanks go to John K. Fairbank of Harvard University for wise counsel on many matters. I am grateful to the University's East Asian Research Center, of which he is the Director, for sponsoring this volume, for bearing some of the costs relating to its preparation and issuance, and for help in putting the manuscript in form for publication. Also I am grateful to the John Simon Guggenheim Memorial Foundation for aiding the work with a fellowship and grant. Finally, I appreciate the help of the staff of Harvard University Press, and their anonymous reader, in advising on the presentation of a complicated subject, and on the division of material between this book and *China and the Helping Hand, 1937–1945*.

For the work as it stands, and for any errors or omissions, those who have helped me are of course in no way responsible.

Arthur N. Young

Pasadena, California
1965

CONTENTS

TABLES

INTRODUCTON. THE PREWAR SITUATION

I. THE PREWAR SITUATION

The outbreak of Sino-Japanese hostilities on July 7, 1937, set the stage for financial events that fundamentally affected China's future. The ensuing disruption and inflation proceeded inexorably and made difficult a recovery from over eight years of bitter warfare.

Attention to the transformed situation since the communist regime took over Mainland China in 1949 has interfered with recognition of the transformation wrought by the National Government between the time of its take-over in 1928 and Japan's attack in mid-1937. In 1928 internal conditions were chaotic. There was no real central authority, and civil war and banditry were rife. Railways were disrupted, and roads and airways hardly existed. The currency was a complicated mixture of silver coins and weights, fluctuating copper coins, and paper money, all varying from place to place. Medieval fiscal practices ruled, except for the foreign-run customs and salt tax services. The debt was mostly in default. The older republican governments were caught in a vicious circle. They could not gain strength or make reforms because of lack of funds. But because of lack of authority they could not install an adequate revenue system.

In 1929–1934 the National Government, under the leadership of Chiang Kai-shek, put down the chief ambitious warlords, and drove the communists from their stronghold in the Yangtze Valley to the far northwest, where they remained a distant and perhaps a diminishing threat. By 1937 China internally was at peace. The government's strength was steadily growing, and Chiang's prestige was high. Yet political generals still controlled many troops, China was strongly regional, and in parts of the country central influence depended upon subsidies, political favors, coaxing, and appeals.

In 1931–1932 Japan seized China's northeastern provinces, commonly known as Manchuria, and set up the puppet regime of "Manchukuo." This began what was in effect a 14-year war with Japan — intermittent at first, and full-scale after mid-1937. The loss of Manchuria deprived China of fertile lands, which provided important exports of soy beans and other agricultural items. The loss also cut off China from rich mineral and hydroelectric resources and a major site of heavy industry. Japan followed by making serious encroachments in North China, whose end no one could foresee. One of these was creation of a puppet regime in East Hopei, north of Peiping, which became a paradise for smugglers of merchandise and pedlars of drugs, and an exit point for smuggling out silver. While these

aggressions caused serious internal problems for China, they also strengthened nationalism and caused the people to look increasingly to the National
Government as the center of authority. More and more the people felt that
civil wars should end in view of the external threat.

Over a century of Sino-foreign conflict had left a legacy of special foreign
rights in and adjoining China. A long Russo-Japanese rivalry over Manchuria had resulted in Japan's ascendancy there, consolidated by the seizure
of the area in 1931. Hong Kong was British, together with the adjacent
Leased Territory of Kowloon. Portugal held Macao, south of Hong Kong.
In several ports there were areas ruled internationally or by foreign governments. Those which were specially important for the finances were the
International Settlement and French Concession at Shanghai, and the
French and British Concessions at Tientsin. On the one hand, China's lack
of jurisdiction in these areas meant that Japan had more or less to respect
them, while seizing adjacent Chinese territory. Thus, the Central Bank
could remain in Shanghai and continue its functions of currency support,
aided by the other government banks, namely, the Bank of China, the
Bank of Communications, and the Farmers Bank. Also, in North China,
the Bank of China and the Bank of Communications stayed at Tientsin
in the French Concession, and maintained the currency in that important
region. Besides, Hong Kong served as an important economic and financial
base for China. This situation persisted until Japan began the Pacific War
on December 7/8, 1941.

On the other hand, China had no authority to control what went on in
these areas, since the laws and regulations enforced there were set by
non-Chinese governing bodies. The areas afforded loopholes for avoiding
Chinese governmental measures. Chinese nationalism understandably had
long been displeased by existence of these foreign-ruled areas. But, on
balance, their existence was definitely advantageous to China during the
fighting prior to the Pacific War.

Foreigners had long enjoyed in China rights of extraterritoriality (extrality), whereby they were subject not to Chinese courts but to courts of
their own nationality. This arrangement was originally desired by China,
because of the peculiar laws and customs of the "barbarians." But the old
agreements came to be regarded as "unequal treaties," and these were
generally ended in the latter part of the war.

The National Government, upon assuming power in 1928, carried out a
program of major financial reforms, without which it could not have
survived for long. In these measures the leaders were T. V. Soong in
1928–1933, and H. H. Kung in 1933–1937, as Ministers of Finance. The
government developed solid revenues. China's recovery of tariff autonomy
led to a big increase in customs receipts. A reformed internal revenue
system taxing salt, tobacco, cotton yarn, and other goods yielded growing

returns. Total nonborrowed receipts in the last prewar fiscal year ending June 30, 1937, were C$870 million, over two-and-one-half times as great as in 1928–1929 (prices meanwhile rose about 10 per cent). *Likin*, an old tax on internal movement of goods, was gradually suppressed. But failure to reform the land tax, in a nation four-fifths agricultural, prevented development of what could have been a major revenue.

In expenditures, however, the record was not as good. A series of civil wars, to put down ambitious warlords and the communists, was necessary for the government's survival. And from the fall of 1931, when Japan invaded Manchuria, it was necessary to arm for defense. The military authorities had the biggest say in the government and a first call upon funds. Many such expenditures were subject to but little control.

Mainly because of heavy military outlay, deficits mounted. The government, nevertheless, was able to avoid paper money excesses. By pledging future revenue, albeit on rather onerous terms, it financed the deficits by borrowing large sums at Shanghai. Without this borrowing, the government could not have stayed in power and pushed its program of unification and resistance to Japanese pressure. Partly offsetting the deficits were payments to retire older debt. In the prewar years these payments totaled well over half the amount of deficit.

In mid-1937 stabilization of the finances was within reach, on the basis of a budget around C$1 billion (US$300 million). The prospective yearly rate of revenue yield was then around C$425 million for customs, C$250 million for salt revenue, C$150 million for consolidated excise taxes, and C$125 million for miscellaneous revenues — a total of around C$950 million. With rapid economic progress and improved internal order, there was a good prospect that revenues would continue to grow. The system of budgets and accounts was improving, and for the first time the government issued fairly full and accurate financial reports. There was progress in public administration. Yet age-old official "squeeze," nepotism, and multiplication of unneeded staff persisted all too often. There was growing respect for the central authority, but regionalism remained a serious problem for the government.

The currency reform of November 1935 succeeded beyond expectation, and was a major strengthening factor. In 1933–1935 the American silver-buying policy, with callous disregard for China's repeated protests, drained away huge amounts of China's silver reserves. It raised China's silver dollar to a high and overvalued level, and brought about a severe deflation, credit contraction, and slump. It forced China to give up her historic silver standard. China then adopted a managed currency, not linked either to the dollar or to sterling (which then was fluctuating). The currency under the new system was commonly known as *fapi*, meaning legal tender notes. The unit, often called the dollar or *yuan*, was variously designated as $, Mex.

(Mexican)\$, CNC\$, NC\$, or C\$. Here the latter symbol is used, and American dollars are designated as US\$.

For the first time in history, China's money had a value stable in foreign exchange, as the Central Bank of China maintained rates at about US\$0.30 and 14½ pence. There was a free market, with no control of exchange or trade. After the reform, the American silver policy at last became helpful to China, as Treasury Secretary Henry Morgenthau, Jr., began purchase of silver from the Central Bank, thus converting it to readily usable dollars and gold. These purchases amounted to US\$66 million by mid-1937. Aided by this addition to reserves abroad, the Central Bank made speculation against China's currency a costly operation for the speculators. The new Shanghai Mint worked on a 24-hour schedule to make subsidiary nickel and copper coins, which were in great demand to replace the old heterogeneous silver, copper, and paper money of uncertain value.

Maintenance of stable exchange at an economic level brought about a favorable balance of payments. With confidence in the currency restored, much capital that had fled during the previous hectic years now returned to China. Exports increased. Total holdings of gold, silver, and foreign currencies as of June 30, 1937, reached US\$379 million. These holdings were about 67 per cent of China's total note issue, estimated at C\$1,897 million, equivalent to about US\$565 million. The holdings, however, included silver equivalent to about US\$168 million. This silver was unsold, and an attempt to realize rapidly upon it would have broken the market. Moreover, most of the silver was at Shanghai, where it was vulnerable to enemy attack.

The Central Bank of China, established in 1928, was first mainly a fiscal agent for the government. But it was steadily taking on more and more functions of regulating the currency, and was growing in prestige at home and abroad. In mid-1937 it held a major part of the US\$211 million of holdings of gold and foreign currencies. Early in July 1937 the government approved a plan to convert that bank into a Central Reserve Bank. But action was prevented by Japan's attack.

The increased confidence created by the monetary reform, together with the favorable balance of payments, cleared the way for settlement of most of the defaulted debts of the old Peking regimes. In 1928 the government resumed service on some of these debts. By mid-1937 it had settled about US\$250 million of debts in arrears. Leading foreign currency issues then sold abroad on about a 5 per cent basis, and at higher prices than comparable Japanese bonds. Internal bonds were traded at Shanghai in mid-1937 on about an 8 per cent basis, compared with yields of 12 to 15 per cent in the earlier 1930's.

China's financial reforms in this period were an impressive example of self-help. The only foreign governmental credits totaled about US$26 million (utilized) from the United States: the Flood Relief Loan of 1931 of about US$9 million, and the Cotton and Wheat Loan of 1933 of about US$17 million.[1]

China had long had important technical help in revenue collection. The Sino-foreign Customs Service, which dated from 1854, assured effective collection of revenue which served as security for the chief foreign loans. Also that service helped to maintain an open door for trade. The Sino-foreign Salt Revenue Service, established in 1913, aided in collection of salt revenue pledged for a number of loans. China also had considerable help from foreign advisers. In 1928 China engaged the Commission of Financial Advisers, headed by Professor E. W. Kemmerer, for a year's service. Most of the fruits of this move were realized through the work of members who remained for varying periods. These included Oliver C. Lockhart, Financial Adviser with special reference to taxation, and who became Associate Chief Inspector of Salt Revenue in 1935; Fenimore B. Lynch, Adviser to the Central Bank of China; and the writer as Financial Adviser with special reference to currency and public credit.[2] J. F. Freeman served as accountant in the Central Bank. For aid in minting, China engaged Clifford Hewitt, formerly of the American minting service, who was succeeded in 1933 by Robert J. Grant, former Director of the Mint of the United States. Also China received advice from European experts. In 1931 and again in 1933–1934 Sir Arthur Salter of the League of Nations visited China to advise on economic and financial matters, and was followed by a number of technical experts in 1933–1934. In 1934 Jean Monnet visited China, with special reference to economic development. In 1935 an international mission to help China with her finances was discussed. But the only representative to come was Sir Frederick Leith-Ross of Britain, who aided in the currency reform of 1935. Cyril Rogers of the Bank of England, who came with him, remained to advise China.

China made notable economic gains in the prewar Nationalist years, despite the hang-over from early days of conditions and institutions unfavorable to development. Over-all conditions in China in the 1930's did not favor formation of capital. The government had no way to avoid heavy demands for funds to promote internal order, to establish nationwide authority, and after 1931 to defend against Japan. These demands un-balanced the budget and led to borrowing which absorbed a material part of the national savings. Japan's seizure of Manchuria in 1931–1932 was a heavy blow to China, and the continuing encroachments in North China disrupted business in important areas and hurt general confidence. The floods of 1931 in Central China were the most serious in decades. The deflation of about 30 per cent in 1931–1935, mainly caused by American silver-buying, had a crippling effect. Considering the adverse factors affecting China in the prewar Nationalist years, the economic progress was creditable and the financial progress outstanding.[3]

The government, and the growing number of China's people with a modern-oriented outlook, were anxious for development, despite the difficulties. In 1937 the government was actively making plans for improvement of rail, road, air, and water communications; for industrial and agricultural development; and for regional development of areas such as the northwest and Hainan Island. These plans were supplemented during and after the war, and were the foundation for communist planning after the take-over. The success of the currency reform of 1935 was stimulating investment of both local and foreign capital. In 1937 the economy was moving strongly upward.

In *China and the Helping Hand, 1937–1945*, I thus summarized the situation on the eve of the hostilities:

. . . in mid-1937 the prospects of continuing and dynamic economic growth were promising. . . . The chief reservations . . . about prospects of progress were two. Would the government overstrain the currency and economy and take the easy but dangerous path of inflationary financing of development, as have so many underdeveloped countries? And would Japanese aggression defeat the growth process? . . .

All things considered, the National Government in its first decade had made a good record in many fields of activity. The over-all contrast between 1927 and 1937 was greatly to its credit. In 1937 its prestige was rising both at home and abroad. The country was prospering — internal peace always made for prosperity in China. After a turbulent decade, the outlook was bright for an era of unprecedented progress for China, if only the country could remain at peace. Grave weaknesses remained, however, which the strain of fighting brought out.[4]

Japan's attack in North China on July 7, 1937, was followed by the spread of fighting to Shanghai and throughout China. The attack ushered in a new era of war, inflation, and internal strife, paving the way for the eventual communist triumph on the mainland.[5]

Part One that follows deals with receipts, expenditure, and fiscal policy; Part Two with debt and foreign aid; and Part Three with currency management and inflation. Appendixes A to H contain basic statistical and other data relating to these matters.

PART ONE. RECEIPTS, EXPENDITURE, AND FISCAL POLICY

II. CASH RECEIPTS AND EXPENDITURE

Expansion of outlay and shrinkage of revenue* were the major factors determining the course of the Chinese government's wartime finance. Needs for money multiplied as the fighting spread. And revenue shrank with early seizure of the main ports and centers of production from which most tax income was derived. It was an enormously difficult task to build quickly a large new fiscal administration under wartime conditions, in areas that were still largely under the influence of warlords, that were living largely as in the Middle Ages, and where traditional "squeeze" was accepted ethics. Loss of the more advanced areas carried with it the loss of men experienced in public administration. For many it was not feasible to leave and go to the interior.

The gap between expenditure and revenue could be filled only by borrowing. Effective mobilization of savings for the war effort was most difficult in the diminishing area that stayed free. Immediate and large recourse to the government banks for money was unavoidable. After the first 15 months of fighting, roughly five-sixths of the credit took the form of increased note issue. The inflation that resulted was essentially of the demand-pull type.

In laying the groundwork for discussion of events and policy, of alternatives available, and of factors that influenced decisions, I present in this chapter the main facts as to wartime receipts, payments, and deficit of governmental cash transactions. Included in the figures are the cash transactions of governmental agencies, not in the budget proper, whose effect upon the inflation was substantially the same as if they had been in that budget. Chapter III contains the data regarding transactions in kind. At the end of that chapter is a summary of the fiscal results during the war period, combining transactions in cash and in kind. Fiscal policy as to revenue, expenditure, and deficit is discussed in chapter IV.

BUDGETARY CASH TRANSACTIONS: RECEIPTS AND EXPENDITURE

Budgetary receipts and expenditure from fiscal 1929 through 1945 are shown in Table 1.† Inclusion in this table of prewar data provides a full

* In this book I use "receipts" to refer to all money received and entered in the accounts, and "revenue" to refer only to nonborrowed receipts.

† Until mid-1938, fiscal years ended June 30. Thereafter they were calendar years, and the second half of 1938 was treated as a separate fiscal period.

TABLE 1. Budgets, expenditure, revenue, and deficits, 1929–1945 (in millions of C$)

Year ending June 30	Budget of expenditure Original	Budget of expenditure Original plus supplementary authorizations	Expenditure, excluding balances at end of the period[a]	Revenue, nonborrowed, excluding balances at beginning of the period[a]	Deficit covered by borrowing
1929	492	—	434	334	100
1930	619	—	585	484	101
1931	712	—	775	558	217
1932	893	—	749	619	130
1933	788	—	699	614	86
1934	828	—	836	689	147
1935	918	—	941	745	196
1936	957	—	1,073	817	256
1937	991	—	1,167	870	297
1938	1,001	1,511	2,091	559	1,532
1938 (2d half)	856	1,294	1,169	297	872
Calendar year					
1939	1,706	2,118	2,797	715	2,082
1940	2,488	4,592	5,288	1,317	3,970
1941	4,610	10,730	10,003	914[b]	9,090
1942	17,311	28,283	24,511	4,592[b]	19,919
1943	36,236	57,560	58,816	15,882[b]	42,934
1944	79,501	149,330	171,690	35,609[b]	136,081
1945[c]	263,844	1,363,577	1,215,089	150,061[b]	1,065,028

SOURCE: Budget data through fiscal 1935 from Chang Wei-ya, *The Money and Finance of China* (in Chinese, Taipeh, 1951), p. 87, and thereafter from the Finance Ministry and the *Statistical Yearbook* (in Chinese, Nanking, 1948), pp. 228–231. Data of expenditures, revenues, and deficit through fiscal 1935 from the Finance Ministry's published reports; for fiscal 1936 and 1937 from that Ministry's unpublished data; and thereafter from the *Public Finance Yearbook* (in Chinese, Nanking, 1948), a pertinent extract from which is in Appendix A.

[a] For the fiscal years before 1934–1935 costs of revenue collection were shown as deductions from revenue. Thereafter they were shown as expenditures, as explained in the *Report for the 23rd Fiscal Year, July 1934 to June 1935*, Ministry of Finance, Nanking, 1936, p. 16n. These costs are here treated as expenditures.

[b] Receipts from interest on unissued bonds are excluded from nonborrowed revenue and treated as part of the deficit, as follows (millions of C$): *1941*, 270; *1942*, 675; *1943*, 635; *1944*, 606; and *1945*, 2.

[c] The data do not permit an accurate breakdown of figures for 1945 to show separately the fiscal results of the war period ending August 15 and the balance of the year. Available data show that about 44 per cent of the outlay in 1945 was for the first eight months of the year. The larger outlay of about 56 per cent in the last four months, after the war, was more a result of the heavy costs of taking over the liberated areas than of higher prices. In the last third of the year, after a drastic price slump, average prices were only about a seventh above the average in the first two-thirds.

series of comparable figures of financial results, based upon the Finance Ministry's accounts, from the time of the National Government's take-over through the war period. The Ministry's figures for the two fiscal years immediately before the war were not published, so far as I know. Others who have dealt with China's wartime finances and inflation have used for those two years data which differ materially from the Ministry's figures, which were given to me at the time as final. I have therefore included details of the data for those two years in appendix A, along with the details for the war years, together with comment upon the differences.

The wartime inflation, together with successive emergencies, disrupted budgetary planning. Supplementary authorizations grew, until in 1945 the total sums authorized were five times the original budget.

The figures for 1937–1945 in Table 1 do not show the full picture of war costs, how they were met year by year, and their bearing upon the inflation. A number of comments and explanations are necessary, some of which are discussed later more fully:

1. The figures do not include some important governmental cash transactions that affected the course of the inflation. The sales of foreign currencies to support exchange were not included. Sales of gold apparently were not included for 1943 and 1944, but were included for 1945. Substantial war savings deposits were accrued in the government banks, with an economic effect like that of public buying of bonds. On the expenditure side, the Joint Committee of the Four Government Banks* made advances to enterprises for war purposes and to sustain and expand the economy.

2. Because of disorganization caused by the fighting, financial returns were often not made with regularity. Thus late entries of receipts distort the year-to-year picture. Especially is this the case as to 1940, for which year "receipts in respect of revenue for previous years" (C$725 million) exceed total nonborrowed revenue (C$591 million). The effect is to exaggerate the deficit for 1937–1939; to understate it for 1940; and to swell nonborrowed revenue in the 1940 accounts to more than that for 1941, despite much higher prices in 1941.

3. Income from unissued bonds is treated as nonborrowed receipts in the accounts for 1941–1945 (see Table 40). Also, for 1939 customs revenue is stated as C$346 million (see Tables 2 and 40), whereas nonborrowed customs receipts were C$33 million. The difference of C$313 million apparently represents Central Bank advances to the Customs to cover loan service, at a time when enemy seizures made current revenue inadequate. The aforesaid items are treated hereinafter as part of the borrowing.

4. Finally, the figures do not include the value of receipts and payments in kind, which began after 1940, from land tax and compulsory purchase

* These banks were the Central Bank of China, Bank of China, Bank of Communications, and Farmers Bank.

TABLE 2. Cash budgetary receipts, 1937–1945 (in millions of C$)

Receipts	1937–1938	1938 (2d half)	1939	1940	1941	1942	1943	1944	1945
Indirect taxes									
Customs	239	128	346ᵃ	38	15	160	377	493	3,321
Salt, including surtax	141	47	61	80	296	—	1,202	13,440	51,725
Salt monopoly	—	—	—	—	—	1,180	1,823	1,089	1,781
Consolidated tax	30	16	22	46	121	309	657	2,046	23,144
Monopolies of cigarettes, matches, sugar	—	—	—	—	—	177	1,333	2,415	488
Wine and tobacco	14	9	20	24	63	273	1,278	2,929	
Stamps	5	3	5	7	16	26	355	1,063	3,140
Minerals	2	1	2	2	5	24	66	186	740
Wartime consumption	—	—	—	—	—	399	718	1,838	304
Subtotal	431	204	456	197	516	2,548	7,809	25,499	84,643
Direct taxes									
Incomeᵇ	19	8	27	44	80	198	765	1,194	2,120
Excess profits	—	—	—	25	70	291	884	1,189	1,833
Business tax	—	—	—	—	—	610	1,785	3,032	7,318
Special business tax	—	—	—	—	—	—	57	45	11
Land excluding tax in kind	—	—	—	—	—	516	4,014	3,392	6,326
Subtotal	19	8	27	69	150	1,615	7,505	8,852	17,608
Other nonborrowed income									
Public enterprises and properties	10	4	7	28	22	102	99	202	6,247
Contributions	3	19	55	33	21	39	21	80	8,556
Receipts in respect of previous years	—	—	—	725	121	123	266	514	3,710
Sales of foreign loan purchases, commodities, gold	—	—	—	—	—	—	—	—	28,663
Miscellaneous	95	62	170	264	83	165	182ᶜ	462	634
Subtotal	108	85	232	1,050	247	429	568	1,258	47,810
Total nonborrowed	559	297	715	1,317	914	4,592	15,882	35,609	150,061
Borrowing									
Sale of internal bonds	}256	}18	}25	8	127	155	3,871	1,647	62,727
Sale of external bonds				—	—	208	15	342	92
Bank loans	1,195	853	2,311	3,834	9,443	20,082	40,857	140,091	1,043,257
Income on unissued bonds	—	—	—	—	270	675	635	606	2
Total borrowed	1,451	872	2,336	3,842	9,841	21,121	45,379	142,687	1,106,079
Balance of previous year	93	12	12	266	137	889	2,091	4,536	10,298ᵈ
Grand total	2,103	1,181	3,063	5,425	10,892	26,602	63,352	182,832	1,266,438

SOURCE: *Public Finance Yearbook, 1948* (in Chinese), Section III, pp. 98–101. A translation of the detailed statement of which this Table 2 is a summary is in Appendix A, Table 40.

ᵃ This item clearly does not represent current customs collections in Free China in 1939, which were C$33 million. See 3 on page 13.

ᵇ Including minor receipts from inheritance tax.

ᶜ In the original table (see Table 40 in Appendix A) one of the tax items apparently should be C$10 million greater than there shown, as the items add up to C$10 million less than the subtotal. The several subtotals add to the grand total, which is presumed correct because it agrees with the total of expenditures. The stray C$10 million is here included with "Miscellaneous".

ᵈ The statement of expenditure in Tables 3 and 40 shows a balance of C$11,142 million at the end of 1944. I cannot explain the discrepancy.

and borrowing of grain. Chapter III deals with the "Rice-Wheat Budget." A further noncash item, for which no estimate is feasible, was requisitioning without payment of labor and materials for the army and for various works.

The various nonbudgetary transactions are further discussed hereinafter, and combined with budgetary transactions to show the over-all picture in relation to the course of the inflation.

Wartime internal borrowing was of two kinds. First, and by far the more important, was creation of bank credit — until July 1, 1942, by the four government banks, and thereafter by the Central Bank. The total of these bank advances to government from mid-1937 through 1945 was C$1,261,921 million (see chap. XIII). Second, there was borrowing from the public, which reduced reliance upon inflationary bank credit (see chap. VI). Also certificates of deposit payable later in gold provided substantial sums (see chap. XIX).

The sources of wartime cash budgetary receipts are shown in Table 2. I have grouped the items by chief categories, since the presentation of items in the original text (see appendix A) is not easy to follow.

CASH BUDGETARY EXPENDITURE

Before the war 40 to 45 per cent of total outlay under the general budget was for military purposes, about 30 per cent for debt, and the balance for various civil expenses. Outbreak of fighting at once called for greatly increased costs, as shown in Table 3. The data do not make possible a precise statement of total military expenditure. Outlay for such purposes as communications, economic development, and subsidies to provincial and local governments was mainly for war ends. On the other hand "emergency" expenditures, which I have classified under military, doubtless contained some nonmilitary components. Certainly most of the total outlay was for purposes of the war.

There remains the question of the receipts and expenditures of provincial and local governments. Figures of realized results are not available. These governments relied partly upon their own revenues, but largely upon subsidies from the National Government, the latter being included in the accounts here presented. The expenditures of these bodies, except as derived from subsidies, were covered by their respective revenues, and do not appear to have had significant inflationary consequences. The budgetary data that follow give some indication of the relative size of provincial and municipal outlay (figures in millions of C$, from *Chinese Statistical Yearbook, 1948*, pp. 228–231):

	Provincial	Municipal
Year ending June 30, 1938	370	203
Second half of 1938	217	174
Calendar year 1939	375	224
1940	493	584
1941	1,077	1,687
1942	1,914	3,468
1943	4,187	10,043
1944	9,240	29,343
1945	58,266	388,023

TABLE 3. Cash budgetary expenditure, 1937–1945 (in millions of C$)

Expenditure	1937–1938	1938 (2d half)	1939	1940	1941	1942	1943	1944	1945
Party, administration, etc.	101	48	153	148	426	1,215	1,514	10,654	58,384
Military									
Ordinary	391	211	443	710	1,179	2,151	6,391	9,553	191,120
Defense, construction	277	121	521	716	1,838	5,515	9,538	21,975	6,888
Extraordinary	720	367	572	2,347	1,861	3,482	7,033	12,478	—
Emergency	—	—	64	139	279	1,028	11,392	73,205	862,389
Provision of food	—	—	—	—	1,458	3,040	8,590	13,869	14,970
Subtotal, military	1,388	699	1,600	3,911	6,616	15,216	42,944	131,080	1,075,367
Development, reconstruction									
Economic	104	71	122	96	213	492	523	1,643	2,288
Water conservancy	7	5	8	22	35	81	142	402	1,741
Agriculture, forestry	—	—	—	—	25	48	108	358	1,410
Communications	57	61	238	439	712	1,648	2,151	9,191	9,339
Northwest reconstruction	—	—	—	—	—	—	392	919	—
Enterprises, capital	—	—	—	23	11	85	147	95	—
Administration and miscellaneous	—	—	—	—	—	—	—	—	3,028
Subtotal, development	168	137	268	580	996	2,354	3,462	12,608	17,807
Subsidies	24	14	54	115	234	51	73	137	461
Provincial, municipal	—	—	—	—	—	1,832	3,394	6,302	30,021
Educational, cultural	36	20	43	116	176	505	1,178	3,790	22,438ᵃ
Health, welfare, relief	1	10	31	47	94	172	457	635	3,219ᵇ
Subsidies to staff	—	—	—	10	72	526	1,347	—	—
Debt	374	242	546	346	480	1,587	3,493	5,220	7,017
Cost of bartered goods	—	—	—	—	906	983	—	—	—
Commodity control	—	—	—	—	—	70	954	836	—
Expenditures of previous years	—	—	—	14	1	2	5	427	575
Balance at year end	12	12	266	137	889	2,091	4,536	11,142ᶜ	51,349
Grand total	2,103	1,181	3,063	5,425	10,892	26,602	63,352	182,832	1,266,438ᵈ

SOURCE: *Public Finance Yearbook*, 1948 (in Chinese), Section III, pp. 98–101. A translation of the detailed statement of which this Table 3 is a summary is in Appendix A, Table 40.

ᵃ Including C$257 million relating to reconstruction.

ᵇ Including C$65 million relating to reconstruction.

ᶜ The statement of receipts in Tables 2 and 40 shows a balance of C$10,298 million at the beginning of 1945. I cannot explain the discrepancy.

ᵈ The items for 1945 in the original Chinese text add to C$200 million more than the total. There is an apparent error in listing the items under Reconstruction. The subtotals (here omitted) for Reconstruction and other main heads add to the total shown, which also agrees with the total for Receipts.

EXTRABUDGETARY CASH RECEIPTS AND BORROWING FROM THE PUBLIC

Counterinflationary cash receipts, both budgetary and extrabudgetary, are shown in Table 4. The main item is the nonborrowed revenue detailed in Table 2. Borrowing from the public comprised the sale of various *fapi* issues, the foreign currency issues of 1938–1940, the dollar-backed issues of 1942, and savings schemes whereby the public made deposits in the government banks (see chap. VI). The counterinflationary receipts also included sales of gold in 1943–1945 (see chap. XIX). Besides, there were sales of foreign currency to support exchange, which absorbed money from the public.[1] The *fapi* proceeds of these sales were mostly impounded, thus restricting the supply of money (the *fapi* impounded when the Pacific War

TABLE 4. Counterinflationary cash receipts, including extrabudgetary
transactions, 1937–1945 (in millions of C$)

| Year ending June 30 | Non-borrowed budgetary revenue | Internal Bonds[a] | | Govern-ment savings schemes (in fapi) | Gold sales[b] | Sales of foreign curren-cies, net | Total |
		Fapi bonds and foreign currency issues of 1938–1940	Dollar-backed issues of 1942				
1938	559	256	—	—	—	499	1,314
1938 (2d half)	297	18	—	—	—	26	341
Calendar year							
1939	402[b]	25	—	3	—	150	580[b]
1940	1,317	8	—	133	—	132	1,589
1941	914	127	—	457	—	525	2,024
1942	4,592	300	483	879	—	—	6,254
1943	15,882	1,000	2,480	1,292	114	—	20,768
1944	35,609	1,989	—	2,508	20,940	—	61,046
1945	150,061[c]	1,056	—	5,067	60,335[c]	—	216,519[c]

SOURCE: Finance Ministry and other governmental organs.

[a] For explanation of these figures see Table 13 and the notes thereto, in chapter VI.

[b] Taking customs revenue as C$33 million; see 3 on page 13.

[c] The item of C$150,061 million includes part of the proceeds of sale of gold, apparently about C$11,365 million, in addition to the item of C$60,335 million under "Gold sales"; see note 2 of this chapter.

broke out in December 1941 fell into enemy hands). Sales of exchange by or for account of the government banks thus enabled them to make loans to the government, to the extent of the *fapi* proceeds, without adding to the total money supply. Sales for currency support were a substantial counter-inflationary factor in 1937–1941, as described in chapters XV–XVII. During the Pacific War these sales were of only minor importance.

Receipts from gold sales were an important source of funds in 1943–1945, with counterinflationary effect, as discussed at length in chapter XIX. In those three years these receipts were, respectively, C$114 million, C$20,940 million, and C$71,700 million, according to data of the Central Bank. But for 1943 and 1944 these receipts are not specified in the accounts, and apparently there are no "catch-all" items that might include them. For 1945, however, receipts from gold are included in the budgetary receipts.[2]

EXTRABUDGETARY CASH EXPENDITURE

The Joint Committee of the Four Government Banks made advances, not included in the budget, which were similar in effect to budgetary appropriations. This organ was created in the fall of 1939, with Generalissimo Chiang as chairman, to succeed a committee constituted two years earlier. The function of these committees was to pass upon advances requested for war needs, and the Joint Committee was created to bring about more effective control of advances.[3] Part of the advances went to

TABLE 5. American military expenditures in China, 1942–1945 (first two columns in millions of US$; last two in millions of C$)

| | Expenditures paid for by the United States | | | | |
| | Nature of payment | | | | |
	Dollars sold at 20-1	Dollars paid under negotiated settlements	Setoff by delivery of surplus property[a]	Fapi provided	Expenditures assumed by China (fapi)
1942	1	—	—	20	600
1943	110	—	—	2,193	4,600
1944					
January	26	—	—	529	
February–December	—	255	—	23,500	22,200[b]
1945	—	—	Value not specified	103,800	107,600

SOURCE: Morgenthau Diaries, vol. 754, p. 55, March 28, 1944; vol. 810, p. 171, January 17, 1945; vol. 859, pp. 28–29, June 27, 1945; and Finance Ministry.
[a] See the New York Times, September 1, 1946.
[b] In all of 1944.

private businesses for work deemed important in the war effort. But the larger part went to public organizations. No breakdown of advances as between public and private organizations is available for the full period; but in 1940 and 1945 about two-thirds of the total was going to public organizations. As inflation progressed, appropriations in the budget commonly became insufficient to accomplish their purpose. Procurement of more money through budgetary channels was slow and cumbersome, hence many public organs sought loans to ease their more urgent problems. Details of the Joint Committee's advances appear in appendix A, Table 41.

These advances tended to be inflationary, because of involving additional credit by the government banks. The amount of increase of these advances was (millions of C$): for 1937–1940, 435*; 1941, 792; 1942, 638; 1943, 8,418; 1944, 21,929; 1945 (through August), 16,200; 1945 (total), 42,644.

The *fapi* costs connected with operations of the American military forces in China during the Pacific War also must be taken into account in considering China's wartime outlay and the course of the inflation. The United States and China divided these costs in roughly equal parts, as shown in

TABLE 6. Budgetary and extrabudgetary cash expenditures, 1937–1945
(in millions of C$)

Year ending June 30	Expenditures, excluding balances at end of the period	Advances through Four Government Banks Joint Committee, net increase[a]	Total
1938	2,091	—	2,091
1938 (2d half)	1,169	—	1,169
Calendar year			
1939	2,797	—	2,797
1940	5,288	—	5,288
1941	10,003	792	10,795
1942	24,511	638	25,149
1943	58,816	8,418	67,234
1944	171,690	21,929	193,619
1945	1,215,089	42,644	1,257,733

SOURCE: See Tables 1 to 5.

[a] Besides the advances shown in this column, C$636 million was advanced in 1937–1939, but yearly figures are not available. At the end of 1940, C$435 million was outstanding.

Table 5. The Chinese government viewed the payments which it assumed as reverse lend-lease, although their status was somewhat ambiguous. The total of both categories in 1944 amounted to more than a fourth of China's total expenditure, and in 1945 to the war's end to more than a third. Although the American government made large payments in dollars and property for *fapi* supplied, an increase of the money supply in China resulted, mostly in the form of bank notes. This increase contributed to the inflation practically as much as if the *fapi* had been provided without payment.

After January 1944, when the American government balked at continuing to buy *fapi* at 20–1, American military costs in China were paid from

* Balance at the end of 1940.

advances of *fapi*. Of these the Central Bank made about 80 per cent and the Finance Ministry the rest. Eventually the American and Chinese governments agreed upon lump sum settlements against dollars and surplus property. There was considerable controversy as to how the two governments should divide the costs, and as to the rate of exchange for the share which the American government assumed. These matters are treated at length in chapter XVIII.

Because the way in which the costs should be shared between China and the United States was uncertain for considerable periods, both the *fapi* advances and the dollar receipts remained for some time in suspense accounts of the Finance Ministry and the Central Bank. The *fapi* payments seem to have been included in due course in the general accounts of receipts and payments, but information is incomplete as to when and how. I have not felt warranted in treating these payments as outside the budgetary accounts herein presented.[4]

We are now in position to supplement Table 3 by bringing together the budgetary and extrabudgetary cash expenditure, in Table 6.

TABLE 7. Cash expenditures; cash receipts; and cash deficit, budgetary and extrabudgetary, 1937–1945 (in millions of C$)

Year ending June 30	Cash war costs, per Table 6	Nonborrowed cash revenue, plus proceeds of bond sales to the public, savings schemes, and sales of foreign currencies and gold, per Table 4	Cash deficit covered by expansion of bank credit	
			Amount	Percentage of cash war costs
1938	2,091	1,314	777	37
1938 (2d half)	1,169	341	828	71
Calendar year				
1939	2,797	580	2,217	79
1940[a]	5,288	1,589[a]	3,699	70[a]
1941	10,795	2,024	8,771	81
1942	25,149	6,254	18,895	75
1943	67,234	20,768	46,466	69
1944	193,619	61,046	132,573	69
1945	1,257,733	216,519	1,041,214	83
Total	1,565,872	310,435	1,255,437	

SOURCE: See Tables 4 and 6.

[a] Revenue of 1940 included C$725 million in respect of previous periods, hence the deficit of 1940 was greater than herein shown, and the deficits of previous periods should be smaller. Omitting the C$725 million, the deficit of 1940 would be 84 per cent.

SUMMARY OF CASH RECEIPTS AND EXPENDITURE,
BUDGETARY AND EXTRABUDGETARY

To show the over-all situation as to the government's cash transactions during the war period, in relation to the course of the inflation, I have combined in Table 7 the various data hereinbefore presented and analyzed. While the data are subject to the various limitations and interpretations herein set forth, Table 7 provides in my opinion as complete a statement as the available data permit.

The cash deficit covered by inflationary credit ranged between 69 and 83 per cent, except in the first year, in which a figure of 37 per cent was attained, mainly because of heavy sales of foreign currencies and large borrowing from the public — resources which were not later available on a comparable scale.

III. THE RICE-WHEAT BUDGET; TOTAL RECEIPTS AND
EXPENDITURE IN CASH AND IN KIND

THE AGRICULTURAL ECONOMY AND TAXATION

China in 1937 was about four-fifths agricultural. There are no accurate prewar production figures because of defects of the crop-reporting system. The best estimates of production are those of Ta-chung Liu and Kung-chia Yeh for 1933, approximately an average year, showing that food crops in China, including Manchuria, totaled 173 million metric tons, including potatoes at their grain equivalent weight. That provided, they estimate, a per capita intake of 1,940 calories daily, about nine-tenths of the total intake from all foods. For the communist period they have made estimates for 1957, which the communists consider an average year, indicating total food crops of 185 million metric tons, including potatoes at their grain equivalent weight. The calory intake from food crops in 1957 they estimate at 1,833 daily per capita, or about 5 to 6 per cent less than in 1933.[1] Communist figures since 1957 are unreliable because Communist China began frankly to use statistics as an instrument of policy and propaganda.[2]

Despite the predominance of agriculture, China in 1937 lacked an effective land tax. The land revenue, such as it was, went to local and provincial bodies and not to the central government. The system was based upon old and obsolete assessments. Professor J. Lossing Buck has stated that in 1937 about a third of the land of both large and small holders was not even on the tax rolls.[3] As far back as 1904, Sir Robert Hart, Inspector General of Customs, urged reform of the land tax to raise much-needed revenue. He remarked that this tax "has hitherto been levied in a way that takes most from the people and hands least to the Government, while both exaction and malpractices flourish under it." He proposed a "chain-letter" plan, whereby a nucleus of ten men would be trained for three months in a selected district in simple procedures of land registration and tax collection; nine of the ten would then go to other districts and each would train ten more; and so on until the reform was nationwide.[4] But the Manchu regime took no serious action. Hart's criticism of the system was still true in 1937. In the spring of that year the government made a start by adopting a basic plan for land reform and land taxation. But outbreak of fighting a few weeks later prevented action.

Thus the government entered the war with a tax system that failed to draw significant revenue from the largest sector of the economy. This seriously handicapped any move to increase tax revenue to cover war costs. As a result, the inflation was worse than it might have been. Significantly a major measure of the communists, after their take-over on the mainland, was a ruthless levy upon income from land, which helped them to control inflation.

It was unfortunate that the National Government failed to deal more effectively with agricultural problems. The Ministry of Agriculture was set up only during the war. It ranked low in power and priority, and had but minor appropriations. If the government could have put into effect on the mainland rural reforms, such as those adopted on Formosa after the war with such success under auspices of the Joint Commission for Rural Reconstruction, the postwar history of China could have been very different. For this neglect of major issues there were two main reasons. The government's leaders throughout were quite fully occupied by urgent problems of survival in the face of threats from warlords, Japan, and the communists. And there was a strong pro-middle class and pro-landlord bias, alike at the levels of national and local government.

COLLECTION IN KIND

In a memorandum of September 11, 1937, responding to Acting Finance Minister Hsu Kan's request for recommendations on wartime financial policy, I suggested considering "new taxes in kind, for example, payable in foodstuffs needed by the military forces. Such taxes if adopted should be of broad application, and should be collected from the owner of the land and out of his share in the produce." But nothing was done until 1940, when a bad crop in West China caused food prices to jump sharply, adding much to the cost of food for the army. Besides the harm to the budget, farmers were holding back food. The situation became so grave that the Executive Yuan on November 13, 1940, adopted a resolution calling for collection of land tax in kind.

In February 1941, Laughlin Currie, when in China as a special representative of President Roosevelt, urged Chiang to reform the land tax. Currie stressed the basic position of agriculture in China, saying that, "Unless the Central Government can draw its revenues from the real wealth and income in the country, it can never hope to cover more than a negligible portion of its war and post-war expenditures through taxation." Further, Currie said that the tax would largely hit well-to-do landowners who were profiting from inflation. He believed that "to proceed along the lines of social justice and equality laid down by Dr. Sun . . . would cut the ground out from under the Communists." Currie also recommended that, if thorough tax reform should not prove possible, "having recourse to a forced rice loan might be seriously explored," as an emergency measure.[5]

Currie's recommendations reinforced the government's earlier decision to proceed with collecting land tax in kind. And the government later adopted also compulsory sale and borrowing of rice and wheat. Collection of land tax in kind took effect July 1, 1941. The tax was handled under direction of the provincial finance commissioners, because of their close relation to provincial governors. Since land tax had been a provincial and local revenue, the government granted subsidies to offset the loss of revenue. There was some element of provinces vying with one another to make a good showing in percentage achievement of quotas. The tax was based on the old rates, and for each dollar of tax the payment was set in fixed quantities of grain.[6] A survey made by Professor Buck of a typical rural district near Chengtu in the summer and fall of 1942 showed that land tax in kind averaged 1.87 per cent of land value, and all taxes 3.44 per cent.[7]

The tax did not bring in as much grain as hoped. So in 1942 a further law required taxpayers to make compulsory sale to the government of an amount of grain equal to that paid as tax. Actually, in 1941–1942 the receipts from compulsory purchase somewhat exceeded receipts from the tax, as shown by Table 8. The plan was to pay 30 per cent in *fapi* and 70 per cent in Food Treasury Notes, which were denominated and payable in kind. In actual practice, these percentages were not followed in all areas, and cash payments were 50 per cent in Kweichow and Anhwei, and 40 per cent in Hupei, Kiangsi, Fukien, and Hsikang. The prices of compulsory purchase were much below the official and free market prices.[8] In the summer of 1943, the government discontinued compulsory purchase and substituted compulsory borrowing, repayable in kind. The term of repayment was six to nine years with 5 per cent interest. The total of Food Treasury Notes issued was about 40.5 million *piculs* (*shih tan*) of rice and 4.8 million bags of wheat, equivalent to about two million and 334,000 metric tons, respectively. As of June 30, 1945, the amounts outstanding where about 26.9 million *piculs* of rice and 2.8 million bags of wheat.[9]

It is not surprising that the system of collection in kind was hard to administer. A tax in kind on land entails far more work and complications than a tax in money. From the political angle, it might have been better to have had the local authorities collect the tax, for handing over to the central government, which was subsidizing them in consideration of their giving up the revenue from land tax. In a memorandum of June 21, 1943, I wrote:

The Ministry of Finance has a separate organization of about 200,000 people to collect the land tax. This could be done by the local government authorities, by adding (say) 25% to the cost of their organization. Besides saving the pay of the 200,000, the work would be better done because the local authorities are in a better position to exercise the necessary authority.

TABLE 8. Yield of land tax and compulsory purchase and borrowing of rice and wheat, 1941–1945 (in thousands of metric tons, converted from *piculs*)

	1941–42	1942–43	1943–44	1944–45
		(*years ending September 30*)		
Land tax in kind				
Rice	995	1,431	1,431	1,334
Wheat	136	291	366	248
Total	1,131	1,722	1,797	1,581
Compulsory purchase[a]				
Rice	1,200	1,340	580	—
Wheat	351	220	100	—
Total	1,551	1,560	681	—
Compulsory loan				
Rice	—	—	654	1,101
Wheat	—	—	107	188
Total	—	—	762	1,288
Total receipts in kind				
Rice	2,195	2,771	2,665	2,435
Wheat	487	511	573	436
Total	2,682	3,282	3,240	2,869

SOURCE: Finance Ministry. The data for the earlier two periods are from the Land Tax Administration of the Finance Ministry, received in the spring of 1944; and for the latter two periods from the Secretariat of that Ministry, received October 31, 1945. The original data are in *piculs* (see note 9). These contemporary data differ somewhat from those cited by Kia-ngau Chang, *The Inflationary Spiral*, p. 144, which are based upon postwar compilations of Chinese government departments and converted to bushels. My contemporary data, converted to bushels, show for the last three periods totals 2 to 3 per cent larger than his, but with a larger proportion of rice compared with wheat. For the first year my data show a total much larger than his, since he did not include noncompulsory purchases.

[a] Including for 1941–1942 certain noncompulsory purchases made more or less at market prices. Available data do not show the amount of these.

The offsetting argument, however, was that local authorities were more susceptible to pressure of influential parties.

There was much unavoidable waste and loss from improper care and storage. Abuses were serious. Collectors were underpaid because of the government's slowness in raising salaries as inflation mounted. They yielded all too often to such temptations as making false returns, stealing grain, adulterating what was turned in, and reporting false losses or "accidents." Moreover, the Ministry of Food, in the judgment of well-informed persons, followed a policy of holding unduly large amounts of grain, thus becoming itself a hoarder.

The tax was not popular. Its burden fell on the rural people, who could not easily evade it, while they saw speculators and hoarders fattening on their gains without paying adequate taxes. Certainly, the measure as operated tended to cause local people to have an adverse attitude to the National Government. Thus, it helped to soften up the country for the communists. Yet as a fiscal measure, it was an indispensable means of covering war costs, and an item to the government's credit. The fault was not so much in the measure as in the failure to take equally strong measures affecting others who could pay, and to carry out a sounder over-all financial policy.

The government announced on V-J Day that, "The land tax will not be collected for one year in the provinces that were occupied by the enemy. Provinces in Free China will be exempted from paying the land tax in the following year." [10] This action, of course, was intended to relieve the people of a heavy burden, in view of the grievous sufferings they had borne in the war. But it was an economic blunder. It left the army without the grain it had been getting in kind, and forced them to buy in the open market, thus greatly bidding up the price. By adding to inflation, it laid other burdens on the people. Politically, the government's loss of prestige from growing inflation more than offset whatever discontent maintaining these burdens as they were would have aroused. The government was forced to amend the measure and keep the tax in modified form. The loss of revenue from suspension of the tax in kind added materially to the government's financial difficulties after the war.

Yield in kind

The yield of land tax, together with compulsory purchase and borrowing of crops, was large as shown in Table 8. The drop in receipts in 1944–1945 was due to extension of the Japanese invasion in Southeast China.

Being based on obsolete and incomplete assessments, these burdens in kind were not fairly adjusted between individuals. Likewise they varied much from province to province. Szechwan, with its rich lands, provided about a fourth of the total. The distribution by provinces of collections in kind and compulsory purchase in the crop year ending September 30, 1943, is shown in appendix A, Table 42.

The measure gave the government definite real value, while the real yield of taxes levied in money terms was shrinking. Being based on prewar rates, it did not increase the real burden of taxes as compared to prewar. Land tax in kind amounted to about 2.5 to 3.5 per cent of the total crop yield, according to estimates of the Land Tax Bureau. Compulsory purchase and loan produced together a little less than land tax. Hence the total realized was about 5 to 6 per cent of production.

About two-thirds of the grain collected went to the army. The amounts were sizable: 1.9 million metric tons in 1941 and 2.2 million in 1942, according to reports of the Ministry of Food. Of the rest about half was reported as used for sustenance of national and provincial and local officials, and about half was sold at official prices to the public.[11]

Receipts in kind from land tax, along with compulsory loan and purchase of grain, became the main single revenue in 1941–1945. The rice and wheat realized were a mainstay in support of the army and of civil officials, and partly offset the constantly shrinking buying power of their pay in money.

VALUE OF RECEIPTS IN KIND

Unfortunately no complete and adequate data are available showing the monetary value of these items. The data of amounts in kind, while stated very precisely in the official figures shown above, cannot be taken as wholly exact in view of defects in the statistical and financial administration under the highly difficult conditions of the war. The quantities were valued at artificially low prices, national or provincial, which varied widely by regions. Had it been necessary to get the grain at actual market prices, the costs would have been bid up to much higher levels. Hence the government, by being able to stay out of the market, refrained from putting additional fuel on the fires of inflation.

The Land Tax Administration supplied the following figures of the value received in the first two years to September 30, 1943, from land tax in kind and compulsory purchase (millions of C$):[12]

	1941–1942	1942–1943
Land tax in kind		
At National Treasury prices	2,315	—
At provincial prices	2,969	15,223
Compulsory purchase		
At National Treasury prices	2,160	—
At provincial prices	3,357	11,338
Total		
At National Treasury prices	4,475	—
At provincial prices	6,326	26,561

No contemporary value data are available for the following two years, but only the quantity data received October 31, 1945, from the Finance Ministry, which are shown in Table 8. The accounts of the Finance Ministry unfortunately do not include either quantity or value of receipts and payments in kind. Collections in kind were handled by the Land Tax Administration of the Finance Ministry, and disposal of collections was by the Food Ministry. Repeatedly I tried to bring about: (1) proper valuations for inclusion in the general accounts, in order to show the over-all financial situation; (2) allocation to fiscal years, either by date of transaction, or by treating crop year receipts in years ending September 30 as pertaining to the fiscal year ending three months later, or by some other tenable principle; (3) accounting for the values of disposal of receipts, at least under heads for the army, civil departments, provincial and local governments, and all other; and (4) analysis of compulsory purchase and loan to determine to what extent the element of tax was involved. Apart from the data shown above, nothing apparently was done.

In the absence of contemporary data showing values for 1943–1945 I have estimated the values, using as a base the C$26,561 million which is the value reported for 1942–1943. Since part of receipts had to be paid back as principal and interest on obligations in kind, issued from the summer of 1943, I have deducted 30 per cent from the estimated totals for each of the last two crop years, representing in the absence of exact data the approximate order of size of these current payments. Estimated receipts (years ending September 30), in thousands of metric tons, were for 1943, 3282; 1944, 3240; 1945, 2869. Indexes of rice prices[13] in Free China (market prices, data of Farmers Bank, approximate) for the same years were respectively 100, 330, and 1740. The approximate value of the receipts, in millions of C$, for 1943 was 27,000; for 1944, 85,000; and for 1945, 400,000. Adjusted approximate values in millions of C$, deducting repayments in kind, were for 1944, 60,000 and for 1945, 280,000.

Summarizing, the value of net collections in kind according to these partly estimated data was approximately as follows (millions of C$)[14]: 1941–1942, 6,326; 1942–1943, 26,561; 1943–1944, 60,000; and 1944–1945, 280,000. Unquestionably these receipts in kind were a major fiscal resource, without which inflation would have been much worse than it was. The effect of land tax in maintaining substantial real revenue is illustrated by the following figures for Chengtu, calculated by the University of Nanking under direction of J. Lossing Buck. The figures show the index of land tax per *shih mou* (0.1647 acre) compared with the University's index of wholesale prices at Chengtu.[15]

Year	Index of land tax	Index of wholesale prices
1937	100	99
1938	149	115
1939	109	211
1940	852*	620
1941	1,295	1,545
1942 (October)	3,689	6,130
1943 (October)	10,297	19,331
1944 (June)	40,573	56,330
1945 (June)	66,086	195,063

* The figure is stated to be based upon a survey of 20 farmers and looks too high to be representative; at that time land tax in kind had not been introduced. See *Economic Facts*, Chengtu, February 1943, p. 47 and *passim*.

VALUE OF TOTAL RECEIPTS AND EXPENDITURE, IN CASH AND IN KIND

We are now in position to summarize the over-all wartime fiscal situation, by combining cash items with the valuation of items in kind. The figures are shown in Table 9, and are subject to the limitations and qualifications previously stated.

TABLE 9. Total receipts and expenditure, in cash and in kind, 1937–1945
(in millions of C$)

Year ending June 30	Cash receipts other than from bank credit	Collections in kind, year ending September 30	Total receipts other than from bank credit	Expenditure in cash	Expenditure in kind, year ending September 30	Total expenditure	Expenditure covered other than by bank credit (per cent)
1937	870	—	870	1,167	—	1,167	75
1938	1,314	—	1,314	2,091	—	2,091	63
1938 (2d half)	341	—	341	1,169	—	1,169	29
Calendar year							
1939	580	—	580	2,797	—	2,797	21
1940[a]	1,589[a]	—	1,589	5,288	—	5,288	30
1941	2,024	—	2,024	10,795	—	10,795	19
1942	6,254	6,326	12,580	25,149	6,326	31,475	40
1943	20,768	26,561	47,329	67,234	26,561	93,795	50
1944	61,046	60,000[b]	121,046	193,619	60,000[b]	253,619	48
1945	216,519	280,000[b]	496,519	1,257,733	280,000[b]	1,537,733	32

SOURCE: Finance Ministry and other governmental organs.
[a] Since revenue for 1940 included C$725 million in respect of previous periods, this figure should be lower and the figures for previous periods higher.
[b] Estimated.

On a cash basis, receipts other than from bank credit covered only 17 to 31 per cent of expenditure in 1938–1945 — the 63 per cent in 1937–1938 being exceptional for reasons explained (see chap. II, Table 7). But, including the value of transactions in kind, the proportion covered other than by bank credit in 1942–1945 was much larger. For the two years 1942–1944, that coverage may be estimated at about two-fifths to half the over-all costs, and for 1945 nearly a third. These proportions are only approximate because some items, notably figures of collections in kind are partly esti-mated. Also for years ending September 30 collections in kind are combined with calendar year data, although the distortion by so combining is not very great, since most receipts came in the harvest months prior to September 30 .

While collections and expenditures in kind reduced inflationary pressures that otherwise would have been met, it was primarily the gap between noninflationary cash receipts and cash costs that caused the inflationary forces to operate.

The rise of average prices by more than 2,000-fold during the war makes it hard to understand real values when stated in *fapi*. Table 10 shows indexes

TABLE 10. Equivalent of revenue and expenditure in prewar currency, 1937–1945
(indexes of revenue and expenditure based on fiscal 1937 = 100)

Year ending June 30	Average retail prices (1st half of 1937 equals 1)	Revenue		Expenditure	
		Cash	Cash and in kind	Cash	Cash and in kind
1937	—	100	—	100	—
1938	1.22	124	—	147	—
1938 (2d half)ᵃ	1.58	50	—	127	—
Calendar year					
1939	2.43	27	—	99	—
1940	5.22	35ᵇ	—	85	—
1941	12.23	19	—	76	—
1942	41.8	17	36	52	65
1943	144	17	38	40	56
1944	478	15	29	35	45
1945	1,919	13	30	56	69

SOURCE: See Table 9 for amounts in current prices and appendix B, Table 48, for prices.

ᵃ The indexes of revenue and expenditure for the second half of 1938 are made comparable by doubling the figures for this half year.

ᵇ Since nearly half of the revenue reported for 1940 was in respect of previous periods, the index figures of revenue for that year should be lower and for previous periods higher.

of wartime revenue and expenditure deflated on the basis of average prices during the respective fiscal periods. Indexes are separately stated for items in cash and for the total values in cash and kind.[16]

Several comments are necessary in interpreting these data. First, the government's base of operations shrank greatly as the war progressed. Free China was productive in agriculture and raw materials, but lacked the incipient industrialization of the large coastal cities and their immediate hinterland. Also, the provincial governments spent substantial amounts for war purposes, besides what the central authorities provided to them by subsidies. Furthermore, a material part of the costs, and especially after Pearl Harbor, was covered by import of specific military items and other materials provided under credits and lend-lease by foreign governments. The value of these imports apparently is not included in the figures stated. The total amount of credits and lend-lease aid utilized by China prior to the Pacific War was equivalent to about US$350 million, and during that war to about US$1.2 billion.[17]

Finally, the Chinese army and civilian officials and the people bore very heavy war costs in ways that do not figure in the government's monetary accounts. The soldiers got little beyond subsistence needs and often hardly that. The civilians' pay fell far short of keeping pace with the inflation, and officials and employees bore much of the real war costs in the form of impaired standards of living. Especially in the zones of fighting, there was extensive requisitioning of labor and supplies, either with no payment or with inadequate payment. All these intangible war costs were still very real.[18]

IV. FISCAL POLICY

REVENUE

Revenue policy. In the prewar years revenue came mostly from customs, salt taxes, and taxes on factory production. O. C. Lockhart, tax expert of the Kemmerer Commission of 1929 and later Financial Adviser and cohead of the Salt revenue administration, advised against income taxation under the conditions existing in the 1930's. China's businessmen did not keep adequate records; they were suspicious of government; self-assessment was not practicable; and the tax administration was not sufficiently developed to run a direct tax system with fairness and efficiency. In 1936 an income tax law was adopted, which applied to public employees and certain income from securities. But its yield never became significant. Land tax was a local and not a national income (see chap. III).

To maintain the yield of revenue and build a largely new system in Free China after the fighting began was at best a hard and slow task. In a little more than a year the enemy seized China's richest areas and forced the government back into the little-developed west. Indiscriminate bombing behind the lines, while stiffening the will to resist, added to the confusion. China's leaders were harassed by constant emergencies. Few in China were qualified to take part in devising and installing a new tax system. When the government was driven from Nanking to Hankow, and then to Chungking, many experienced administrators could not follow. In the underdeveloped provinces of Free China there were few who could replace them. Moreover, revenue policy, especially during the early part of the war, was influenced by the view that the people's tax burden should not be made heavier because they were already so poor and suffering so much. To sympathize with the government in its troubles is easy, especially for those who shared some of the trials. Nevertheless, that view aggravated an unavoidable inflation, which allocated the burdens haphazardly and contributed to eventual collapse.

The distribution of receipts in 1937–1945, including those in kind from rice and wheat and also cash items outside the budget, is shown in Table 11. Indirect taxes, comprising mainly customs, charges on salt, and excises on factory products, shrank in importance after the first 18 months. The yield of direct taxes grew, but never became a relatively large proportion of total receipts. After the fall of Canton and Hankow in October 1938, yield from customs became a minor item. Loss of major cities cut the yield of the

TABLE 11. Distribution of receipts, 1937–1945 (in percentages)

Year	Indirect taxes	Direct taxes	Other	Sales of foreign exchange and gold[a]	Borrow- ing from the public	Revenues in kind from taxes and receipts in kind from borrowing	Total receipts excluding bank credit	Deficit covered by bank credit
1937–
38[b]	20.6	0.9	5.2	23.8	12.3	—	62.8	37.2
1938[c]	17.5	0.7	7.3	2.2	1.5	—	29.2	70.8
1939	5.1[d]	1.0	8.3	5.4	1.0	—	20.8	79.2
1940	3.7	1.3	19.8[e]	2.5	2.7	—	30.0	70.0
1941	4.8	1.4	2.3	4.9	5.4	—	18.8	81.2
1942	8.1	5.1	1.4	—	5.3	20.1	40.0	60.0
1943	8.3	8.0	0.6	0.1	5.1	28.3	50.4	49.6
1944	10.1	3.5	0.5	8.3	1.8	23.6	47.7	52.3
1945	5.5	1.1	3.1	3.9	0.4	18.2	32.3	67.7

SOURCE: See Tables 2, 4, and 9.
[a] Sales of exchange in 1937–1941; sales of gold in 1943–1945.
[b] Year ending June 30, 1938.
[c] Second half year.
[d] See note a to Table 2 concerning customs revenue in 1939.
[e] Including 14 per cent from unspecified revenues in respect of previous years.

consolidated taxes on factory products. Revenue from salt fell both from loss of territory and from failure to raise the specific rates as inflation progressed. Taxes in kind and borrowing in kind became a major item in 1942–1945, roughly half of these receipts being from taxes and half from the borrowing. Borrowing in cash from the public, after the success of the Liberty Loan in the fall of 1937, never became a very significant source of income. Other important items of noninflationary revenue were sales of foreign currencies for support of the exchange market in 1937–1941, and sales of gold in 1944–1945.[1]

Direct taxes were introduced by the government only in 1936, and the income tax of that year had no wide coverage when the fighting began. In 1938 the income tax was broadened to cover income from rentals and business profits. But its yield was of only minor importance in the early war years. In 1942–1945, however, the government made an extensive effort to tax business through taxes on capital, profits, and turnover. These taxes brought a moderate growth of yield. The Direct Tax Administration tried hard to make them work, but their operation was unsatisfactory. The system relied largely upon self-assessment, despite the inadequacy of accounting practices and of business records. There was widespread evasion, falsification, and concealment of records, and the poorly paid and largely inexperienced administrators could not cope with the problems, especially under conditions of wartime disturbance and acute inflation.[2]

Rapid wartime loss of most of the customs revenue was a serious blow to the finances. Before the war, customs revenue was well over half of total revenue from taxes. By 1939 about 90 per cent of customs revenue had passed into enemy hands. The situation was as follows (amounts in millions of C$): In 1937 (July to December) — Free China, 90, for occupied areas, 67, totaling 157; 1938 — Free China, 77, occupied areas, 178, totaling 255; 1939 — Free China, 31, occupied areas, 300, totaling 331; 1940 — Free China, 38, occupied areas, 372, totaling 410; and 1941 — Free China, 67, occupied areas, figures not available. The figures of the Customs were for calendar years and on an accounting basis different from that of the Finance Ministry. The yield increased much less than average prices — which in 1941 averaged about 12 times as high as in mid-1937. In occupied areas the Japanese cut the duties, especially on Japanese goods, in the first half of 1938. In the fall of 1939 China reduced to one-third of previous rates the duties on authorized imports and later banned a list of nonessentials. After outbreak of the Pacific War in December 1941 foreign trade almost disappeared, as did customs revenue.

The Salt administration, as a result of the government's policies, made a sorry showing in revenue collection in the first four years of hostilities. Yields according to the accounts of the Finance Ministry were (millions of C$): On a basis of the year ending June 30 — for 1937, 197; 1938, 141; and 1938 (2d half), 47. On a basis of the calendar year — for 1939, 61; 1940, 80; and 1941, 296. The government, wishing to avoid adding to the people's burdens in a time of stress and also to assure the supply of salt, was unwilling to increase materially the existing salt charges. Some were even reduced. These charges were set in specific amounts of money and not *ad valorem*. So yield failed to increase along with the general price rise, besides shrinking with loss of territory to the enemy. Only as from September 1941 did the government raise the rates on salt and other important items from the prewar levels fixed in *fapi*, despite the great rise of general prices. Until then the yield in 1941 from salt had been at the annual rate of about C$100 million. The system was complicated. As many as 31 different items of tax, surtax, and fee were collected in the districts as of August 31, 1941, the number in individual districts ranging from 6 to 16. Failure to consolidate these multiplied paper work. By 1941 the salt operation had become a source of cost rather than revenue, thus aggravating inflation. Salt merchants found their capital shrinking due to the war and inflation. They prevailed upon the government to provide large sums for salt transportation and loans. By the end of 1940 the four government banks had provided C$160 million in loans relating to salt. During 1941 they provided C$409 million more, plus C$40 million in cash and C$44 million which the Salt administration was allowed to deduct from revenue. Thus in 1941 the outlay totaling C$493 million far exceeded the yield of C$296 million.

The government's proposed solution was that salt become a government monopoly, along with tea, cement, wine, sugar, tobacco, and matches. Tea, cement, and wine were later dropped from the project. The stated aim was to add to revenues, improve the supply of salt, and check the increase of its price. In December 1940 the salt administration at the direction of the Finance Ministry prepared a plan for monopoly, not consulting Associate Director General Lockhart. The government was to buy and transport the entire output of salt, at an estimated yearly cost of C$3 billion, and sell it at wholesale to merchants agreeing to distribute it at fixed prices. The plan called for initial costs of C$80 million and a capital outlay of C$1.5 billion for purchase and transport of salt. The government banks would lend the money, mostly of course from proceeds of the printing press. Also, there was talk of changing the status of the foreign staff from administrators to advisers, without participation in the purchase and transport of salt. Foreign participation in the collection of customs and salt revenue is discussed in the following sections of this chapter.

Lockhart learned of the monopoly scheme only at the end of 1940, just as he was about to leave for medical attention in the United States. He at once pointed out to Finance Minister H. H. Kung the serious objections to the scheme, but his views were not well received. I was then in Washington aiding in negotiations for American aid, and I then and later called attention to the objections. Monopoly as proposed would have disrupted the existing salt trade, taking it out of the hands of the established and experienced merchants. It would have substituted a vast bureaucracy with infinite possibilities of inefficiency and corruption in the existing conditions of war and inflation. The cost would have aggravated inflation, being a needless outlay when every avoidable expense should have been postponed. Moreover the scheme was in violation of assurances to bondholders and their governments that China intended to maintain the Salt administration substantially as it had been constituted.[3] The scheme would have created new problems to be solved at a time when unavoidable problems surely were great enough. Better measures were available — such as to raise drastically the taxes, consolidate all charges in a single rate, keep tax rates abreast of price increases by measuring rates in terms of the price of a given quantity of salt, substitute subsidies for provincial surtaxes and retentions, and give proper pay to the staff.

Fortunately the scheme met with such opposition that the government, instead of introducing it as projected, materially raised the salt tax rates in the fall of 1941. Nominally the monopoly took effect on January 1, 1942, but in actual operation the plan was much less far-reaching than first contemplated. Producers paid to the government the difference between officially set buying and selling prices. But retail prices remained without effective control, and rose steadily along with the inflation.

The operation of the monopolies on salt and other goods gave rise to such difficulties and criticism that before the war's end they were replaced by commodity taxes.[4]

The revenue in 1942–1945 from the salt monopoly and from the tax (including surtax), according to the accounts of the Finance Ministry, was (in millions of C$): for 1942 — salt monopoly, 1,180, salt tax, none, totaling 1,180; 1943 — salt monopoly, 1,823, salt tax, 1,202, totaling 3,025; 1944 — salt monopoly, 1,089, salt tax, 13,440, totaling, 14,529; and 1945 — salt monopoly, 1,781, salt tax, 51,725, totaling, 53,506. In 1944–1945 salt became the most productive source of revenue, excepting rice-wheat taxes in kind.

Early in 1942 the government decided to set up a system of consumption taxes. These were applied to movement of goods. Clearly the method was far from good, and in a memorandum of January 15, 1942, I warned of the danger that such taxes would degenerate into a system of endless barriers to trade and movement, as the old *likin* had. But revenue needs were deemed paramount. Rates as adopted ranged from 5 per cent on basic necessities to 25 per cent on luxuries. In a memorandum of April 15, 1942, I recommended that the Customs collect the new taxes. That service would not be busy during the war with customs duties. Also it could easily be withdrawn at the end of the war, when such taxes ought to be abolished. I pointed out that, "China's experience shows how hard it is to abolish any organization that once creates a vested interest in any form of tax collection." The Customs service was charged with collecting these taxes. But there was resistance to using the Customs and the government failed fully to utilize them. Influential warlords in Szechwan wanted their own henchmen to collect the taxes. And there was objection from some who felt the bite of the taxes and preferred to deal with local officials.

The multiplication of taxes on many kinds of goods, levied in many places, led to setting up numerous controls on roads, rivers, airports, and railways all over Free China. To the original fiscal purpose was soon added a security check. The result, as feared, was to restore an obstructive system similar to the old *likin* or transit tax, the abolition of which in the early 1930's, though not wholly effective, had been one of the fine accomplishments of the National Government. Vehicles, despite the serious shortage of transport, were delayed futilely for long hours at many points for taxes and "squeeze." The revenue raised was minor compared with the cost of collection, economic loss, and inconvenience to the public. *Ta Kung Pao* of Chungking editorialized on October 24, 1942:

How can goods be transported? How can people travel? We have roads but we blockade them. We have cars and steamers but we keep them from running. We have goods but we hold them up and let them deteriorate. We have men but we create troubles for them. There can be no more foolish actions but we tolerate them.

This condition, they said, "is more or less our own making and not due to the action of the enemy."

In a memorandum of June 24, 1943, I wrote:

The present interference with movement of goods by road and water greatly hampers production and delivery of necessary goods, and is an important factor aggravating the rise of prices. It is creating once more abuses like the old *likin*. The following action is strongly recommended:

1. The various transport control bodies to be at once abolished at all points except at the limits of Free China.

2. Licenses to vehicles and water craft to be promptly and effectively issued on application in a few leading cities, good for periods of say six months and entitling them to circulate freely within Free China without paying any further fees or taxes.

3. Movement of duly licensed vehicles and water craft to be freed from interference, other than verification of having the necessary papers.

But a vested interest had been created, which profited from operating the system. The consumption tax was abolished early in 1945, but numerous restrictions on internal movement of goods and persons remained.

The pledged revenues and their administration. The outbreak of fighting threatened not only the yield of pledged revenues, but also the integrity and working of the Sino-foreign agencies collecting customs and salt taxes. Their personnel was international and they were affected with a strong international interest, because of foreign trade and business investment and the large foreign holdings of Chinese bonds. China's credit had never stood higher than when Japan attacked. Debt receiving service was equivalent to about US$1.1 billion. Of this about three-fourths was secured upon customs and salt revenue, mainly the former, and most of the remainder was railway debt. The foreign currency debt secured upon those revenues was about half as great as the internal debt so secured. In mid-1937 prospective annual yields were at record levels, equivalent to about US$125 million for customs and US$75 million for salt. The annual foreign currency debt payments where equivalent to about US$25 million and US$5 million, respectively.

The venerable Maritime Customs, dating back to 1854 and built up largely by the remarkable leadership of Sir Robert Hart, had long been the mainstay of China's credit. This British-dominated though internationally staffed service was a Chinese government organ. Under the 1898 Loan agreement China was obligated to maintain it "as at present constituted during the currency of this loan," that is, until 1943. The Inspector General was to be British so long as British trade with China predominated. In 1936 China's total trade with the British Empire, including the large *entrepot* trade through Hong Kong, exceeded trade with the United States and other countries, though trade with Britain proper was less than with the United States, Japan, or Germany. In 1937 the Inspector General of Customs was Sir Frederick W. Maze, an experienced career Customs officer.[5]

The Salt revenue administration was set up pursuant to the Reorganization Loan agreement of 1913, with a Chinese Chief Inspector and a foreign Associate Chief Inspector. That agreement provided for joint Sino-foreign collection of salt revenues, deposit in foreign banks, payment of collection costs and debt service, and turning over the surplus to the government. In 1913 President Wilson made his famous statement that the American government would not ask American bankers to participate in that loan, the conditions of which "include not only the pledging of particular taxes, some of them antiquated and burdensome, to secure the loan but also the administration of those taxes by foreign agents." China and the other national groups, however, went ahead, and the Salt administration was duly organized under British auspices. At first it had been under British leadership, but since 1930 the Associate Chief Inspector had been an American. The incumbent in 1937 was Dr. Oliver C. Lockhart, who, since 1929 as Financial Adviser with special reference to taxation, had played an important part in improvement of China's revenue system.[6]

Between 1913 and 1937 China, while keeping a system of joint Sino-foreign administration, departed from some terms of the 1913 agreement. That was of only nominal importance to holders of the 1913 loan, since in 1917 pursuant to the 1913 agreement its service was transferred to the Customs, a better security. In 1936–1937, however, China referred to the Inspectorate General of Salt Revenue in announcing settlement of certain salt-secured loans, creating a moral though not a contractual obligation to maintain the substance of the collecting system as it then existed. Shortly before the hostilities, China adopted a new Organic Law for the Salt administration. Members of that agency drafted it and took it up with the Legislative Yuan without the courtesy of consulting Lockhart. Parts of it could be interpreted as impairing the position of the foreign Associate Director General and the foreign staff. The bondholders' representatives inquired, and in reply the Finance Ministry stated in a letter of May 25, 1937 (translation), that "in our interpretation and implementation of this law the foreign associate officials continue to have joint responsibility as to essential functions and thus no material change in the established practice is being introduced."

Besides the revenue from customs and salt a number of internal taxes, notably the "consolidated taxes" on cotton yarn, tobacco, and cement, were pledged for the service of certain internal loans. The Internal Revenue Administration, benefiting from Lockhart's advice but entirely operated by Chinese, already had much improved the administration of these taxes.

Participation of foreigners in administration of the customs and salt revenues understandably aroused the nationalistic feelings of many Chinese. Yet thoughtful persons well realized that China not only was bound by agreements, but that the agreements worked for China's benefit. It was not merely that the foreign personnel were technically well qualified and generally efficient. They also could better resist pressures for unsound measures and for practices of favoritism and squeeze that were opposed to China's interest. On the whole the Sino-foreign Customs and Salt organizations worked smoothly and effectively in 1937 as an important part of China's administration. They were making more and more use of trained Chinese personnel. After the National Government came into power in 1928, the Customs service had ceased recruiting foreigners, but those already in that service were retained. Both the Customs and Salt services were becoming more and more integrated in the over-all financial administration of the Ministry of Finance and the Central Bank. China was making rapid strides in improvement of the working of government, and was moving gradually to a position in which in due time Chinese would be ready and able to operate effectively these important services. As to the foreign participation in the Customs and Salt services, the tendency in China in 1937 was to recognize the value to China of abiding by agreements made, and to make changes by evolution and negotiation rather than by violations and seizures.

The hostilities and the Customs. Japan quickly seized Tientsin and the other major ports of North China after fighting broke out in the summer of 1937. At Shanghai the Chinese-controlled area was captured in November after bitter fighting. The International Settlement and French Concession there and the foreign concessions at Tientsin kept most of their prerogatives, although with difficulty, until seized at the outbreak of the Pacific War in December 1941.[7]

The enemy seizures of ports and territory at once raised issues concerning the integrity of the Customs service, the application of pledged revenues for debt service, and maintenance of a uniform tariff which sustained the "open door" policy. To the Western countries these issues were important because of their support of China's integrity and the "open door" policy, and their nationals' stake in investment and trade. Britain felt specially concerned, because of the large British economic interest and her leading part in development of the Customs service.

To avoid complications and maintain debt payments, the British bond-holders' representative suggested to me on August 25 a plan for depositing both customs and salt revenues in the Hongkong and Shanghai Banking Corporation as a trustee. On August 27 as a first step Maze, Lockhart, and I forwarded to Acting Finance Minister Hsu Kan a message to be telegraphed to Minister Kung, in Europe, saying that temporarily the idea had much to recommend it.

Questions at once arose about payments due to Japanese creditors. The customs-secured Japanese portion of the Boxer Indemnity was due in monthly installments of about £33,000, equivalent to nearly US$2 million yearly. China naturally was unwilling to help finance her enemy. So payments of these monthly installments were accrued in a special account in sterling in the Hongkong and Shanghai Banking Corporation, pending a later settlement. At one stage the Ministry of Finance ordered the Customs not to pay the monthly installment due on the "Japanese portion" of the Reorganization Loan of 1913. But these payments were restored, though through the neutral banks, after I pointed out that Japan's original participation was only nominal, and that hardly any of the bonds were currently held by Japanese but rather by foreign nationals and to a large extent also by Chinese. To have stopped these payments would have damaged China's credit needlessly.

On August 30 the Japanese Consul General at Tientsin stated to the local Commissioner of Customs that Japan had no desire to interfere with the Customs service in Japanese occupied or controlled areas, if regular foreign loan quotas were remitted, and if the surplus were deposited in the Yokohama Specie Bank or other acceptable means devised to guarantee that the surplus would not be "improperly administered." The Customs would have to undertake not to admit arms and ammunition for China. Payments on internal loans could not be considered unless they concerned foreigners or until international agreement was reached. Refusal of these conditions would cause Japan to take over the Customs in these areas. The arrangement would apply at first to Tientsin and Chinwangtao, but Japan contemplated extending it to Tsingtao and even Shanghai. Maze recommended that the Finance Ministry accept the arrangement as a provisional compromise, but negotiate to include provision for regular quotas for internal loans.[8]

In mid-September, while the Ministry of Finance and the Customs Inspectorate were debating what to do, the American, British, and French governments gave support by pressing Japan at Tokyo to safeguard the Customs and Salt administrations. At Nanking and Tokyo they urged the plan put forward by the bondholders' representatives for having a single depository and trustee, namely the Hongkong and Shanghai Bank, with sub-deposits by it in American and French banks. That was designed to avoid confronting China with an unacceptable demand for deposit in the Yokohama Specie Bank.[9]

The Japanese Consul General's proposal of August 30 led to active negotiations, in which China sought deposit in neutral banks and quotas for internal loans. But in October the Japanese military put pressure on the Japanese negotiators, and the local Commissioner of Customs at Tientsin agreed on October 22 to put collections in the Yokohama Specie Bank, with withdrawals only for expenses and nothing for foreign loan quotas. The British embassy at Nanking thought that the commissioner had exceeded his authority, but it developed later that his yielding was affected by the garbling of instructions sent to him through that embassy. The instruction authorized him to deposit collections in "a reliable bank of good standing" but remittances of loan quotas were "to be made therefrom as due and if considered necessary by you any balance remaining is to be left to accumulate in the Bank." The words "due and if" were somehow omitted.[10] Maze managed to stave off the Japanese demand to extend the system to Shanghai, but only by agreeing after that city fell in November that collections be put in the Hongkong and Shanghai Banking Corporation and in effect blocked there. Minister Kung only learned of this six months later, and the arrangement was to be a cause of trouble in connection with British efforts for a temporary adjustment of the Customs issue.

On November 22 Customs officers, representatives of the bondholders, British officials, and I evolved a compromise plan to create an international bankers' commission with American, British, French, and Japanese members to receive all customs revenue, deposit it equally in banks of the four nationalities, and apply it to all customs obligations in order of priority. Maze would operate the arrangement for the commission during the hostilities. The British backed this plan at Nanking and Tokyo. The United States sought Japanese assurances not to impair the Inspector General's authority or disrupt the service, and to safeguard the revenues for expenses and foreign loan service. Throughout this period the United States felt it should not back any specific plan of settlement.[11]

During January, negotiations continued, mostly at Shanghai, but also at Tokyo. On February 2 in an instruction from Minister Kung to Maze China again indicated willingness to agree to a compromise plan, with a neutral bank and the Yokohama Specie Bank as cotrustees to apply the revenue to debt payments, any surplus to be disposed of after the hostilities.[12] Civilian Japanese officials wanted a settlement. But the military became more and more difficult to deal with. About February 1 General Matsui, commander-in-chief for Central China, stated in a press interview that he might have to take over the Customs, since "the new Chinese regime whatever it may be called . . . must draw its financial resources from the customs." Payments for foreign loans could be negotiated, "but it must be understood that the sum to be allowed for such services will be much lower than before." [13]

Throughout this period Maze was in a very difficult position.* He faced the hard task of trying to safeguard the integrity of the Customs and the debt service, which both China and the friendly powers desired, in difficult negotiations which his subordinates had to carry on with the militant Japanese as they strengthened their grip on China's ports. He was subject to Chinese government instructions. But he hoped the powers would dissuade China from issuing to him instructions that "might possibly conflict with the policy which the interested powers may deem it desirable to adopt in the best interests of China herself." [14] He early had to face in North China a Japanese-sponsored regime claiming authority, and he felt if he were not amenable to some extent to Japanese demands he might be replaced by a Japanese. If the powers wished, he was even ready to "extend limited recognition" to such regime, pending a Sino-Japanese settlement. He wanted the guidance of the friendly foreign powers and hoped they would treat him "not only as a servant of the Chinese Government but as a trustee of foreign interests." In forwarding Maze's views to Washington, Consul General Gauss commented from Shanghai on January 9 that he felt "the present Inspector General is inclined too much to seek the instructions and support of the three interested powers." Washington decided to make no reply to Maze. London, however, instructed its embassy in China to advise Maze to keep the embassy fully informed and follow its advice, and to give him such support as possible. British Ambassador Clark Kerr asked the Chinese government to authorize Maze to reach a settlement with the Japanese, to be subsequently submitted to China for approval. But Chinese Foreign Minister Wang Chung-hui (not to be confused with Wang Ching-wei, who later defected to the puppet regime) replied that China would have to maintain its right to examine and approve any plan prior to acceptance.[15]

One matter on which the Japanese brought pressure was for use of more Japanese in the Customs work. Maze resisted this well, and yielded by

* After this book was in type Nicholas R. Clifford's article, "Sir Frederick Maze and the Chinese Maritime Customs, 1937–1941," appeared in the *Journal of Modern History*, March 1965, pp. 18–34. This informative article is based mainly upon Maze's papers at the University of London and views the situation through his eyes. It supplements what I state here but does not alter statements of fact or judgments. It describes his action, in the face of Japanese pressure, in trying to maintain the integrity of the Customs as "a single unit at least nominally under his own and the central government's control" (p. 21), a task which he performed with considerable skill. Clifford also brings out the viewpoint of many Customs men in their concern for service integrity, which Maze's successor L. K. Little has described as "almost an obsession" which led to "temporizing and compromising with whatever authority held power" (p. 33). That view led some Customs men to be ready to put loyalty to the service above loyalty to the government that employed them and to be ready to serve the Japanese and their puppets (p. 29). Clifford concludes, I think rightly, that Maze "shared much of the Customs outlook," but would only compromise on what he considered unessentials, and not give the Japanese the full cooperation they wanted but which he deemed inconsistent with his responsibility to the government of China (p. 34).

assigning Japanese already in this international service to more important posts and by employing additional Japanese in lesser "outdoor" work. He was an adroit politician and succeeded well in preventing full Japanese control of the Customs at any port. He deserves credit for maintaining the integrity of the service as well as he did. He reported these pressures to Minister Kung, who was in a difficult position and for the record had to send instructions tending to restrain Maze. But in practical effect he allowed Maze enough latitude to handle the problem. The alternative would have been full Japanese control and breaking any semblance of integrity of the service. Maze was confronted also with the possibility of being formally appointed Inspector General by a Japanese-sponsored regime. The American, British, and French governments made representations against this at Tokyo in October 1939.[16] The contingency did not arise.

When in January 1938 the Japanese announced through the Peiping regime a new tariff for North China, Minister Kung instructed the Inspectorate General not to recognize that tariff, and the American, British, and French governments at once strongly protested at Tokyo. Maze proposed, with British backing, that China revert to her 1931 tariff of lower rates. Kung pointed out to the British embassy that there was no assurance that Japan would allow that tariff to be applied in North China or even Shanghai, and that China did not wish to be drawn into an undignified competition with the puppet regime in cutting rates.[17] Agreement to Maze's plan would have been viewed as a sign of weakness. Meanwhile at Shanghai Japanese importers were bringing in goods without paying any duties. Import of military items was used to cover ordinary imports, and ordinary steamers were designated as "transports." On May 9, 1938, a Japanese embassy spokesman admitted that duty was not being paid on goods for the Japanese community. He said that these goods would pay the proper duties. After conclusion of the Anglo-Japanese Customs agreement, and introduction of the new tariff in Central China on June 1, they apparently did so.

Adjustment of duties to favor Japanese trade and legalized smuggling at Shanghai and elsewhere were of course very objectionable to non-Japanese business men. Customs integrity, effective control of trade, and uniform rates not grossly favoring any foreign country were vital to maintain the Open Door. Japanese armed forces also seized and on occasions attacked customs craft, thus interfering with antismuggling work. They also made it harder for ships to use the port of Shanghai, by detaining dredging equipment needed to keep the harbor safely navigable, and for a year there was no dredging.

As the difficulties mounted, Britain took over the effort to devise a specific working arrangement for the Customs. The hope was that the Customs service could somehow be sustained throughout the hostilities, since afterward it could greatly aid China in the period of rehabilitation, and that meanwhile the bondholders would be paid. In December the British government proposed to Washington that negotiations be shifted to Tokyo, instead of continuing in China where the Japanese military were bringing pressure on the Inspectorate General and the Commissioners of Customs. Washington raised the question of "who or what agency is to represent the Chinese in these negotiations." The British reply on December 31 was that China of course would not be present, but that "an endeavor would later be made to persuade the Chinese to accept any understanding which might be reached." [18]

It was not, however, until the latter part of February 1938 that the negotiations were concentrated at Tokyo, with the British seeking a concrete agreement. On March 8 the British diplomatic representative at Hankow wrote to Minister Kung that "His Majesty's Government desire that the utmost effort should be made to persuade Your Excellency to acquiesce in any arrangement that it may be possible to reach." Kung replied that he had not been "informed with particularity concerning these negotiations" which "touch upon vital Chinese interests," and restated his views on the chief matters at issue.

China's firm attitude reflected the patriotic surge caused by the fight for existence and the unexpected success in resisting a far stronger enemy. To many foreigners in China, including some officials, the fighting seemed an incident like former Sino-foreign clashes that would somehow be compromised, with most of the *status quo* remaining. But to the Chinese government and to the Chinese people generally it was clear that Japan was making an all-out effort to dominate China and destroy the position and influence of Western countries and their nationals. China's leaders saw little gain in handing over the Customs organization to collect revenue for the enemy and grant favors to Japanese trade. They saw no promise for the future in giving way on matters of principle, and opposed "appeasement."

Negotiations went ahead actively at Tokyo. On March 24 the British ambassador, Sir Robert Craigie, gave the American ambassador, Joseph C. Grew, the text of a proposed agreement, which was refined in further talks. About mid-April Ambassador Clark Kerr orally informed Minister Kung of the subject matter under discussion but did not indicate that agreement was imminent. On April 26 press reports from Japan stated that a full agreement had been reached and was shortly to be initialed. Kung at once wrote to the British Diplomatic Mission's Hankow representative (the ambassador having left):

Since this matter is chiefly of concern to China, I assume that the Chinese Government will be fully informed of the proposed terms well in advance, before any such understanding is reached, in order to ascertain whether the terms would be acceptable to the Chinese Government. Pending receipt of further information and full consideration of all material aspects of the situation, the position of the Chinese Government is of course fully reserved.

The British reply of April 29 was that no agreement had been reached but that a draft text had been established which London was considering.

On April 29 Ambassador Quo Tai-chi telegraphed from London the substance of a personal communication from Sir Frederick Leith-Ross, Economic Adviser to the British government, summarizing the proposal and stating that his government had not yet definitely approved it. Sir Frederick felt it was the best obtainable, and that some such plan was better than to leave Japan in complete control of the customs revenue. He said that London thought it best not to consult China officially, but hoped that if and when agreement was reached China would find it possible to offer no objection.

On May 2 the agreement was hurriedly completed at Tokyo. The urgency arose because the Japanese Finance Ministry told the Foreign Office that the military were bringing such pressure that they would not accept the terms of the proposal unless it were concluded by that date.[19] A summary of the agreement was made public the same day at London. On that day Ambassador Clark Kerr telegraphed from Shanghai to Generalissimo Chiang and Minister Kung that the matter suddenly had become urgent and that the agreement had to be concluded at once to prevent Japanese take-over of the Customs. To prevent this, and because clearly Japan would not meet China's minimum terms about the Customs, Britain he said had deliberately refrained from consulting China during the negotiations. China of course could disavow responsibility; but he hoped China would not do anything to make the measures unworkable. He believed that the arrangement was much preferable to unconditional Japanese seizure of the Customs.

The announcement referred to "unofficial conversations" at Tokyo, which led Japan to notify Britain of "the temporary measures proposed to be taken during the period of hostilities," concerning foreign debt payments and other Customs matters. The revenue collected in occupied areas was to be paid to the Yokohama Specie Bank. Quotas for foreign debt service would be remitted to the Inspector General's account at that bank in Shanghai, and the Inspector General would arrange to convert them into foreign exchange. The customs revenue accumulated in the Hongkong and Shanghai Banking Corporation in occupied ports, about C$27 million, was to be transferred to the Yokohama Specie Bank for future foreign debt quotas. The arrears of the Japanese portion of the Boxer Indemnity accumulated in sterling in that Bank since September, then equivalent to well over US$1 million, and further sums as due were to be paid to Japan. Japan expressed in the agreement the intention of resuming duty payments by Japanese importers, and of returning seized customs craft, "except those specially required for military purposes," and allowing them to resume preventive work. The entire arrangement might be reconsidered "in the event of a radical change in the economic conditions under which the above measures are proposed." [20]

The British announcement mistakenly said that the American government would offer no objection to the arrangement. British Ambassador Craigie had put that statement in the draft, hoping that the United States could be persuaded to take that stand, altering its previous view. Craigie thought that here would be time to modify the wording if necessary. But, when the announcement was hurriedly issued, the United States still maintained that it would not be right to comment pending knowledge of China's views. The mistake embarrassed both the United States and China. [21]

China at once told Britain she regretted that a Chinese administration had been "the subject matter of an agreement between two foreign states," and fully reserved China's rights and freedom of action about the Customs. [22] But China, being so dependent upon British sympathy and aid, refrained from positive action to oppose the agreement. Such action, however, was not necessary because the agreement could not come into effect without China making certain payments to Japan. These were (1) the accumulated and blocked monthly installments of the Japanese portion of the Boxer Indemnity, about £33,000 each, then totaling £260,000; and (2) custom funds of about C$27 million accumulated and blocked in the Hongkong and Shanghai Banking Corporation at Shanghai. [23] No Chinese official could put himself in the position of handing over money to the enemy. Japan, on the other hand, argued that if she released part of the revenue of occupied areas to benefit other foreign interests, she should get her contractual share in debt payments which the quotas covered.

In favor of the agreement, from China's standpoint, was that it was designed to preserve a measure of "integrity" of the Sino-foreign service, which could still be useful to China in case of a stalemate or Japan's eventual defeat. On the other hand, there was little chance that a victorious Japan would tolerate continuance of that service and allow the Open Door.

Besides the broad issues of principle and policy, the financial side was important. That involved China's position as to both local and foreign currencies. Japan was to receive at once the C$27 million, plus sterling funds equivalent to about C$8 million, a total of about C$35 million (about US$8 million). But China would receive C$19 million as of July 1, and about C$4 million monthly thereafter. Thus until November China would not benefit financially. From November, however, the payments of about C$4 million monthly would reduce the supply of money at Shanghai, and thus tend to check inflation. Meanwhile, China feared that Japan, which was short of foreign currencies and in July mobilized the foreign assets of her nationals, would use the C$27 million to be turned over at once to buy exchange at Shanghai.

Moreover, China would have had to provide all the foreign currencies needed for debt payments. Reserves abroad were shrinking, and Japan was interfering with the supply of exchange from exports. It seemed only a matter of months until China would have to suspend payments on the foreign debt, unless large aid available in foreign currency were obtained. There was no such aid in sight. Thus the appearance that quota payments under the agreement would help the holders of foreign currency debt was mostly illusory.

For over a year China examined from time to time the possibility of finding some indirect way to implement the agreement. But any plan for Japan to provide loan quotas would have implied that continuance of debt service was assured. Also any change in the agreement would have involved further British negotiations with Japan, and meanwhile China's hands would be tied as regards suspension of debt payments. And, in the unlikely event that Japan would agree to changes that China could accept, and if thereafter China suspended payments in foreign currency, it was doubtful that Japan would continue to allow remittance of quotas in Chinese currency. So the agreement remained inoperative.

When China suspended payments on the privately held foreign currency debt early in 1939 (see chap. VII), China anticipated that suspension would bring renewed urging on behalf of British bondholders to give effect to the agreement. Hence a Chinese spokesman stated, when suspension was announced, that Japanese remittances of customs funds had been made "dependent upon conditions which China could not accept." He specified these conditions. In response to British urging at London that China implement the agreement, Kung telegraphed on January 20 to Ambassador Quo Tai-chi that China "could not sanction such action in midst of war and any Finance Minister doing such acts would be punished as traitor. If they put themselves in China's position would they do it? They should realize suggested action politically impossible."

The British government, when it decided in March to go ahead with a currency credit to China (see chap. XVI), weighed whether to condition it upon China implementing the Customs agreement. But Ambassador Clark Kerr telegraphed in February that difficulties for China were matters of principle, and that these views were "held in all quarters." [24] Britain then granted the credit without this string on it. But Britain continued to press for some means of implementation.

With the currency situation becoming acute in the spring of 1939, China would have benefited if it had been possible to obtain under the agreement the payment of C$40 million of accrued debt quotas. [25] Payment to China of that sum, and of about C$5.5 million monthly of future quotas, would have materially tightened money and tended to support the exchange market. Cyril Rogers of the Bank of England, who began supervision of stabilization operations with the aid of the new British credit early in April (see chap. XVI), repeatedly urged me to try to work out some arrangement to implement the agreement. With Minister Kung's acquiescence I exchanged views with Ambassador Clark Kerr. We made progress in seeking a formula of set-off to which China would not object. The American government helped on June 23 by authorizing a fresh approach at Tokyo, to press Japan for contributions for debt service.[26] But a further Anglo-Japanese understanding would have been necessary. There was doubt whether Japan would any longer be ready to transfer a large sum to China and remit current loan quotas, a year after the agreement was made and after suspension of payment of China's debt in foreign currency. The chance of successful negotiations practically vanished in the second half of June, when Britain and Japan came close to the breaking point over the Tientsin blockade (see chap. XVI). In July China's currency broke badly. And on September 1, World War II broke out. The Anglo-Japanese Customs agreement, which had caused so much difficulty and controversy, stayed in abeyance.[27]

Appraisal, with benefit of hindsight, shows that the British correctly felt that no deal which both China and Japan could formally accept was feasible. The difficulty was inclusion of provisions calling upon China to turn over funds to her enemy. Especially with the financial advantage favoring Japan for the first half-year, it was too much to expect that any Chinese official could take such action. But Japan would not have agreed to terms materially less favorable to her than those of the agreement of May 1938. Hence it is doubtful that there was a real basis for agreement at that time. Probably the only chance for an agreement was in September 1937 when the Japanese consul general at Tientsin indicated that Japan was ready to make a limited provision of debt quotas. But then China sought better terms, the Japanese military intervened, and the opportunity passed.

Although the agreement failed to help the holders of China's foreign debt, it did divert the attention of the Japanese military from the idea of seizing the Customs organization. Thus it preserved a measure of integrity until outbreak of the Pacific War. Also, it led to ending the Japanese import of goods without duty, although the trade continued under a new tariff designed to favor Japanese trade. But a by-product of the agreement was to magnify Sino-British friction, which increased as the fighting progressed.

Meanwhile, stimulated Chinese nationalism, which naturally resulted from the fighting, was reflected in continuing pressure on the Customs, and also on the Salt revenue service. On June 26, 1938, China promulgated a new Treasury Law, but with a provision (article 32) that the date and area of enforcement were to be determined by governmental decree. That law, if strictly applied to the operations of these services, would have materially changed their status in using pledged revenues for debt payments. Also it would have hampered their day-to-day working by tying up in red tape and delays the receipt and payment of funds. I strongly urged the Ministry not to change the status of these two agencies. But there was all too much of the idea that such a law could and should override international commitments. When Lockhart wrote to me from Shanghai about prospective difficulties in the law, I replied on August 14, reflecting the climate of the time:

> I suppose I must put in another memorandum on the subject; but I rather hate to do it as it is a sore subject. It is hard to get the powers that be to see that China will want credit again, and that the way to get it most readily and on the best terms is to follow religiously the letter and spirit of existing agreements. Their answer is likely to be that other countries do not abide by their treaty obligations to China . . .
>
> You and I have gone on record so many times on these matters . . . that it is a question how far to risk continuing irritation and possible prejudice to future usefulness by again arguing them.

Consul General Gauss commented from Shanghai on September 15 that it was

> astounding . . . that at a time when China is so dependent upon the foreign Powers and their financial resources, and when it is evident that she will be dependent upon them for many years to come in any reconstruction following the hostilities with Japan, China goes merrily on her course of gradually breaking down foreign control and influence in the Customs and Salt services, to the prejudice of her own interests through resulting lack of confidence on the part of foreign bondholders and financial and banking interests in the integrity of the Chinese Government and the integrity of the security of existing loan services.[28]

As a result of the objections raised by the Customs and Salt services, and by bondholders supported by foreign governments, China postponed for the time being the application of the new law to those services.

After outbreak of the Pacific War, the Japanese seized the Customs headquarters in Shanghai and captured Sir Frederick Maze. In a memorandum of December 13, 1941, I recommended transferring the head office to Chungking, appointing a foreigner as Acting Inspector General, and leaving the setup substantially unchanged, in view of loan commitments to maintain the existing arrangements for Customs administration. The government concurred, and appointed C. H. B. Joly, a British member of the service, as Officiating Inspector General. Because foreign trade practically ceased after 1941, on account of the blockade, the Customs had little to do. The Customs participated in collection of certain internal taxes, as described in the first section of this chapter.

Nationalism gave rise after 1941 to growing pressure to alter the former Customs arrangements. Efforts to undermine the setup were partly forestalled by the action of the Finance Ministry. But it was clear that nationalism could not be denied, and that some change in the old arrangements would have to take place. The problem was how to avoid unilateral action and sabotage, and to work out an orderly agreed change. In 1942 after long postponement the government applied to the Customs the Treasury Law of 1938. This unilaterally changed the handling of pledged revenues, in disregard of loan agreements. From the administrative side, a serious difficulty was how to maintain a living wage for the foreign and Chinese personnel, and to prevent their being dragged down to the level of grossly underpaid civil servants in general. The result was a long struggle, in which the Customs had only partial success. In 1943 Minister Kung appointed L. K. Little, an American, as Acting Inspector-General and later gave him the definitive title. Everyone agreed that he was an admirable choice. He did all that he could do to maintain the service. But the wartime and postwar disorganization made his task a hard one. The Chinese Customs, a unique international civil service with nearly a century of worthy history, gradually became an all-Chinese organ in Taiwan.

The hostilities and the Salt revenue administration. The fighting brought increasing difficulties to the Salt revenue administration. Major salt-producing areas were not far from Tientsin and Shanghai, and were overrun early in the fighting. Foreign and Chinese officials were forced to leave. By early 1938 the revenue of districts yielding over half the salt income either was not being collected or had been taken over by the Japanese or their agents. Loan quotas no longer came forward from these districts. Also loan quotas from Free China fell into arrears. The local authorities had need of funds for large wartime costs. So they fell back upon the practice of the days of the warlords, and under one guise or another kept much of the locally raised revenue. These inroads became more and more serious as time passed. The Central Government tended to acquiesce, although it would have been better to maintain revenue rights, and grant local subsidies if necessary.

Beginning in August 1937 the Japanese set up rival local organizations to administer salt revenues in North China and elsewhere. They made use of renegade Chinese, some of whom had formerly been in the service and had left with none too savory reputations. There were reports that the Japanese might try to set up a rival organization at Shanghai for general control. To hold back such schemes, about December 1937, Lockhart with Ministry acquiescence called back for service two Japanese who had been on leave, one of whom, however, did not return. The apparent alternative was military pressure to take on other Japanese who would have been less amenable. That move helped to tide things over.

The administrative offices of the Salt revenue were divided between Shanghai, Hankow (until its capture in the fall of 1938), and Chungking;

and later further divided in other places in Szechwan Province. There was nationalistic pressure to close the Shanghai office. But Lockhart pointed out that its retention was important to keep contact with conditions in nearby producing areas, which were partly occupied; to stay in touch with banks representing the bondholders in matters of loan service; and to avoid giving the enemy an excuse for setting up a rival puppet organization which could take over by default if the lawful authorities abandoned the field. Minister Kung approved keeping that office, and instructed Lockhart to divide his time between Shanghai and Free China.

In the fall of 1937 the friendly powers, while making representations at Tokyo about the Customs, also indicated their interest in safeguarding the salt-secured debt and the integrity of the Salt revenue administration. Plans were discussed among Chinese officials, creditors' representatives, and friendly governments for seeking loan quotas from the occupied areas and depositing them in neutral banks. The British considered trying to devise a concrete plan, but waited because the Customs issue, which impinged more sharply upon foreign rights and interests, was viewed as a test case. After China's adverse reaction to the Anglo-Japanese Customs agreement of May 1938, however, they were unwilling to try for a deal about salt without a definite request by China. But China was not ready to make such a request while the Customs question remained unsettled.

Sad experience with the Customs made clear an inherent difficulty in any scheme for cooperation with Japan to maintain "integrity" of these Sino-foreign agencies. Integrity meant in practice turning over to Japan the services, in occupied areas, of experienced revenue-collecting organs. In connection with schemes for the Salt administration that had been discussed in 1938, Lockhart wrote to me on October 29, 1938, from Shanghai that neither he nor his Chinese colleague could approve a "proposal to work alongside the Japanese in supplying salt to Japanese-controlled areas, even if thereby we were permitted to *share* the right of taxing." If anything would have fitted the salt revenue situation, it would have been international pressure on Japan to remit loan quotas on as fair a basis as could have been negotiated, without involvement in any arrangement to collect revenue for Japan's benefit.

Meanwhile, the war-stimulated nationalism was having its effect in efforts to reduce and eventually end the foreign participation in handling the pledged salt revenues. While Associate Director General Lockhart stayed much of the time at Shanghai for reasons stated, Director General T. C. Chu stayed in the interior to look after problems of the revenue and supply of salt. Each had his representative with the other, but that was far from an ideal system of operation. In the prevailing atmosphere of strong nationalism, Chu's tendency to disregard his colleague grew. He and some of those working with him started early in the war to undermine the system by intrigue and indirection, rather than by frankly trying to change it by agreement or openly casting it aside.

Preparatory to possible negotiations with Japan, Ambassador Clark Kerr wrote to Minister Kung on March 22, 1938, through the British Diplomatic Mission at Hankow, urging "the necessity of maintaining the authority of the foreign staff." In his reply of March 24, Kung said:

> . . . in principle I consider that as to essential functions the joint responsibility of the Directors-General and of the subordinate foreign and Chinese officers should be maintained substantially as it existed during the years prior to the outbreak of hostilities. I am issuing instructions to the Salt Administration to the effect that there should be no derogations from this principle except to such extent as is unavoidable during the emergency, and that any such derogations are only temporary in character.

Kung repeated the assurance in August 1939 to the bondholders' representatives at London in connection with negotiations for partial resumption of debt payments.

Clearly the commitments of 1938–1939 should not have been subject to unilateral change. Yet the instructions based on the letter of March 24, 1938, issued after some delay, did not stop the decay. The system of joint authority and responsibility remained the announced policy of the Ministry of Finance. But the attitude of numerous persons in the Salt administration and elsewhere made it hard in practice to give effect to the policy. In the summer of 1939, despite Kung's aforementioned assurance at London, came the plan to apply to the Salt revenue administration the Treasury Law of 1938 (see the preceding section). Both Lockhart and I repeatedly argued against unilateral change, whether directly or by indirection. After foreign debt payments were suspended early in 1939, some within the government argued that there was less use in keeping the foreign participation. The abortive scheme for a salt monopoly, proposed in 1941 and mentioned earlier in this chapter, would have further departed from the letter and spirit of China's international commitments. There was all too much of the notion that China could unilaterally override such commitments, rather than negotiate for changes in the light of new conditions. In a memorandum of February 20, 1942, reviewing the situation, I wrote:

> . . . under stress of war and the growth of more intense nationalism, many Chinese inclined more and more to push for further nationalization of the Salt Administration. Much of this pressure was not a frank urging of modification of the set-up by agreement, but rather took the forms of resistance to the practical operation of a system of joint authority and responsibility, encroachment with a view to gradual complete taking over, and efforts to hold the foreign officers responsible for results even though in fact they had not been accorded the corresponding authority and power to act. The situation was further complicated by the long continuance in office of T. C. Chu as director general, and by the illness

and absence in Shanghai and the United States of the associate director general, Dr. O. C. Lockhart.

The position of the foreign staff steadily worsened during the war. Their pay and allowances failed to keep abreast of the inflation. They were further discouraged by living conditions which became increasingly hard, separation from families, lack of home leave, and infringement upon their prerogatives. In August 1939, Ambassador Johnson reported to the State Department his impression that the presence of foreigners was coming to be viewed by the Chinese as "a reflection on their capacity as Chinese"; and that it seemed "regrettably probable that . . . more sinister reasons of financial irregularity have crept in." Washington authorized Johnson to use his good offices informally "to the end that the service conditions of the foreign personnel . . . may be improved." [29] But the deterioration could not be checked. Many resigned, and by the fall of 1941 the number of foreigners in the service had fallen to 16, half the number in mid-1937. Lockhart resigned in 1941, having left China at the end of 1940 because of illness. During the Pacific War the other foreign officers gradually left. The struggle to uphold China's international commitments by maintaining joint authority and responsibility was lost.

Supply of salt for China's huge population was a problem throughout the war. Without enough salt there would have been serious riots and disturbances. Salt merchants and the government worked hard to remove stocks from exposed points. Fortunately enemy action did not lead to serious shortages of salt for any long periods in the country as a whole. In all the confusion salt merchants managed somehow to meet the people's need during the fighting. There was much smuggling from producing areas. This helped meet the need, but naturally cut into the revenue in Free China.

EXPENDITURE, DEFICIT

Expenditure. Thanks to the printing press, the government never lacked money during the war. Hence objects of outlay did not get the cold and careful scrutiny that was so needful. Budgetary procedures were faulty. The various branches of government put in requests which, as customary everywhere, were well padded. There was no system of priorities for expenditures, nor was there an adequate procedure for comparison with past appropriations, for examining requests and requiring justification in detail by the asking organizations, or for determining the real merits under war conditions. The final decision was made by the National Defense Council, which included the heads of Yuans which (except for the Executive Yuan) were actually somewhat remote from the main work of the government. The budgets were more a matter of negotiation than of financial planning. H. H. Kung, as Finance Minister and President or Vice-President of the Executive Yuan, often struggled against avoidable spending. T. F. Tsiang, as a leading official of that Yuan, was a constant advocate of restraint and good sense, as were a few others. But the pressures for spending all too often were too strong to be withstood.

As inflation progressed, original budget estimates soon became outdated and had to be increased by supplementary authorizations (see Table 1). Actual payments rose to twice the original budgets or more, and in 1945 were more than four times as great.

Military costs, as listed in Table 3, were by far the biggest item, amounting to 60 to 70 per cent of cash outlay according to the budgetary accounts. Including payments in kind in rice and wheat, the proportion was about the same. War costs, however, should logically include a good part of the outlay for communications, economic affairs, and payments to provincial and local governments. Also, much of the large cost of collecting land tax in kind could be considered a war cost, since the chief object of this measure was to supply the armies. Furthermore, payment for goods delivered under commodity agreements and barter transactions mostly with the United States and Russia was in exchange for items for the war effort.

Under the conditions that existed, it could hardly be said that China spent too much for military purposes. But, as is usually the case in a war, the money often was not well spent. China supported far too many troops, many of whom were so badly equipped and poorly trained that they had little fighting value. Hitler once said that the wolf does not care how many sheep there are. China would have been better off with much smaller armies, making use of the best-trained leaders and men, and concentrating with them most of the available weapons and supplies. Part of the difficulty was the government's lack of control of local warlords. But, despite this, much more could and should have been done to improve the armies, especially when the United States was providing military aid and advice. Feasible measures of improvement were urged by the German military advisers until they left in 1938, by the Americans after arrival of the military mission in 1941, and also from time to time by influential Chinese both within and outside of the government.[30]

Furthermore, military expenditure was never brought under proper fiscal control. Commanders of units were given large lump-sum payments, based upon the reported number of troops. This invited corruption. The practice was a hangover from prewar days, from regimes long dominated by the military leaders. The German General Hans von Seekt, while acting as military adviser in 1933, strongly urged reform of the army financial system, with proper budgets and controls. But his recommendation had little positive result.[31] Only toward the end of the war was there a serious effort at reform, which was stimulated by the successful results of the training by

American officers of Chinese units in India, where the men were regularly and adequately paid.

Development outlay, generally termed reconstruction, comprised about a tenth of the budget in the first six years (Table 3). Large early items related to transplanting essential industries to the interior. Emergency moving of supplies, machinery, and personnel was necessary, to set up a base of resistance beyond the enemy's reach. From 1939 the Extraordinary National Congress of the Kuomintang adopted the policy of "resistance and reconstruction." A declaration adopted at Hankow April 2, after calling for strengthened military action and internal solidarity, dealt with economic matters in the following clauses:

17. Economic reconstruction should revolve around military needs. At the same time, attention should be given to improving the people's livelihood. With these objects in view, economic planning should be enforced and investments at home and from abroad should be encouraged in order to increase the nation's production during wartime.

18. To devote full energy to the development of rural economy, establishment of cooperatives, readjustment of food supply, reclamation of wasteland, and inauguration of water conservancy projects.

19. To develop the mineral resources so as to lay the foundation for the nation's heavy industry. Light industries will be encouraged while local handicraft industries will be promoted.

20. To enforce a war time taxation system, and to thoroughly reform the financial administration.

21. To control the banking business following which adjustments will be made in the industrial and commercial activities.

22. To strengthen the legal tender, control foreign exchange, and manage imports and exports in order to stabilize the currency.

23. To adjust the network of communications, undertake through water-land-air traffic, and construct more railways, and highways, and open additional airways.

24. To strictly prohibit unscrupulous merchants from speculating in and manipulating the market, and enforce a price-equalization system.

Partly underlying this declaration was the idea, common to so many wartime inflations, that the major cause of the price rises was scarcity rather than multiplication of note-issue, and that the chief remedy was more production.

Results of the ideas embodied in the declaration were not slow to appear in the form of projects for increased expenditure, partly outside the general budget, to be financed by credit inflation. The determination to modernize while fighting is understandable, given the undeveloped state of the free areas into which the government and its armies were being forced. Unfortunately there was inadequate realization of the limitations of the economy, a failure to distinguish between what was essential to the war effort and what could and should have been postponed, and no procedure to set priorities and allocate the scarce resources of money, goods, and men accordingly. The availability of printing-press money made restraint harder.

Spending for development was partly under the general budget, and partly from advances through the Joint Committee of the Four Government Banks. In nonmilitary affairs much was spent for avoidable projects, such as bridges and tunnels for railways which could not be finished for use in the war, notably those in Szechwan Province and the northwest. Considerable sums were spent to develop production of iron and steel but of such poor quality that it was of little use — a project which could be considered a prelude to the later unsuccessful communist experiment with "backyard iron furnaces." Also there were expenditures for roads, irrigation works, river conservancy, and improvement of navigation which, however desirable projects in themselves, could not be justified when they added to an inflation that already was getting out of hand. It is ironic that this aggravation of inflation tended to help the communists to come to power, and thus to inherit both completed projects and various planned and partly completed projects which they have since been carrying forward. Avoidable spending for development undoubtedly bid up prices of some relatively scarce items, such as machines and tools, certain materials, and transport. The lack of restraint in spending for development, moreover, was hurtful to general confidence in the finances.

Outlay for debt was 18 per cent of the total in the first year, but thereafter it was a much smaller part. This was partly because of suspension of payments on foreign loans early in 1939, and partly because payments to the public on the *fapi* debt were fixed in amount, while inflation was swelling the figures of the budget. Also there was relatively little borrowing from the public after the first year.

Administrative and general costs took about 5 per cent or less of the total.

Efforts for reform. Repeatedly during the war I urged building up revenues and cutting avoidable costs. Shortly after the fighting began, Acting Finance Minister Hsu Kan asked my views on war finance. The reply of September 11, 1937, urged defraying from taxation as much as possible of public expenditure, including consideration of land taxes in kind; borrowing from the public to the extent possible, and pressing the well-to-do who largely escaped taxes "to subscribe to Liberty bonds in proportion to their ability"; limitation of government spending to what is absolutely essential; and use of credit facilities "only for essential ends."

A few of the many efforts made for a better fiscal policy during the war will be noted. In a memorandum of September 26, 1941, for Generalissimo Chiang, I said:

. . . by far the greatest cause of the price difficulty is the heavy issue of *fapi* as the result of financing the war mainly by borrowing from the four Government banks. The remedies therefore have to be sought chiefly in the strictest possible measures to control the further growth of fapi issues. Other measures such as price control, rationing, encouragement of production et cetera are only palliatives. They can be applied only to a limited extent under actual conditions, and cannot much influence the main trend in China as a whole.

Roughly there are two main sorts of remedial measures: — first, to get back from the public as many as possible of the *fapi* already issued and spend them again instead of issuing more; and, second, to refrain religiously from issuing more *fapi* than absolutely necessary. . . .

. . . unless drastic action is promptly taken, runaway inflation cannot be avoided.

Specific proposals as to revenue were: increased taxation; adequate pay of the revenue services; abandonment of the scheme for government monopolies of salt and other goods, which called for an initial outlay of C$1.5 billion for salt alone, and would have diverted trained men needed more elsewhere; and more borrowing from the public with measures to safeguard against currency depreciation. As to expenditure, the memorandum urged seeking means to control spending not essential to the war effort and reduction of surplus personnel while raising the pay of needed staff, since it is "poor economy to have responsible work done by persons not paid a living wage." As to the military, a program for "smaller but better trained and equipped personnel" should be considered. With regard to a proposed Three Year Plan for economic and social development, the memorandum urged "no expansion of any government organization, or addition to staff, unless clearly proven necessary for the war effort." A further recommendation called for better control of loans by commercial and provincial banks and of provincial spending schemes.

Generalissimo Chiang approved these ideas for the most part, and directed the Executive Yuan to issue appropriate orders to the various offices concerned. Shortly after this Sir Otto Niemeyer of the Bank of England arrived in China. He and I combined forces during his brief stay, in favor of a better fiscal policy, and helped bring about some improvements in the budget for 1942. A. Manuel Fox, American Representative on the Stabilization Board, when in Washington in early 1942, was critical of what was done, especially of Sir Otto. In a memorandum of February 18, 1942, to Secretary Morgenthau he said that the restraints were helping to "set in motion a deflationary movement. This had a bad effect and tended to retard production of essentials and various new industrial developments." [32] Actually the inflation was going ahead faster than at any earlier period, mainly because of damage to confidence caused by enemy military successes in the early weeks of the Pacific War, and fears caused by China's greater isolation.

Although from time to time there was some stiffening of policy, the problems were too deeply rooted in a weak fiscal and governmental system that was steadily made weaker by the ravages of the enemy and the less tangible ravages of inflation. So there was no drastic change in the way things were going. As pressures for useless or unimportant spending continued, I urged in a memorandum of April 24, 1942, that the government adopt a set of principles stringently regulating fresh expenditures or credit: they should be clearly essential to the war effort, capable of being completed in time, the cost should be commensurate with the result expected, existing organizations and facilities should be used as far as possible, and the burden of proof should be on the proposers. T. F. Tsiang, a senior official of the Executive Yuan, wrote to me on April 27 that adoption of these proposals "would do China infinite good." Yet waste continued, despite efforts by him and others of the same mind.

From time to time the press urged sounder policies. Thus *Ta Kung Pao* of Chungking, September 21, 1942, argued for better coordination and organization of the government to effect economy, and against creation of fresh bodies and undertaking enterprises that were not essential to war. Again on October 24 they argued for a much smaller army to be better paid and provided for, reform of taxation, and compulsory allocation of bonds to those able to buy them.

When the government began consideration of the budget for 1943, I made the following recommendations to Minister Kung in a memorandum of August 25, 1942:

Despite the dangers, many offices and many influential members of the Government unfortunately are trying actively to expand their expenditure — not only to keep pace with real war needs and with higher prices, but also for the sake of having a larger program in fields where it could and should be postponed in the interest of the war effort. There are schemes for extension of railways and for industrial establishments that are not really necessary for the war effort, that would take well over a year to complete, and for which the needed imported materials are not at hand and cannot be obtained. Also there are schemes for enlargement of the functions of various offices and creation of new activities unessential to the war effort . . .

Many branches of the Government that now complain of lack of funds could do their necessary work properly if they stopped expansion, curtailed postponable activities, reduced personnel and used their resources for adequate support of a minimum program appropriate to the present emergency. Cannot a plan be worked out to select the essential lines of work and the essential personnel in the various offices, and to hold them to hard work with a high standard of efficiency and properly to pay them?

The great need is, first, firmly to establish the principle that avoidable expenditures are to be cut out of the new budget; and second to have a careful and impartial examination of all proposed expenditures in the light of past outlays and future needs for really essential purposes, in order to find the minimum amount that has to be appropriated.

In a memorandum of June 24, 1943, I called attention to a Japanese announcement that Japan had discharged 125,355 civil employees, stating that thereby administrative efficiency was increased; and said, "China might profit by following the example of its enemy in this regard," of course with proper severance pay. The same memorandum urged simplifying the tax system by reliance on taxing substantially a few goods of wide consumption, whereas, "Efforts to tax a large number of goods all over the country do not add much to revenue, but are sure to add to costs of collection and multiplication of tax officials."

The problem of China's inflation involved the issue of the causes of inflation. Economic analysis showed clearly then, and is amply confirmed by hindsight, that far and away the main factor was excessive creation of money, and that scarcity of goods was only a minor cause of the continuing and growing rise of general prices (see chap. XX). There were capable economists in the government and the universities who understood the issues, but they were not the policy makers. To many officials, engineers, and businessmen in China the scarcity factor was paramount. The issue was not confined to China. I debated the issue with Donald M. Nelson in Washington in the fall of 1944, just before he went to China to set up a War Production Board. But he was unconvinced and told a group of officials and bankers in Chungking on November 22 that "in the long run increased production was the only sound means of offsetting inflation." [33] In a memorandum of November 20 to Kung I said:

> In the case of Mr. Nelson's program, I would strongly recommend concentrating fresh outlay on urgent production for the war effort; and avoiding in principle any large expenditure merely to increase the supply of civilian goods, e.g., of iron and steel, or to prepare at this stage for future industrialization. China's capacity to carry a war burden is limited, and the nature of the burden chosen should be that which will do the most good.

Planning for postwar financial stabilization. The major postwar financial problem appeared clearly to be to bring about stabilization through control of outlay and building up noninflationary income. These measures were a fundamental prerequisite to monetary reform, since only thus could the inflation be slowed and brought within bounds, if not ended. Some of China's leaders saw clearly the need for careful financial planning for the future. Thus T. F. Tsiang, interviewed April 15, 1942, by a representative of the American Office of Strategic Services, was quoted as follows: "Dr. Tsiang expressed very strongly the opinion that China's main problem in the near and further future is to save the Chinese financial system from the complete collapse experienced by Germany."[34]

By early 1943 it seemed prudent to begin serious financial planning in anticipation of the war's end. I submitted a series of memorandums on the prospective problems. A memorandum of May 8, 1943, said:

There are two vitally important problems bearing upon China's financial and economic rehabilitation and progress to which I venture to call attention, although as political problems they are not directly within the field of my work, namely: (1) external security, and (2) internal political stability . . .

Especially in the immediate post-war period of rehabilitation, it will be important to keep military outlay at a minimum consistent with national security, and to defer so far as practicable to a later period any large and unavoidable costs for development of the military establishment.

As to the internal situation, the history of the decade before 1937 shows that when China was politically tranquil great strides could be made in economic and financial progress and in promotion of the people's welfare. But in the periods of internal disturbances the progress was stopped, and the Government incurred heavy unproductive expenditure and large deficits and debts — not to speak of the loss of lives and destruction of property . . . if unhappily the end of external war should be followed by serious internal disturbances, the financial problems and the already grave difficulties of rehabilitation would be infinitely complicated and the program of reconstruction delayed . . .

The means to accomplish external security and internal political stability are of course outside my province. I venture, however, to stress the vital importance on economic and financial grounds of doing all possible well before the end of the war to ensure external and internal peace after the war.

Also an improved social climate was basic for solid financial rehabilitation. To that end a memorandum of July 28, 1943, called attention to the land problem, and the need for reforms centering upon "land registration, land taxation, and land tenure and utilization." To devise a sound and workable program, I urged constituting a group of Chinese and foreign experts.

The receipt in Chungking early in 1943 of the American and British plans for monetary arrangements after the war, the White and Keynes plans, opened the way for study of China's prospective financial problems. Minister Kung referred the plans to me and I prepared a careful analysis, the substance of which is contained in appendix G and discussed in chapter XX. The conclusion was that, while the earliest practicable stabilization of postwar exchange rates was important, the plans needed changes to take account of the problems of countries such as China whose finances were disrupted by the war. On September 3, 1943, the Chinese ambassador at Washington communicated to the American government China's views on these lines.[35] Unfortunately they received no serious attention, and there was no international provision to aid war-smitten countries to recover financial stability. But at the Bretton Woods Conference members of the Chinese delegation were able to procure the inclusion of provisions for transitional arrangements concerning exchange rates, for the benefit of these countries.[36]

In arranging for international aid for physical reconstruction, there was good progress, through the United Nations Relief and Rehabilitation Administration (UNRRA). In September 1944 China requested UNRRA to provide imported requirements of US$945 million, for food, clothing, shelter, public health, transport and communications, agriculture, industries, flooded areas, welfare services, and displaced persons. I participated in preparing the program, which was reasonably realistic except as regards clothing, public health, and industrial rehabilitation. The request, however, covered only 37 per cent of China's estimated need of US$2.5 billion of imports for full relief and rehabilitation. Eventually UNRRA's aid provided US$519 million of imported supplies and over 1,000 foreign personnel. Meeting internal costs in China, however, was a serious problem, and here the planning fell short. These costs were projected as equivalent to C$2.7 billion, being figured in prewar currency because inflation made it impossible to estimate effectively in depreciating money. That figure, equivalent to over US$800 million, compared with the government's *total* prewar yearly expenditure of about C$1 billion (about US$300 million). The estimates for UNRRA went much beyond relief and rehabilitation and included much new development — so anxious were China's leaders to begin development immediately after the war was over. An instance was the public health proposal. Commenting on this I said in a letter of August 18, 1944, to Tsiang:

As to the financial side, I cannot see how it is possible to contemplate expenditure in the first year of CN$247 million, of which CN$112 million would be for capital purposes and CN$135 million for running expenses. The total outlay of the Government for *all* civil expenditures before the war in the last year for which figures were published (1934–35) was CN$231 million. The total revenue of the National Government in 1936 from customs, salt and consolidated taxes was CN$666 million, and total revenues, according to my recollection, were around CN$800 million. It will be some time before the tax revenue can be restored even to that level. Meanwhile, the demands upon the national revenue will be enormous . . .

For some time I have been convinced that in the initial period the meeting of internal costs will be a more difficult problem than external costs. In my opinion China's interests will be best served, and the people's welfare promoted, by concentrating in the first couple of years upon the restoration of monetary stability. In order to do this, many desirable projects will have to be postponed, and only the most essential things done. There is a heavy burden of proof on those who wish to start immediately after the war developments that go beyond restoration of what previously existed, until a general restoration has taken place all along the line.

Tsiang tried to get the public health program cut down to size, but Chungking insisted on keeping it substantially as it was.

A memorandum of April 30, 1945, given to several Chinese leaders, analyzed further the financial problems of economic rehabilitation. It was clear that the program would have to be spread over considerable time because of its size and cost and the scarcity of some items. Part of the costs could be met by the Chinese government's program of selling food and clothing to raise noninflationary revenue; private foreign contributions; private investment by Chinese and foreign capital, for which the government should create a proper climate; and by some rehabilitation which the American army of liberation could be expected to do — which latter unfortunately did not materialize. On the inflationary angle I said: "Inflationary methods of finance must be given up at the earliest possible moment, since it is of vital importance to restore the currency in order to facilitate rehabilitation and pave the way for a successful program of development. Also in the early period borrowing internally will have to be ruled out almost wholly because interest rates will be prohibitive. These deficits, therefore, can best be met from sales of foreign exchange and goods." I urged making every possible use of sale of consumers' goods, and that the government's and UNRRA's programs of import and sale be closely coordinated.

Recapitulating the situation, I said in a memorandum of May 26, 1945, given to Foreign Minister T. V. Soong at Washington:

Decisions on many of these matters are becoming more and more urgent. While emergency war-time matters have to be dealt with largely by improvising, the main principles of action ought to be carefully worked out and agreed, because the action taken will strongly affect the restoration of China's economic and financial system and the beginning of the program of development. No successful plan can be carried out piece-meal. There should be a tightly-knit plan covering the over-all situation. Each major part of the plan affects other parts, hence it should be conceived as a whole. Above all, the work should be well coordinated. Otherwise action taken in some fields will defeat efforts being made in others.

Without the adoption and carrying out of a sound and practicable plan, China cannot within a reasonable time restore war damages and resume its national progress. It is better to take this action deliberately than to wait the failure of opportunistic and uncoordinated action which may set back China's progress for decades, with grave consequences for the future.

Both the prospective amount of foreign currency funds and the amount that can be spent internally for rehabilitation and new development are limited. It will be very important tentatively to determine these amounts together with priorities and allocations within these limits, so that the different agencies of the Government can proceed with their plans on a sound basis. . . .

The foregoing deals only with financial and economic problems. These interlock with international and internal political problems. Many of the latter will have to be faced and dealt with as separate problems, but nothing would do more to help solve them than a wise policy in the financial and economic field.

Appendix H contains the text of a comprehensive memorandum of June 18, 1945, given to Foreign Minister Soong, which summarizes my proposals for financial rehabilitation after the war. Unfortunately the government made no serious effort at financial planning. Nor did such planning receive adequate encouragement from outside, by American or international action.[37]

APPRAISAL

In trying during the war to narrow the gap between expenditure and noninflationary income, the government faced enormous difficulties. The wartime economy was tragically weak, and the structure of government far from ready for the strain of total war. Even with the greatest zeal and efficiency a serious deficit was bound to occur, most of which had to be covered by printing-press money. Only the fact of having introduced a managed currency system, 20 months before the fighting began, made even that financial recourse feasible. The central fiscal problem was how to minimize use of the printing press. The obvious action was to do all possible to rebuild revenues from taxes and other contributions by the public, and to avoid unessential outlay.

Clearly the government was wrong in the early decision to refrain from adding to the burden of taxation, and in keeping unchanged so long the rates of internal taxes in terms of *fapi*, despite the inflation. Also, the delay until 1940 in moving to draw greater revenue from land, in a country that was about four-fifths agricultural, was unfortunate. Dropping the loan campaign in the early months of fighting, thus yielding to objection from influential people irked by pressure to buy the Liberty Loan, made matters worse — although loss of the chief financial centers and the steady progress of inflation made it impossible to raise a sizable part of war costs by borrowing from the public. Throughout the war it was unfortunate that the government failed to find ways to lay heavier burdens on the well-to-do and on those enriching themselves, including some civil and military officials, at a time when so many were sacrificing lives and property. Such measures, however, were difficult, given the absence of conditions making possible effective use of direct taxes or compulsory lending to the state. The government continued too often the old practices of over-staffing offices, and of undue nepotism and favoritism in appointments.[38] The government neither paid enough in the first instance to attract the more desirable workers, nor kept up a reasonable standard of pay in the face of inflation. At times Minister Kung tried to do more for underpaid staff but was rebuffed. No way was found to solve the problem of how to exact better services from key officials such as tax collectors, and give them adequate pay, while tolerating overstaffed and underpaid organs in the government generally.

In expenditure, the biggest fault was failure during most of the war to put the military under better fiscal control, and to improve the army's effectiveness by reducing numbers and up-grading quality. In civil affairs, there was no effective system of priorities to allocate the limited fiscal resources to the most important needs. The ease of getting printing-press money operated to prevent adequate control of its use.

Commenting on China's wartime fiscal policy, Joseph M. Jones of the State Department said in a memorandum of April 14, 1941:

The Government of Chungking has aroused the admiration of the world for the way in which it has resisted aggression and maintained internal services under great difficulty, but at the present time it does not seem fully to appreciate the immensity and complexity of the economic and financial problem or the necessity of equal sacrifice for all classes in a protracted war, and these facts are necessarily having their effect upon the functioning of the economic system and upon the national morale . . .

Even were China's finances managed with the greatest science, zeal, and honesty, there would remain at the present time a great disparity between revenues and expenditures, but the rate of economic deterioration would be sharply reduced.

The memorandum, which was critical of Finance Minister Kung, went on to urge the need of land reform, measures against hoarding, and development of cooperative production, suggesting that if such steps were taken "a large part of the attractiveness of the Communist Party at the present time (by comparison) would have disappeared." [39]

Part of the trouble was the general lack of understanding of the real

TABLE 12. Percentage of cash expenditure covered by noninflationary receipts, by China in 1937–1945 and by Great Britain, France, and Germany in 1914–1924.

Year	Great Britain[a]	France	Germany	Year	China[b]
1915	40	21	39	1937–1938	63
1916	22	13	10	1938 (2d half)	29
1917	27	14	11	1939	21
1918	27	12	21	1940	16[c]
1919	35	21	19	1941	19
1920	80	34	[d]	1942	25
1921	119	41	38	1943	31
1922	104	50	45	1944	31
1923	113	55	36	1945	17
1924	106	64	12		

SOURCE: For China, Table 7; and for European countries, John P. Young, *European Currency and Finance*, Commission of Gold and Silver Inquiry, U.S. Senate, Serial 9, vol. 1, Washington, 1925, pp. 302, 334, 392–393.

[a] Year ending March 31.

[b] The figures show the estimated cash deficit covered by bank credit, and exclude the value of transactions in kind.

[c] Excluding receipts in 1940 in respect of previous years. The inclusion of these receipts would raise the percentage to 30 per cent; but actually they should be included in the preceding periods, although this cannot be done because these receipts were not allocated by periods.

[d] Not available.

nature and main cause of the wartime inflation, namely, the growth of note issue brought about by the fiscal gap. The crux of the issue is thus summed up in a memorandum I made on June 19, 1942: "The close connection between the budget and the price rise is not sufficiently realized either by the Government or by the public."

While it is well and good to set forth standards of performance in fiscal matters, it is something else to expect that under conditions of stress they will be applied in practice beyond a certain point. China's showing in the first four years of war, as regards the proportion of noninflationary revenue to total wartime expenditures, compares not unfavorably with the situation in European countries in 1914–1918 during World War I. While the figures may not be perfectly comparable for the different countries, the general situation is indicated in Table 12 showing percentages of coverage of expenditures by noninflationary revenues.

China's showing in the whole period of fighting should not be judged too harshly, considering the difficulties and the fact that China fought alone longer than the duration of World War I, and with allies nearly four years after that.

PART TWO. DEBT AND FOREIGN AID

V. THE DEBT SITUATION IN MID-1937

China's credit, internally and externally, was at its peak in mid-1937. The chief internal obligations, following the consolidation of February 1936, recorded the highest prices ever, and were on better than an 8 per cent basis. That was a great improvement over the former yields of up to 15 per cent. Senior foreign currency obligations sold at or above par to yield about 5 per cent, thanks to action in 1928–1937 that restored regular payments on foreign debt equivalent to about US$250 million, which the former Peking regimes had allowed to fall into arrears.

SUMMARY OF TOTAL DEBT AND CURRENT PAYMENTS

As of July 1, 1937, the debt comprised the equivalents of about US$1,138 million of debt being paid, and about US$118 million of original principal amount in arrears, a total of about US$1,256 million. The debt being paid is summarized below:

		US$ equivalent
Foreign currency debt		
Finance Ministry	US$276 million*	
Railway Ministry	163 million	
Communications Ministry	17 million	
Total		US$456 million
Chinese currency debt		
Finance Ministry	C$2,028 million	
Railway and Communications		
Ministries, etc.	257 million	
Total	C$2,285 million	682 million
Grand total		US$1,138 million

* Including: (1) the relief and commodity credits granted by the American government in 1931–1933, US$14.7 million; (2) the capital amount of future Boxer Indemnity annuities, US$27 million, which figure excludes annuities pledged for service of loans included above; and (3) the Kwangtung Harbor Loan of 1937, US$2 million, an internal loan issued in dollars.

Of the foreign currency debt, making up about two-fifths of the total, 66 per cent was in sterling, 13 per cent in dollars, 9 per cent in yen, and 12 per cent in other currencies. Of the Boxer Indemnity of 1901, a capital amount equivalent to about US$27 million was still owed. But most of what remained in 1937 had been remitted for China's benefit.

Customs and salt revenue were pledged for the equivalent of about US$200 million and US$75 million, respectively, of foreign currency debt under charge of the Finance Ministry. About 90 per cent of the internal debt under charge of that Ministry was customs-secured and the rest was secured by taxes on salt and by other internal revenues. The railway debt was mostly secured by the property and revenues of the several lines. Certain railway obligations involved also the Finance Ministry. The two Tientsin-Pukow Railway loans of 1908–1910, although paid from the revenue of the railway, had a contingent claim upon customs revenue. The Hukuang Railway loan of 1911 was primarily paid out of the salt revenue, with a contingent charge upon the customs, and therefore is included with the debt under charge of the Finance Ministry rather than with the railway debt.

Although the foreign currency bonds were floated abroad, many banks and private investors in China had bought them originally or over the years. It was estimated that something like a third was held in China in 1937, but definite data are not available.

The payments in 1937 for current debt service were approximately as follows as of July 1, 1937 (figures in millions):

	Foreign currency debt, equivalent in		Fapi debt	Total, equivalent
	US$	C$	C$	C$
Finance Ministry				
Customs-secured	26	86	131	217
Salt-secured	4.5	15	14	30
Secured on consolidated taxes	—	—	8	8
Other	—	—	4	4
Railway Ministry*	13	43	29	72
Communications Ministry	1.5	5	—	5
Other	—	—	5	5
Total	US$45	C$149	C$191	C$341
				About US$100

* The figures represent the annual rate of payment as of August 1937. In 1937 prior to the hostilities the Railway Ministry contracted sizable debts for new construction. The figure of current payments is derived by using as a base the figures I compiled as of January 1, 1937, showing total annual payments equivalent to US$7 million (equivalent to C$24 million) for foreign debt and C$22 million for internal debt, a total (rounded) equivalent to C$45 million. In August I sent these figures to the Railway Ministry to be checked and brought up to date, and they advised me that the total was C$27 million greater, that is, C$72 million. Because of the outbreak of hostilities and the evacuation of Nanking it was not possible to obtain a breakdown. In a letter of September 9 Minister Chang advised me that monthly payments on foreign debt, both funded debt and material loans, were equivalent to £216,666 — equivalent to a yearly total of about US$13 million or C$43 million. The difference between the total of C$72 million and the latter figure is C$29 million, which is shown above as the yearly cost of service on internal railway debts.

After 1937 yearly payments were scheduled to increase slightly for five years, and then to fall.

The total of foreign currency payments, equivalent to about US$45 million in 1937, was not a very heavy burden upon China's balance of payments under conditions as of mid-1937. More serious, however, was the budgetary problem of covering payments on the foreign and internal debt. Over-all revenues were small relative to needs, despite the considerable progress which the National Government made in developing revenue in 1928–1937. Debt payments took over half of the revenue from customs, the best regarded security, and about an eighth of the salt revenue. Of the total equivalent to about C$341 million of debt payments in 1937, C$259 million was included in the general budget. The balance of C$82 million was not so included, being the responsibility of the Railway and Communications Ministries and other organs whose finances were practically autonomous. The C$259 million for which the Finance Ministry was responsible was more than a fourth of the budget for the fiscal year 1937–1938. About a third of total debt payments in 1937 was for amortization; and the proportion was scheduled to grow year by year.

FOREIGN CURRENCY DEBT RECEIVING SERVICE

Finance Ministry. A list of the obligations showing amounts, interest rates, maturities, and security of foreign loans equivalent to US$247 million is given in appendix A, Table 43. In addition was the Boxer Indemnity, equivalent in total capital amount to US$27 million. There was also the Kwangtung Harbor Loan of 1937, US$2 million, an internal loan issued in dollars and secured on a surtax of the Canton Customs.

Since the triumph of the National Government in 1928, quotations had roughly doubled. In 1928 the salt-secured debt was in default, and the position of the chief customs-secured debt precarious. The settlement of the greater part of the defaults and the fiscal and monetary reforms instituted, had brought a vast improvement in China's credit in foreign markets. In mid-1937 leading Chinese issues were traded on a lower yield basis than comparable Japanese bonds.

Railway Ministry. A list of obligations is given in appendix A, Table 44. As of January 1, 1937, the foreign currency railway debt was equivalent to US$163 million, of which over 60 per cent was in sterling. During 1937 the Ministry contracted various additional obligations to build new railways and improve existing lines. Details of the amounts outstanding in mid-1937 are not available because of wartime disruption.

The Railway Ministry, like the Finance Ministry, made a series of settlements of debts in arrears in the years preceding the hostilities, and by July 1937, nearly all the defaults had been cured. The result was a large rise in prices of railway bonds. Railway credit had improved to an extent that made it possible to obtain in the spring of 1937 commitments in London to finance new railway building. Unhappily the onset of fighting prevented giving effect to these plans.[1]

Communications Ministry. Particulars of the obligations are given in appendix A, Table 45. This Ministry as of January 1, 1937, had a foreign currency debt equivalent to US$17 million. In 1938 this Ministry was merged into the Railway Ministry. Most of the communications debt was in yen and owed to Japanese creditors. These were obligations which the former Peking regimes incurred in connection with development of electrical communications. They had gone into default, and were being paid under settlements of 1934–1935.

INTERNAL DEBT RECEIVING SERVICE

Finance Ministry. Particulars of the outstanding loans are given in appendix A, Table 43. As of July 1, 1937, these totaled C$2.0 billion. More than 70 per cent comprised the five issues of the Consolidated Loan of February 1936, issued to convert 33 issues of varying interest rates and maturities. Nearly all of the issues outstanding in 1937 bore 6 per cent interest. About 90 per cent were secured on customs revenue, and the rest on salt and other internal taxes. The Inspector General of Customs or other revenue-collecting officer handed over the funds needed for current service to the Central Bank, for account of a supervisory commission which included representation of private bankers. The paying procedure worked smoothly.

The conversion of 1936 was a forced conversion. Current and near-time principal payments were then very heavy, and the savings of about C$85 million yearly were essential to bring the budget nearer to balance, and thus to support the monetary reform of November 1935. At the time holders of converted bonds complained and bond prices slumped. But holders were soon to benefit, since the improvement in economic conditions and in general confidence, resulting from success of the monetary reform and related measures, brought a dramatic rise in the price of internal bonds. In mid-1937 the yield of the consolidated issues was about 7¾ per cent, compared with about 11 to 11½ per cent a year earlier.[2] Before that, yields were even higher, in the range of 12 to 15 per cent. So China's credit on the eve of the war stood high, as compared with other of the less developed countries. The situation reflected a growth of prestige of the National Government. Some internal obligations of the former Peking governments remained in arrears, and presumably settlements would have been made had not hostilities supervened.

Railway Ministry. Particulars of the various obligations are given in appendix A, Table 44. As of January 1, 1937, the internal debt comprised C$130 million of funded loans and advances, C$39 million of debts of individual railways for materials, etc., and C$58 million of floating debt, a total of C$227 million. As of July 1, 1937, the amount was larger because of loans for new construction, but precise figures are not available.

Communications Ministry, etc. This Ministry's internal debt as of January 1, 1937, was about C$17 million, being advances for electrical communications. The National Construction Commission and other organs had internal debts totaling about C$13 million as of that date. Particulars are shown in appendix A, Table 45.

DEBTS IN ARREARS

When the National Government took over in 1928 it recognized most of the debts of the former Peking regimes. At that time only the senior customs-secured obligations were being paid. Before the take-over, foreign governments had pressed for settlement of defaulted obligations, but without avail because the Peking regimes had become financially impotent. The National Government, however, was able to resume payment of the chief loans having a claim on the salt revenue and on other internal taxes, and also of the debts with a contingent claim on customs revenue, viz., the Tientsin-Pukow Railway loans of 1908–1910 and the Hukuang Railway loan of 1911. The government also in 1928–1937 settled the chief outstanding debts in arrears of the railways and of the Communications Ministry. The total principal amount of the debts on which payments were resumed was equivalent to about US$250 million. This was a creditable record indeed, in a world where uncured defaults and repudiations were widespread.

As of mid-1937, however, there remained recognized debts in arrears with an original principal amount equivalent to about US$118 million. A list of the obligations in arrears is given in appendix A, Table 46. Most of these had been in arrears from the early 1920's or longer; hence there were also large arrears of interest.[3] The foreign currency obligations, equivalent to about US$54 million of original principal amount, were due mainly to European and Japanese creditors. About US$49 million of this pertained to the Finance Ministry, and about US$5 million to the Railway Ministry. The internal debts in arrears totaled about C$216 million, equivalent to about US$64 million, in original principal amount. These included four loan issues of about C$71 million and about 350 items of floating debt totaling about C$144 million.

In addition to the obligations above-mentioned, there were the so-called Nishihara Loans which the government did not recognize. These originated in 1917–1918, and were made to the "Anfu Clique" at a time when Japan was pressing an aggression upon China, taking advantage of the pre-occupation of the United States and Europe in World War I. These loans were in the original principal sum of about Y154 million with 7 to 8 per cent interest; and about Y150 million (equivalent to US$43 million) was outstanding as of July 1, 1937. Also bonds were issued in the early years of these loans for part of the large arrears of interest, calculated at 8 to 14.4 per cent per annum. In view of Japan's resumed aggression, by seizure of Manchuria in 1931 and by continuing encroachment in North China, the government understandably would not consider settling the Nishihara Loans.

Had not fighting broken out in 1937, the government presumably would have made settlements covering most of the old obligations, under its general program of settling the obligations in arrears. Negotiations were pending with regard to the chief non-Japanese obligations; but settlements of the obligations then due to Japanese creditors would have depended upon a change in Japan's aggressive attitude toward China. The outbreak of fighting forced the government to abstain from fresh commitments to holders of unsettled obligations.[4]

VI. INTERNAL BORROWING

The government sporadically tried to borrow from the public, but with only moderate success. Since borrowing was inevitable, most of it had to be by creation of bank credit.

BORROWING FROM THE PUBLIC AND BANK ADVANCES IN FAPI

At the time of outbreak of fighting the prices of internal bonds were at the highest level in China's history. The Consolidated Bonds of 1936, Series A, ranged from 87.20 to 87.95 in the week July 5–10, to yield about 7.7 per cent. In the next week, as the seriousness of the July 7 incident began to appear, prices dropped to a range of 75.50 to 82.20. In the latter part of July the government pegged prices at 76 for this issue, with corresponding prices for other leading issues. This action avoided a market crash that had been feared. But on August 13, when fighting broke out in Shanghai, the government closed the Exchange. Thereafter, with reduced trading, prices slumped further and the range to the end of 1941 was from a low of 42.50 for Consolidated A bonds in 1938 to a high of 81.65 in 1941. At these prices, yields ranged between about 10 and 18 per cent. During the Pacific War prices after mid-1942 were quoted at Shanghai in puppet currency and are not comparable with prices in *fapi*.[1] Quotations in *fapi* after mid-1942 during the war are not available. Toward the end of the war speculation about possible postwar valorization of the bonds, to offset the currency depreciation, caused wild gyrations in prices. But valorization did not prove feasible.

The government issued the following series of bonds denominated in *fapi* during the war:

1937	Short Term Treasury Notes	C$500 million
	Liberty Loan	500
	Kwangsi Currency Readjustment Loan	17
1938	National Defense Loan	500
	Relief Loan	30
1939	Reconstruction Loan	600
	Military Supply Loan	600
1940	Military Supply Loan	1,200
1941	Military Supply Loan	1,200
	Reconstruction Loan	1,200
1942	Allied Victory Loan	1,000
1943	Allied Victory Loan	3,000
	Loan for Readjustment of Provincial Loans	175
1944	Allied Victory Loan	5,000
	Total	C$15,522 million

Interest on the issues was 6 per cent, except that the Liberty Loan, Kwangsi Currency Loan, and the Relief Loan bore 4 per cent interest. The term varied but was usually about 25 years. For the loans issued in 1937–1939 the government pledged specified revenues, except for the Liberty Loan and the Relief Loan. After 1939 only the general revenues were pledged, except in the case of the Allied Victory Loan of C$1 billion, issued as of July 1, 1942. Article 5 of the regulations of that issue provided (translated):

> Payment of interest and repayment of principal of the loan shall be made by allotment from the £50 million loan from the British Government, to be deposited in The Central Bank of China and converted into national currency.

British willingness to support such a loan had been indicated in a general way early in 1942 by Sir Otto Niemeyer of the Bank of England while visiting China. But in mid-1942 China and Britain had reached no definitive agreement regarding the £50 million credit — this was not formalized until 1944 (see chap. IX). The security for the Victory Loan was only of academic interest, because payment of interest and principal depended upon the output of the printing press.

Despite the closing of the Shanghai Exchange on August 13, 1937, and the uncertainties caused by the fighting, the government went ahead with public sale of bonds to finance war costs. It made a good start by announcing the Liberty Loan a few days after the fighting began at Shanghai. This issue of C$500 million was put out on terms involving a large element of contribution by subscribers — interest was 4 per cent, the term 30 years redeemable by yearly drawings, and there was no pledge of specific revenues. Just before outbreak of the fighting in North China, customs-secured internal issues yielded nearly twice as much as the new Liberty Loan, and these yields became much higher after fighting began, as stated above. Nevertheless patriotic fervor, supported by the surprisingly strong stand of China's armies at Shanghai, made the issue succeed beyond expectation. Sales were made throughout Free China. The correspondent at Canton of the *North China Daily News* reported on September 15, "In one week over C$6,000,000 has been invested in national defence by the people of this one province, and selling continues brisk, even though the people must make great sacrifices." A committee headed by T. V. Soong, Chairman of the Bank of China, promoted sales, which were aided by pressure on well-to-do persons and enterprises. Public subscriptions in China were C$146 million, and abroad C$37 million, a total of C$183 million equivalent to about US$55 million. For China's weak economy, disrupted by war, that was a good showing. The rest of the issue was pledged to the government banks for advances.

Unfortunately the pressures to subscribe, together with anti-T. V. Soong sentiment, caused repercussions at Nanking and Hankow that interfered with efforts to repeat the success of the Liberty Loan. Further factors making it difficult to gain public subscriptions were the progress of inflation, the slump in bond prices, and the succession of military reverses. As a result of these factors, public issues in terms of *fapi* played but a minor part in war finance after the early months of fighting. Most of the bond issues were pledged as security to the government banks, and not sold publicly.

Beginning in 1940 the government again sought public subscriptions for bonds. Up to the end of 1941 C$487 million was subscribed for bonds issued in 1940, but as of December 31, 1941, only C$238 million actually had been paid in. The demand was mostly for the 1940 issue denominated in dollars, described in the next section.[2] Beginning in the fall of 1942 there was an effort to require compulsory subscription to *fapi* bonds by individuals and businesses with large incomes or properties. The scale of required subscriptions was progressive. Quotas were assigned to provincial governments. But the difficulties were serious. Efficient operation of direct taxes or of compulsory charges on income or capital requires prevalence of adequate accounting records, an adequate experienced administration, and general acceptance of an obligation to support the state according to capacity. These conditions were not then present in China. Nevertheless, much could have been done to press the well-to-do and especially civil and military officials profiting during the war and inflation, had there been a strong will to do so. As the campaign progressed, however, inequities and dissatisfaction grew. Governmental agencies which received part of their support from the Central Government often paid from their own funds instead of collecting quotas. By February 1944, subscriptions to the *fapi* bonds of the Allied Victory Loan of 1942 totaled C$100 million, and by the end of 1944, C$700 million. Late in 1944 subscriptions to the *fapi* Allied Victory Loan of 1943 also totaled C$700 million, and it was expected that C$1 billion would be subscribed by the end of 1944.[3] Figures for 1945 are not available. Since note issue grew C$114 billion in 1944 and C$842 billion in 1945, it is clear that compulsory subscription to internal bonds was only a minor source of revenue.

Besides the sale of bonds, the government beginning in 1940 sought funds from the public through savings certificates and deposits in terms of *fapi*. These comprised "Thrift and Reconstruction" certificates and deposits, "Public Works Savings Deposits," and "Lottery Savings Deposits," of which the certificates were the most important.

Because the government's urgent need for funds could not be met from tax revenue and borrowing from the public, it was necessary to rely mainly upon creation of credit. The four government banks created this credit up to July 1, 1942. In this period the Central Bank provided about half; and of the remainder, the Bank of China provided considerably more than the Bank of Communications and the Farmers Bank. From July 1, 1942, the advances were made by the Central Bank. The amounts advanced in the respective years by the four government banks were (millions of C$):[4] for *1937–1938*, 1,195; *1938* (2d half), 853; *1939*, 2,311; *1940*, 3,834; *1941*, 9,443; *1942*, 20,082; *1943*, 40,857; *1944*, 140,091; and *1945*, 1,043,257.

Before the war the practice had been for the government to pledge bonds to the banks to secure advances, and the banks in turn would cover these by selling the bonds gradually on the Shanghai Stock Exchange. But, when the bonds were no longer readily marketable because of the hostilities, pledging of bonds to the government banks continued, the latter holding them without regard to marketability. With the privilege of note issue (for the Central Bank alone after June 30, 1942), they had no problem in providing money to the government. The total of *fapi* bonds issued during the war was C$15.5 billion; and the internal foreign currency issues of 1938–1940, which were mostly pledged to the government banks, had an equivalent value of about C$5 billion at the official rates of exchange. Total government borrowing during the war was well over C$1 trillion; hence the bond issues pledged to the government banks provided security for only a minor part. The balance was covered by issuance to the banks of Treasury Certificates.

Maintenance of payments on the internal issues gave rise to no serious difficulty. In these days of managed currency, governments no longer are likely to default on internal debt. When customs revenues fell off, because of enemy seizures, so that the yield was not enough to cover external and internal debt payments, the Central Bank made advances to the Customs, these totaling about C$175 million up to the time when payments on the external loan issues were suspended early in 1939.

When China had to suspend payments on the foreign currency debt in January 1939, the real difficulty was that of transfer. But for psychological reasons the suspension of payments on foreign issues was attributed to Japanese seizure of customs revenue, to avoid hurting confidence in the currency by drawing attention to the shortage of foreign currency. With a view to justifying continued payment of internal debt while not paying foreign debt, the government as from January 31, 1939, made the *fapi* payments in Chungking instead of Shanghai, in six equal monthly installments instead of semiannually, and paid in *wei wah* or transfer money (see chap. XV) instead of ready cash.* A further reason for the six installments was to avoid suddenly putting into the market the large sums due January 31, which would have made it harder to tighten money and support the rate of exchange.

* Also the government set aside in the Central Bank in local currency a share of foreign debt service proportionate to the collections of pledged revenues in Free China.

INTERNAL FOREIGN CURRENCY ISSUES OF 1938–1940

With inflation growing, the government found it hard to get the public to subscribe to issues payable in *fapi*. It therefore had recourse to issuing the following series of bonds denominated in dollars, sterling, and customs gold units (CGU):[5] in 1938 — U.S. Dollar Loan US$50 million, Sterling Loan £10 million, CGU (customs gold unit) Loan CGU 100 million; and in 1940 — U.S. Dollar Loan US$50 million, Sterling Loan £10 million. The approximate equivalent of the total of these was US$260 million, at exchange rates of May 1938.

The 1938 issues, as of May 1, were 5 per cent 16-year bonds secured on the salt revenue. The 1940 issues, as of May 1, were 5 per cent 27-year bonds secured only on general revenue.

When the 1938 issues were proposed, the purpose stated was to attract overseas Chinese subscriptions. I recommended against sale in China, especially because such issues in foreign currency would be thought to reflect adversely on confidence in Chinese currency. Also, I recommended not using salt or customs security for such issues, because of complications about these revenues already pledged for outstanding foreign obligations.

Sales of the 1938 issues were disappointing. Figures by years are not available, but as of the end of 1942 sales had been: US$2,772,850 of dollar bonds, £92,090 of sterling bonds, and CGU5,510 of those in customs gold units. The sum of these sales was equivalent to only a little over 1 per cent of the total issues authorized. Total sales as of September 1, 1945, increased slightly to US$3,570,000 and £122,000, respectively; and the sales of the CGU issue were still insignificant, CGU80,110 as of December 31, 1945. Sales abroad as of September 1, 1945, were only US$497,000 of the dollar issue and none of the sterling issue, despite the originally declared purpose of seeking overseas subscriptions. Part of this failure to enlist support of overseas Chinese was due to the restrictions of American law.

In 1940 the case against issuance of this type of bond was even stronger than in 1938. Nearly all of the 1938 bonds remained unsold. Moreover, after the 1938 bonds were issued China had suspended payment, early in 1939, on the prewar foreign currency debt. It was thus not surprising that holders of the old foreign debt were taken aback to note in the press on March 2, 1940, an announcement apparently published for the first time, advertising the payment of the coupons and drawings of the 1938 foreign currency internal loans. They promptly complained. I felt obliged to urge the government not to proceed with the proposed 1940 bonds scheduled for issuance as of May 1, 1940, since the foreign currency internal issues of 1938 were hurting China's credit, and, with most of the 1938 issues unsold, there was neither need for further issues nor significant benefit from them.

I recommended against incurring further foreign currency liabilities unless absolutely necessary.

Nevertheless the government went ahead with the two 1940 issues. This time there was more of a sales compaign. As of the end of 1942, sales of the 1940 issues were US$11,750,620 and £700,455, respectively, most of the sales being in 1940–1941. After 1941, only a minor proportion of these issues was sold to the public, and as of September 1, 1945, the outstanding amounts sold were US$12,828,000 and £716,000, respectively. Sales abroad as of September 1, 1945, were US$552,000 of the dollar issues and none of the sterling issues.

To summarize: Of the total of these issues equivalent altogether to about US$280 million at exchange rates of 1945, only the equivalent of about US$20 million or about 7 per cent was sold to the public. The rest was pledged to the government banks for advances. Nevertheless the unissued bonds were, on paper, a sizeable addition to the government's eventual liability in foreign currency, and at best a confusing item in the debt accounts. Early in 1943 I recommended canceling the CGU obligation by paying to the holders the CGU5,510 outstanding plus accrued interest; withdrawing from sale the unissued dollar and sterling bonds, especially because of the pending issue of dollar obligations backed by the US$500 million American credit of 1942; and arranging with the government banks to take *fapi* obligations in place of the 1938–1940 issues then pledged as security for advances, mostly by the Central Bank. Later I repeated this recommendation but no action was taken.

The dollar-backed issues of 1942

In a memorandum given to Generalissimo Chiang September 26, 1941, at a time when he was specially worried about inflation, I pointed out that borrowing from the public in China would tend to check inflation if suitable means could be devised. In 1941 such borrowing was only C$457 million, roughly 5 per cent of the deficit. I proposed seeking new means for such borrowing. He asked me to prepare a "concrete and practicable plan." In November in Hong Kong I talked with H. Merle Cochran of the American Treasury and Sir Otto Niemeyer of the Bank of England with regard to possible guarantee by the American and British governments of securities to be issued in China with some form of protection against Chinese currency depreciation.[6] Niemeyer was independently thinking of a similar scheme, and we pooled our ideas.

Preparation of a plan raised various problems. Would issuance of a loan in foreign currencies hurt confidence in national currency? Should China issue fresh internal loans in foreign currency when transfer of prewar foreign currency debt was suspended since early in 1939? Would existence of freezing of foreign currency funds make the public hesitant to subscribe? If these obstacles were not too serious, at what rate would subscriptions be received? At what rates would payments of interest and principal be made? Would such a loan be too costly? And would the United States and Britain be ready to back such a scheme?

In December and January the scheme was actively discussed at Chungking. At first Niemeyer and I preferred an issue in Chinese currency repayable at the equivalent of specified sums in dollars and sterling at the market rate of exchange when payments were due. But gradually it became clear that an issue directly payable in foreign currency would have the best appeal to the public. A tentative outline of such a scheme was telegraphed to Washington and London, where it was generally accepted as desirable in principle. In the latter part of January 1942 the British government was ready to support the plan.[7] In February the granting of the American credit of US$500 million and the British credit of £50 million (see chap. IX) cleared the way for action. But action was delayed by Kung's illness and the Generalissimo's absence.

On March 24, the government announced the issuance of two kinds of securities. First were the U.S. Dollar Savings Certificates of US$100 million. These were of one-, two-, or three-year term, with interest respectively of 3, 3½, and 4 per cent. Second was the allied Victory U.S. Dollar Loan of US$100 million, a 4 per cent 10-year issue, as of May 1. The announcement stated that the US$200 million would absorb about C$4 billion, "or roughly one out of every four dollars in circulation." Note issue as of February 28 was C$16.8 billion, so the actual size of the note issue was officially indicated for the only time after the early part of the war. The rate of exchange was set at US$0.05 for the Certificates. Some months later the government made that rate the official rate of exchange, instead of US$0.05⅝₆. For the 10-year loan, the government set a more favorable rate: US$0.06.

The agreement of March 21 for the US$500 million credit contained no provision requiring China to consult the United States about use of the money. But, in a letter accompanying the agreement, Foreign Minister Soong stated that China would keep the United States "fully informed from time to time as to the use of the funds." After the announcement of March 24, the American Treasury complained that they had not been informed, and indicated that they would criticize some parts of the plan. Kung, however, had talked with Treasury Representative Adler on March 18 about the plan, and presumed Adler had informed Washington. The available record does not show what Kung told Adler six days before announcement of the final plan.[8] Kung wanted immediate transfer to China of the US$200 million, because he believed that large currency reserves, even though they could not be used immediately, were essential "to convince the people that use was being made of the loan without delay to prevent inflation." The

Treasury wanted to transfer funds only as needed, because they would have had to borrow and pay interest to deposit the whole US$200 million. But Morgenthau transferred the full US$200 million on Soong's advice, having in mind the friction in the spring of 1942 about possible strings on the loan (see chap. IX).[9]

Before the rates of exchange for subscription were set, there was long discussion. China's currency already was much overvalued at the official rate of US0.05\frac{5}{16}$ set in August 1941. That rate gave the money a value of about 18 per cent of prewar. But, at the price level of early 1942, money had less than 5 per cent of its buying power five years earlier. If the official rate remained unchanged, the disparity was bound to get worse as prices rose. The secretary of the Wartime Public Loan Commission proposed a rate of US$0.07. I urged US$0.05, pointing out that, because of the over-valuation of the currency, buyers at that rate would have a great bargain, and that at higher rates the loan would be a costly piece of financing since it would not draw in a large enough equivalent in national currency.

Clearly the loan would not be an automatic success. From the start Kung said it would not be easy to get the public to buy bonds. In a memorandum of February 2, I said:

> Of course, the issue must be supported and promoted by patriotic appeals and by various forms of pressure upon persons and business organizations able to subscribe, and particularly upon hoarders and speculators. With a carefully pre-pared program carried into effect, such an issue should be a real success and help materially to check inflation.

The issue should be accompanied by tightening of bank credit and the government banks should not make advances to finance purchase of the bonds or buy them themselves, since such action would defeat the issue's purpose. Niemeyer urged that the sales compaign be accompanied by sale of rice collected from the land tax in kind, to help to break the existing high prices. That, he argued, would frighten rice hoarders into selling and let them find a place for their money in buying the bonds. He pointed out that steps to lower the price of the people's main food, together with drawing in currency through sale of the bonds, could have a very worthwhile effect in checking the inflation. *Ta Kung Pao* of Chungking said on March 27, 1942, that it would be necessary to press the well-to-do to buy the securities and to force hoarders to take them in place of goods, since the ordinary people had little capacity to subscribe. Ambassador Gauss reported on May 5 that the government could force speculators and landlords to buy. But he doubted that it would be done, because "the Government . . . is itself closely allied to banking and land-holding interests."[10] That prediction proved right, and there was no real pressure to subscribe. Nothing was done about Niemeyer's proposal to attack speculation and hoarding by sale of some of the rice collected as tax in kind. Instead, reports indicated that the government held rice over and above what the army and public employees needed for current use plus reasonable reserves.

To strengthen confidence I urged, as part of the plan, using the Federal Reserve Bank of New York as trustee, and setting aside there funds from the US$500 million loan *pari passu* with sales of the securities in China. That would have facilitated subscriptions, since with a purely national set-up the public would wonder whether the government would pay the dollars at maturity.[11] But the plan adopted provided that US$100 million would be set aside in the Central Bank of China for payment of the Certificates; and, for the 10-year bonds, funds for payments would be appropriated from the US$500 million credit. So the government failed to use a valuable means of adding to the effectiveness of the issues.

Failure to fix a relatively brief time limit for subscriptions at the very favorable prices offered was the most serious mistake. Niemeyer and I had planned a well-secured issue to be sold promptly, with the aid of pressure on hoarders and those well able to subscribe. But subscriptions stayed open for 18 months at fixed rates for dollars, while the internal buying power of the national currency fell to about 15 per cent of what it was in early 1942. Those intending to subscribe could wait, while increasing their local currency funds by speculating in goods, hoarding, or lending to speculators at 3 to 6 per cent monthly interest.

The Certificates became specially attractive to American army personnel. The men were paid in American currency notes (see chap. XVIII), which they could sell for *fapi* in the free market and buy Certificates at 20 to 1. In the first seven months of 1943, rates for dollar notes ranged from C$44 to C$95 per dollar. Thus each American dollar of notes could be converted into from two to nearly five dollars in Certificates. After subscriptions closed, the Certificates and Loan sold at a large discount compared with rates for dollar notes (see below). Purchase of these securities by army personnel was eventually forbidden by an order of September 21, 1944. Previously the American ambassador had forbidden the embassy staff to buy them.

Sale of the Certificates was slow for many months. In the first week at Chungking, only US$36,390 were sold. Less than a tenth of the US$100 million was sold in eight months. Sales spurted in December, because of rumors that the issue would be closed at the year end. By June 1943, after 15 months, US$47 million had been subscribed. But in July and the first three days of August, until the issue was closed August 3, US$56 million were taken up, bringing the total to US$103 million. Cumulative sales by months were as follows (millions of US$):[12]

	1942		*1943*
April	0.5	January	27.2
May	1.3	February	30.5
June	1.9	March	34.8
July	2.6	April	38.7
August	4.2	May	43.8
September	5.6	June	47.4
October	7.6	July	73.0
November	9.9	August	103.4
December	24.2		

For some time before sale of Certificates closed, I urged ending the sale of both issues, unless there could be radical readjustment of the rates of exchange at which they were sold. About US$150 million of the US$200 million had not then been used. When the sale of Certificates ended on August 3, 1943, I urged immediately ending sale of the Bonds. For these, because of 10-year maturity, subscriptions were even slower than for the Certificates. By the end of 1942, after eight months only US$130,160 had been taken up. By October 12, 1943, subscription totaled only US$18 million, on which only the equivalent of US$11 million had been paid. On that date the closing of subscriptions was rumored, and there was a rush to buy. Subscriptions were closed October 15. The public took up about 45 per cent of this issue of US$100 million, and the government through the Central Bank and the other government banks took up the part that was not otherwise sold. Altogether, the public took about US$150 million of the two issues.

For a time some certificates were issued in bearer form. This was stopped, however, in March 1943, when the American authorities pointed out that it was contrary to the freezing regulations. In November 1944 the American Treasury issued regulations providing: (1) payments could be made to beneficiaries outside Free China only if they acquired the Certificates there, unless they were obtained from a member of the immediate family employed in Free China by the United States; (2) payments to a blocked national, including Chinese, could be made only to blocked accounts in the United States; (3) payments could not be made to enemy or specially blocked nationals; and (4) payments to persons residing outside Free China would be limited to US$10,000 per month.[13]

An active market developed in China for these securities. About December 1, 1943, matured one-year certificates sold for C$53 per dollar; and certificates due August 4, 1944, a year after subscriptions closed, sold for C$37 per dollar. In December 1943 black market for dollar notes ranged between 73 and 95 to 1. The prices and exchange rates in 1944 and 1945, which appear to be averages, are shown below (C$ per US$):[14]

	US$ Savings Certifi- cates	US$ Allied Victory Loan	US$ Notes in Chung- king	US$ Savings Certifi- cates	US$ Allied Victory Loan	US$ Notes in Chung- king
		1944			1945	
January	72	60	84	335	260	515
February	113	101	164	327	277	552
March	132	120	240	402	338	677
April	125	110	220	520	517	738
May	126	100	209	640	633	827
June	132	98	192	1,380	1,410	1,705
July	135	104	197	2,300	2,275	2,850
August	132	108	198	1,750	1,600	2,185
September	151	109	264	—	—	—
October	180	113	267	—	—	—
November	295	184	487	—	—	—
December	315	216	570	—	—	—

These securities thus sold at a large discount as compared with American notes. There were wide fluctuations in the discount. It was roughly of the order of a third and a half, respectively, for certificates and bonds up to the spring of 1945; but thereafter, with better news in the war, prices relative to notes rose to a discount of the order of 20 per cent up to the end of the war.

The figures of US$ Savings Certificates and US$ Allied Victory Loan outstanding as of the end of the war are not available, but as of December 7, 1945, the amounts were US$58.9 million and US$99.6 million, respectively. Early in 1945 about US$73 million of certificates was outstanding.

The real financial benefit which China gained from the sales cannot be exactly measured. Figures of the government's monthly deficits in this period are not available, to compare with the proceeds of sale. But a rough calculation shows clearly that the benefit was not of much over-all signifi- cance. In about a month, from July 1 to August 3, 1943, the proceeds may have covered something like a quarter of the deficit; and in December 1942 and October 1943, perhaps a tenth. In the rest of the period the proportion was much less.[15] A later offsetting benefit was that those obtaining the funds could use them after the war in China's rehabilitation. But the extent of such use probably was not very great, because of continuing inflation and other disturbances.

There is, of course, no way to estimate what amount could have been realized if the dollar-backed securities had been sold under a better plan, for example, with the Federal Reserve Bank of New York as trustee, to hold and disburse the dollar funds; with governmental pressure on those able to subscribe; and with readjustment of exchange rates for subscribers of successive *tranches*. The securities offered a recourse to those anxious to preserve the purchasing power of their money, instead of speculation and hoarding. But buyers were reluctant because of uncertainty about when and how they could use the dollars at maturity, with China blockaded and the war's outcome in doubt. Also the maintenance of fixed overvalued rates of exchange raised doubt about the eventual rates at which the money could be brought back to China. With benefit of hindsight, the attempt to issue 10-year bonds was a mistake. But whatever the amount that could have been sold, the dollar assets could not possibly have brought in a real return in China comparable with the purchasing power of dollars in the United States, because of the China market's low purchasing power. While a sizeable sacrifice of dollar assets was justifiable in the emergency, much of the sacrifice that took place could and should have been avoided.[16]

The prompt sale, even at the rate of C$20 per dollar, of a sizable first *tranche* of Certificates, say US$25–50 million within a time limit of a few weeks, could have forced substantial de-hoarding. The effect would have been greater if combined with Niemeyer's idea of sale of some of the rice gotten from collections in kind. Sale of other *tranches* could have followed, at rates of exchange raised successively somewhat in line with the rise of prices. Besides the effects of such a program in limiting hoarding and checking inflation, there would have been important social and political gains. To require well-to-do persons and hoarders to buy the issues, as contemplated in the original proposal, would have partly offset inequities of the tax system, whereby persons with the greatest ability to pay bore far less than a fair share of the war costs. Such a measure would have strengthened the government at one of its weakest spots. But instead, the government's good name suffered from the manner of successively closing subscriptions to the two issues, with rumored large buying by insiders. Secretary Morgenthau, reporting to the President on December 18, 1943, said that this US$200 million of aid "had little effect except to give additional profits to insiders, speculators, and hoarders and dissipate foreign resources," and "made no significant contribution to the control of inflation." [17]

SUMMARY OF INTERNAL BORROWING FROM THE PUBLIC

The sums realized from the public by means of the various schemes of borrowing from the public, not including deposit certificates payable in gold,[18] are shown in Table 13. In 1937–1941 while China fought alone, borrowing from the public through issuance of *fapi* obligations produced about C$1 billion or about 5 per cent of the total outlay. The showing was

TABLE 13. Proceeds from internal borrowing from the public (excluding borrowing in kind and certificates of deposit payable in gold), 1937–1945 (in millions of C$)

Year	Internal bonds, including foreign currency issues of 1938–40[a]	Savings schemes[b]	Dollar-backed securities of 1942[b]	Total
1937–38[c]	256	—	—	256
1938[d]	18	—	—	18
1939	25	3	—	28
1940	8	133	—	141
1941	127	457	—	584
1942	300	879	483	1,662
1943	1,000	1,292	2,480	4,772
1944	1,989	2,508	—	4,497
1945[e]	1,056	5,067	—	6,123

[a] The data of proceeds from sale of internal bonds in 1937–1941 and 1944 are from the table of official accounts in appendix A, Table 40. That table does not show separately the proceeds in 1942 and 1943 from sale of the dollar-backed securities of 1942, but appears to include most or all of the proceeds in the item for 1943, C$3,871 million. For these two years I have made a different breakdown showing approximately the same total as the official accounts for the two years, but estimating the proceeds from sale of obligations other than the dollar-backed issues. For 1945 the figure comprises for internal sales the figure of C$964 million contemporaneously received, and for external sales the C$92 million shown in the official table, which is confirmed by the contemporary data. Nearly all the total of C$62,727 million shown in the official accounts for 1945 as proceeds from internal bonds represents the proceeds from sale of gold certificates (see chap. II, note 2).

[b] The data for savings schemes are from the Central Bank *Bulletin* (in Chinese), February 1946, p. 101, and included Thrift and Reconstruction Certificates and Deposits, Public Works Savings Deposits, and Lottery Savings Deposits. The figures for savings schemes do not include deposits payable in gold, since these are separately included as receipts from gold. Nor do they include receipts from dollar-backed Savings Certificates, since the latter are included above in the third column. The figures for dollar-backed securities in the third column are the contemporary data of the Central Bank.

[c] Year ending June 30, 1938.

[d] Second half year.

[e] To August 31.

best in the first war year, when the figure was about 10 per cent. After 1941, during the Pacific War, borrowing through issuance of *fapi* obligations was of lesser importance, which is understandable in view of the growing inflation. In 1942–1943 the sale of dollar-backed obligations boosted the proportion of total costs covered by borrowing from the public to over 10 per cent in 1943. More important in drawing resources from the public in this period was the compulsory borrowing and sale of grain for public use (see chap. III). The money value of such receipts from grain in the years 1942–1945 I estimate, respectively, at C$4 billion, C$13 billion, C$27 billion, and C$125 billion. These sums far exceeded the totals of borrowing from the public in cash.

VII. THE PREWAR FOREIGN DEBT

Nearly all of China's prewar foreign debt was owed to private persons. The relatively small intergovernmental debt comprised remaining portions of the Boxer Indemnity of 1901, amounting to only about 8 per cent of the original sum; and certain credits granted by the American government in 1931–1933. Appendix Tables 43 to 46 list the foreign debt items.

PRIVATE FOREIGN DEBT

China tried hard in 1937–1938 to maintain payments on the prewar foreign debt. The efforts aided by friendly governments to protect pledged revenues and preserve the Sino-foreign revenue-collecting services, in the face of enemy seizures and interference, are described in chapter IV. But it was not the loss of pledged revenues that forced consideration of suspending payments. Rather it was depletion of foreign currency reserves, inability to build them up from current transactions, and failure to obtain abroad credits available in cash.

While during 1938 the Central Bank's funds abroad shrank toward minimum working balances, China faced a grave dilemma. The likelihood of American and British credits was growing. But, in the prevailing political climate in Washington and London, credits had to appear justifiable as a commercial risk. China feared that suspension of debt payments would spoil the chance of getting credits. Finally at the year end, when American and British credits at last were announced, they were not usable in cash to pay debts. After exchanges with Washington indicated that the United States would not object, China reluctantly decided upon suspension.[1]

On January 15, 1939, the government issued the following statement regarding customs-secured obligations:

For over a year the Japanese authorities, despite their assurances, have been detaining all the revenues pledged for debt service that have been collected in the areas under their military occupation, except for a single remittance from the Shanghai Customs last June. In order to make up the amounts that should have been remitted from these areas the Chinese Government has advanced about $175,000,000. The Central Bank of China moreover has provided all the foreign exchange required although the Japanese have been interfering with the Chinese currency and forcing the acceptance of several forms of yen, military and puppet notes which has reduced the collections in legally valid currency on which obligations of the Government are secured.

Notwithstanding all difficulties the Chinese Government has provided for service of China's debts thereby demonstrating the utmost consideration for the holders of its obligations.

Under existing conditions the Chinese Government very reluctantly has been forced to the conclusion that this situation has become too anomalous to be continued. The Government therefore has been obliged to reject the Inspector-General of Custom's request for a further advance. As from this date, however, the Government is prepared to set aside in special accounts in the Central Bank of China a share of the long-term debt service, proportionate to the collections in the areas not subject to Japanese interference, of the revenues pledged to all such debts outstanding before the hostilities. It is hoped that remittances of the share attributable to the pledged revenues from the areas under Japanese military occupation may similarly be forthcoming, and that interference with Chinese currency will cease, so that service of these debts may be duly effected. This measure is a temporary arrangement in view of present abnormal conditions.

In the case of salt-secured loans, action followed a different course. In the fall of 1938 the government, while duly paying interest on the foreign currency loans secured by the salt revenue, suspended amortization payments. Lockhart, Associate Director General of the Salt revenue, and I opposed the action, which originated with some of his colleagues and gained Ministry approval. The suspension was unfortunate, because it singled out these loans and was done apart from general policy with regard to all of the foreign debt. Japan was seizing a much larger share of revenue from customs than from salt. Nevertheless, the action was accepted without undue shock.

When the government on January 15, 1939, announced suspension of payments on foreign currency customs-secured debt, it delayed action concerning salt-secured debt, mainly because the next payments on that debt were not due until the latter part of March. A further factor in the situation was the state of negotiations in London for a credit to support China's currency. When that credit was arranged early in March, China undertook to make a proposal for resumption of debt service. On March 21 China initiated negotiations by proposing partial resumption of interest payments, but with no payments of principal. Meanwhile, China was in no position to make payments on the salt-secured foreign currency debt.[2] So the following statement was issued on March 26:

Dr. H. H. Kung, President of the Executive Yuan and concurrently Minister of Finance, announced today that the Government has initiated negotiations with a view to effecting an arrangement in respect of the service of customs and salt secured loans. Pending conclusion of these negotiations, the Government is taking action in relation to salt secured loans similar to the action of January 15 concerning customs loans.

It will be recalled that on January 15 it was announced that in view of Japanese interference with the pledged revenues and with the currency the Government was forced temporarily to discontinue full provision for the service of customs secured loans and that the Government was prepared to set aside in the Central

Bank of China certain funds in respect of the long-term debt service. Such funds are being duly set aside.

With reference to loans secured on salt revenue, Dr. H. H. Kung announced that the Anglo-French loan coupon due April 5 will be paid at the usual time, inasmuch as the fiscal agents already have on hand out of payments previously made to them a sum sufficient for this purpose. In the case of the Crisp Loan, the Government is setting aside out of salt revenue a share of the interest due to bond-holders on March 30. The Government having regard for China's obligation and for the interests of the bondholders, has been much concerned to continue debt service despite the unprecedented difficulties caused by the Japanese invasion. It does not wish to permit continuance of the situation resulting from the measures which circumstances have forced it very reluctantly to take in relation to customs and salt loans without endeavouring to arrive at a reasonable arrangement to maintain debt services as far as practicable, having regard to the abnormal conditions obtaining and to the vital necessity of prosecuting the war and preserving China's financial and economic stability.

In the negotiations that followed China's proposal of March 21, China's negotiators felt that China could not afford to pay more than the equivalent of about US$5 million yearly on the foreign currency debts, and that only on a temporary basis, in the absence of large foreign aid available in cash for debt payments. Such aid was not in prospect. A major issue related to priority. The British negotiators felt obliged to press a strictly legal view, the result of which would have been to apply to payment of principal of the senior loans most of what China could afford to pay. China, however, felt it preferable to allocate the payments to cover interest owed to a larger number of creditors than the few whose bonds would be drawn for payment, and to postpone principal payments for the time being. The British also pressed for payment of the Tientsin-Pukow Railway loans of 1908–1910, which had a contingent claim upon customs revenue. Payment on these loans was suspended early in the war when the enemy seized the line.

In July the negotiators in London reached substantial agreement on a plan which amounted to paying full interest in 1939 on the senior customs- and salt-secured loans of 1898 and 1908, respectively, and half interest on the rest of the foreign currency loans under charge of the Finance Ministry. The creditors, however, yielded as to payments on the Tientsin-Pukow Railway loans. China insisted that she ought not to make these payments, since Japan had seized the entire railway and its revenues. But the plan for resumption of debt payments never came to fruition. On July 17 China was forced to suspend support in the foreign exchange market because of exhaustion of foreign currency funds. On July 27 China reluctantly had to advise the creditors that she was unable to proceed with the debt negotiations. China negotiated in good faith, and her leaders were genuinely distressed that the negotiations had to be ended. I accept part of the responsibility for the breakdown, because I was handling the negotiations under general authorization by and frequent reference to Minister Kung, and delayed because of the deterioration in the reserve position. Neither China nor the creditors would have gained, but rather there would have been severe detriment, had China announced an offer which she would not have been able to implement.[3]

Prices of China's foreign obligations during the war reflected the vicissitudes of events. The outbreak of fighting in North China caused a considerable break in prices; and the break extended drastically when the fighting spread to Central China on August 13. The quotations that follow show the situation in the summer of 1937, and indicate for comparison the quotations of Japanese issues, which also slumped severely.[4]

	Chinese Loans	July 1	August 9	August 27
4½%	loan, 1898, British issue	103½	98	92
5%	loan, 1925	104½	95	88½
4½%	loan, 1908	100	99	93
5%	loan, 1912 (Crisp)	94½	83½	66
5%	Reorganization loan, 1913	99½	91	78½
8%	Sterling notes (Vickers), 1925	43¼	—	24½
5%	Peiping-Liaoning Railway	100	94	72½
5%	Honan Railway	85½	71	50
5%	Hukuang Railway	75½	61	42
5%	Lung-Tsing-U-Hai Railway	45	35½	25
5%	Shanghai-Nanking Railway	90½	71	45
5%	Tientsin-Pukow Railway, British issue	76	61	42
5%	Canton-Kowloon Railway	57	—	33
	Japanese loans			
5%	Sterling loan, 1907	82¼	74½	62
6%	Sterling loan, 1924	93¼	81½	68

In comparing quotations of the various items, it should be noted that some were debts formerly in arrears that were being paid under settlements recently made in 1936–1937 under which interest payments were reduced, especially in the earlier years.

Thereafter quotations during the war were affected by the course of the fighting, China's finances, the extent and prospects of foreign help, the suspension of debt payments, and the breakdown of negotiations to resume payments. Quotations at London of the largest loan, the 5% Reorganization Loan of 1913, London issue, were:

Year	High	Low	Year	High	Low
1937	101½	61	1942	—	—
1938	73	48	1943	60½*	—
1939	54	25	1944	57½	44
1940	45	18	1945	76½	47½
1941	44	26½			

* To December 2.

The position of the private foreign currency debt under charge of the Finance Ministry at the end of the war, compared with the prewar position, is shown in appendix A, Table 43. The dollar equivalent of outstanding principal fell from about US$247 million to about US$180 million because: (1) about four-fifths was in sterling, and sterling exchange fell after mid-1937 from about US$4.95 to US$4.035; and (2) a substantial amount of debt was paid off during the war, prior to suspension of payments early in 1939.

Details of the railway debt are shown in appendix A, Table 44. The principal amount outstanding as of January 1, 1937, was equivalent to US$163 million, and the postwar equivalent was about US$104 million.[5] Relatively little railway debt was paid off during the war, because payments on the debt of a railway were suspended when the enemy had seized the line. The decrease in value of principal was a result largely of the fact that most of the debt was in terms of European currencies which fell in value during the war in terms of dollars; and also to the elimination as of 1945 of debt to Axis creditors, mainly Japanese, since it was assumed that in the postwar settlements the Axis governments would be required to assume these debts. The preceding figures do not include railway debt originating after January 1, 1937, as to which particulars are not available because of wartime disruption.

Of the prewar foreign debt of the Communications Ministry, equivalent to about US$17 million, about US$14 million was owed to Japanese creditors. On the assumption that China would be relieved of the latter obligation, the postwar figure would be about US$3 million.

To summarize the foregoing, the dollar equivalent of the principal amount of China's postwar private foreign currency debt according to the preceding data totaled about US$287 million, compared with about US$427 million in mid-1937. Those figures do not include the principal amount of prewar foreign currency debt in arrears, equivalent to about US$54 million in mid-1937. Much of that was owed to Japanese and other enemy creditors and, excluding that, the postwar equivalent was of the order of US$15 million. Thus China's postwar obligations to private foreign creditors did not appear as extremely burdensome if China could be rehabilitated.

THE BOXER INDEMNITY OF 1901

This indemnity originally was equivalent to about US$334 million. Following the example of the American remissions to China in 1908 and 1924, the British and Belgian portions were remitted in 1925 and the Netherlands portion in 1933. The Japanese portion was allocated to educational and cultural purposes in 1923, but Sino-Japanese friction interfered with the procedure. About half of the indemnity payments outstanding after World War I were canceled: the German and Austro-Hungarian portions in the peace settlements, and the Russian portion by voluntary renunciation in 1924. The French portion was made security for loans of 1925 and 1930, part of the proceeds of which was used for China's benefit. Also, the Belgian and part of the British portions were used to secure loans for China's benefit. These various loans are included in appendix A, Table 43. The Italian portion, per agreements of 1933–1934, became security for an internal loan in terms of Chinese currency. The Portuguese, Spanish, and Swedish-Norwegian portions, equivalent in capital amount to about US$50,000 as of July 1, 1937, had not been remitted to China. Prior to the dates of the special arrangements mentioned, much of the indemnity had been retired by payment.[6]

As of mid-1937, the outstanding capital amount was equivalent to about US$27 million, apart from the loans mentioned, as follows:

Portion	Date of final payment as scheduled in 1937	Capital amount outstanding July 1, 1937
American	1947	US$8,469,280
British*	1946	£1,903,841
Japanese	1945	£1,747,332
Netherlands	1940	Fl. 353,545
Portuguese	1945	£ 4,822
Spanish	1940	Fr.fr. 127,648
Swedish and Norwegian	1940	£ 2,371
		US$8,469,280
		£3,658,366
		Fl. 353,545
		Fr.fr. 127,648

* Excluding the outstanding amount of the 1934 loan, namely, £1,164,000 as of July 1, 1937.

Indemnity payments were suspended as of January 1, 1939, along with payment of other customs-secured obligations. As from that date, under instructions of the Minister of Finance, the Inspectorate General of Customs made monthly deposits in special accounts in the Central Bank of China of sums in Chinese currency representing for the several customs-secured obligations, including indemnity payments, a share of debt service corresponding to the proportion of customs revenue collected in Free China to total customs receipts of the entire country. The government, in order to aid in continuing activities supported by indemnity payments, arranged for loans by the government banks to the American and British trustees having charge of the activities.

The American and British treaties abolishing extraterritoriality, effective May 20, 1943, also canceled as between the two countries and China the 1901 protocol which provided for indemnity payments. Later in 1943 Belgium made a similar treaty with China, as did France after the war. On February 16, 1943, shortly before finalization of the Sino-American treaty, former ambassadors Sao-ke Alfred Sze and Hu Shih telegraphed from Washington:

We have learned from certain friends in the American State Department, in explanation of the new treaty, that indemnity payments should cease as soon as the treaty goes into effect, but the Chinese Government seemed under moral obligation to continue to pay to the China Foundation and the Tsing Hua University the amount that was overdue under moratorium; as to the existence of the China Foundation, the American Government would say, when questioned, that it is always interested in the Foundation and would like to see it continue to exist.

About 64 per cent of the overdue payments of the American portion was due for support of Tsing Hua University and about 36 per cent for the China Foundation. For both of these, substantial endowments had been accumulated, and their activities in support of education of Chinese students and for other cultural and scientific purposes have continued.

These treaties of course did not cancel China's obligation to complete payment of the loans secured on the Belgian and French portions and on part of the British portion of the indemnity. The amounts of these loans outstanding at the war's end were:

1925 Gold loan	French portion	US$22,136,650
1928 Gold loan	Belgian portion	US$ 828,900
1930 Sino-French Educational Fund Advance	French portion	US$ 265,000
1934 Canton-Hankow Railway Loan	British portion	£ 972,000

The total principal amount of these was equivalent at 1945 exchange to about US$27 million. Also China remained liable for payments equivalent to about US$100,000 in respect of the Netherlands, Portuguese, Spanish, and Swedish-Norwegian portions, which were not canceled.

There was also the Japanese portion, which China assumed would be canceled after the war. Beginning in September 1937, payments of that portion were put in a special account in the Hongkong & Shanghai Banking Corporation at Shanghai and not turned over to Japan. When all foreign currency debt payments were suspended as of January 1, 1939, the accumulated total of the account was about £525,000. The total of unpaid annuities remaining after that date was about £2.15 million. The grand total of the Japanese portion unpaid as of the war's end was about £2.7 million, equivalent at exchange rates of 1945 to a little over US$10 million.

OTHER INTERGOVERNMENTAL DEBT

The only intergovernmental debt existing in mid-1937, other than the Boxer Indemnity, comprised the American flood relief loan of 1931 and the cotton and wheat loan of 1933.[7] These were consolidated before the war into a combined obligation of which US$14,700,000 was outstanding June 30, 1937. The debt bore 5 per cent interest, was secured on a customs surtax, and final payments were due in 1942.

In view of further American credits beginning in December 1938, China maintained payments on this debt during the war, although with some agreed lightening of the burden. China completed repayment before the end of the war. Further particulars are contained in chapter VIII.

VIII. THE FOREIGN PURCHASE CREDITS OF 1937-1941

The start of fighting brought urgent need for large purchases abroad, partly for costly military hardware and partly for other essential items. China rapidly drew down her monetary reserves by purchases begun immediately, as well as by support of exchange (see chap. XV). It was clear that the reserves, with only meager chance of replenishment by exports, would not long suffice to finance China's needs for purchases abroad.

Aid came at once from Russia, in the form of credits to buy military items. But the first American wartime credit was announced only after 18 months, and because of the neutrality law could not be used for war materials. These were not obtainable from the United States without cash payment prior to the lend-lease law of March 1941.

After the Brussels Conference, held in November 1937 under the 1922 Nine Power Treaty, failed to take effective action either to curb Japan or aid China, the Chinese government asked for a loan equivalent to US$500 million from the United States, Britain, and France. The money was sought to buy war materials, a list of which China submitted. The loan was to have been secured on customs and salt revenues and by oil concessions.[1] Although the figure looked big, it was I believe eminently realistic as to the amount China could well have used. But the request received little consideration. Britain and France were busy with the threat of Hitler, and wanted no further risks in Asia. The United States, neutralist and isolationist, would not give a lead that might have brought serious action to aid China.

This chapter deals with purchase credits in 1937–1941. Financial aid for currency support is treated in Part Three because it was intimately related to currency management. The American government's purchases of China's silver beginning in 1937, which greatly helped China by converting silver reserves into usable dollars, and which did not involve credit, are also treated in Part Three.

In *China and the Helping Hand, 1937–1945*, I have dealt at length with all forms of aid, including military, and how it developed and was used. Here I present the situation from the angle of finance, and include financial data not suitable for inclusion in that book. I refer the reader to it for a fuller treatment of the internal and international setting in which the aid was provided, and its results.

A summary of wartime credits to China is contained in appendix A, Table 47.

RUSSIAN CREDITS

Russia's policy *vis-à-vis* China was changing in 1936–1937, after years of friction. Because of Japan's growing encroachments in northeast Asia, Russia felt a common interest with China in checking Japan's expansion. Eight days after large-scale fighting broke out at Shanghai on August 13, 1937, Russia and China signed a "nonaggression" pact. At that time Russia promised China a credit of C$100 million (about US$30 million), and at once began providing aid "short of war." The aid consisted mostly of military items, including planes, together with "volunteer" pilots. Not being bound by legal requirements, Russian aid began as an emergency measure, well before conclusion of the formal agreement. When that agreement was signed, March 1, 1938, the amount was raised to US$50 million. Further credits followed in 1938–1939, bringing the eventual total authorized to US$250 million.

Russian aid developed promptly. On September 29 the American embassy at Nanking reported that 300 Russian planes were being sent to China via Lanchow. A few days later a Russian pilot was reported found in a plane shot down near Shanghai. On October 14 Ambassador Davies reported from Moscow that 400 Russian planes and at least 40 instructors had already been sent to China. Caravans were taking supplies on the long trek through Central Asia, and at least 200 trucks were working on that route. Also heavy items were sent via Indochina, and later via Rangoon and the Burma Road.

Russian aid continued actively during 1938 and until the outbreak of war in Europe in September 1939. Russian arms sufficed to equip about 10 reorganized Chinese divisions in 1938–1940. By the fall of 1939 Russia had provided about 1,000 planes together with about 2,000 "volunteer" pilots in rotation. Russian pilots took active part in the aerial war. Russia also sent military advisers, altogether about 500 including some leading generals. These partly filled the gap caused by Hitler's withdrawal in mid-1938 of the German military advisers who had served China well since 1927. For the Russians the fighting was also a laboratory for training pilots, observing Chinese and Japanese war operations, and learning what they could about the German equipment used by China and the methods and organization which the German advisers had taught the Chinese army.[2]

Russian aid, however, gradually petered out. The war in Europe forced attention to matters closer to Moscow. Fear of a two-front war led Russia to appease Japan with a five-year "neutrality" treaty in April 1941, which both sides observed until Russia disregarded it by attacking Japanese forces in Manchuria just before the war ended in August 1945. In June 1941, Hitler's attack on Russia posed the issue of Russian survival. Thereafter

Russian shipments to China practically ceased, although some Russian military advisers and technicians stayed in China until mid-1944, apparently without much influence. Even though a large part of the third Russian credit of US$150 million had not been utilized, Russia provided to China after 1941 little more than technical aid through military advisers, and aid in maintaining transport through Central Asia for delivery of goods from China for payments on the debt. Several times efforts were made to arrange transport through Russia of trucks and heavy equipment which could not otherwise be sent to China because of the blockade and loss of the Burma Road. But these efforts failed, apparently in part because Russia feared to risk causing Japan to attack her.[3]

Russian aid went correctly to the National Government and not to the Chinese communists, even after the United Front between the Nationalists and communists had broken down. There is no evidence of Russian material aid to the latter until the end of hostilities.[4]

Russian aid was important to China in the critical first two years of fighting. It gave both weapons and moral support. China's leaders, however, had no illusions about this aid, and felt that Russian imperialism was only in abeyance. China took pains to avoid too great dependence upon Russian supplies, believing that Russia would provide no more aid than was necessary to maintain resistance against Japan.

Russia's wartime aid to China was provided under three agreements:[5] March 1, 1938, in the amount of US$50,000,000, to be repaid October 31, 1943; July 1, 1938, US$50,000,000, to be repaid June 30, 1945; and June 13, 1939, US$150,000,000, to be repaid June 30, 1952 — a total of US$250,000,000. The credits bore 3 per cent interest, and were payable by delivery to Russia of agricultural and mineral products, half of each kind. Transactions were for the Russian fiscal periods from November 1 to October 31. China shipped the barter goods under interim agreements, after which a settlement was made in respect of each year. The agricultural materials were bought and shipped by the Foreign Trade Commission and later the Central Trust of China and included tea, bristles, silk, and wood oil. Minerals sent included tungsten, tin, antimony, mercury, bismuth, and molybdenum, and were handled by the National Resources Commission.

Table 14 shows the schedule of total payments to Russia due by years on the three credits, together with the payments which China actually made. The wartime payments were less than those scheduled. This resulted, first, from the fact that while all of the first two credits was used, the third credit for US$150 million was used only in part. Second, deliveries fell behind because of difficulties of procuring and forwarding the goods under war conditions. Of total payments of US$131 million in the period ended October 31, 1945, US$60.5 million were in agricultural and US$70.5

TABLE 14. Russian credits of 1938–1939: scheduled and actual payments, 1938–1952 (in thousands of US$)

| Year ending October 31 | Schedule of payments | | | Amounts due | Actual payments | | |
	Principal	Interest	Total		In agricultural products	In minerals	Total
1938	1,667	2,500	4,167	—	2,555	—	—
1939	10,000	2,950	12,950	13,593	7,505	—	—
1940	15,000	2,650	17,650	16,709	8,424	—	—
1941	20,000	6,700	26,700	22,976	8,919	—	—
1942	27,500	6,100	33,600	23,127	6,216	—	—
1938–1942	—	—	—	76,405	33,619	38,516	72,135
1943	33,333	5,275	38,608	24,006	8,386	11,940	20,326
1944	25,000	4,275	29,275	13,339	7,015	10,357	17,372
1945	20,000	3,525	23,525	33,611	11,483	9,700	21,183
Subtotals	152,500	33,975	186,475	147,361	60,504	70,513	131,017
1946	15,000	2,925	17,925	31,527[a]	—	—	18,300
1947	15,000	2,475	17,475	8,561	—	—	14,300
1948	15,000	2,025	17,025	8,342	—	—	5,700
1949	15,000	1,575	16,575	8,122	—	—	—
1950	15,000	1,125	16,125	7,903	—	—	—
1951	15,000	675	15,675	7,684	—	—	—
1952	7,500	225	7,725	5,027	—	—	—
Totals	250,000	45,000	295,000	224,527	—	—	—

SOURCE: Schedule from Finance Ministry memorandum, *Supply and External Requirements of Chinese Agricultural Products, 1938–1961 (re-estimated in July 1942)*; amounts due and payments from letters of June 5, 1946, from Central Trust of China, and July 20, 1946, from Finance Ministry, and for 1946–1948 from International Monetary Fund, *Balance of Payments Yearbook, 1948–1949*, p. 115.
[a] Comprising US$23,968,000 of agricultural products and US$7,559,000 of minerals.

million in mineral products. Arrears of deliveries at that date were US$16.3 million. In the circumstances, China made a creditable record of performance.

Only partial data are available as to the commodities which comprised China's actual deliveries to Russia. Table 15 shows the estimated quantities of the chief items programmed for delivery, with total values for the respective years sufficient to meet the scheduled obligations if the total credits of US$250 million were utilized. These items were of obvious importance to Russia.

For 1945–1946 China programmed payments to Russia of US$31.5 million, comprising US$24 million in agricultural products and US$7.5

TABLE 15. Products assigned for payment of Russian credits, 1938–1945[a]

Year ending October 31	Mineral products (tons)			
	Tungsten	Antimony	Tin	Mercury
1938	1,500	2,000	300	—
1939	5,000	5,000	1,000	—
1940	3,300	5,500	3,300	110
1941	5,600	4,400	5,600	220
1942	3,200	8,000	5,600	300
1943	3,800	8,000	6,200	400
1944	2,200	8,000	5,600	200
1945	1,000	8,000	5,600	200

	Agricultural products[b]				
	Tea (cases)	Sheep and camel wool (piculs)	Wood oil (tons)	Bristles (piculs)	Silk (piculs)
1938	200,000	—	—	—	—
1939	250,000	60,000	1,680	500	500
1940	300,000	103,000	2,240	1,000	—
1941	450,000	106,000	2,240	2,000	1,000
1942	60,000	100,000	500	5,000	1,500
1943	60,000	110,000	500	5,800	2,500
1944	200,000	60,000	2,000	2,000	1,000
1945	120,000	60,000	1,500	1,600	1,000

SOURCE: Ministry of Finance memorandum, *Supply and External Requirements of Chinese Agricultural Products, 1938–1961 (re-estimated in July 1942)*.

[a] The estimated total value for each year was estimated to be sufficient to cover the payments scheduled. But because the credits were not fully utilized, the amounts actually due by China were less. Other products also were delivered.

[b] The unit of measurement for wool, bristles, and silk is the "new" *picul* of 50 kilograms.

million in minerals. Apparently over two-thirds of these payments were to meet arrears of deliveries, especially of agricultural goods, not delivered during the war. The schedule as of 1946 called for future payments of about US$8 million yearly, to liquidate the debt by 1952. A tenth of total payments was to be handed over in dollars to cover the costs of transport. The shipments of agricultural goods contracted and under negotiation for the year 1945–1946, as of June 1946, included 5,500 tons of wood oil, 3,500 *piculs* of raw silk, 8,000 *piculs* of bristles, 1,000,000 goatskins, 240,000 chests of black and green tea, and 1,250,000 pieces of brick tea — all valued at about US$18 million.[6]

The first two credits of US$50 million each were all utilized, and US$73.2 million of the third credit of US$150 million, making a total of US$173.2 million utilized, according to data of the Ministry of Finance as of June 1945.[7] I estimate that practically all of this, perhaps US$170 million, was utilized prior to the Pacific War. The transactions were handled with special secrecy, part of the time by the Generalissimo directly, and data of the amounts utilized by years are not available.

Despite Russia's violation of agreements, by actively aiding the Chinese communists at the end of the war, China felt obliged to continue for some time payments to Russia, lest Russia make the situation even worse. By June 1946 the debt due and unpaid was about $55 million. Payments continued into 1948. The eventual amount of unpaid principal, according to official Chinese figures, was US$46 million.[8] There were disputes about the quality and prices of deliveries, and hence different calculations of sums to be credited. As of January 1946, yearly settlements with Russia had not been made since November 1, 1942.[9] Hence the amount claimed by Russia in respect of unpaid balance is not known. It would be interesting to know whether Russia held the Chinese communist regime responsible for the balance, as successors to the Nationalists.

It is a striking fact that the terms of Russia's postwar aid to communist China appear to be quite similar to those on which Russia aided Nationalist China during the war.

AMERICAN CREDITS

While Russia immediately after the fighting broke out was providing credits for military items and "volunteer" pilots, the United States was backing away from involvement in Asia.[10] Washington refused passports to Americans engaged before the hostilities to go to China as aviation instructors, and even considered trying to block pilots of the Sino-American civil air line, the China National Aviation Corporation (CNAC), from flying in China. Washington was carrying out the neutrality law and the policy of isolationism. But Ambassador Johnson was disturbed, and on September 3, 1937, telegraphed to Secretary Cordell Hull that ". . . sooner or later . . . we must consider whether we are to abandon all hope of saving something, even our self respect, from the wreckage of 150 years of cultural and commercial efforts in China." [11]

American policy gradually began to change. Among those wanting to do something to help China was Secretary Morgenthau.[12] In the summer of 1938, a year after outbreak of the fighting, he invited to Washington K. P. Chen, who had negotiated with him previously about sale of silver. Chen arrived in September and began his talks at the Treasury. Opinion in Washington was divided, with Morgenthau and some members of the

State Department and the Export-Import Bank favorable to granting a loan, and Secretary Hull and others opposed. The project had a setback in October when China lost to the enemy both Canton and Hankow. But Generalissimo Chiang made it clear that China had both the capacity and the will to keep on fighting. Finally, after Hull left for a conference abroad, Morgenthau got Roosevelt's approval.

On December 15, 1938, Chairman Jesse Jones of the Export-Import Bank announced a credit of US$25 million to China. The credit was granted under an agreement with the Universal Trading Corporation of New York, organized for the purpose by the Chinese government. The proceeds were to be used ". . . in financing the exportation of American agricultural and manufactured products to China, and the importation of wood oil from China." The announcement went on to say that since 1931 China had gotten US$27 million of American credits which that Bank was handling, and that China had repaid US$14.4 million and was repaying the balance as it matured.[13] To placate congressional and other American opinion, Jones took special pains to have the loan appear as a commercial deal with maximum security. Besides China's pledge to repay by delivering wood oil, he insisted upon an unconditional guarantee by the Bank of China, an essentially commercial bank of good standing partly owned by the government.

In China the effect of the credit was inspiriting, especially since similar British action followed. The American embassy in Chungking reported that the Chinese construed the action ". . . as indicating the commencement of action by those powers to prevent Japan from achieving its aims in the Far East," and that it had ". . . immensely stimulated and stiffened the Chinese will for prolonged resistance." The Japanese Foreign Minister, however, called the loan "a regrettable act" and "economic pressure," and declared that "the Japanese people will undoubtedly find new grounds for strengthening the proposed new order in East Asia." Writing after the war, former Japanese Foreign Minister Mamoru Shigemitsu said that this and the following Western credits were viewed by the Japanese army as "an insult" and the only thing that made possible China's continuing resistance.[14]

Pursuant to the agreement signed on February 8, 1939, between the Export-Import Bank and Universal Trading Corporation, the Bank was to provide "commercial credits" to Universal up to US$25 million, to buy American agricultural and manufactured goods. Interest was 4½ per cent. Payment was to be by shipment of 220,000 tons of tung oil (wood oil), beginning with 25,000 tons the first year and rising to 60,000 the fifth and final year. China agreed to use half the proceeds from the tung oil to repay the credit, and the other half to buy other American goods. The credit could not be used for arms, ammunition, or airplanes. In practice, however, the American side took a liberal view of items that could readily be converted into military use.[15]

This credit was the forerunner of three somewhat similar credits. Although China badly needed them, they did not come easily. American opinion was divided, and isolationism was strong. In the fall of 1939 China asked for a further credit of US$75 million. Most of the first credit had been committed for purchases. Also China wanted what Ambassador Hu Shih termed a "life-saving injection," to sustain morale at a time when Japanese pressure on France threatened closing of the route via Indochina.[16] But the lending authority of the Export-Import bank was limited, and only US$20 million was approved, being announced in February 1940. The agreement between the Bank and the Universal Trading Corporation was signed April 20. The terms were a little more liberal than those for the previous loan of US$25 million. The Bank dropped the requirement in the previous credit that China agree to spend in the United States, over and above repayment of the credit, a sum of equal amount. Interest was 4 per cent instead of 4½ per cent, and the money could be spent for commercial but not military planes. The security was export of tin, and again the Bank insisted upon a Bank of China guarantee.

In mid-1940 China sought a third purchase credit. The funds provided under the earlier credits were by then mostly committed. But negotiations lagged. Roosevelt, while anxious to aid China, felt he should move cautiously in view of the uncertainty created by Hitler's great drive against France and Britain. Meanwhile, Secretary Morgenthau explored the possibility of a triangular deal with Russia. The scheme was that the United States buy strategic minerals from Russia, and that Russia in turn use the funds to provide military supplies to China — which the United States could not do under the neutrality law. The State Department opposed the scheme, in view of its unhappy experiences in trying to deal with Russia since recognition in 1933. But Morgenthau and Jones got the President's authority to go ahead. The Russian ambassador stated that Russian aid to China was limited by availability of materials and not by finance; and also that while Russo-Chinese and Sino-American relations were good, Russo-American relations were a "blank." So the matter was dropped.[17]

The third credit was granted in September 1940. The issue came to a head because of Japan's encroachment in Indochina. The terms were similar to those of the previous two, but this time the credit was granted to the Central Bank. Without limiting that Bank's obligation, the credit was secured by export from China of tungsten to be provided by China's National Resources Commission. Interest again was 4 per cent. The schedule of repayment was more liberal, with half the credit due in five years. As before, the credit could not be used for munitions, but purchase of commercial aircraft was allowed.

On October 18 Generalissimo Chiang again asked for aid. The recently announced purchase credit of US$25 million was helpful, but he wanted planes and, if possible, American volunteers. More than the Japanese army, he feared "the defiant Communists." Ambassador Johnson strongly supported Chiang's plea, saying that "aid short of war" was not enough. "We give nothing," he said, "neither life nor treasure, to help those who are fighting against those who, if they succeed, must inevitably unite to fall upon us." American aid, he said, "is offered only at a high cost which is draining the country of the money and resources which might otherwise back the currency and prevent soaring prices." The United States, he said, should not by inaction force the Chinese people "to choose between the Japanese and Communism," and "failure of the United States and Great Britain to afford timely aid to China may in the end result in Communist ascendancy in China." [18] These pleas promoted before the end of the year action which led to formation of the American Volunteer Group, Chennault's famous Flying Tigers. The pleas also were part of the background for Roosevelt's revealing on December 17 the idea of what came to be lend-lease aid.[19] A more immediate result was announcement on November 30 of credits to China totaling US$100 million. Half of these was for currency support, and this is discussed in chapter XVI. The other half was a fresh credit for purchases.

The purchase credit of US$50 million was formalized by an agreement of February 4, 1941. The loan again was a credit to the Central Bank. Specific security was to be provided by export of "tin and other strategic materials." Interest was 4 per cent, and repayment was extended over seven years.[20]

This was the last of the four purchase credits, the total of which was US$120 million. Of that amount I estimate that about US$95 million was utilized up to outbreak of the Pacific War December 7/8, 1941. As of the end of the war US$104.5 million had been utilized. The total eventually utilized was US$117 million, US$3 million of the first credit having been canceled. China repaid US$66 million through 1945, and the remaining US$51 million after the war, mostly in 1945–1948.

After adoption of the American lend-lease law in March 1941, there was little need for further purchase credits. Under that law the United States could provide military items without China's assuming any specific financial obligation. The total of lend-lease aid furnished to China in 1941 was US$25,821,000.[21] Lend-lease aid after outbreak of the Pacific War is discussed in chapter IX.

BRITISH CREDITS

In the spring of 1938 the British government began thinking of possible financial aid to China, and in June Cyril Rogers flew to London to press for aid. The Foreign Office then favored a large loan to China, and there was much British public support for it.[22] In a letter to the London *Times*, July 4, 1938, Lord Lytton, who headed the League of Nations commission on the Manchurian affair in 1931–1932, said that Britain should help prevent the collapse of China's currency. Otherwise, he said, "not only shall we be open to the charge of placing a quarantine on the victim of aggression instead of the aggressor, but we will also be neglecting our own manifest interests." In France Foreign Minister Henri Bonnet told American Ambassador Bullitt on July 6 that "he was certain that both Great Britain and France would be prepared to advance money to the Chinese Government at the present time if the United States should be able to take similar action," which would be "separate but simultaneous." On July 13 the State Department sent a telegram to Ambassador Joseph P. Kennedy authorizing him to indicate the American government's sympathy for the proposed British action, along with doubts about joint as compared with separate action within the limits of each country's situation. But Washington got cold feet, and canceled the message the next day before Kennedy had acted. On July 15 the British government announced in Parliament an adverse decision, apparently influenced by a wish to avoid antagonizing Japan in view of the tense situation in Europe. The British Cabinet were divided, and the canceled American message might have weighted the balance in favor of the loan. Britain also considered purchase credits to China under the export guarantee procedure, but negotiations at this stage led to no definite result.[23]

By November the progress of the American negotiations led Chiang to press for British aid. On December 20, after announcement of the first American credit of US$25 million, London announced a credit of £500,000 mainly for motor lorries for the Burma Road. The announcement forecast further credits.[24] The credit of £500,000 was formalized by an agreement of March 15, 1939. Under this agreement China used £223,000 for lorries and parts. China paid a fourth in cash and the remainder (£167,000) in serial notes with Bank of China guarantee, bearing 5½ per cent interest, and maturing during four years. The Board of Trade guaranteed the other three-fourths. China did not use the rest of the credit, since other credit arrangements became available under which no cash down payments were needed, and later lend-lease.

On July 20, 1939, London told Ambassador Quo Tai-chi that Britain would grant a further purchase credit. In the summer of 1939 the situation in China was critical. Aggressive Japanese measures against the Tientsin British Concession were damaging confidence. The exchange market had slumped badly and was almost in panic. Japan was insisting publicly that Britain stop aid to China. A joint Anglo-Japanese statement of July 24 was widely taken as British appeasement.[25]

On August 18, on the eve of World War II, the agreement, for £2,859,000 to buy British goods, was signed. The Board of Trade guaranteed payment to exporters. Interest was 5 per cent, and payments were spread over 10 years. There was no specific security of Chinese goods, but it was understood China would earmark enough exports to cover the payments due. The British also required a Bank of China guarantee, because the Americans had insisted on it, but stated that otherwise they would not have asked for it.

In the latter part of 1940, when China's situation was specially difficult, as described in the preceding section, Britain joined the United States in announcing a further purchase credit, and a credit for currency support (see chap. XVI). Each of these British credits was for £5 million. The Generalissimo had hoped for a larger amount, but the British felt that they could do no more at a time when they had far-reaching commitments for the war, and were seeking financial aid from the United States. The purchase credit was formalized in an agreement of June 5, 1941. The credit was secured by export of bristles, tea, silk, antimony, or other commodities to be agreed upon. Purchases were to be made in the sterling area. Interest was 3½ per cent, and payment was to be completed within 10 years. There was no Bank of China guarantee. China used the whole of this credit, £3.7 million by the end of 1945 and the remainder by June 1948.

Altogether British purchase credits to China in 1938–1941 totaled £8,359,000. These credits, like those from the United States, helped China to get a variety of useful goods and services and relieved some of the strain on assets abroad. China used all of these credits excepting £277,000 of the first credit of £500,000. About £7 million altogether was used up to the end of 1945, and the remainder of the credits of £2,859,000 and £5 million by June 1948. The £223,000 used from the £500,000 credit apparently was paid in full. But, according to Chinese records, about £1.3 million of the credit of £2,859,000 remains unpaid; and about £4.1 million of the credit of £5 million.[26]

FRENCH CREDITS

France was the first Western nation to give official backing to wartime credits to China. By an agreement of April 22, 1938, a French banking group, in association with the China Development Finance Corporation, financed building a railway from the Indochina border to Nanning in Kwangsi Province. They advanced about 150 million French francs (against an authorized 180 million French francs) and £144,000, equivalent in total to about US$5 million. The French Government Credit Insurance Department insured 80 per cent of the advances. Interest was 7 per cent, principal repayment ran from the 4th to 15th years, and the security was the surplus of salt revenue and the mining taxes of Kwangsi Province. Unfortunately the railway did not prove of much value, since soon after its completion the Japanese captured Nanning.[27]

The French group and the China Development Finance Corporation, by an agreement of December 11, 1939, also agreed to advance up to 480 million French francs (about US$10 million) to finance a railway from the Kunming terminus of the Indo-China Railway to Suifu on the upper Yangtze River above Chungking. There was to be an 80 per cent guarantee by the French Government Credit Insurance Department. In May 1940 the puppet regime at Nanking issued a statement repudiating the loan.[28] During the first part of 1940 the French group placed orders in France for a considerable part of the materials required. But these remained there in storage when in May-June Hitler overran France. Soon afterward Japan's encroachments in Indochina blocked that route for shipments to China. So it was not possible to proceed with the project as contemplated. Apparently a substantial amount was advanced under the agreement, but definite figures are not available.[29]

The French group also contemplated financing the Chungking-Chengtu Railway, but information is not available whether funds were advanced for that purpose.

GERMAN BARTER AGREEMENTS

Under an agreement of 1936 with "Hapro," a concern controlled by the German War Ministry, German interests provided China with materials for railway construction and industrial projects. The maximum of German credits outstanding in mid-1937 may have reached about 100 million marks, say US$40 million, this being an estimate subject to an error of some 20 per cent either way. These credits were being repaid by shipment to Germany of agricultural and mineral products.[30] In China the Central Trust of China administered the purchase and shipment of the barter goods. In the two years ended in August 1938, the government provided about C$70 million, say US$20 million, to Central Trust for purchases. These included 6,257 tons of tungsten, 3,635 tons of antimony, 760 tons of tin, 32,234 tons of vegetable oils, and 15,500 tons of shelled groundnuts.[31] These shipments were of obvious strategic importance to Germany, and continued up to the outbreak of World War II in September 1939.

Arms shipments from Germany were said to have been included among the barter goods, but I do not have definite information on that matter.

IX. FOREIGN CREDITS AND LEND-LEASE DURING THE PACIFIC WAR

When Japan attacked on December 7/8, 1941, China and the Western powers became allies. There was no need for further credits on commercial terms. Instead, China's allies granted credits whose repayment in money was tacitly not expected, on terms somewhat analogous to lend-lease.

As Japan quickly overran much of Southeast Asia in the early fighting, the possibility of large-scale material aid faded. Such aid came to depend upon expansion of the tenuous air route over the "Hump" from India, which was explored only two weeks before Pearl Harbor, and upon fighting through from India to complete the Stilwell Road, opened only in January 1945. While quick material aid was out of the question, there was no doubt about the ability of the United States to provide promptly such financial aid as China could use. It was natural to turn to financial aid, because China's financial difficulties were as grave as the military. But at this stage the difficulties were not primarily related to lack of funds abroad, but were internal. By the end of 1941 prices had risen about 20-fold above the level of 1937. How to cope with acute and ever faster inflation in an overstrained economy, and how to finance the growing American military effort in China, stood out as major problems. Moreover, there were questions of China's morale. It was vital that China be able to continue fighting. A Sino-Japanese peace would have been a terrible blow to the Allied cause.

For some time before Pearl Harbor China had been talking of really big credits. The outbreak of the Pacific War brought need for decisions and action.[1]

THE AMERICAN CREDIT OF US$500 MILLION

In November 1941 Minister Kung broached to H. Merle Cochran of the American Treasury, then visiting Chungking, the idea of a large credit. Cochran reported on this to Secretary Morgenthau, who sent word to Kung on December 16 that the matter was receiving sympathetic consideration. On December 30 Generalissimo Chiang told Ambassador Clarence E. Gauss that he wanted about a billion dollars — US$500 million and £100 million. On January 9, 1942, President Roosevelt gave his blessing to the idea of a large loan. It was warmly supported by the State Department for reasons of morale and, in the words of Stanley K. Hornbeck, "to tie China into our war (which is still her war) as tight as possible." [2] Secretaries Stimson and Knox also favored the proposal. Secretary Morgenthau had misgivings as to the amount, but finally went along with the others. At the Cabinet meeting on January 30 it was agreed that the President would promptly send a message to Congress urging the loan.

On February 7 the President signed a Joint Resolution which both houses of Congress passed unanimously, providing

That the Secretary of the Treasury, with the approval of the President, is hereby authorized, on behalf of the United States, to loan or extend credit or give other financial aid to China in an amount not to exceed in the aggregate $500,000,000 at such time or times and upon such terms and conditions as the Secretary of the Treasury with the approval of the President shall deem in the interest of the United States.

A bill appropriating the funds was signed February 13. Thus it took only two weeks to complete action after the administration had made its decision.

Morgenthau told the House Appropriations Committee that to sustain the war in China "the Chinese financial and monetary system should be made as strong as possible"; that "in waging this war China has performed economic and military miracles," but that its financial system had been "severely strained in the process"; that China had made payments on schedule or even ahead of schedule on the wartime loans already granted, had shipped strategic commodities to the United States under the most difficult conditions, and had "carried out to the letter every obligation to us which it has assumed." But off the record he told a member that "we might not get a dollar back," to which a member replied, "Even so, we might consider ourselves amply repaid by Chinese participation in the war." [3]

In China the loan was welcomed as a measure of friendship and encouragement. All elements, including the communists, applauded it.

Chiang at once telegraphed instructions to T. V. Soong, who was representing China in aid negotiations at Washington. There should be no specific security, no interest or fixed term of repayment, and no conditions for use of the money. The deal should be like lend-lease and not like the stabilization agreement of April 1941, which the Generalissimo and Kung felt was too "legalistic and stern" (see chap. XVI).

The draft agreement which the Treasury gave Soong on February 21 provided for making available US$500 million "in such amounts and at such times as the Government of the Republic of China shall request." The final determination of the terms would wait "until the progress of events makes clearer the final terms and benefits which will be in the mutual interest of the United States and China." Article II of the draft provided that China would "keep the Secretary of the Treasury . . . informed as to the use of the funds . . . and . . . consult with him from time to time as to such uses"; and also would discuss with him "technical problems that may from time to time arise." The Generalissimo at once objected to even these slight "strings" on the credit. The feeling in high Chinese circles in Chungking was that China, by her sacrifices in resisting aggression alone for over four years, was entitled to a completely free hand in use of the money. The State Department, however, wanted to keep the proposed provisions, and sought a formula through an exchange of letters. Hornbeck told Morgenthau that this would avoid a precedent of China's "laying down terms to us," and that China was trying to score a "first-class diplomatic victory the consequences of which in the long run will be good neither for this country nor for China." [4] But China remained adamant. Finally on March 20 the Cabinet agreed to dropping the proposed provision. The agreement was signed on March 21, and Soong wrote a letter stating that China would keep the United States informed of the use of the credit.[5]

When China asked for the large credits there was no complete plan for their use. Minister Kung had the idea that their mere existence would strengthen confidence and give support to the currency. I pointed out repeatedly that little continuing effect could be expected from merely adding to the reserves, so long as the multiplication of money proceeded, and that the benefits had to be sought in measures within China which the credits made possible. There was support, in American as well as Chinese circles, for the idea that somehow the credit could be used to encourage production in China. I pointed out in a memorandum of February 7 that such projects had to be carried out almost wholly with materials and labor already in China, and paid for in *fapi*. Hence "the merits of schemes for fresh expenditure ought to be judged exactly as they were judged before the credits were granted."

The preamble of the agreement for the credit said that the credit would help China to

(1) strengthen its currency, monetary, banking and economic system

(2) finance and promote increased production, acquisition and distribution of necessary goods

(3) retard the rise of prices, promote stability of economic relationships, and otherwise check inflation

(4) prevent hoarding of foods and other materials

(5) improve means of transportation and communication

(6) effect further social and economic measures which promote the welfare of the Chinese people

(7) meet military needs other than those supplied under the Lend-Lease Act and take other appropriate measures in its war effort.[6]

The credit eventually was used as follows (figures in millions):

To secure dollar obligations issued in China	US$200
To acquire gold for sale in China	220
To pay for bank notes	55
To pay for textiles shipped to China	25
Total	US$500

In chapter VI I described the issuance of the dollar-backed securities, which involved blunders by China and the wasteful use of the US$200 million allocated. The procurement and sale of gold, which was intimately related to currency matters and is discussed in chapter XIX, fell short of its potential because of obstruction on the American side.

It is my opinion that the credit would have been of greater value to China, and later Sino-American friction reduced, had China agreed to the relatively slight "strings" asked by the United States and which involved consultation and cooperation but not control. This judgment, however, must be qualified in the light of the Treasury's later obstructive dealings with China in relation to gold, under the influence of Harry D. White. Hornbeck, I believe, was right in his prediction quoted above that China's success in avoiding "strings" would be "good neither for this country nor for China."

In the latter part of 1943, when Chiang met at Cairo with Roosevelt and Churchill, he sought a billion dollar loan from the United States. Such a loan, he felt, was needed to sustain morale at a difficult time and to check the deteriorating situation in China. He and Kung believed that a big loan would have great psychological value in retarding inflation, because it would show a large backing for the currency. Chiang pressed the proposal after Roosevelt, at Churchill's urging, withdrew the promise of an amphibious operation as part of a plan to recover Burma. Chiang felt that a big loan was needed to sustain morale at a difficult time. The proposal led to much friction, being related to the controversy about how to cover the cost of American military operations in China (see chap. XVIII). Although the friction continued, the immediate difficulties were patched up, and the billion dollar proposal was dropped. Such a loan, for reasons explained above, would not have helped much to check the deterioration in China, however useful a large fund might have been for postwar restoration.[7]

THE BRITISH CREDIT OF £50 MILLION

When in late December 1941 Chiang sought a credit of £100 million, London felt that such a big sum was out of the question. Britain was ready to grant to China all possible lend-lease aid. But Britain was not prepared to grant a large "psychological" credit. Worry about the postwar balance of payments made Britain unwilling to give China an unrestricted call after the war on any unused portion of the credit. The British reply proposed a credit of £20 million, to be secured upon postwar customs revenue.

The Chinese reaction was emotional. Chiang and his colleagues felt that China, after years of fighting alone against Japan, rated larger aid. Sino-British friction had been building up. Most recently there was the temporary closing of the Burma Road under Japanese pressure in 1940, and the friction on financial issues (see chaps. XVI and XVII). In the background was the memory of Sino-British friction during many decades. China rejected the proposal of customs security as "colonial."

The American agreement to grant an unrestricted credit of US$500 million cut the ground from under the British position. On February 3 London announced willingness to "lend to China for war purposes an amount up to 50 million pounds, at such times and upon such terms as may be agreed between the two Governments." [8] But the negotiations went badly, as Britain felt obliged to keep her basic position, and by mid-1942 they had practically come to a halt.

After intermittent negotiations, an agreement was signed on May 2, 1944. The official British statement said that the agreement "carries out the offer made . . . some time ago . . . for the financing of goods and services required by China in the sterling area for the purposes arising out of the war." Britain was to finance the rupee needs of the Chinese forces in India and Burma. Also Britain would provide funds during the war to pay for transportation, for bank notes, and to help to cover the cost of orders already placed under the 1939 and 1941 purchase credits; for further purchases for war purposes; and for other purposes that might be agreed. The agreement also provided that Britain would provide sterling backing for a loan up to £10 million to be issued in China on terms to be agreed, to withdraw redundant purchasing power. As of July 1, 1942, however, China had issued the "31st Year Allied Victory National Currency Loan" of C$1 billion, to be secured by allotments from the £50 million credit, not waiting for conclusion of the formal agreement.

China's use of the £50 million credit for purchase of goods and services in the sterling area was limited because of unavailability of transport. Total drawings were £8.1 million, of which £3 million was charged by the end of 1945 and the balance by July 1948. [9] The internal loan secured by the credit was denominated in *fapi* and hence not attractive to the public. Little of that loan was used except as security for advances to government by the Central Bank.

AMERICAN LEND-LEASE

The lend-lease act became effective March 11, 1941, and on May 6 the President formally declared China eligible under the act. On March 31

T. V. Soong presented at Washington a comprehensive request for planes, armaments for 30 divisions, and transport equipment. A year or two earlier American producers could have filled such orders. But now, with the war in Europe at a critical stage, Britain had the chief priority. And the United States was beginning to rearm. Planes and many items of artillery and ammunition were in very short supply for some time. But transport equipment and some other items sought could be provided to China.

Considerable shipments of transport items and miscellaneous supplies went forward promptly to Rangoon. Much piled up there and later had to be destroyed or was lost to the enemy early in 1942. An important cargo of artillery, machine guns, and ammunition was sent in October. But little was done to meet China's need for planes.

In 1941 total lend-lease aid "furnished to China," according to American Treasury data, was US$25,821,000 or 1.7 per cent of the total to all countries. Lend-lease was so slow to start that China bought supplies of many kinds, especially for needs of the air force, from the proceeds of the Export-Import Bank credits. These supplies were shipped to China and proved invaluable later after the Japanese cut the Burma route early in 1942. Lend-lease comprised both goods and services. Shipments to China began with 7,552 tons in May and totaled 66,675 tons through December.

China's relatively small share in lend-lease reflected American concentration upon events in Europe, and the strategic view that Hitler's defeat was the prime objective. Indeed lend-lease, in the view of the American public at this stage, was almost equated with aid to Britain. The prevailing view, especially in the War Department, was that scarce items should be allocated with priority to Britain, or to rearm the United States.[10]

In 1942, after outbreak of the Pacific War, China's newly found allies were hard pressed on many fronts. Aid was slow to materialize. Planes were in greater demand than ever. Serious delays occurred in meeting promises to develop an effective air route over the Hump. China's leaders accepted with fairly good grace the principle that defeat of Hitler had first priority. But they felt that China deserved better treatment after her years of sacrifice as the first to resist aggression. They resented a degree of emphasis on Europe that denied to China the minor proportion of aid that China could receive and use. The Generalissimo complained to Roosevelt on April 19, 1942, that "China is treated not as an equal like Britain and Russia, but as a ward." [11]

It was not until the latter part of 1943 that the Hump route moved 10,000 tons monthly. Eventual development of that route to a peak of 73,691 short tons in July 1945 was a remarkable feat, and has been termed the beginning of mass air lift. The total tonnage airlifted to China was about 650,000 tons. But this was only equal to the capacity of 70 Liberty ships, and was small relative to China's need. It was not until about mid-1944 that the tonnage equaled the Burma Road's peak in 1941. The opening of the Stilwell Road in January 1945 permitted by the spring of 1945 further shipment to China of about 28,000 tons monthly, including the weight of vehicles sent to China. Also the opening of the pipeline from India to China in the spring of 1945 provided a further capacity of over 10,000 tons of gasoline monthly.

The improved access to China led to stepping up lend-lease aid in 1945. Also the end of the war in Europe in May eased the pressure to furnish lend-lease to fight Germany. The table below shows total lend-lease aid to all countries and to China by years (millions): [12]

		China	
Year	All countries	Amount	Percentage of total
1941	US$ 1,540	US$ 26	1.7
1942	6,893	100	1.5
1943	12,011	49	0.4
1944	14,940	53	0.4
1945	13,713	1,107	8.0
1946	1,751	210	12.0
Totals	US$50,847	US$1,546	3.0

China got about half of its 1945 total after the Japanese surrender of September 2, 1945. About US$300 million represented the cost of flying Chinese troops to such centers as Shanghai, Tientsin, and Peiping to take control and receive the Japanese surrender — the only Chinese forces near to those centers being communist. Lend-lease to China continued into 1946, because of the large number of enemy troops in China and because of the need to equip the Chinese troops. From V-J Day through February 1946 lend-lease aid of about US$600 million went to China.[18]

BRITISH LEND-LEASE

Britain also provided lend-lease aid to China, but in a much smaller amount, since the United States assumed the primary burden of aiding China. British lend-lease aid to China totaled £11 million, mainly supplies and services for Chinese forces in India and Burma and sterling freights on military supplies. British lend-lease supplies provided in India for Chinese troop training there were equivalent to about US$18 million (say £4.5 million).[14]

Part of this lend-lease aid was provided while negotiations for a formal agreement were pending. On May 2, 1944, when the agreement for the credit of £50 million was concluded, a further agreement was made regarding lend-lease. The British official statement announcing these agreements said:

Pending signature of the agreement the cost of goods and services required by China from the Sterling area for war purposes has been met from earlier British credits, and munitions have been provided on Lend-Lease terms in anticipation of the present agreement. The limit of our assistance to China remains, as always, therefore, one of transport and not one of finance.

LEND-LEASE GOODS TO CHECK INFLATION

Early in 1944 Minister Kung sought means to import to China limited quantities of consumers' goods, to be sold to check inflation. Calculations which I made indicated that the amounts that could be realized in China compared favorably with the value of an equal weight of bank notes, which were being imported over the Hump at the rate of about 150 tons monthly. Of course, Hump tonnage was limited, and there were many urgent calls on it. Yet if inflation got out of hand the military program would be jeopardized. While the proceeds of any conceivable import of consumers' goods at that time could not have been large, it was believed that arrival of goods for sale would help confidence and force some de-hoarding. Ambassador Gauss and the supply section of the American army sent to Washington, with their endorsement, a proposal I prepared for experimental shipments of goods available in India. But the War Department refused to furnish transport for that purpose.[15]

Early in 1945 the proposal began to have serious consideration. The tonnage over the Hump was improving, and the Stilwell Road from India was opened in January. China asked for 23,000 tons of textiles, and both Ambassador Hurley and the army HQ supported the request. The British were ready to help with procurement in India. Opinion in Washington was divided, but finally in May the War Department approved a program of 15 million yards of cloth monthly for six months, to use to procure food and supplies for the Chinese forces. Also 4,000 trucks were to be provided for civilian use. But the war ended before such imports could have a significant effect.[16]

A related matter came up in connection with planning the proposed American landings in China. The American military authorities were worried about how to meet local costs, if they had to land in an area plagued by inflation and almost bare of supplies, and where the population would be largely undernourished. At the invitation of General R. L. Maxwell of the General Staff, I conferred with a group of officers at the Pentagon on October 6, 1944. I urged bringing in supplies such as wheat, flour, and cotton cloth, that could be used in kind to exchange for local goods and labor services. Such a program would not only help to meet military needs, but would administer minimum relief to the area. At the request of Assistant Secretary of War John J. McCloy I developed the subject further in a memorandum, with specific recommendations as to the kinds of goods to be brought in and means to avoid local profiteering and to insure that the goods would go into use and not into hoards.[17]

Unfortunately there was no American landing in China during the war. There was a shift to the strategy of island-hopping in the Pacific. As was the case in Europe, a strictly military view prevailed. Little serious attention was given to rescuing China after her long ordeal. In *China and the Helping Hand* I said:

Such a landing would have enheartened China after long years of war-weariness, and strengthened the government's prestige. It could have helped to stave off the worst stage of wartime inflation. The government would have gained experience in rehabilitating recovered territory, and at the war's end its civil organization and troops would have been located nearer to China's main economic centers. In such a postwar situation, the government would have had a better chance to put China again on the path to stability and progress.[18]

X. SUMMARY AND APPRAISAL, DEBT AND FOREIGN AID; PLANNING FOR POSTWAR

FOREIGN CREDITS AND LEND-LEASE, 1937–1941

In the period before the Pacific War China received foreign credits equivalent to US$513.5 million, plus US$26 million of American lend-lease, a total of US$539.5 million. All of the credits were to pay for goods and services, excepting US$93 million for currency support (see chaps. XVI and XVII). For goods and services, Russia granted US$250 million and the western nations US$170.5 million, of which US$120 million was from the United States, US$35.5 million from Britain, and US$15 million from France. For currency support, Britain provided US$43 million and the United States US$50 million. China may also have received some goods from Germany in this period, under the barter agreement of 1936, but definite information is not available.

Of this aid authorized, however, only about US$350 million or about two-thirds was utilized in this period. The totals utilized of Russian and Western aid were about equal: about US$170 million of Russian and US$180 million of Western aid. The latter comprised about US$127 million of purchase credits, about US$27 million of the British stabilization credits, and US$26 million of American lend-lease "furnished to China." Parts of the American and British purchase credits were used after 1941 during the Pacific War, and even after the war. But only an estimated US$3 million of Russian aid was utilized after 1941.

Appendix A, Table 47 contains a summary of the main facts concerning wartime credits and lend-lease for China. A full account of this aid is given in *China and the Helping Hand*, telling of its development and use.

The purchase credits helped China greatly to pay for a large amount of goods and services needed for the war effort. Without them, China would have found it hard to carry on. Russia granted aid immediately upon outbreak of hostilities, comprising mostly military goods and the services of "volunteer" airmen. But the American and British credits could not be used for military purchases — although the restriction was liberally interpreted. It was not until 1941 that the American government followed Russia's example of "volunteers," by allowing organization of the famous Flying Tigers. Also, compared with the Western credits, the terms of the Russian credits were more liberal, with 3 per cent interest.

There were no political strings. The aid went to the National Government, which Russia viewed as fighting a vicarious war against the common enemy Japan, and not to the Chinese communists. In the first two and a half years Russian aid utilized was nearly three times as great as Western aid. But thereafter Russian aid tapered off, while American and British aid grew.

The various Western purchase credits were fairly sufficient, once they started. Transport difficulties, with China so largely blockaded, interfered with import. Also many goods deteriorated while awaiting shipment from the tropical ports of Southeastern Asia. Large quantities of supplies were lost when Japan overran Indochina and later Burma. For currency support, however, Western aid was slow and inadequate, apart from American purchase of China's silver, which did not involve credit. To anticipate Part Three, China should have had US$100 to 125 million more for currency support in 1938–1941, beginning in mid-1938.

China fully repaid the American purchase credits, US$66 million by the end of the war, and the rest (less US$3 million canceled) thereafter. The American stabilization credit was terminated in 1943 with nothing owed by China. Of the British purchase credits totaling £8.4 million, about £8 million was used. About £5.4 million of this remains unpaid. The British stabilization credits were liquidated before the end of the war. Of the Russian credits, US$46 million remains unpaid.

The credits involved for China a serious offsetting detriment. To pay interest and principal, China had to pay her producers in local currency for the metals, wood oil, tea, and other goods exported. In 1938–1941 these payments totaled the equivalent of about US$85 to 90 million, of which about two-thirds was for Russia. In addition, the equivalent of about US$20 million was spent for barter goods for Germany, mostly it appears under the 1936 barter agreement. These heavy payments aggravated the inflation, because the additional money needed could come only from the printing press. Moreover, governmental trade in these goods removed from the exchange market a supply of exchange, and made harder the task of currency support. But at this stage outright grants or soft loans were not politically feasible in the Western countries. And Russian foreign aid characteristically, during the war and since, has been in the form of loans rather than grants.

As to military supplies, the inability of the United States, under the neutrality law, to provide credits handicapped China and contrasted with Russian liberality. It is difficult to estimate how much China could have used well for military purchases abroad in 1937–1941. It was hard to get sizable supplies to places where they were needed, as Japan's blockade tightened. Also, to provide military aid quickly and with good effect to underdeveloped countries is far from easy, as the United States has been finding out. "Strings" on such aid, properly operated, are essential for optimum results. Russia's supply of military items was accompanied by sending advisers and "volunteers." Had similar American aid been provided, it would have been desirable to act on the same lines as did Russia. Of course the United States was not ready for such action in the early war years.

China's request in November 1937, at the Brussels Conference, for a credit of US$500 million from the United States, Britain, and France, for military supplies received no serious consideration. The international situation, especially with strong American isolationism, did not make such a credit feasible. But the amount was reasonable. Had such a grant been practicable, especially with proper strings on its use, it might have changed history for the better.

In *China and the Helping Hand* I thus appraised foreign aid while China fought alone against great odds for four years and five months, a period longer than World War I:

> Friendly nations helped but, over-all, their help in these years was too often too little, late, and not the kind best suited to strengthen China's resistance and add to her chance of survival as a free nation.[1]

FOREIGN CREDITS AND LEND-LEASE, 1942–1945

Early in the Pacific War the United States granted a credit of US$500 million. Of this something more than US$300 million was used during the war, comprising: US$200 million turned over to China to secure the dollar-backed internal loans, although only part was actually disbursed during the war; US$67 million of gold, being the amount received in China before V-J Day; and about US$40 to 50 million for purchase of bank notes and textiles. The rest of the US$500 million was used after the war.

No strings were attached to this credit. Its use failed to bring to China the benefits that should have resulted. China managed badly the sale of the dollar-backed securities. And the American Treasury largely defeated the purpose of gold sales in China by deliberately obstructing shipments, despite China's relatively good handling of sales up to the time when shipments were withheld (see chap. XIX).

In addition to the US$500 million credit, the United States provided large amounts of dollars to China through payments made to acquire local currency. Since the dollars were provided at rates much above the fair value of the *fapi*, these payments may be considered to involve aid. The United States paid cash for currency, instead of claiming it as reverse lend-lease, because of China's weak financial position. For army costs the United States paid China US$392 million: US$1 million in 1941–1942;

US$110 million in 1943; US$51 million in 1944; and US$230 million in 1945. Besides, to buy strategic goods from China, the United States paid about US$48 million to mid-1944. These various payments totaled US$440 million, and afforded some offset for the damage to China from the faster inflation caused by American military operations. The funds were especially valuable to China as resources for postwar needs.

The United States provided lend-lease aid totaling US$1,546 million as follows (millions of US$): in *1941*, 26; *1942*, 100; *1943*, 49; *1944*, 53; *1945*, 1,107; and *1946*, 210. The lend-lease aid utilized during the war was about US$800 million, including US$26 million in 1941. After the war lend-lease aid continued, a chief item being the cost of airlifting Chinese troops to take over in areas liberated at the war's end. Deliveries continued into 1946, largely to provide equipment for the Chinese army.

Britain agreed to provide to China early in 1942 a credit of £50 million, but the agreement was not concluded until 1944. China used only £3 million up to the end of 1945, and about £8 million altogether to July 1948. During the war use of the credit was hampered by difficulties of transport. Britain also provided lend-lease aid equivalent to about US$44 million. Major items were payments for support and equipment of Chinese troops training in India, and for freights on supplies for China.

Total aid to China by credits and lend-lease utilized during the Pacific War was about US$1.2 billion, comprising something over US$300 million of credits and about US$850 million of American and British lend-lease. Those figures compare with a total of about US$350 million utilized before Pearl Harbor, while China fought alone.

The financial aid granted to China during the Pacific War was helpful as support for morale. But, apart from its important psychological value, it was of little direct use in holding back inflation (see chap. IX). In 1943–1944 China sought a billion dollar loan as a means of support at a critical time when Roosevelt at Churchill's instance withdrew a promise to mount an amphibious operation as part of a plan to recover Burma. That loan was refused after some rather bitter exchanges. Had the loan been granted, it would not have helped much to check the wartime deterioration in China.[2]

Material aid to China was far from adequate. China suffered from the Allied decision to give priority to defeat of Hitler. Also the loss of most of Burma early in 1942 cut off the vital land route into Southwestern China, and import of strategic goods depended upon development of the air route over the Hump from India. China's share in total American lend-lease aid was only about 1½ per cent in 1941 and 1942; about half of one per cent in 1943 and 1944; and in 1945 about 4 per cent up to the end of the war. China accepted with fairly good grace the strategy of Europe first. But more aid could and should have been allocated to China, to develop more promptly the Hump route and to furnish military goods for delivery over the Hump. Appraising the situation in *China and the Helping Hand* I said:

The United States failed to meet promises of aid and for some time did not send even the relatively small volume of items that could have been used . . . In the Fall of 1943, the Lend-Lease Administration told the State Department — both being favorable to greater aid to China — that the War Department mistrusted China and "works to prevent the transfer to China of otherwise needed, available, and deliverable supplies." China after enormous sacrifices while fighting Japan alone for over four years, felt ignored and discriminated against. Hornbeck, as early as August 17, 1942, pointed out that the President had promised aid to China, but that various operating agencies of the government were impeding performance. He said with prophetic foresight: "China and the whole Far East can be lost as effective allies and, if lost, can be turned against the Occident — in absence of and for want of a little more effort on our part to convince the Chinese that we mean what we say when we praise China for the fight she has made . . . and when we promise to send her aid."[3]

Further particulars of aid to China during the Pacific War are contained in appendix A, Table 47.

INTERNAL BORROWING

Expansion of bank credit covered from 69 to 83 per cent of cash war costs after the first year (Table 7). The over-all proportion was about four-fifths, weighted heavily by the expenditure in 1945 which was swollen by inflation. The totals from July 1, 1937, to December 31, 1945, were (billions of C$): bank credit, 1,255; sales of securities to the public, 8; savings schemes, 10; sales of gold, spot and forward, 93; sales of foreign currencies, 1.3; and taxes and nonborrowed revenue other than the aforementioned, 198. These total C$1,566 billion.

The money equivalent of costs in kind is estimated at C$373 billion, of which C$169 billion or about 45 per cent was the proceeds of compulsory borrowing and sale of grain. Thus, of total costs in cash and in kind, estimated at C$1,939 billion, about 65 per cent was covered by bank credit, and the balance by payments directly provided by the public.

The use of internal borrowing from the public to realize a significant part of war costs presented difficulties which the government could not overcome, after the early months of the war. These were the loss of Shanghai, with the only important market for securities; the forcing back of the government to areas where securities were not well known, where there was relatively little liquid wealth, and where, in general, banking was not well developed; the disruption of the administrative system by invasion; and the inflation, which penalized investment in fixed value obligations. Moreover, the government was at fault, first, in its reluctance to press well-to-do persons and enterprises to subscribe to bonds; and, when the American credit of US$500 million was available in 1942, in mishandling the issuance of the dollar-backed securities (see chap. VI).

THE DEBT SITUATION AT THE WAR'S END

Inflation almost wiped out the prewar *fapi* debt, together with the relatively small amount of *fapi* obligations issued to the public during the war. The privately held foreign currency debt receiving service in mid-1937, which remained in arrears from early 1939, was reduced during the war to the equivalent of about US$287 million in principal amount. The reduction resulted in part from depreciation of European currencies. Partly it is explained by calculating the figure on the assumption that China would require Japan and other Axis countries to assume debts due to creditors of their nationalities. Of the prewar foreign currency debt that was in arrears in mid-1937, much was due to Axis creditors, and it was assumed that this also could be written off, leaving for settlement a principal sum of the order of US$15 million (equivalent).

Of the prewar intergovernmental debt, the Boxer Indemnity was ended for practical purposes by agreements made during the war with the friendly powers, and by victory which precluded the possibility of renewed payments to Japan. The other prewar intergovernmental debt, comprising US$14.7 million of debt to the United States, was repaid during the war.

Of the American wartime purchase credits of US$120 million, a balance of US$51 million was outstanding at the end of 1945. Well over half of the wartime British purchase credits, totaling about £8.4 million, was then unpaid — probably £5–6 million (there were some postwar purchases, and about £5.4 million eventually remained unpaid). Of the Russian credits of US$250 million, about US$173 million in all was used; and about US$55 million remained unpaid in June 1946, and eventually about US$46 million.

To summarize, China's debt position at the war's end was relatively favorable. The *fapi* debt had been mostly wiped out by inflation, although there was need to consider whether any revalorization of part of it was feasible. The principal sum due to private (non-Axis) holders of foreign currency debt was of the order of US$300 million (equivalent). The unpaid balance due to governments in respect of purchase credits was of the order of US$150 million (equivalent). The total principal sum of these foreign currency obligations was of the order of US$450 million (equivalent). As regards the Pacific War credits of US$500 million and £50 million, China could reasonably expect to negotiate political settlements whereby the

American and British governments would not call for cash repayment. These credits bore no interest and were in effect analogous to lend-lease. Apparently no eventual settlements have been made.

PLANNING POSTWAR DEBT SETTLEMENTS

In 1945, when it became clear that China was on the winning side, I made a series of studies of the debt position.[4] As to policy, I urged the desirability of prompt settlement of the intergovernmental credits granted after outbreak of the Pacific War and of lend-lease, the final terms of which were left open until after the war. Until China knew how settlements would be arranged, it would be difficult either to settle the private debt in arrears from 1939, or to contract fresh private loans for postwar needs. I concluded that the governmental creditors ought to be lenient, and said, referring to the terms of the agreements:

China can well represent, and the United States and Great Britain agree, that payment of the credits would not be consistent with maintaining a "healthy and stable economic and financial situation" in China and throughout the world; and as to lend-lease, that the "benefit" is China's great contribution to the defeat of Japan and to the security of these countries.

The pre-Pacific War credits from the United States, Britain, and Russia, of which a total equivalent to about US$150 million was outstanding at the war's end, were being paid on terms calling for fairly heavy yearly payments. Spreading out the payments would make it easier for China to settle the private foreign debt and to contract new loans. But:

On the other hand, the good record China has made in retiring these debts has been favorably commented upon in the United States, and has strengthened China's credit rating with the American Government and public. It may be in China's interest not to propose a revision of these schedules, since repayment of the old debts would help to clear the way for fresh credits.

As to prewar private external debt, the recommendation was as follows:

Early resumption will help China's credit. Improvement of credit is important both to add to confidence in the Chinese Government and to facilitate foreign investment and new borrowing. China, however, should not prematurely assume an undue burden of debt payments. China should not risk a breakdown of the arrangements. Negotiations for final arrangements therefore may wait until China is definitely on the path to economic and financial recovery, and until China's internal situation and the international situation affecting China show a fair prospect of stability.

I recommended adoption of a new schedule of gradually increasing payments, for example, with half of the interest due to be paid in the first year, full interest in the second year, and amortization to begin not before the third year and spread over an extended period, with preference in amortization given to senior debt. It would be reasonable to seek cancellation of arrears of interest, or at least to figure them at 1 per cent per annum and issue non-interest-bearing scrip for them to be redeemed over an extended period.

As to railway debt, restoration of service would give opportunity for fundamental changes which I had recommended just prior to the war. These provided for unifying the railways and issuing, in place of the many loans secured on specific railways, obligations secured by the unified system and with the guarantee of the Finance Ministry. The plan was thus summarized:

Inasmuch as the various railway obligations are of differing quality, because of the varying earnings and financial position of the lines pledged as security and differing interest rates and periods of payment, the debt reorganization must provide for differential treatment of the old debts. These should be divided into several different clases having regard to: (1) interest rates, present and future; (2) the schedule of amortization of principal; (3) specific security; (4) record of interest and principal payments; and (5) pre-war market quotations, if any. Under the new debt plan, these classes should receive different treatment as to interest and amortization.

An exchange of bonds of most of the debt under charge of the Finance Ministry was not advisable, partly because most of the old bonds bore moderate rates of interest, and partly because an exchange, if the bonds were to be traded in the principal market at London, would be subject to a tax of 2½ per cent and would involve other sizable costs.

As to debts in arrears, I favored a prompt settlement, along with settlements covering the prewar debt receiving service, to clean up the obligations not included in settlements made before the war. Such a move would strengthen China's credit.

The issue of revalorizing the *fapi* debt was sure to arise, in view of the extreme currency depreciation during the war. The depreciation had caused great loss to many holders. On the other hand, the bonds were bearer bonds, and had been traded actively during the war. It would be hard to establish what would be equitable. I concluded that it would not be possible to devise and put into effect a fair and practicable scheme of revalorization of *fapi* bonds.

As to internal foreign currency debt, I recommended redeeming the Customs Gold Unit issue of 1938, of which less than CGU100,000 was in the hands of the public. The rest of the issue of CGU100 million was held by the government banks, along with most of the dollar and sterling internal issues of 1938–1940. It would be desirable to arrange to give these banks in exchange Treasury Notes in *fapi*, and to cancel their holdings of dollar, sterling, and CGU bonds — thus clearing the slate of the greater part of issues which gave an artificially inflated appearance to the debt payable in foreign currency. The public holdings of these issues at the war's end were US$16.4 million and £836,000, equivalent in total to about US$20 million. It would be anomalous for these bonds to remain in a better position than the senior prewar foreign debt, and I recommended that in conjunction with a general postwar debt settlement, the schedules of payment of public holdings of these wartime issues be readjusted to a basis not more favorable than those to be arranged for the older foreign currency debt.

Unfortunately the conditions in which China could be warranted in making settlements to readjust her debt after the war did not develop.

PLANNING POSTWAR BORROWING

By the first half of 1945, China had built up assets abroad of nearly a billion dollars, thanks largely to the credit of US$500 million and American payments for military outlay in China. While these assets were much more than the US$379 million held at the start of the war, it was clear that they would be fully needed as currency reserve and for financial stabilization. Certainly they would not suffice to meet the major needs of funds abroad for relief and rehabilitation, and for beginning a program of economic development.

For relief and rehabilitation, China's estimated needs were US$2.5 billion to pay for imported goods. China sought from UNRRA a grant of US$945 million, to avoid borrowing for those needs. In the negotiations I was able to convince UNRRA that China could not pay for these imports in foreign exchange. Eventually UNRRA provided about 2.5 million tons of supplies costing US$518 million. China, I argued, also would need help in obtaining imported goods to sell to raise funds in local currency for internal costs of relief and rehabilitation. The eventual program entailed internal costs estimated as equivalent to US$191 million, of which China provided about three-fifths and the rest came from sale of UNRRA goods and special UNRRA contributions.[5]

China's urge for economic development dates back to Sun Yat-sen's imaginative but grandiose plans for communications, industry, and agriculture. Some progress was made before the war, but the war sadly impaired the program. Nevertheless, the government sought to continue during the war with a program of "resistance and reconstruction," the latter meaning development. As a wartime program, inflation was worsened to the extent that money was spent on things that could and should have been postponed. With China's racial pride and nationalism, the urge to redress economic backwardness was renewed as the end of fighting came into view, and it has carried through into the communist phase.

The roots of communist China's Five Year Plans for industrialization are to be found in the plans made during the war by the National Government. It was on future development of industry, mining, and transport that wartime planning placed by far the greatest emphasis. It was then commonly said in China, and also by many in the United States, that China should be developed speedily to supplant Japan as the chief industrial factor in Asia. The experts of the various Ministries worked hard and in general intelligently on specific plans for future progress. China already had a large backlog of such plans, especially for railways, highways, and water conservancy. In the 1930's and even in the 1920's, many competent Chinese and also foreign experts had studied China's development. Part of the credit claimed by the communists for whatever they have accomplished in these fields should go to their predecessors as to planning and preparation.

The plans for development were brought together in the summer of 1945 in a scheme calling for total external costs of about US$2 billion. The objects of expenditure were worked out in detail. Over 40 per cent was for transport and communications and over 50 per cent was for industry and mining. There was provision for engineering costs and training of Chinese experts. The plans were to be carried out by a combination of public and private enterprise. These plans, like the later plans of the Chinese communists, suffered from neglect of agriculture, which constituted about four-fifths of the total economy. The emphasis upon building promptly a strong industrial base is, however, understandable in the light of China's many unhappy experiences in decades of contact with the West, Russia, and Japan.

During the spring and summer of 1945 Soong sought in Washington large long-term credits for these projects. In memoranda of May 9 to Morgenthau, he suggested joint preparation of a program of development.[6] The Generalissimo and other leaders attached great importance to the program of development with the aid of big American loans. Why the loans were not forthcoming after the war is another story.

On the financial side, there was unfortunately a big gap in planning postwar development. While there was careful planning of how to spend large foreign credits, there was little attention to how to meet internal costs. There was scant recognition of the hard fact that, for every dollar spent abroad on imports of equipment and supplies, a sum of the same order of size would have to be spent in Chinese currency for labor and materials. Such money could be printed. But how long could that continue? In Washington there were divided counsels. Some wanted China at once to embark upon a big plan of development, regardless of the unchecked inflation. Others realized that a program of development was bound to be illusory, unless China's finances were first put in order. Believing that the big schemes were quite unrealistic for the immediate postwar period, I explained my view on both the American and Chinese sides.[7] But with little success. A comprehensive memorandum stating my analysis of these problems is reproduced in appendix H.

In internal and international affairs, the issues with the Chinese communists and Russia were the critical factor. In economic and financial affairs, the critical factor was the disruption of the economy, the inflation, and the fact that the budget was out of control. In Part Three, which follows, I discuss the wartime happenings and problems of currency, monetary management, and inflation.

PART THREE. CURRENCY, MONETARY MANAGEMENT, AND INFLATION

XI. THE CURRENCY SITUATION IN MID-1937

CURRENCY

China abandoned her historic silver bullion standard in 1934–1935, primarily because of the American silver-buying policy which drained away huge quantities of the monetary reserves and caused severe deflation. China's first measure in October 1934 was to impose a flexible duty on export of silver. Then in November 1935 came the nationalization of silver and adoption of a managed currency system.[1]

The decree of November 3, 1935, and the accompanying official announcement contained the following main provisions:

1. Notes of the Central Bank of China, Bank of China, and Bank of Communications became full legal tender. Notes of other banks were to be gradually retired, and these banks could not increase their circulation. The Central Bank was to be reorganized as the Central Reserve Bank, and to have the sole right of issue after two years.

2. Banks, firms, and all private and public institutions were to hand over their silver holdings to the newly created Currency Reserve Board, in exchange for legal tender currency (*fapi*).

3. The three government banks aforementioned were to keep "the exchange value of the Chinese dollar stable at its present level." To that end they were to "buy and sell foreign exchange in unlimited quantities."

The official statement announced that the government had made plans to balance the budget within 18 months, was determined to avoid inflation, and would "take energetic measures to deal with speculation."

China did not adopt a definitive parity of exchange, but rather undertook to maintain the "present level" at the time of the reform. That level was about 14½d. and US$0.30. It compared with varying earlier levels under the old silver standard, which were roughly US$0.45 from the latter part of 1926 to the spring of 1929, and which slumped during the depression to about US$0.20 early in 1933. Under the impact of American silver buying, rates rose sharply to above US$0.40 in 1933–1935. From about US$0.37 in September 1935, rates fell to about US$0.30 at the time of the reform of November 3, 1935, the drop being aided by operations of the government banks. The new level of about US$0.30 was approximately the average of the five years 1930–1934. Certainly that level, which I had recommended in a memorandum of October 2, 1935, did not overvalue the currency. In such situations it is well to avoid overvaluation.

The Central Bank's official buying and selling rates after the reform were originally 14⅜d. and 14⅝d. for sterling, and US$0.29½ and US$0.30 for dollars. Sterling exchange fluctuated in the year after the reform between about US$4.90 and US$5.05, not being tied to gold. The Bank's middle rates of 14½d. and US$0.29¾ reflected a crossrate of about US$4.924, the approximate rate in November 1935. When in the following months the Bank's rates became out of line because of changes in the crossrate, the Bank first made small changes in the dollar rate. The larger proportion of transactions in the market was in sterling, and the Bank feared that to lower the sterling rate would be deemed a devaluation and hurtful to confidence. These considerations were of real importance, since the public in China were "exchange-minded" to an unusual degree. China insisted throughout that her currency was independent and not linked to either sterling or to the dollar. The solution, in September 1936, was to widen the spread between buying and selling rates for both currencies — to 14¼–14¾d. and US$0.29½–0.30½, respectively, to prevent arbitrage dealings through the Bank and to avoid if possible further changes in the official rates.

Accompanying the reforms, the government introduced a new system of coinage, to substitute subsidiary coins of dependable fixed value for the conglomeration of silver, copper, and paper subsidiary money of fluctuating value. The public avidly welcomed the new coins. These comprised 100 per cent nickel coins of 20, 10, and 5 cents, weighing respectively 6, 4½, and 3 grams; and copper coins of 1 cent and a half cent, weighing, respectively, 6½ and 3½ grams. The Shanghai Mint went on a 24-hour schedule making the coins, with the effective aid of Robert J. Grant, former Director of the Mint of the United States.

The reform was buttressed by sale to the American Treasury of 187 million ounces of silver for a total price of US$94 million, from the date of the reform to July 8, 1937. Confidence was strengthened at the time of the reform by a British Order in Council requiring British nationals to transfer obligations from a silver basis to the national currency, thus implying approval of the reform.

The reform succeeded beyond expectations in the 20 months before the hostilities. A strong upsurge of economic activity in China followed. Foreign trade in the first half of 1937 was up 40 per cent over the first half of 1936. Aided by repatriation of capital, there was a large favorable balance of payments. Speculative efforts to force a break in the rates were a costly failure for the speculators. The Central Bank was on balance a heavy buyer of foreign currencies.

On June 30, 1937, on the eve of hostilities, China's holdings of gold, silver, and foreign exchange totaled the equivalent of US$379 million, as shown in Table 16. These were the total note reserves, plus banking funds

TABLE 16. Holdings of gold, silver, and foreign exchange, June 30, 1937
(in millions of US$)

	Abroad and in transit abroad	In China	Total
Gold (at US$35)	32.8	12.4	45.2
US dollars	73.9	—	73.9
Sterling (at US$4.95)	92.0	—	92.0
Yen (at US$0.29)	0.1	—	0.1
Silver (at US$0.45 per oz.)	49.4	118.3[a]	167.7
Total	248.2	130.7	378.9

SOURCE: Central Bank of China.
[a] Silver reserves as of June 26, 1937.

abroad, of the Central Bank, Bank of China, Bank of Communications, Farmers Bank, and Kwangtung Provincial Bank. The equivalent of banking funds abroad was US$74.6 million for the Central Bank, and US$22.2 million for the Bank of China and Bank of Communications. In mid-1937 44 per cent of the reserves, equivalent at the current price of US$0.45 per ounce to US$168 million, was still unsold silver. This was a weakness; and since the silver was mostly at Shanghai, it was vulnerable to enemy attack.

The Central Bank of China was growing in prestige. Created in 1928 and wholly owned by government, it was at first little more than the government's fiscal agent. But, after the monetary reform of 1935, it took the main responsibility for regulating the exchange market. In mid-1937 the government approved a plan to convert it into a Central Reserve Bank, with control of the money market and with its base broadened by giving private bankers a voice in its control.[2] But the outbreak of fighting prevented action.

From the start the Central Bank shared note issue with other banks, notably the Bank of China and the Bank of Communications which were older and whose issues were well established. It was only in mid-1942 that the Central Bank was accorded a monopoly. Meanwhile, at the time of the 1935 currency reform, the government took control of the other two banks and the Farmers Bank of China, which with the Central Bank became known as "the four government banks." At that time the government coordinated the note issue of these and most of the other important banks through the Currency Reserve Board. Early in 1937 the government took control of the Kwangtung Provincial Bank of Canton, to extend the currency reform to South China. In mid-1937 the holdings shown in Table 16 were equal to 77 per cent of the total note issue of the banks under the Currency Reserve Board, C$1,642 million or about US$490 million. If we include provincial and other issues not under the Board, the total note issue is estimated at C$1,897 million (see Tables 21 and 62) equivalent to about US$565 million, and the coverage about two-thirds.

When fighting began China was in a far stronger position to finance the heavy costs of warfare than at any previous time. Reserves were much larger than ever before. There was good reason to feel that the United States would be ready to buy the unsold silver. Credit stood high, aided by the settlement of debts in arrears of the former Peking regimes (see chap. V), and by the growing prestige of the National Government at home and abroad. Confidence in the currency was well established. This permitted the government to put out an indefinitely growing volume of paper currency with only gradual impairment of confidence. Without that recourse, China could not have resisted for long.

BANKING

In mid-1937 China's banking system had many elements of modernity, along with characteristic features deriving from earlier days.[3] Modern-style banking was relatively well developed in Shanghai and the other treaty ports. Development of a system of branches of leading banks was helping modern-style banking to penetrate throughout the country. The banking system comprised the four government banks; provincial and local banks; the modern-style private Chinese banks; the native banks; and the foreign banks.

The Central Bank of China did little commercial business. The Bank of China, established in 1912, had long been the leading private bank, but early in 1935 the government took over its control. The Bank of Communications, established in 1907, also had been prominent as a private bank. The government took over its control in 1935, along with that of the Bank of China. The Farmers Bank of China, established in 1933 under government auspices, operated mostly in the interior and with reference to rural credit, and was the fourth government bank. These banks as a group had in 1937 well over two-thirds of the resources of the modern-style Chinese banks.

Most of the provinces had provincial banks, and there were several municipal banks. All were relatively small, except the Kwangtung Provincial Bank at Canton, which operated a separate currency that was not merged into the national system until 1936–1937.

The private modern-style Chinese banks, numbering about 75 in 1937, went through some vicissitudes in the 1930's. Some were hard hit by the deflation accompanying the draining off of silver and had to be reorganized. But the stronger of these banks, such as the Shanghai Commercial and Savings Bank and the Kincheng Banking Corporation, were progressive and gaining strength on the eve of the hostilities.

The native banks were partnerships of family members or of close associates, and were strictly local. They took deposits and granted local credit. The slump of 1933–1935 hit them hard and many failed. On the eve of hostilities there were perhaps 800 of these banks, the number having been roughly cut in half in the prewar decade. These banks, however, maintained a definite place in the financial structure because of their local standing and knowledge of credit.[4]

The foreign banks numbered about 25 in 1937, and were American, Belgian, British, Dutch, French, German, Italian, and Japanese. They handled primarily foreign trade, and some of them from time to time handled foreign loans and investments in China. They were the leading factor in the foreign exchange market, although the Chinese banks, notably the Bank of China, were becoming increasingly active in that market.

The chief offices and branches of the foreign banks in China were located in the foreign settlements and concessions. Being subject to the laws of their respective governments, under the system of extraterritoriality (extrality), they were not subject to Chinese regulation. The leading American and European foreign banks, however, fell in line promptly with the Chinese banks in accepting the monetary reform of 1935, and turned over their silver. The Japanese banks in Shanghai at first were hesitant, but finally turned over their silver in the spring of 1937.

Hong Kong and Macao were economically, in effect, part of China, but being under separate jurisdiction they represented potential leaks in application of financial measures by China. The Hong Kong authorities, in particular, were disposed to cooperate with China.

Existence of these international settlements and concessions, and of Hong Kong, permitted Chinese and foreign banks to operate free of Japanese control from mid-1937 until outbreak of the Pacific War. This unusual condition, events were to prove, afforded aid to China in maintaining her currency, despite the special problems posed. These places after hostilities began became islands surrounded by the Japanese tide.

The four government banks issued notes, but the Central Bank was to have the sole right of issue after being reorganized as a reserve bank. The chief private banks also issued notes, but in 1935–1937 their issue was being taken over by the Currency Reserve Board. Previously the foreign banks issued notes, but by 1937 these had been practically withdrawn from circulation. The provincial and local banks had some issue, about a fifth of the total in mid-1937. Most of this, however, was the issue in Kwangtung and Kwangsi provinces, which was in course of being taken over. There remained the issue of the Hopei Provincial Bank in North China, about C$55 million in mid-1937,[5] which was out of control because of the Japanese penetration. The silver reserves in North China, about 40 million ounces, were immobilized there for the same reason.

PRICES

The most representative prices in the prewar period were those at Shanghai, which for 1926–1937 are shown in Table 17. Fluctuations reflect the vicissitudes of China's currency. These were intimately bound up with silver prices, which are also shown in Table 17. China had a silver bullion

TABLE 17. Prices and cost of living at Shanghai, silver prices at New York, 1926–1937

Year	Wholesale prices	Export prices	Import prices	Cost of living	Silver price at New York[a]
1926	100.0	100.0	100.0	100.0	62
1927	104.4	106.1	107.3	106.7	57
1928	101.7	104.5	102.6	102.5	58
1929	104.5	105.2	107.7	107.9	53
1930	114.8	108.3	126.7	121.8	38
1931	126.7	107.5	150.2	125.9	29
1932	112.4	90.4	140.2	119.1	28
1933	103.8	82.0	132.3	107.2	35
1934	97.1	71.7	132.1	106.2	48
1935	96.4	77.6	128.4	106.6	65
1936	108.5	96.1	141.7	113.3	45
1937[b]	123.8[b]	—	—	118.7[b]	45

SOURCE: Prices and cost of living for 1926–1930 from the Bureau of Markets, Finance Ministry, and for 1930–1937 from the National Tariff Commission; silver prices from reports of the United States Director of the Mint.

[a] Cents per fine ounce.

[b] Average of the first six months. The compilation of export and import price indexes was temporarily suspended for revision of method at the end of 1936. Because of the hostilities the compilation was not resumed, and the other series were interrupted.

standard with free export and import of silver, until 1934. Then the American silver-buying policy forced China to abandon her age-old silver standard: first, by imposing a flexible duty on silver exports in October 1934, and then by adopting a managed currency in November 1935.

Under the old silver standard general prices in China tended to move inversely with the world silver price, but with a lag and to a much lesser extent. In foreign exchange, however, rates closely followed silver, because silver could profitably be imported or exported when rates diverged from bullion parity enough to justify costs of shipment. Imports of silver tended to add to bank reserves and to increase the supply of money. Conversely, silver exports tended to tighten credit.

In 1921–1928, after the sharp bulge in silver prices accompanying World War I, silver prices were steady. In those years prices in China showed little change. The slump in silver from US$0.58 per fine ounce in 1928 to US$0.28 four years later led to a sharp rise in general prices in China. That rise offset in China much of the effect of the world-wide depression. The drop in exchange rates maintained Chinese exports, despite the depression elsewhere. But, beginning in 1933, the American silver-buying policy reversed the trend. It pushed silver prices from a low of about US$0.25 in 1932–1933 to an average of US$0.65 in 1935, with much higher levels at times. Exchange rates for China's silver dollar, containing slightly over three-fourths of an ounce of fine silver, rose sharply. Hundreds of millions of ounces were drained away from China, credit was severely contracted as bank reserves shrank, and acute deflation resulted with failures of banks and businesses. The index of wholesale prices at Shanghai, based upon 1926 as 100, fell from a high of 130 in August 1931 to 91 in July 1935. After repeated protests failed to change the American silver policy, China had no choice but to abandon silver. Fortunately China could finally turn the situation to her advantage by selling her silver reserves to the United States at prices well above those obtainable had the market been free.[6]

With abandonment of the silver standard in 1935–1936, general prices in China recovered promptly and advanced, especially during the latter part of 1935 and in 1936. Following the slump, a moderate rise was economically beneficial. During the first half of 1937, however, on the eve of hostilities, prices were relatively steady — the cost of living being practically unchanged and wholesale prices rising about 3 per cent.

Note issue grew materially from November 1935 to mid-1937, especially during 1936. The larger part of the increase represented replacement of silver money and of notes of private banks. Bank deposits grew by 20 per cent during 1936 and a further 10 per cent in the first half of 1937.[7] There was in this period a notable surge of economic recovery. The managed currency presented a risk of inflation, depending mainly upon credit policy and how the government implemented its declaration to balance the budget. The latter gave promise of being difficult, in view of continuing aggressive acts by Japan and the urge to modernize the nation with governmental participation and support. But in the months just before the outbreak of fighting there was no pronounced inflationary tendency.

XII. PRICES, EXCHANGE, INTEREST RATES

THE MEASUREMENT OF PRICES

Various indexes of prices were compiled during the war. At Chungking official indexes were compiled by the Central Statistical Bureau, the Central Planning Board, the Ministry of Economic Affairs, the Central Bank, the Joint Office of the Four Government Banks, the Farmers Bank of China, and the Municipal Government. Nankai University, under the direction of Franklin Ho and T. Y. Wu, compiled for Chungking indexes of wholesale prices and cost of living. The University of Nangking at Chengtu, under the direction of J. Lossing Buck and W. Y. Yang, compiled indexes of wholesale prices and cost-of-living indexes for three groups in Chengtu: laborers-peddlers, merchants-storekeepers, and the military-official-education group; and also indexes of prices paid and received by farmers in rural districts.* A number of provincial and municipal governments likewise compiled local indexes.

The indexes must be taken with some reserve, because of the uneven quality of the investigators in the various places, and the difficulty of their task. I would record, however, my praise of the devotion of the economists and statisticians who faithfully gathered and compiled the data. They did their part in providing a basis for governmental policy decisions, even though policy makers gave less than adequate consideration to the data and their implications.

The base of the indexes was commonly the first half of 1937, but some used the entire year or the year ending June 30, 1937. The price level in January–June 1937 was fairly stable, although agricultural prices ruled higher than in the previous half-year, a common seasonal phenomenon. The prices shown by the indexes were generally retail prices. The number of items varied, some indexes using as many as 100 and others only 15. Some indexes were distorted by using imported items that soon became very scarce, or by giving undue importance to items such as metals that were in special wartime demand. The common method was use of the simple geometric mean. There were at least two weighted averages, but statisticians generally felt that they did not have enough information for proper weighting. The indexes were usually monthly, but in the latter part of the war when

---

* A full set of *Economic Facts*, monthly, which contains the price and cost-of-living data together with economic studies published by the University of Nanking, is in the Library of the Department of Agriculture at Washington, D.C.

inflation was acute some agencies compiled them on a half-monthly, 10-day, or weekly basis.

There were wide variations in prices from place to place. Transport and communications have always been difficult in China, and during this period it was commonly difficult or impossible for goods to move very far from regions of low prices to where prices were higher. Also prices were higher in places of heavy concentrated government spending, like Chungking and Kunming. Often money could not be transferred from place to place without a considerable premium or discount. In 1939–1941 the premium on Shanghai funds ranged from 7 to 54 per cent at Chungking and Kunming (see appendix C, Table 60, and a following section of this chapter). Even within Free China there were premiums on some inland transfers, sometimes up to about 1 per cent and occasionally more.

The wide regional price differences make it impossible to say that data for any one place are representative for all of Free China, whose area shrank with successive enemy drives. Thus at the end of 1941 when the Pacific War began, retail prices were 12 to 15 times the 1937 level at Shanghai and at such places as Kanchow in inland East China and Lanchow in the northwest. But in Chungking and Kunming they had risen about 27- and 35-fold, respectively. At the end of the war the peak ranged from nearly 2500-fold in Chungking to about 7500-fold at Kunming, and 1250-fold at Sining in the northwest.

For showing the wartime price movement in Free China as a whole, I used contemporaneously and use herein the retail price indexes compiled by the Farmers Bank of China. These were developed under the general direction of Y. C. Koo, a competent economist, formerly a chief officer of that bank, then Vice-Minister of Finance, and at this writing Treasurer of the International Monetary Fund. They covered 16 cities originally, though the number shrank as various cities fell to the enemy. In the introduction to appendix B, especially the part pertaining to Table 48, I explain the statistical effects of dropping cities from the averages. The index comprised 25 items: 11 for food (rice, flour, salt, eggs, pork, etc.); 5 for fuel (coal, charcoal, vegetable oil, firewood, matches); 4 for clothing (2 shirtings, sox, lcoth shoes); and 5 miscellaneous (tea, towels, soap, grass paper, cigarettes). There were some small variations regionally in the list of items. The base was the first half of 1937. The method was the simple geometric mean.

Compilation of indexes was complicated after 1942 by efforts at price control, which I discuss in a following section of this chapter. Since the control was not effective, the more representative prices were the free prices and not the official prices. I received at the time from Franklin Ho of Nankai University the following comparison of index numbers of whole-sale prices at Chungking in April 1943 (based upon July 1936 to June 1937 = 1):

	Market	*Official*
All commodities	100.48	75.31
Food	67.68	52.89
Clothing materials	161.91	113.18
Metals and products	296.46	192.05
Building materials	117.21	78.82
Fuels and light	202.77	154.38
Miscellaneous	28.97	26.21

In some centers the "economic police" were often rough on dealers in the black market, and investigators found some difficulty in getting the free prices. The Farmers Bank, however, was able to collect these prices in the principal cities for confidential use — in addition to official prices of controlled items. Availability of indexes of market as well as official prices is a further reason for using the price data of the Farmers Bank. A comparison of indexes of market prices with those of "composite" prices, which include official prices, is shown in appendix B, Table 50.

Table 48 in appendix B and the chart at the front of this volume show the average market prices by months for the war period, using data of the Farmers Bank for the cities of Free China. That bank during part of the time compiled simple averages of the prices in the several cities. Because of the wide variations from place to place, however, I have computed a simple geometric mean of the local indexes. The series presented in appendix B, Table 48 is, I think, the most representative index available of the price movement in Free China as a whole in these years. Other representative price data for Free China are shown in appendix B, Tables 49 to 56.

Because of differences in method and content, the several indexes kept during the war differ. But the general trend which the figures show is wholly clear.

THE COURSE OF PRICES IN FREE CHINA

During the war until August 1945, inflation progressed without pause. The rate of increase grew, with occasional slackening, and quickened dangerously from the latter part of 1944 until August 1945. At the war's end a sharp but brief drop took place. The figures that follow show by years (December to December) the percentage increase of the average of monthly indexes of retail market prices, based upon the data of the Farmers Bank (appendix B, Tables 48 and 49): for *1938*, 49; *1939*, 83; *1940*, 124; *1941*, 173; *1942*, 235; *1943*, 245; *1944*, 231; *1945*, 230; and in *1945*, to August, 251. The monthly rate of increase varied considerably, as shown in appendix B, Table 49, being affected especially by seasonal variations in crops, war news, international events, and the government's financial policy.

In the first year the rise was moderate, considering the seriousness of the invasion. By mid-1938 average prices in Free China rose to about 40 per cent above the prewar level of mid-1937. A major factor holding back the rise was the sale of foreign currencies to support exchange, equivalent to US$121 million in the first eight months, thus withdrawing *fapi* from circulation and checking the inflation. But the government lacked the resources to continue sales at that rate (see chap. XV). A further factor was China's surprisingly strong resistance to Japan's superior might. But Japan's strength told and, as fighting dragged on, the course of the war was adverse to China until 1945. Although Japan could not conquer China's vast reaches, she overran the richest areas and won most of the battles. The shock of defeats as well as the overrunning of productive regions urged on the inflation. A constant upward pressure on prices resulted from the issue of more and more notes to finance the deficit. To about a 20-fold rise up to the outbreak of the Pacific War was added a rise of about 130-fold to August 1945. By the war's end the average level was about 2,600 times that of mid-1937.

Beginning late in 1944 the price rise became definitely faster. A shock to confidence resulted from the strong Japanese drive in the second half of that year to take the whole length of the Canton-Hankow Railway and capture the American air bases in East China. This drive even threatened Chungking. The slowness of Allied aid and the failure of the American Treasury to deliver gold also hurt confidence (see chap. XIX). The price rise caused growing worry. In February 1945, General Wedemeyer felt that inflation was "almost as great a threat to U.S. Army operations in China as the Japanese." [1] The rate of rise reached about 25 per cent monthly early in 1945. It threatened to pass to the almost irreversible stage of hyper-inflation,[2] and to financial collapse, before the war's end.

In August 1945 when Japan's surrender seemed near, prices broke sharply. The drop was about a third on the average, but was from 50 to 60 per cent in Kunming and Lanchow. According to the intramonth indexes which the Farmers Bank was then compiling, retail prices moved as follows (January–June 1937 = 1):

1945		Chungking	Kunming	Lanchow
July		2163	6894	1672
August	1–10	2404	7962	1870
	11–20	2483	7325	1467
	21–31	2192	6695	1289
September	1–10	2138	4797	1029
	11–20	1914	3275	907
	21–30	1878	3682	877
October		2107	4548	1046

That was the only real drop during China's wartime and postwar inflation.

Unhappily China was not able to use this breathing spell, with American and other aid, to get the situation in hand. From October the inflation resumed its course unchecked.

Among commodities the rise was uneven. Food production in Free China as a whole was not seriously interrupted. But food prices, borne along by the flood of inflation, showed greater or less rates of increase than the general indexes, under influence notably of the size of crops. Until 1940 the price of rice lagged much behind the increase of general prices. But from the end of 1939 to the end of 1940 the price of rice almost tripled, under influence of a poor harvest, and drew abreast of the general advance. Thereafter prices of rice and goods in general moved more nearly together, although factors such as variations in crops and availability of transport affected the general average.[3] The average prices of rice are shown in appendix B, Table 56.

Imported items such as some kinds of cloth and many manufactured goods and metals became more and more scarce in the interior and prices soared. Fuel prices rose faster in the interior because of scarcity coupled with demand by war industries. Gasoline and kerosene became very scarce. Export goods, on the other hand, could not readily be moved, and prices of such items as wood oil and bristles fell considerably in the early war period. When the rise became general they did not keep pace with other local goods. The Chengtu indexes of wholesale prices prepared by the University of Nanking showing the movement of prices of domestic goods, import goods, and export goods are given in appendix B, Table 54.

Indexes of wholesale prices at Chungking compiled by the Institute of Economics of Nankai University are shown in appendix B, Tables 52 and 53. This index moved in a way broadly similar to that of retail market prices at Chungking compiled by the Farmers Bank (see appendix B, Table 51). The wholesale index showed wide variations in the movement of prices of groups of commodities. Food products were particularly affected by variations in crops and by seasonal factors, and for the period as a whole rose less than the average of commodities in general. The indexes of metals and metal products and of fuel and light, on the other hand, greatly outran the general average, these items being in special demand for war industries.

The varying effects of inflation upon the cost of living of different social classes were studied by the University of Nanking at Chengtu, and also by Nankai University at Chungking. The former kept indexes of cost of living in Chengtu for three classes: laborer-peddler, merchant-storekeeper, and military-official-educational. These indexes are shown by 6-month periods in appendix B, Table 55. For laborers-peddlers, rise of prices was mostly below the average, and notably so as the inflation worsened after 1943. For the merchant-storekeeper class, the costs tended to be fairly near to the average. But for the military-official-educational class the costs tended to outrun the average, especially after 1943. In contrast, the Nankai University indexes of cost of living at Chungking showed no significant differences in the increase of cost of living of the three classes for which they collected data: merchant-landowner; official-schoolteacher; and laborer.[4]

Regardless of whether costs of living for different social classes moved unevenly or more or less together, the effects of inflation involved the extent to which income grew along with costs. The changes in income of different classes were very far from even. I discuss this subject in chapter XXI.

PRICE CONTROL

During the war the government took various steps to regulate prices and assure the supply of necessities, especially to public employees and the army. The most important of these measures was land tax in kind, which despite defects of administration not only assured a supply of food for public needs but was an important source of revenue to help reduce the deficit.

A measure of December 22, 1937, authorized the Commission on Militars Affairs to take action to assure essential supplies to those producing itemy of national importance. This measure authorized control of selling prices and profits. But little was done under this measure. Also little was done under regulations of October 6, 1938, authorizing the Ministry of Economic Affairs to fix prices. In February 1939 the government authorized provincial and municipal authorities to control prices through price stabilization committees composed of the local authorities and business organizations.

The price rise was becoming so acute that in May 1939 the Ministry of Economic Affairs pressed local authorities to set up price stabilization committees. This was done extensively to regulate the prices of several essential commodities such as rice, cloth, salt, coal, vegetable oil, and fuel. On December 5, 1939, that Ministry issued regulations on hoarding. These authorized investigations to determine what stocks of necessities were available and permitted the authorities to force hoarders to dispose of excess stocks at fixed equitable prices, or alternatively the stocks might be taken over by the authorities at a "fair price." A week later the Ministry issued further regulations, that wholesale profits should not exceed 5 per cent and retail profits 20 per cent of cost.

In July 1940 the Price Stabilization Bureau of the Ministry of Economic Affairs began direct operations of purchase and sale. It supplied coal and charcoal to residents of Chungking, through local stores established in that city. In 1940–1941 the authorities issued repeated orders prohibiting speculation, manipulation, and hoarding and set up special organizations to administer production and distribution of such items as cotton yarn, cement, and fuels.

Effective rent control began at Chungking in 1940. There had been a great influx when the government moved the capital there in 1938. And enemy bombing from May 1939 reduced greatly the supply of available buildings, despite much new construction. Rent control could work because of its limited and specific application, and the interest of renters in its enforcement. The control greatly benefited renters, as shown by the fact that in 1941–1942 the index of rents was but half as high as the index of cost of living; in 1943–1944, a third as high; and in 1945 a sixth. It was correspondingly onerous for landlords. The following tabulation shows the indexes (for December of the years listed, except as otherwise noted):[5]

	All commodities	Excluding rent	Rent
1937	1.10	1.10	1.15
1938	1.42	1.41	1.50
1939	2.82	2.82	2.87
1940	11.8	12.7	6.83
1941	29.3	31.8	15.6
1942	62.9	68.2	32.8
1943	183	205	60.6
1944	528	588	175
1945, August	1,822	2,074	320
1945	1,788	2,033	382

Because of the importance of rice, the government established the National Food Administration, August 1, 1940. This body created subordinate organizations of provincial and local authorities. Nevertheless, food prices rose even more drastically than before because of the poor crops of 1940–1941. On June 16, 1941, the government created the Ministry of Food. Because of land tax in kind, adopted in 1941, rice was available for supply both to the army and to civilian officials. This measure had considerable rough and ready effectiveness, though its operation left much to be desired (see chap. III).

On the eve of the Pacific war a memorandum of October 1941, prepared in the Central Bank, analyzed price control measures to date, and termed them a "complete failure." Price control in China, said the memorandum, was impracticable because of the Japanese occupation of part of China, defects of organization within China, and public ignorance and indifference. Enforcement was uncoordinated, being left to local authorities. These adopted varying bases of regulation and used different degrees of zeal, so that goods were diverted from some areas and to others. A dispatch of October 15, 1941, from the American embassy at Chungking quoted Franklin Ho, a respected economist, as saying that price control would do more harm than good.[6]

Early in 1942, the government set up the Bureau of Commodities of the Ministry of Economic Affairs to take charge of measures to stabilize prices and prevent an abnormal rise, to check speculation, and to improve supply and distribution of goods. This Bureau was given a fund of C$450 million, of which C$200 million was from the government and C$250 million a loan from the four government banks. This Bureau first paid attention to the supply of necessities for public employees, who already were entitled to buy rice at controlled prices. Beginning in April 1942, it put into effect a scheme whereby government employees and their families were entitled to buy each month at controlled prices 30 kilograms of charcoal or 50 kilograms of coke, 12 ounces of vegetable oil and 1⅓ pounds (1 catty) of salt; and 20 feet of cloth per year. While this measure helped those benefiting from cheaper prices, the government's going into the market to buy the goods raised the prices for other buyers.

In the fall of 1942 discussion in the United States of the anti-inflation law adopted early in October 1942 was telegraphed to China and had considerable repercussions. The thought was that if the United States was establishing control of prices, similar measures ought to be adopted in China. Feelings were reflected in the comment that "free prices are not adopted nowadays by any country in wartime." In view of the active discussion of price control, I gave the government on October 1, 1942, the following memorandum on price control.

The constant increase in the volume of purchasing power caused by creation of fresh bank credit, together with scarcity of goods, transport difficulties and other factors, is steadily pushing up the general level of prices at the rate of 10% or more per month. If this purchasing power is dammed up in some places it will overflow in others.

Fixing of prices in China cannot be applied so as to affect to any considerable extent either the monetary factor, the scarcity of goods or difficulties of transport. In other words, it cannot greatly affect the fundamental problem because it neither increases the total supply of goods nor reduces the demand.

Price regulation cannot be applied generally throughout the country, but only in limited areas or places. Control of producers and owners of goods as a whole cannot be complete enough to force them to sell in the controlled markets. Fixing of lower prices there will tend to cause these people to take their goods elsewhere, thus causing local scarcity. Also announcement of such measures may lead to increased hoarding of goods by producers or merchants or speculators, since people will be reluctant to sell at fixed prices. There will be some uneconomic movement of goods to be sold at places other than their normal markets, thus adding to costs of production. Finally the public will not believe in the efficacy of price control, will not understand it, will evade it, and the injury to confidence may even add to the rate of increase of prices.

Any shortage of supply of goods needed in controlled areas will have to be made up by purchases elsewhere. This means setting up a considerable business organization, which cannot be as efficient as the ordinary channels of trade. The buying and movement and handling of the goods will entail expenditures that will bid up the price of goods and services in other regions. Thus any reduction in some areas would be at the cost of increases elsewhere. The fund for purchase will have to come out of the budget, thus adding to the deficit and increasing the amount of note issue. There may be a business loss — which might be justified if the net results were good, but which in the present circumstances might be suffered in vain. Ordinary trade will be dislocated.

In existing conditions, the net result of price control, over a period of time, may well be to increase rather than to check the rise in the general level of prices. Finally, if the Government commits itself to such a policy, and the policy should fail because of evasion and inability to maintain the fixed prices and dislocation of trade, the failure may impair confidence and hurt the Government's prestige.

In a further and more detailed memorandum of October 5, 1942, I further analyzed price control schemes. I pointed out that it would be unwise for the government to become committed to "ceilings" of prices, because these could not be maintained. Nevertheless something could be done. The surplus of goods obtained through the tax in kind, after meeting needs of the army and of public employees, should be sold at cheap prices. It was important that these goods should not be hoarded by the government or needlessly held off the market. In any event if the government should decide to adopt price-fixing it would be advisable to begin experimentally with a very few essential goods in a few places, and without the appropriation of large funds. It could be limited to meeting specific needs or specially acute situations, and the actual results could be observed before the government became committed to a large-scale and costly program.

The government nevertheless adopted the price control program. The Kuomintang Central Executive Committee, on November 12, 1942, adopted a resolution to enforce price control. On October 29 the Third National People's Political Council (PPC), to whom the Generalissimo had proposed the program, endorsed it unanimously. The report which the Council adopted blamed the price rises primarily on hoarding, speculation, and manipulation. It said that the government had been equally responsible for following a policy of "hands off." The report also made broad recommendations for the curtailment of expenditures and for the improvement of revenues.

In a circular telegram of December 17, 1942, Chiang ordered that the price measures take effect from January 15, 1943. Provincial and local authorities were to put the measures into effect at important centers in their respective regions. Prices and wages prevailing November 30, 1942, and especially prices of food and salt, were to be taken as standards for fixing price ceilings; special attention was to be paid to necessities. Shops were to post the fixed prices and black markets were to be strictly prohibited.

Press comments in Chungking indicated various pertinent queries about the proposed measures. What would be the effect on costs of production and on profits, and would this situation affect the movement of goods? Would production be reduced? How could manufacturers continue production if their costs rise and selling prices are fixed? What about the considerable price rise that already had occurred since November 30, 1942?

Would enforcement of price ceilings cause goods to flow to the occupied areas? Would merchants evade the measures and would black markets exist?[7]

Chiang, in addressing the officials who were about to leave on December 24 to administer the price control in different parts of the country, was quoted by Central News Agency of that date as follows: "Stressing the importance of spiritual solidarity and unity of purpose, Generalissimo Chiang said that the seriousness of the problem of commodity prices is not due to the effect of currency but to the divergence of social psychology and spirit and will." In view of the sacrifices of those at the front and the civilians in the occupied areas, he said, "the gentry, rich business men and social leaders should be stimulated to a high pitch of patriotism and induced to abandon their mean designs of profiteering."

Although the price control compaign began with a certain amount of energy and enthusiasm, it almost immediately became clear that it could not succeed. In an editorial February 2, 1943, the important paper *Ta Kung Pao* of Chungking reported that "every purchaser and seller are violators," and asked whether the authorities expecting to punish violators had available "thousands or tens of thousands of cells for the imprisonment of black market violators."

There were numerous difficulties. Although the Generalissimo's instructions stated that price ceilings should be applied first to daily necessities, the controls at Chungking covered over a thousand items. The *Bulletin* of the China Information Committee, January 13, 1943, thus reported on the program:

With the publicity week started on January 11, the entire nation has completed preparations for the restriction of prices to be enforced on January 15 in accordance with a circular order of Generalissimo Chiang Kai-shek issued on December 17, 1942. Chungking will be a model for the new price control measure.

The strengthened price control program in Chungking is handled by the Municipal Bureau of Social Affairs. From the 50,000 kinds of commodities, the prices of which were reported by 98 trade guilds (including the Chamber of Commerce), the Bureau has selected 1,000 kinds of commodities for control. Commodity valuation has been completed. Beginning January 15, all controlled commodities will be sold at the fixed prices to be labelled on the commodities upon the publication of the list of controlled goods. Prices prevailing on November 30, 1942, as ordered by Generalissimo Chiang, are taken as the standard, using the prices reported by the trade guilds as reference. The legitimate profit for merchants has been fixed at 10 per cent. Constant inspection will be conducted by the newly organized economic police headed by Police Commissioner Tang Yi. Punishment will be imposed on those merchants who do not label their goods with the fixed prices, or violate the restriction rules, as well as on those who engage in illegal business transactions.

The new program is applied in Chungking not only to the eight kinds of necessities (food, salt, paper, cooking oil, fuel, cotton, cotton yarn, and cotton piece goods) as listed by Generalissimo Chiang, but also to other daily-used articles.

It was not surprising that the relations of prices among the controlled items were often wrong. Thus for cotton the price was set at C$3,000 per *picul* and for cotton yarn C$12,500 per bale, though mills needed about five *piculs* to make a bale. Price ceilings in places of production were sometimes higher than where the goods were to be consumed. Within a given region with various sources of supply, price ceilings differed too much from place to place.

Merchants held back goods from sale, or sold only lower grades at official prices. They reduced weights and measurements, and adulterated goods, for example, mixing impurities with coal. *Ta Kung Pao* of Chungking, February 2, 1943, reported (translated): "Pork is according to the fixed price $14 a *chin* but its weight is not enough and usually carries with it large pieces of bones and intestines. Everything considered it is even higher than in the black market." Where controls were strictly enforced many shops closed.

The restrictions interfered with production and supply of goods. Farmers refused to come to Chungking and other cities because of fear of inspections and lack of understanding of the measures, consequently the supply of food became less. In regions accessible to the occupied areas the control tended to prevent goods from flowing to centers in the free areas but instead to go to the occupied areas. A missionary in the interior wrote on January 28: "Price control has been a complete washout and adds to the difficulty. Nothing can be bought anywhere throughout this province except at twice the fixed price and on a black market. This has made it worse for the poor people." On March 1 I wrote from Chungking to a friend: "The price control here has not worked, and clearly will not work. There are active 'black markets' and people hesitate to bring in goods for sale." Control at Chengtu was lenient and floating capital moved there from Chungking, bidding up prices there. Professor Buck of the University of Nanking wrote from Chengtu on April 12 that most business there was done at open market prices. He said: "People hear about shortages due to control in other places and consequently they are buying ahead for future needs."

On March 14 I wrote to Mrs. Young:

Just now there is a silly program of meat rationing going on here. There is no shortage of meat in Szechuan, nor is it being shipped nor could it be shipped anywhere else. But still they are controlling it and putting in force all sorts of foolish regulations. The Chinese-American Institute of Cultural Relations restaurant was closed the other day for serving meat. Yesterday I heard how the black market for meat works. It is held at different times after midnight — say at 4:00 a.m., and at different places fixed by agreement. Quite a lot of people attend it. The price regulation scheme is doing more harm than good and putting actual prices higher — all of which I clearly predicted. There are no illusions about it in the Ministry of Finance, but it is being done by some impracticable people who have sold to the Generalissimo the idea that the price problem is one of wickedness instead of economics . . . Just because they have price controls abroad some people want to have them here — even though they do not have the conditions in which they are possible.

A week later I wrote that it was difficult to get meat in Chungking "except occasionally, though there is no real shortage but only the dislocation caused by the price-fixing."

A resolution adopted at the fifth meeting of the Central Executive Committee of the Kuomintang on September 11, 1943, admitted that under price control "no outstanding results have been achieved." The resolution recommended increase of production, improvement of transport, increase of revenue, retrenchment of expenditure, and absorption of idle capital through such measures as the sale of gold and encouragement of capital to invest in productive enterprises.

The price control measures gave rise to a dual price system. The official price indexes made public after 1942 were generally for "composite" prices, that is, official prices plus certain free but unregulated prices. But for use in limited governmental circles the Farmers Bank gathered actual market prices, which reflected the great bulk of actual transactions. Appendix B, Table 50 shows indexes of the two sets of prices. Average market prices in leading cities were higher than "composite" prices by 14 per cent in 1943, but by 1945 the margin grew to 67 per cent. For rice, average market prices in this period ruled 20 to 40 per cent above "composite" prices. In the year ending December 1942, average market prices rose 3.3-fold. In the following year, after the price control measures described, the rise was 3.4-fold; in 1944, 3.3-fold; and in 1945, to August, 3.5-fold. Of course so many factors were affecting prices that one cannot easily generalize about the effect of price control *per se* on the extent of the rise.

Attempts to control prices continued during the rest of the war, but with no better results. As inflationary pressure grew price ceilings were raised, somewhat in line with the rise of general prices. Prices of services which the government fixed or controlled, like postage, light and water charges, and fares for buses, railways and airlines, lagged far behind general prices. This eased the burden for users and helped them to cope with inflation. But this was at the cost of adding to the deficit of the budget, and so aggravating the general price rise.

In March 1945 the Chinese government invited to China Leon Henderson, former head of the American Office of Price Administration. His visit was recommended by Donald M. Nelson, who was then in China advising on increase of war production. In talking with Henderson in Washington before his departure, he told me Nelson had suggested that he come to "help with an installation," apparently meaning price control. Before he left I gave him a memorandum of March 19 on the situation which said, "No remedy can be found in economic controls." I stressed views repeatedly pressed on the Chinese government as to the need to control expenditures and increase revenues, and the importance of beginning to get essential civilian goods into China in order to add to the supply and realize non-inflationary revenue from their sale.

When Henderson reached China, Adler, the Treasury attaché, gave him a memorandum of March 19 which contained strikingly similar views. The first point in the memorandum was:

The abolition of price control, except perhaps for a few strategic commodities whose supply and distribution are comparatively centralized. This measure is essential if production, both agricultural and industrial, is to be increased and if the wheels of commerce are to move more smoothly. In the long run it will assist in retarding the increase in prices and in diminishing hoarding; it will also enable the government to curtail unnecessary staff.

The attempts at price control in the last few years have been unsuccessful: they have resulted in a decrease in production, as in the case of cotton, and an increase in hoarding and in the size of the government bureaucracy. The abolition of price control is, therefore, indispensable to an anti-inflation program.

With the adoption of this measure, it may be advisable for the government to pay its officials increasingly in kind. But as this tendency is growing in prevalence, no excessive complications should ensue.[8]

The memorandum urged strong measures against hoarding, both public and private. Some public agencies held too large stocks of food, cotton yarn, and other supplies, which should have been sold for the good of the market. The rest of the suggested program comprised measures that I had repeatedly urged during the course of the war. These included import and sale of cotton textiles, sale of gold, reduction of government personnel, reduction of the army, curtailment of avoidable expenditure, improvement of taxation, and increase of production.

Henderson's conclusions after reaching China, instead of finding a panacea in price control, stressed the humdrum subject of better balance of expenditure and revenue. He urged reduction of the numbers of China's army to 3.5 million. I noted in my diary written at Washington April 21, 1945:

Leon warned CKS [Chiang Kai-shek] on inflation — got him to stop a plan to build a lot of new barracks all over the place for newly trained Chinese troops. Also warned U.S. army — told them that when they could not buy eggs for CN everything would have to come over the Hump.

Appraising China's experience with wartime controls, it is clear that price control did little good and much harm. It diverted attention from the need for fundamental measures to keep inflation in check. It was a great pity that the effort spent on price control was not used to build revenues, improve public administration, and cut avoidable expenditure.

As to rationing, the collection and distribution of foodstuffs gotten from the land tax in kind, though far from perfect, was of great value in assuring a supply for the army and public employees. Their lot was hard enough, but without this would have been almost intolerable.

As to hoarding, much more should have been done. Hoarding was largely a result of inflation, and in turn played a part in worsening it. Many of the worst offenders were officials, both military and civil. From time to time the government sporadically went after hoarders, and punished some by imprisonment and even execution. But hoarding remained widespread and in general the government was lax in dealing with it, failing to attack it persistently and ignoring the worst offenders while from time to time finding scapegoats. The government itself was a hoarder of food and other supplies.

The unhappy results of price control, as described, were no reflection on the Chinese people compared with others. As to American price control, *Life*, May 24, 1943, described the program's effects, which were similar in general nature to those described above in the case of China though not as extreme. *Life* said that the problem of policing American price ceilings with inadequate agents was, in the words of P. G. Wodehouse, "like a one-armed blind man trying to shove a pound of melted butter into a wildcat's left ear with a red hot needle."

Price control in wartime is helpful only when conditions are such that it can work with a fair prospect of success. That means not only an effective administration, but enforcement of a strong policy to hold inflation in check by removing surplus buying power through such means as heavy taxation, compulsory savings, patriotic pressure for subscription to war loans, control of credit and rationing of production and consumption. In China in 1937–1945 such conditions simply did not exist.

THE COURSE OF PRICES IN OCCUPIED AREAS

Indexes for the war period were compiled in Tientsin, Peiping, and Shanghai, both before and during enemy occupation. Prices shifted gradually from *fapi* to puppet money as use of the latter became general. In the North China cities the shift to Federal Reserve Bank (FRB) notes was in 1938–1939 (see chap. XIV). In Shanghai the shift to Central Reserve Bank (CRB) notes was in the latter part of 1941 and early 1942 (see chap. XIV). Data for Tientsin are not available after 1941, and for Peiping before 1942. The two cities are near together, and a combination of the two series gives an approximately continuous picture of the price movement in terms of FRB currency. Table 18 shows the course of prices in occupied areas, compared with prices in Free China.

In occupied North China inflation in terms of FRB notes was much less extreme than in Shanghai in terms of CRB notes. It also was much less extreme than in Free China until the summer of 1945, when prices rose sharply and somewhat surpassed the figures for Free China as the war was

TABLE 18. Comparison of prices in occupied areas and in Free China, 1937–1945

Period	Wholesale prices			Averages of retail market prices in Free China
	Tientsin	Peiping	Shanghai	
1937, January to June	1.00	1.00	1.00	1.00
1938, average	1.29	—	—	1.45
1939, June	1.77	—	1.64	2.26
December	2.47	—	3.18	3.23
1940, June	3.70	—	4.51	4.87
December	3.48	—	5.23	7.24
1941, June	3.61	—	8.03	10.5
December	—	5.84[a]	15.6	19.8
1942, June	—	7.22	29.4	35.9
December	—	11.7	44.7	66.2
1943, June	—	18.6	104	132
December	—	33.5	214	228
1944, June	—	81.6	560	466
December	—	351	2,490	755
1945, June	—	1,455	21,300	2,167
August	—	3,791	85,200	2,647
September	—	1,460	54,200	1,799

SOURCE: The wholesale price data for Tientsin and Peiping are from unspecified sources. The Shanghai data are from the China Institute of Economics, whose data by months are detailed in appendix B, Table 57. The base used by that Institute was 1936, but the figures in this table are converted to a base of January–June 1937 for comparison with the other series.

[a] January 1942.

ending. In North China the growth of circulation of *fapi* was limited by Japanese measures (see chap. XIV). Moreover, the Japanese in that area were more conservative financially than in Central China, and especially in 1940–1941 restrained the Federal Reserve Bank from rapid overissue of currency and increase of credit. By the end of 1943 the price level in North China was only about 15 per cent of that in Shanghai and in Free China. But then in the occupied areas galloping inflation set in, influenced by Japan's worsening prospects in the war. People wondered whether the Japanese-sponsored currency would eventually have any value at all. During 1944, and again in the first eight months of 1945, the rise in occupied North China was more than ten-fold. At the peak prices there were close to 4,000 times the level of 1937.

Until the Pacific War, Shanghai was linked to Free China economically and financially because it remained on a national currency basis. This was despite full occupation of the Chinese city by the Japanese, and their surrounding the International Settlement and French Concession, from

November 1937. Until 1942 prices in Shanghai rose less than in Free China generally. This appeared to be caused by continued access to outside supplies as well as to many local sources. Rice, for example, was extensively imported from South Asia. Another factor was the premium on remittances from the interior to Shanghai, which tended to limit the influx of money to Shanghai (see the following section and appendix C, Table 60).

After Pearl Harbor the Japanese forced the use at Shanghai of the notes of the puppet Central Reserve Bank, which until then had made little headway. In early 1942 prices there began to be generally quoted in that currency. For a time, influenced by relative moderation of issue and by Japanese military successes, the rate of the price rise was slower than in Free China. But by the early part of 1944 the level in Shanghai had caught up with that of Free China, and thereafter rose much faster. During 1944 Shanghai prices rose about 12-fold, compared with 3.3-fold on the average in Free China. In 1945 hyperinflation of the puppet currency set in at Shanghai. Both available indexes show that in 1945 prices rose 34-fold up to collapse of the puppet currency in August–September as Japan went down in defeat. At the peak the level was close to 100,000 times that of 1937 (see appendix B, Table 57).

FOREIGN EXCHANGE POLICIES AND RATES

During the war the government maintained a system of official rates of foreign exchange, with few changes. During most of the period, however, this was combined with (1) authorized derogations from official rates, and (2) a free market departing more and more from official rates, which was tolerated but subject to frequent fulminations against it by some government leaders. The foreign exchange situation in different periods of the war is described below, and market rates of exchange are shown in appendix C, Table 59.

1. July 7, 1937, to March 12, 1938. The prewar official rates of 14½d. and US$0.30 continued. The Central Bank supported exchange at a selling rate of 14¼d. and the equivalent in dollars at the sterling-dollar cross-rate — this because a drop in the sterling rate, which was the most important in the market, would have shocked confidence. Rates in the free market were close to the official rates, ranging from 14.13–14.75d. and US$0.2944–0.3025.

2. March 14, 1938, to August 18, 1941. When it became necessary to end support at the prewar level, the government adopted as a temporary measure a system of rationing exchange. Rationing became largely nominal after about three months. From June 1938 to August 18, 1941, official operations to support free market rates and minimize fluctuations were conducted: first by the Bank of China working with the Hongkong and Shanghai Banking Corporation, and then by the Anglo-Chinese stabilization

committee (see chap. XVI). Official rates were not changed, and were used during the war in intragovernmental transactions, and for over a year for sale of rationed exchange supplied by the Central Bank and sold by commercial banks to the public (see chap. XV).

The range of rates in the free market in this period was as follows:

Year	Sterling	Dollars
1938, from March 14	7.97–14.13d.	US$0.1565–0.2938
1939	3.22–8.50	0.0625–0.1650
1940	3.06–5.03	0.0444–0.0825
1941, to August 18	2.84–3.61	0.0475–0.0575

On July 3, 1939, the government announced measures of partial exchange control. These nominally applied to the whole country, but actually had limited application in Free China. The official rates could not realistically be applied to commercial transactions. The government did not change them, but announced that approved exchange would be supplied to the market and export exchange bought on the basis of the official rates, subject, respectively, to a charge or a supplement determined by the difference between these rates and rates announced from time to time by the Bank of China and the Bank of Communications. By not using the Central Bank, the government avoided the delicate issue of changing the official rates. The rates announced were 7d. and US$0.13⅝, which were then near to the free market. Frequent adjustments, however, were not made, and these rates stood until August 1940, when they were reduced to 4½d. and US$0.07½. There was no further change in announced rates until August 19, 1941, when the Sino-American-British Stabilization Board of China began operations.

3. August 19, 1941, to the end of the war. Effective on August 19, 1941, the Stabilization Board announced its official rates, 3⅝₃₂d. and US$0.05⅝₁₆. These were the approximate average rates in July 1941, and when announced were about 10 per cent above the market rates. The dollar rates worked out at C$18.82 for US$1. As from July 10, 1942, the rate became 20–1. The Board provided large sums for "legitimate" imports and personal needs up to outbreak of the Pacific War December 7/8, 1941. Thereafter trade became only a trickle, but personal demand for exchange continued. The Board was wound up as of March 31, 1944 (see chap. XVIII), and handed over its work to the Commission for the Control of Foreign Exchange Assets and the Central Bank. Beginning August 19, 1941, exporters were required to deliver to the Board the proceeds of their sales. But because the rates were so out of line with the free market the Board received only relatively minor sums. This requirement was waived before the end of the war. Such exports as moved were nearly all for official account, comprising mainly goods bought by official Chinese agencies and shipped out to meet

payments on the various barter credits, and also strategic goods bought by the American official agencies partly on the basis of the 20–1 rate, and partly against payment in gold.

Because the 20–1 rate was so out of line with the free market, foreign agencies and individuals in China, both official and private, were pinched in their sales of foreign currencies. In response to pressures for a remedy, the government in April 1943 provided a "supplement" of 50 per cent in *fapi* for sales of exchange by foreign embassies and consulates. A month later this was extended to "all cultural, missionary and philanthropic institutions," and the supplement was made 100 per cent in the case of remittances for famine relief. In November the 50 per cent supplement was extended to overseas Chinese remittances and to foreigners not connected with their governments. In January 1944 the 50 per cent supplement was raised to 100 per cent. That, however, still greatly overvalued *fapi*. The government finally authorized philanthropic organizations to sell exchange in the open market through the United Clearing Board, whose sales began in June. The average rates which that Board realized are shown in appendix C, Table 59.

The growth of American military activities in China after 1941 gave rise to more and more serious problems of financing. From the fall of 1942 personal expenditures of American military personnel, and also American diplomatic and consular outlay, were covered by sale of American currency notes. China acquiesced in this procedure, and other foreign governments took similar action. The military expenditures of the American government were met first by purchase of *fapi* at 18.82–1 and 20–1, until early 1944; and thereafter by advances of *fapi* for which settlements eventually were reached after great difficulty and friction.[9]

The range of rates in the free market in the three and two-thirds months from August 18, 1941, to outbreak of the Pacific War was approximately 2.00–2.91d. and US$0.0325–0.0503. Thereafter there was no large market for exchange other than for foreign currency notes, mostly dollars. The range of rates for dollar notes was (C$ per US$): for *1942*, 26–50; *1943*, 44–98; *1944*, 86–680; and *1945* (through August), 470–3250. Rates for sale of drafts by the United Clearing Board ranged from 82–228 in June–December 1944, and 290–1505 in January–August 1945.

Monthly rates for sterling and dollars during the war are given in appendix C, Table 59, and the movement of rates for dollars is shown in the graph at the front of the book.

INLAND EXCHANGE

While a free exchange market was maintained at Shanghai, restrictions began to be imposed in the interior in the latter part of 1937. At the temporary capital of Hankow, the Central Bank under Finance Ministry instructions was not selling freely either foreign exchange or remittances to Shanghai. The Bank limited such sales to special cases, such as to meet proven import bills or for expenditure in Shanghai in local currency. Moreover, exports were not moving out of the Hankow area: first, because of the enemy blockade of the Yangtze River; and, second, because export freight was hardly moving on the Hankow-Canton Railway. The railway was under military control, and the army deemed quick turn-around of trains so urgent that they would not allow much time for loading outbound cargo from Hankow on trains that otherwise were almost empty. Thus the supply of foreign exchange from exports was cut down.

It was not surprising, therefore, that in mid-November Shanghai funds began to command a premium, which soon reached 3 to 4 per cent. The discount on the currency in the temporary capital was somewhat disturbing to general confidence. Studies showed that exchange could be brought up to only about 2 per cent below par, roughly reflecting the cost of shipping notes to Shanghai, by providing to the Hankow market exchange roughly equal to what could be realized if outbound trains were made available to move exports to Hong Kong, with car permits conditioned on delivering or agreeing to deliver the relative exchange. The railway situation was gradually gotten in hand, but before anything was done about the exchange discount the problem changed, when exchange rates generally slumped after the market was unpegged March 14, 1938.

The final policy decision was to let the premium in the interior on Shanghai funds continue, as it tended to check remittances and thus made it easier to sustain the Shanghai exchange market. The premium in interior cities on Shanghai funds soon became larger, and continued until the outbreak of the Pacific War ended regular communications. The range of rates on Shanghai was:

Year	Chungking	Kunming
1938	1003–1165	—
1939	1144–1665	—
1940	1185–1420	1190–1540
1941	1065–1387	1140–1445

Monthly rates are given in appendix C, Table 60.

Within Free China during the war the range of premium or discount on inland remittances usually did not exceed 1 to 2 per cent. Costs of remitting to some of the less accessible cities, however, sometimes ran to 10 to 15 per cent. At the war's end there was a large demand for remittances from West China to Shanghai. The premium on these remittances at times reached 20 per cent.

INTEREST RATES

The Central Bank had the lowest rates — 0.7 per cent monthly or 8.4 per cent yearly much of the time. The rates of the other government banks were somewhat in line with those of the Central Bank. Private commercial banks had higher rates, while rates of native banks were higher yet. Table 19 shows the average of monthly market rates.

TABLE 19. Interest rates per month in Free China, 1937–1945

| Year | Commercial banks | | | Native banks | |
	Chungking	Chengtu (per cent)	Kunming	Neikiang[a]	Sian (per cent)
1937	1.0	1.4	1.1	2.3	1.4
1938	1.2	1.2	1.0	1.6	1.4
1939	1.3	1.2	1.8	1.4	1.9
1940	1.5	1.2	2.4	2.9	2.5
1941	1.9	2.7	2.9	5.6	5.2
1942	2.8	3.7	3.4	6.1	5.8
1943	6.0	4.0	4.0	8.4	8.2
1944	8.5	8.0	8.0	10.1	8.2
1945, August	12.0	9.0	17.0	13.0	12.0
September	9.4	8.0	11.0	8.0	12.0
October	7.2	7.0	10.0	8.0	—

SOURCE: Farmers Bank, *Monthly Bulletin*, Index Numbers of Retail Prices, October 1945.

[a] Neikiang is midway between Chungking and Chengtu, and was an active center for small business.

In the first half of the war, broadly speaking, the government felt that the increase of production for war needs was so important that it provided fairly liberal credit. Interest rates rose but moderately. In the second half of the war, there was a stricter hand on credit. Also the government tried to regulate market interest rates. The controls were largely evaded and there was a black market with higher rates. The inexorable rise of general prices made for rising interest rates. But the extent of increase of interest rates was much less than that of general prices. Shun-hsin Chou has shown that interest rates in real terms were actually negative during most of the war period, so that borrowers gained at the expense of lenders.[10] Hence commodity speculation and hoarding with use of borrowed funds became very attractive. Many and perhaps most of the private modern-style and commercial banks, unable to operate profitably in the ways formerly customary, found their main activity in buying and hoarding goods, directly or indirectly. The government failed to control such activities effectively.

XIII. CREDIT, NOTE ISSUE, DEPOSITS

Wartime borrowing involved, of course, both the government and the private sector. In chapters II, IV, and VI I have dealt with the wartime growth of credit to the government. Kia-ngau Chang has described and analyzed the wartime growth of private credit. Shun-hsin Chou has studied in detail bank credit and its velocity as bearing upon the inflation.[1] I shall not duplicate their treatment, but include herein a statement of some of their data and conclusions.

THE EXPANSION OF CREDIT

The comparative growth of credit to the public and private sectors, per figures compiled by Chang, is shown in Table 20. By far the greatest ex-

TABLE 20. Credit granted to the public and private sectors, 1937–1945
(in millions of C$)

Year	Increase of total credit to the private sector	Advances to the government	Total increase of credit	Per cent of increase of private credit to the total
1937–1938	—	C$1,195[a]	—	—
1938 (2d half)	C$357	854	C$1,211	29
1939	1,092	2,310	3,402	32
1940	408	3,834	4,242	10
1941	1,475	9,443	10,918	13
1942	5,813	20,081	25,894	22
1943	11,356	40,857	52,213	22
1944	17,665	140,090	157,755	11
1945	132,046	1,043,257	1,175,303	11

SOURCE: Kia-ngau Chang, *The Inflationary Spiral*, p. 187.

[a] Advances in 1937–1938 much exceeded the deficit caused by inflationary bank credit, because sales of exchange for currency support withdrew C$499 million from the market from July 7, 1937, to March 12, 1938 (see chap. XV).

pansion was the creation of credit by means of advances to government by the government banks for war needs. Increase of credit to the private sector after the first 18 months was from about a fifth to a tenth of the total increase. Prior to 1942 the government did not strictly control the granting of private credit, but instituted direct control in that year. Through the

Four Banks Joint Committee the government, beginning early in the war, provided private credit for purposes deemed important to the war effort, as well as credit to public enterprises (see chap. II). The relation of credit expansion to inflation was not clearly understood in some influential circles of the government and the public, and at times there was considerable pressure from private banks and private enterprises to receive credit. As a result credit was granted at times for purposes not essential to the war effort (see chap. IV).

NOTE ISSUES

From the time of the currency reform of November 1935 to mid-1937 the issue of the four government banks expanded rapidly, from C$458 million to C$1,407 million. This resulted from: (1) substitution of notes for nationalized silver; (2) replacement of notes of private banks, whose circulation shrank greatly in this period; and (3) meeting the increase in the demand for money resulting from the notable economic improvement that followed the successful reform and the stabilization of rates of exchange.

The growth of total note issue in Free China from 1937 to 1945 is shown in Table 21. Monthly figures of the issue of the four government banks are in appendix D, Table 61. They are shown graphically in the chart at the front of the book, in comparison with the course of general prices and foreign exchange rates. From mid-1942 the Central Bank took over the issues of the Bank of China, the Bank of Communications, and the Farmers Bank. In mid-1937 the issue of the Kwangtung Provincial Bank and the Kwangsi Provincial Bank, in South China, came under National Government control, and the total issue of these banks shrank slightly thereafter. The various provincial banks issued largely one-dollar and fractional notes. These issues little more than doubled in the first five years of the fighting, and thereafter gradually dropped from circulation because they were of small denominations. They were not a serious factor in the inflation. These issues are shown in appendix D, Table 62.

The supply of enough notes became a demanding problem for the Issue Department of the Central Bank, which was resourcefully run by Lea Tsing-yao. Much of the money was made in China, and machinery and supplies were moved to the interior. A leader in effectively organizing note production in China was Henry Lin, reported to have been killed by the communists after their take-over while serving as president of Shanghai Baptist College. A great part of the notes had to be imported, also bank-note paper and ink. These came mostly from the United States, though in the early part of the war some came also from Great Britain.

After 1941 notes were flown in over the Hump, mostly by the China National Aviation Corporation (CNAC). In 1943–1945 the monthly aver-

TABLE 21. Note issue outstanding, 1937–1945 (in millions of C$)

End of year	Four government banks	Provincial and local banks[a]	Private banks	Total
1937 (June 30)	1,407	418	72[b]	1,897
1937	1,639	425	—	2,064
1938	2,305	433	—	2,738
1939	4,287	510	—	4,797
1940	7,867	565	—	8,432
1941	15,133	675	—	15,808
1942 (June 27)	22,975	—	—	—
	Central Bank			
1942	34,360	957	—	35,317
1943	75,379	—	—	75,379
1944	189,461	—	—	189,461
1945 (August 31)	556,907	—	—	556,907
1945	1,031,932	—	—	1,031,932

SOURCE: The data for the four government banks are from the Finance Ministry and the Central Bank. For the source of the data for provincial and local banks, see appendix D, Table 62.

[a] The figures for June 30, 1943, are roughly similar to those for the end of 1942. Figures are not available for mid-1942, or after mid-1943.

[b] As of May 29, 1937. These issues greatly shrank thereafter, but figures are not available.

age weight of notes, including some banknote paper, was about 150 tons. This flying was not without incident. In my capacity as a director of CNAC I received the following telegram dated March 13, 1944:

Captain Hall in plane 85 left Dinjan for Kunming at 3 p.m. local time, March 13. After 1 hour and 40 minutes the oil pressure in the left engine dropped to zero and the propeller would not feather. Captain Hall decided to return and 15 minutes later found that he could not maintain altitude. As he was flying on instruments in over-cast weather, he ordered the co-pilot to throw out the cargo . . . The cargo consisted of 21 packages of bank notes and one zinc slab. Plane 85 arrived at Dum Duma at 6:48 local time.

This happened in the northeastern part of Burma, over wild and mountainous country which was largely uninhabited. We asked that anything practicable be done to recover the cargo, but there was no trace of it. Kung expressed his concern to W. L. Bond, who was in general charge of CNAC operations. Bond replied, "Dr. Kung, you may be surprised, but every case fell in the middle of the Salween River!"

The government became reluctant to increase the size of denominations of notes. When the largest notes were C$100, rumors about issuing C$500 and C$1,000 denominations caused an increase in free market exchange rates and sensitive prices; and this went on in similar fashion from time to time as prices rose. Convenience called for larger notes, and when they were not issued the public had to use large parcels of smaller notes. The making of a large purchase might require carrying a briefcase or even a suitcase full of notes. Banks would make up parcels of 20, 50, or 100 notes, writing on them the value and sealing them with a paper band with their "chop." These were commonly taken at the value stated without counting.

The cost of notes was large. Reluctance to issue larger denominations meant that more pieces of money were needed, hence printing costs grew during the war. Of the US$500 million loan of 1942, no less than US$55 million went for banknotes, paper, and ink.

The Central Bank stopped publishing figures of note issue as from mid-1940. After hostilities began, a part of the issues had been excluded from published figures, because of a fear that the true figures would hurt confidence. The government decided to omit giving out any data of issue after mid-1940. It was then pretty generally believed that the published figures were not complete, and this in itself hurt confidence. Actually "informed quarters" in the market somehow had a fairly good idea of the truth. Thus *Finance and Commerce* of Shanghai estimated total issue as C$5,700 million in mid-1940, when the true figure was C$6,063 million and the published figure C$3,962 million. And for the end of 1940 they estimated C$8,000 million, when the actual figure was C$7,867 million.[2]

The rate of increase of total note issue grew considerably during the war, as is shown by the following figures (in per cent): *1938*, 33; *1939*, 75; *1940*, 76; *1941*, 87; *1942*, 124; *1943*, 114; *1944*, 152; and *1945*, to 8/31, 194, and to 12/31, 444 (see Table 21).

We have seen (chap. II) that the cash deficit was covered primarily by advances to the government by the government banks. The government's procedure of borrowing was to obtain credits from these banks — after mid-1942 from the Central Bank — on the security of bond issues or against delivery of Treasury Certificates. Table 22 sets forth the data as to deficit and the note issue of these banks.

The explanation of variations in percentages of increase of note issue to deficit is not entirely clear, but certain comments may be made:

1. The data for notes seem fairly accurate as to time periods, but there were irregularities in reporting budgetary transactions. Thus the budget accounts for 1940 show C$725 million of receipts in respect of previous years (see chap. II). As a result, the accounts show a smaller deficit than the actual for that year, and correspondingly larger deficits for preceding years.

2. In 1937–1938, mostly before March 12, 1938, the Central Bank received C$499 million net from sales of foreign currencies, thus reducing

TABLE 22. Cash deficit and increase of note issue, 1937–1945
(in millions of C$)

Year	Estimated cash deficit	Increase of note issue, government banks	Percentage of increase of note issue to estimated cash deficit
1938[a]	777	320	41[b]
1938[e]	828	578	70
1939	2,217	1,982	89
1940	3,699	3,580	97[b]
1941	8,771	7,266	83
1942	18,895	19,227	101[b]
1943	46,466	41,019	88
1944	132,573	114,082	86
1945	1,041,214	842,471	81

SOURCE: Finance Ministry and Central Bank.
[a] Year ending June 30, 1938.
[b] For 1938, 1940, and 1942 the percentages are out of line with the other years. See headings 1, 2, and 3 in the accompanying text for comment.
[e] Second half year.

the need to increase its note issue. In 1939, 1940, and 1941, the approximate net proceeds of these sales were, respectively, C$150 million, C$132 million, and C$525 million.

3. For 1942 part of the higher ratio of notes to deficit seems related to the Central's Bank's receiving as of July 1 the exclusive privilege of note issue. Between the usual Saturday report of June 27 and July 1 that Bank's issue expanded about C$2 billion or 9 per cent from C$22,975 million to C$24,945 million. The increase reflected adjustments with the Bank of China, Bank of Communications, and Farmers Bank in connection with their relinquishing the right of issue.

To generalize from Table 22, after the first year and a half of fighting about 80 to 90 per cent of the cash deficit gave rise to corresponding growth of note issue.

DEPOSITS

In 1937–1938, before Japan captured the large cities of Canton and Hankow in October 1938, more transactions in Free China were handled by checks than after loss of those large cities. Then the government was forced back into areas where modern-style banking was only beginning to penetrate. In 1945 after the war China recovered the areas in Central and Eastern China where modern style banking was more important.

Note issue grew during the war much faster than deposits, as shown in

TABLE 23. Increase of total note issue and bank
deposits, 1938–1945 (in millions of C$)

Year	Increase of note issue	Increase of bank deposits
1938	674	847
1939	2,059	1,905
1940	3,635	1,777
1941	7,376	5,979
1942	19,509	9,146
1943	40,062	12,784
1944	114,082	69,614
1945	842,471	432,553

SOURCE: Note issue from Table 21; bank deposits
from Kia-ngau Chang, *The Inflationary Spiral*,
p. 191.

Table 23. Besides the backwardness of so much of Free China, the shrinking
value of money led people to prefer ready cash to funds in a bank. The
ratio of notes to deposits (per totals in Tables 21 and 24) was (for the end
of each year):[3] *1937*, 0.61; *1938*, 0.66; *1939*, 0.79; *1940*, 1.08; *1941*, 1.14;
1942, 1.54; *1943*, 2.11; *1944*, 1.80; and *1945*, 1.94.

The breakdown of deposits in 1937–1945 is shown in Table 24. The
amounts of current and fixed deposits, respectively, in other than the gov-

TABLE 24. Bank deposits, 1937–1945 (in millions of C$)

Year	Government banks, deposits				Commercial and provincial banks, all deposits	Total deposits, all banks
	Current	Fixed	Savings	Total		
1937	1,318	685	188	2,191	1,115	3,306
1938	1,808	928	251	2,987	1,166	4,153
1939	2,408	1,906	312	4,626	1,433	6,059
1940	3,297	2,172	533	6,002	1,884	7,836
1941	6,446	3,382	1,104	10,932	2,833	13,815
1942	15,039	1,782	2,976	19,797	3,164	22,961
1943	22,811	891	7,387	31,089	4,656	35,745
1944	78,887	1,213	15,456	95,556	9,803	105,359
1945	466,190	5,289	55,693	527,172	10,740	537,912

SOURCE: Kia-ngau Chang, *The Inflationary Spiral*, p. 191. Whether government
deposits are included is not clear.

ernment banks is not available. About 60 per cent of the deposits in government banks in 1937 were current. If we assume a like proportion for the other banks, the total of current deposits in 1937 would be about C$2 billion, roughly equal to the total of note circulation. Whether the figures include government deposits is not clear. Kia-ngau Chang calculated that increase of deposits compared with increase of total credit in the following proportions (in per cent):[4] *1938*, 70; *1939*, 56; *1940*, 42; *1941*, 55; *1942*, 35; *1943*, 25; *1944*, 44; and *1945*, 37.

Much of the increase of deposits reflected rapidly rising prices and increased credits, rather than savings; but precise data on this point are not available. Certainly the growth of deposits from savings during the war was not a major factor in providing funds available for lending, and hence not an important check on inflation. Commercial banks could not create credit by note issue during the war. Provincial banks did not do so extensively (see the preceding section). Hence the credit which commercial and provincial banks granted grew somewhat in line with their deposits plus any credit granted by the government banks. The total deposits in commercial and provincial banks grew less than 10-fold during the war. Since average prices increased about 2,600-fold to the end of the war, such deposits shrank greatly in real value.

Chou noted several important changes during the war in the over-all banking situation. The share of private banks in total deposits and loans was 36 and 29 per cent, respectively, in 1937, but fell almost to 2 and 1 per cent in 1945. The Central Bank's share grew relative to the other government banks. Much of the shift in favor of the government banks was caused by transactions with government. The capital funds of private banks before the war were on a conservative basis, about a sixth of deposit liabilities. But capital funds did not keep up with inflation, and the proportion fell to about 3 per cent by 1946, leaving the banks greatly weakened. Also the investment portfolios of private banks fell from under 20 per cent of deposits before the war to about 1 per cent in 1945. Over-all, the position of private banks suffered greatly during the war. The government was lax about allowing expansion of banking, by allowing many new private banks, and increase of the number of offices of private, provincial, and municipal banks.[5]

XIV. PUPPET, JAPANESE, AND COMMUNIST CURRENCIES

Japan, taking advantage of China's pronounced regionalism and wishing to strengthen it as a divisive force, set up several more or less separate regimes in occupied China. Each had its own currency. Also the military, not fully trusting the civilian side, relied extensively upon military yen (*gunpyo*), which were issued beginning late in 1937 for use mostly in Central and South China. "Manchukuo," after Japan's seizure of Manchuria in 1931, already had its own currency. The Mengcheng Bank began in 1937 to issue currency for use in Inner Mongolia. The Federal Reserve Bank (FRB), first termed the Federated Reserve Bank, began operations in North China in March 1938. In Central China the Japanese first set up the Hua Hsing Bank in May 1939, but it never attained much importance. The Central Reserve Bank (CRB) began operations at Nanking and Shanghai in January 1941. In South China the Japanese created the Kwangtung Provincial Bank late in 1940, with headquarters at Canton — this bank being designed to take the place of the Nationalist bank with the same name which withdrew ahead of the Japanese invasion of South China in October 1938. Besides, the communists issued their own money.

Figures of the Japanese-sponsored currency issues are given in appendix D, Tables 63 and 64.

The Chinese government resisted the Japanese monetary moves, fearing them as important measures to promote enemy control of China. In this resistance China had the support of Britain, France, and the United States.

The Japanese wartime efforts to introduce and maintain new currencies illuminate several aspects of monetary experience. Japanese purposes, as they developed first in North China, were to redeem Japanese yen and Bank of Chosen notes, which were used extensively to finance Japan's military outlay in North China from the beginning of hostilities and which quickly went to an embarrassing discount of 10 to 20 per cent in terms of *fapi;* to finance the expenditures in China of the Japanese armed forces and civilian organs; to tie the occupied areas into the yen bloc, that is, the home islands and colonies including "Manchukuo"; to finance puppet regimes and their armies and other organs; to promote and help to finance Japanese exploitation by industrial enterprises and procurement of goods for export; and finally to discredit and displace *fapi*, and thus attack the National Government and further control of the occupied areas. In *China and the Helping Hand* (chaps. V and VIII), I have described the broader aspects of the currency war and its relation to the support given to China by Britain, France, and the United States. Here I shall supplement that general account with further particulars especially related to currency matters. These include the working of Gresham's law; the competition between *fapi*, freely convertible into foreign currencies, and FRB notes subject to exchange control; the competition among the several kinds of Japanese-sponsored currencies; and Japan's monetary problems of financing an invasion and occupation.

PUPPET CURRENCIES IN NORTH CHINA

At the time of outbreak of hostilities the chief currency in North China was the issue of the Bank of China and the Bank of Communications, more largely the former, the total amounting to about C$250 million. Central Bank notes were a relatively small part of the circulation there. In 1935–1937 the Japanese, as part of their pressure on China, pushed the circulation of notes of the puppet Hopei Provincial Bank as a rival issue. As of mid-1937 that bank's issue was reported to be about C$55 million.[1] The notes of the Bank of China and the Bank of Communications that circulated in North China were made payable at Tientsin, and a smaller amount at Tsingtao. This limitation was a hang-over from silver standard days. Silver was heavy and bulky in relation to value, and to move it from one branch of a bank to another was slow and costly. Hence the banks chose to limit the issue of notes in particular areas to amounts related to the silver reserves kept in financial centers in those areas. After the currency reform of November 1935, the marking of notes for local redemption continued, although the original reason for it no longer existed. Central Bank notes, whose issue for all China before that reform was only about a fourth of the total issue of the four government banks, were not issued with limitations as to redemption in various centers. At the time of the reform about 40 million ounces of silver remained in the vaults of the Bank of China and the Bank of Communications in the foreign Concessions at Tientsin and in the Legation Quarter at Peiping.

After the fighting began, one result of the regional limitation of note issue was to hold back the growth of *fapi* issues in North China. Shipments of notes could not easily go through the enemy's controls, since early in 1938 Japan embargoed import of *fapi* notes. For a time notes could be smuggled in, and methods even extended, with British cooperation, to including parcels as supplies for the British garrison, brought in by a British warship.[2] But, as a result of the restrictions, these notes became relatively scarce in North China. This tended to create a vacuum into which new puppet currency could flow. Inland exchange between North China and Shanghai, which formerly was done at par subject to small remittance charges, became dislocated at times.

The first puppet bank was the Mengcheng Bank for Chahar and Suiyuan provinces, in Inner Mongolia. This bank was set up in November 1937 to be the sole bank of issue for those provinces and to be an instrument of Japanese exploitation. The bank's notes circulated along the Peiping-Suiyuan Railway, prior to creation of the Federal Reserve Bank hereinafter described. The notes were linked at par to the yen, and later also to FRB currency. Because of this latter link, the bank became associated with the difficulties which the Federal Reserve Bank met in maintaining the value of its notes. The Mengcheng Bank operated controls of foreign exchange and trade. Its note issue was small compared with that of the puppet banks for North and Central China, and was managed with relative conservatism until the latter part of the war. Figures of issue are shown in appendix D, Table 63.

When the Federal Reserve Bank opened in North China March 10, 1938, its notes promptly went to a discount in terms of *fapi*. This continued in spite of the slump of *fapi* in the foreign exchange market when exchange was "unpegged" as from March 14 (see chap. XV). The puppet authorities tried to legislate *fapi* out of circulation by decreeing that they could circulate in North China for only one year. In August they proclaimed a discount of 10 per cent against *fapi*. On February 20, 1939, they raised the discount to 40 per cent. And as of March 10 they forbade entirely the circulation of *fapi* in North China. But these measures failed to have the effect desired and were disregarded outside the range of Japanese gunshot. During 1938 FRB$100 could be bought in the Concessions for about C$95.50 to C$99. In the spring of 1939, instead of a 40 per cent discount against *fapi*, FRB$100 could be had for as little as C$74. It was not until *fapi* slumped seriously in the summer of 1939, when the Anglo-Chinese stabilization fund broke down, that CRB notes gained the upper hand in market quotations. Then, for a year, sometimes one and sometimes the other was at a premium. After mid-1940 the advantage of FRB notes grew. From early 1941 *fapi* slumped rapidly in terms of CRB notes, and by summer were worth only about half as much. The causes of this slump, I noted in a memorandum of April 8, 1941, were:

(1) deflationary action by North China authorities, including restriction of note issue increase, restriction of bank loans and compulsory liquidation of commodity holdings; (2) increased export of bristles, eggs, and peanuts from Shantung, and of opium from North China; (3) restriction of imports into North China; (4) lesser use of *fapi;* (5) fear of freezing American assets and of extension of the war to the Pacific.

Quotations of FRB notes in terms of *fapi* are given later in this section.

Outside the range of Japanese force the people of North China firmly rejected the new notes as an alien currency and maintained a remarkable confidence in *fapi*. Japan's control was limited to leading cities, various "strong points," and lines of communication. Elsewhere the Chinese authorities and guerrilla forces forbade use of FRB money, and even executed as traitors those found with them. As to the attitude of the Chinese public, Professor George E. Taylor, who was in the region in this period, wrote:

There are few things which make the goodwill of a conquered people more difficult to secure than the imposition of a worthless currency. If the Japanese had wished to make the Chinese people nationally conscious they could have invented no better way than that of attacking the national currency.[3]

Within areas of Japanese control and in the foreign Concessions, however, FRB notes gradually made some headway. By the fall of 1938 these notes may have constituted about 10 per cent of the total actual circulation in all North China. As to conditions in the Concessions and occupied areas a report of August 8, 1938, by the Bank of China's branch at Tientsin said (translated):

At the present time, new notes are circulating in the market freely and very actively. Old notes are still obtainable in the Concessions in Tientsin, but outside the Concessions and in Peiping, it is almost rare to find old notes used.

Gresham's law was working:

All classes of people, with or without means, spend the new notes first whenever they receive funds. Moreover, as prices are quoted in terms of the new notes, no allowance is given to the buyer who pays in the old notes. Thus the market is full of new notes and they are being used everywhere and with rapidity. . . .

Nevertheless, the report continued,

Not only are foreign merchants unwilling to accept new notes but even Japanese shops are not altogether happy to receive them — although they obviously cannot easily refuse them. If relatively large amounts of new notes are paid to Japanese merchants for the purchase of their goods, they invariably inquire politely whether it is not possible to pay a portion in old notes. Since the status of the new notes seems clearer to the Japanese than to our own people, the Yokohama Specie Bank and the Bank of Chosen are extremely careful in their dealings with the Reserve Bank, and are noticeably adopting an attitude of half-hearted co-operation.

By December 1, 1938, the new notes had made such headway in the Tientsin Concessions that the authorities there, under Japanese pressure, were obliged to agree to accept the notes for payment of taxes, etc. China protested strongly to the British and French governments, but without avail. The protests correctly pointed out that the progress of the new currency was quite certain to lead to Japanese control of foreign exchange and trade, which would operate contrary to the Open Door principle. But the notes had made such inroads and Japanese force was so strong that the British and French authorities could not avoid yielding despite their sympathy with China's views.

By mid-1939 the circulation of FRB notes had grown to FRB$264 million, compared with FRB$162 million at the end of 1938. But a major part, perhaps something like half, was held by Japanese banks and puppet organs and not in actual circulation. Chinese currency designated for North China comprised as of September 30, 1939, C$275 million of Tientsin notes and C$105 million of Tsingtao notes, a total of C$380 million. About C$20 million was estimated to circulate in the Tientsin concessions and the rest was in the guerrilla areas of North China or hoarded.

While FRB notes were making headway as a circulating medium in the Concessions and in Japanese-controlled areas, because of the working of Gresham's law and enemy pressures, *fapi* remained in special demand. They were desired for hoarding by the public, by banks for reserves and clearings, to pay for goods bought from the interior, and for dealings in foreign exchange. *Fapi*, as China's national currency and aided by maintenance of convertibility in exchange, retained public confidence to a degree that surpassed expectations. Even the Japanese, when they sought to buy goods from the interior, had to pay for them in *fapi*.

The convertibility of *fapi* into foreign currencies in a free market, which was maintained after exchange was allowed to drop when the Federal Reserve Bank was created, was an outstanding advantage in favor of *fapi* in North China. Existence of the foreign Concessions at Tientsin and the Legation Quarter at Peiping allowed maintenance of this market by the foreign and Chinese banks there, despite Japanese occupation of the surrounding areas. The link between the free market in the International Settlement at Shanghai and North China was kept, even though at times restrictions and difficulties caused some divergence of foreign exchange rates for *fapi*. *Fapi* remained freely convertible into foreign currencies until China, with American and British participation, applied an exchange control at Shanghai in August 1941.

FRB currency, on the other hand, was not freely convertible. Moreover, it was overvalued in foreign exchange. When the FRB scheme was begun on March 10, 1938, it was based upon parity with the yen at 14d. But the National Government followed this move at once by ending support of *fapi* at the prewar level, which in sterling was in the selling and buying range of 14¼d. to 14¾d. When rates for *fapi* fell in three months to about 8d., the value of FRB currency in the free market followed and fell even lower. Its parity was with the yen, which was subject to exchange control and tied to sterling at 14d. until linked to the dollar at US$0.23⁷⁄₁₆ in September 1939, after outbreak of war in Europe. With FRB notes at a discount compared with *fapi*, and the market rate for *fapi* held at about 8d. for a year from June 1938, the puppet bank found it hard to operate in foreign exchange. Japanese merchants, who had to take the new notes, soon became loaded up with them and could not even use them to pay their bills in Japan. In the summer of 1938 the Japanese forbade sale of various Japanese goods including machinery and cloth for FRB notes. A Japanese spokesman said at Peiping in September, "The depreciation of exchange below 1s.2d. was not envisaged in the original plan." [4]

As from March 10, 1939, the Peiping regime decreed export control of 12 leading items, and as of July 17 extended the control to all items. This was hard on exporters, who were forced to take FRB notes at par of 14d. (equivalent to about US$0.27). In the free market in the spring of 1939 FRB notes were worth only about 6d., compared with about 8d. for Chinese currency. These events disturbed the market which quickly realized that, with exporters forced to surrender their foreign currencies to the bank and at a very unfavorable rate, little cover would be available to pay for imports. This led to heavy buying of foreign currencies to pay for imports of cereals, oil, tobacco, chemicals, et cetera. Foreign exchange rates at Tientsin fell below rates at Shanghai. The demand for *fapi* to buy exchange raised the premium over FRB notes to 20 to 35 per cent in the spring of 1939. There was heavy demand for remittances to Shanghai to buy goods. The premium at Tientsin on Shanghai funds, which had been nominal at times and not over 5 per cent, rose momentarily to 40 per cent. The government banks met the demand for remittances up to daily limits of C$300 per person, C$2,000 for firms, and quotas for foreign banks. Also there was smuggling of notes out of Tientsin to take advantage of the disparity. In turn the government banks at Shanghai had to resort to restrictions to relieve the pressure, for example, limiting cash redemption of Tientsin notes to C$50 and redeeming by remittances on Tientsin, or by accepting these notes only for fixed deposit. By October, however, Tientsin rates on Shanghai moved back toward par.

These Japanese measures were an attack upon the business interests of the United States and other countries friendly to China, and not merely moves against China's currency. The American, British, and French governments at once protested. The American communication called the measures discriminatory and not in accord with treaty rights, and "a virtual nullification in that area of the Open Door so far as import and export trade are concerned." There were reports that the measures were to be applied less stringently against Japanese, German, and Italian interests.[5]

The various Japanese measures raised difficult questions for the foreign banks. The American, British, and French governments pressed the respective banks to maintain a common front against Japanese pressure. But they recognized that the banks might have to yield somewhat to safeguard their individual interests, as otherwise they might be virtually eliminated from business.[6]

In the areas of Japanese military control, the people had to sell goods and give services for payment in puppet notes. But the Japanese were not accomplishing their aim to exploit North China by drawing from it for export large amounts of food and raw materials. The fighting disrupted trade and communications. Under urging by the Border Government the farmers made a rather remarkable shift from planting export crops such as cotton to wheat and other subsistence crops. British ambassador Craigie reported from Tokyo on June 24, 1939, that the causes of failure of the puppet bank up to then were "inept management on the spot, inconvertibility, insistence on link with the yen and trade control," and "refusal of Chinese population living in areas under guerrilla control to deal with new currency." [7]

A key factor that so largely frustrated the Japanese drive for full economic control of North China was the existence of the British and French Concessions at Tientsin. The Japanese brought increasing pressure on the Concession authorities. A Tientsin dispatch of December 12, 1938, stated that the Japanese in a meeting with leaders of the foreign communities in Tientsin threatened "to take steps to bring the Concessions to their heels" unless Japanese wishes were met as to (1) police control, (2) delivery of silver, and (3) recognition of FRB currency. Although the British felt obliged to yield in some matters, such as acceptance of FRB currency in payments to the authorities in their Concession, they were firm in refusal to make that currency the legal tender there.

The Japanese suddenly blockaded the foreign concessions at Tientsin on June 13. The excuse was British failure to hand over some Chinese accused of a political murder. On the pretext of a search for *fapi*, the Japanese held up traffic with the Concessions, causing long delays and expense because of forcing the unloading of cargo, even coal, in the streets. [8] This was hurtful to confidence in the currency generally, especially because of fear that the blockade might be extended to Shanghai. The blockade issue was settled by negotiations, leading to issuance of a joint statement at Tokyo which was interpreted as showing a weak British attitude. Nevertheless, the British remained firm on the essential issues regarding currency. The British embassy advised the State Department July 26, 1939, that "the British Community in Tientsin have expressed the view that to give way on the questions of currency and silver reserves would jeopardize the currency, undermine Chinese resistance and give to the Japanese an even greater stranglehold on trade in North China than they now possess." The American chargé at Tokyo was authorized on August 2, 1939, to say, "The Government of the United States could not be expected to give assent to any measures arranged by third States which would purport to make illegal the use in any part of a sovereign State of the currency of the recognized government of that State." [9]

At the time of allowing the exchange value of *fapi* to slump in March 1938, the Chinese policy-making authorities foresaw that the slump would in itself be a defense against rapid spread of FRB notes. They rightly guessed that these notes would not easily be moved from their tie with the yen at 14d., and that accordingly the overvalued currency would find it harder to make its way. That is what happened. Despite Japanese efforts to keep FRB notes at par with yen, their foreign exchange value in the free market in this period followed roughly that of *fapi*, at a somewhat lower level.

It was only in mid-1939 that the Japanese, through the Yokohama Specie Bank as agent for the Federal Reserve Bank, allowed merchants to "link" imports and exports on the basis of a rate of 8d. According to this system 89 per cent of the proceeds of exports could be used to pay for imports (10 per cent being reserved to meet personal requirements, etc., and 1 per cent commission). The system, however, was not very attractive to traders, as the Japanese would provide import exchange only five months after sale of the export exchange. Also the system was clumsy because it was hard to "marry" import and export transactions, and there were link brokers who tried to effect a match. Some smart merchants who had already settled their import exchange imposed on the Japanese by keeping the exchange and declaring the intended imports against fresh cover through exports. Linking gave some stimulus to trade, but the total situation was not favorable to a large volume. In July 1939 the national currency fell to as low as about 4d. and thus undermined the new "link" rate of 8d. for FRB notes. When sterling slumped at the outbreak of the war in Europe, September 1, 1939, and the Japanese tied the yen to the dollar at US0.23\frac{7}{16}$, the puppet Federal Reserve Bank followed suit with a nominal tie to the dollar at the same rate. To adapt the linking system to this situation, links were based on US0.13\frac{7}{8}$, the approximate equivalent of 8d. with sterling at about US$4.00. Although actual rates in Tientsin were lower than 8d., the Bank did not wish to change its rate because of face and confidence. It acquiesced in dealers certifying at that rate transactions actually done at a lower level, for example, 5d. The Bank's report for 1939, the only one available, stated that in that year it had taken in proceeds of exports amounting to £2,058,000 and US$5,068,000, and had sold most of these sums for imports.

In North China *fapi* remained up to Pearl Harbor the medium for dealings in free foreign exchange. The Japanese had to use them if they wished to buy goods from regions outside their military control. But in other dealings FRB notes were gradually taking a more and more important place. In the first part of 1940 about 70 per cent of the commercial accounts in foreign banks in Tientsin were in FRB. By the spring of 1941 FRB notes had become the chief currency of occupied North China. *Fapi* were no longer used there in ordinary buying and selling. But they remained up to the Pacific War the unit for foreign trade; and throughout continued to be the principal currency of the area outside the reach of Japanese force.

The growth of FRB circulation, 1938–1945, is shown by the following figures for the end of each year (in millions of FRB$): for *1938*, 162; *1939*, 458; *1940*, 715; *1941*, 964; *1942*, 1581; *1943*, 3762; *1944*, 15,841; *1945* (August 10), 73,131; and *1945* (August 31), 83,506.[10] This rate of growth was only half of that of national currency in 1940–1941, and the growth partly represented displacement of the latter. Because the Japanese more strictly controlled credit expansion in North China, prices and cost of living in Tientsin in terms of FRB in the second half of 1941 ranged from about 4 to 6 times the prewar level, while in Free China the range was about 10 to 20 times the prewar level.

After outbreak of the Pacific War Japan took full control of the foreign Concessions, and her currency moves could no longer be contested there. The rise of prices in the occupied areas of North China continued, but for a time at a rate much lower than in Free China. At the end of 1944 prices in North China, despite a 10-fold rise during the year, were still well below the level in Free China, probably by more than 50 per cent. In 1945, however, deterioration in North China, with another 10-fold rise in the first eight months, was much faster than in Free China. Prices in North China at the peak in September 1945, from which they then fell back a little, were at a slightly higher level than prices in Free China (see chap. XII).

A full series of quotations of FRB-*fapi* rates is not available. Table 25

TABLE 25. Rates of exchange between notes of the Federal Reserve Bank, Tientsin, and Chinese currency, 1938–1941 (cost of FRB$100 in C$)

1938		1939		1940		1941	
		January	96 to 99	January	98 to 106	January 18	120
		February 25	88	February	84 to 101	February	119 to 131
March 10–31	96 to 100			March	95 to 101	March 12	135
April 1	99	April 11–30	74 to 92.5	April	97 to 99	March 28	149
						April	153 to 202
May 1	98.5	May	74.5 to 85.5	May	94 to 101	May	168 to 200
June[a]	95.5	June	82 to 91			June	137 to 174
		July	91 to 102	July 12	106	July[a]	187
August	97 to 99	August 1–20[b]	96 to 104	August 2	105	August 27	187
		September 6–30[b]	110 to 123			September 27	213
		October	101 to 120	October 18	126	October 28	250
		November	104 to 114				
December	96 to 98	December	104 to 110	December 31	115		

SOURCE: Advices to the Finance Ministry and Central Bank and press reports.
[a] The data at hand do not indicate the dates of rates for June 1938 and July 1941.
[b] The market was closed from August 21 to September 5, 1939.

shows for 1938–1941 partial data of the cost of FRB$100 in terms of *fapi*. Only fragmentary quotations of exchange rates between *fapi* and FRB currency are available for the period after 1941. For a time the premium on FRB currency over *fapi* continued to grow and reached about 5–1. From about 1943, however, the exchange value of FRB notes slumped drastically, accompanying the galloping inflation which developed in occupied areas as it became more and more clear that Japan was nearing defeat. By the war's end *fapi* held a considerable premium over FRB money in North China.

Liberation of the occupied areas in 1945 at once raised the problem of getting rid of the puppet money. The issue arose first as to the CRB money of Central and South China, but action there was bound to influence developments in the FRB area of North China. In September 1945, it was announced at Shanghai that CRB money would be exchanged for *fapi* at 200–1 (see a following section of this chapter). That rate was very adverse to CRB, because relative market prices in August and September were about 30–1 *vis-à-vis fapi* (see Table 18). I had recommended taking careful account of relative prices in puppet money and *fapi*, but was en route from Washington when the decision was made. The market rate of exchange for CRB money was then about 250–1. But that rate reflected, first, a temporary scarcity of *fapi* in the liberated areas, and also official intimations that a rate adverse to puppet money was to be set. In liberated Central and South China the 200–1 rate led to a price rise of several fold.

The setting of a rate for the FRB money of North China came up in November. Prices there slumped after the war from a peak in August of 3,791 times the prewar level to 1,460 times in September. Then followed a rise to about 3,000 times in November. That was about 50 per cent above the level in terms of *fapi* at Shanghai or Chungking. I recommended on November 14 a rate of FRB$2 for C$1, stressing the bad results of what was done as to CRB money. But the market rate of exchange had been ruling at about 4.5–1, influenced by the adverse treatment of CRB money. Finally a rate of 5–1 was fixed.

THE NORTH CHINA SILVER

From the time of the 1935 currency reform, the removal from Tientsin and Peiping of the silver stocks of about 40 million ounces, handed over then by the local Chinese and foreign banks to the Currency Reserve Board when silver was nationalized, was blocked by hesitation of the regional authorities plus Japanese pressure. The National Government counted that silver in its currency reserves. The currency no longer was redeemable in silver, but the government used its reserves freely to support the currency, including that circulating in North China. I estimate that the total cost of currency support in North China in the war period 1937–1941 was of the order of US$18 million. That figure is about equivalent to the value of the silver at 45 cents per ounce, which was about the average price realized from silver sales in that period. Thus the Chinese government had a moral as well as a legal right to the silver.

From the early days of the fighting the Japanese had their eyes on this silver. Its seizure would have been a blow to confidence in *fapi*, since the people thought of it as currency reserve. Repeatedly the Concession authorities prevented Japanese interference with it. In the summer of 1939 delivery of this silver to the Federal Reserve Bank was one of the key Japanese demands made to the British authorities. These authorities, however, took a strong line. Foreign Secretary Lord Halifax telegraphed to the British ambassador at Tokyo August 17, 1939, that Britain could not recognize the authority of the puppets; that China's claim to the silver was strong; that other powers were interested; that yielding would depress *fapi* and strengthen FRB currency and would "deal a damaging blow to the confidence of the Chinese Government (and other friendly powers) in ourselves." [11] London consulted Washington, and the State Department strongly supported the British position against appeasing Japan by yielding on silver.[12] Britain was disposed to take a strong line in the event of failure of the negotiations with Japan, which involved besides silver and FRB currency certain police matters in the Tientsin Concession and the possibility of a renewed anti-British agitation and blockade of the Concession. A Foreign Office memorandum of August 21, 1939, for the Cabinet proposed in that event: (1) denouncing the Anglo-Japanese commercial treaty, following the American lead; (2) advising British women and children to leave occupied China, the men to be so advised later; (3) imposing on Japan a financial clearing arrangement, which had been under consideration and would be hurtful to Japan; and (4) granting further financial aid to China. The consensus of views, including British commercial interests in China, was that "the danger of surrender on vital principles is greater than that of a breakdown of the conversations," and that "it is better to face the situation now"; and that a firm line might well give Japan pause.[13]

As a compromise the sealing of the silver "for the duration" was discussed. Finally after difficult Anglo-Japanese negotiations a formula for sealing was found. The American and French governments offered no objection. The British ambassador in Chungking took it up with the Chinese government. China maintained that the silver was the property of the banks and could not be touched without Chinese consent, but acquiesced in it being sealed by the British consul general and in the release of the equivalent of silver valued at £100,000 for relief of victims of flood and drought in North China. The Anglo-Japanese agreement in the words of a United Press report of June 19, 1940, from London, provided:

A total of 100,000 pounds sterling of Chinese silver in the Bank of Communications at Tientsin will be used for North China relief purposes, while the remainder will be placed under an Anglo-Japanese seal at the Bank of Communications pending future Anglo-Japanese agreements for its disposal.

British officials will not hinder circulation of the Peiping Federal Reserve Bank notes in the British Concession.[14]

The relief was to be administered by an international committee including British, Japanese, French, and Chinese. The British also agreed to cooperate in repression of terrorist activities and in censorship.

On the strength of this agreement, the Japanese lifted the blockade of the Concessions, though threatening to renew it "if there is imperative need." The blockade was not renewed, but 18 months later Japan seized the Concessions at the outbreak of the Pacific War.

Most of the silver remained in North China, and was recovered after the war.

PUPPET CURRENCIES IN CENTRAL AND SOUTH CHINA

The lack of success of Japanese currency maneuvers in North China delayed similar ventures in Central and South China and led the Japanese to be cautious about further monetary moves. They had quite a debate on what to do. The army extremists wanted to destroy the Chinese currency. But the moderates and business elements felt that relative stability of this currency would be better for Japanese trade and investment. Japanese business men did not like the strict controls that they faced in North China and Japan.

Early in 1939 the Japanese decided to set up the Hua Hsing Bank at Shanghai. Its opening was announced at the end of April and it began business May 10. Its capital of HH$50 million was put up in equal shares by the puppet regime and by six Japanese banks with branches in Shanghai. The new bank's notes occupied the strange position of being pegged to the Chinese currency. This seemed to reflect the troubles met in trying to maintain a higher value for FRB currency in North China. The Hua Hsing Bank intended to issue its own notes convertible into foreign exchange.

When the opening of the Hua Hsing Bank was announced, the Chinese government telegraphed at once to its embassies in Washington, London, and Paris asking them to urge the respective governments to do all possible to prevent the proposed action, and particularly to ask banks of their nationality not to accept the proposed notes or to deal with the puppet institution. The Japanese scheme was called an opening wedge to force control of the financial system centered in Shanghai, which thus could be a serious threat to foreign as well as Chinese commercial interests.

On May 20 the State Department instructed Consul General Gauss at Shanghai to advise the American banks there of its position that

. . . the Department is interested in the position which American banks with branches in Shanghai propose to take in regard to the Hua Hsing Bank and its note issue; that it is our impression that the establishment of the new bank is an initial step in a Japanese program for the establishment in Central China of financial and economic control similar to that which the Japanese have attempted to set up in North China; that it does not seem to the Department that advantage would accrue to American or other foreign banks through assisting the new bank in the launching of its note issue; and that, while the Department recognizes that American banks have responsibilities of their own and have to protect their own interests, the Department would welcome the maintenance by foreign banks in China of a united front against the new Japanese financial measures and hopes that American banks in central China will see their way clear to refraining from action which might assist the Japanese in establishing the new bank and launching the new currency.[15]

After the Stabilization Fund withdrew support of the Chinese currency July 18, 1939 (see chap. XVI), the Hua Hsing Bank suspended its link to Chinese currency, and instead announced that it was pegged to sterling at 6d. Once more Chinese currency gained the competitive advantage of having a lower value in foreign exchange than puppet money.

On August 31, 1939, the puppet regime issued a notification that customs duties henceforth were to be paid in Hua Hsing Bank notes. Chinese currency would continue to be accepted for duties at rates to be announced, and which involved at the outset about 6½ per cent rise in duties.

The Hua Hsing Bank never amounted to much except as providing a unit of account for customs collection. The government forbade Chinese banks to deal in its notes. The circulation of Hua Hsing notes grew as shown in the following figures for 1939 at the end of each month (in thousands): May, 221; June, 607; July, 1,408; August, 1,249; September, 3,291; October, 3,184; November, 4,035; and December, 5,075. Thereafter until the bank ceased to be an official bank of issue early in 1941 its total circulation was around HH$5 to 6 million. As of February 19, 1941, the Hua Hsing Bank redeemed its entire circulation by exchanging it for notes of the newly formed Central Reserve Bank (CRB). Its issue of about HH$5 million was exchanged at the rate of CRB$175.75 to HH$100.

The next Japanese-sponsored bank to be created was the puppet Kwangtung Provincial Bank, set up by the regime at Canton late in 1940. Like the Hua Hsing Bank, its notes were linked to *fapi*. Particulars of the amount of issue are not available, but it was not an important factor in the total monetary situation.

Prior to announcement of the creation of the Central Reserve Bank at Nanking and Shanghai, a debate on policy went on behind the scenes. Agents kept Chungking well posted on such matters during the war. In a memorandum of February 29, 1940, prepared after visiting Shanghai, I summarized the situation:

Reliable information has been received to the effect that the proposed puppet regime wish that the contemplated new currency replace all other currency in China, but that the Japanese wish to retain the Federal Reserve notes and also to push the Hua Hsing currency. The puppets wish temporarily to retain the old Chinese currency and not to attack it as this would disrupt economic and financial conditions and disturb the public. They would gradually substitute the new currency. The Japanese on the other hand argue that the existence of the old currency is of great advantage to Chungking and to third powers and seek its total collapse. The Japanese, however, are deterred from drastic measures by fear of the consequences upon relations with third powers. It is indicated therefore that the Japanese would be sensitive to pressure against introduction of a new currency or other new currency measures. But it would be harder for them to yield to pressure if they have previously taken overt steps toward setting up the new currency.

The Japanese favor a tighter control against Chungking and third powers. The puppets, however, wish to operate trade and exchange control themselves as a sovereign right; but are prepared to accord "economic cooperation" to Japan, which is taken to mean trade preferences and measures discriminating against third power interests. The discussions are characterized by definite antiforeign attitude.

At about this time Chow Fu-hai, who was to become the "Minister of Finance" of the puppet regime at Nanking, made the following proposal, as per copy procured by Chungking's agents:

II. The FRB and the Hua Hsing Bank

The Hua Hsing Bank has not been long established and the notes issued by it amount to little more than $1,400,000. Representations should be made to the Japanese, as soon as the new Government is formed, to stop the issue of HH notes, and to arrange redemption after the issue of new notes by the Central Reserve Bank of China. As regards the FRB the treatment should be different because of its long history and standing. First: their right of issue to be stopped as soon as the new Government is formed. Second: liquidation of the actual assets of the FRB. Third: reorganization as a branch office of the New Central Reserve Bank of China. After reorganization, the FRB notes to be replaced by the new legal tender notes or to be recognized as legal tender by having a special chop placed upon them. This problem can be satisfactorily brought to an end when the political conditions prior to the "Lukochiao" Incident are restored.

III. The Military Yen Problem

The amount of military yen forced into circulation stands at a high figure. The issue of military yen should be stopped as soon as the new Government is established. The Japanese should also place some funds at our disposal for the redemption of military yen.

IV. We should seek the recognition by the Japanese of the necessity for maintaining the old *fapi*. Unlike merchants and economists, the Japanese militarists and politicians, as a rule, want to destroy the old *fapi*. This is a mistaken policy. If we permit the use of the old *fapi*, we should make it clear to the Japanese that: (1) they should recognize that the old *fapi* circulating throughout the country has become a part of the peoples' property and not the private property of "Mr.

Chiang"; (2) all efforts to destroy the old *fapi* will be in vain, and only throw the market into confusion. The experiment in North China should serve as an object lesson.

The creation on March 30, 1940, of the puppet regime for Central China headed by Wang Ching-wei cleared the way for announcement of establishment of the Central Reserve Bank. In April the regime announced creation of a preparatory committee to draw plans for the bank's opening. The plans derived from the discussions mentioned above. The Committee borrowed the title and part of the scheme from the plan which the Chinese government adopted about July 1, 1937, but was never able to put into effect because of Japan's attack. The scheme contemplated that while the new bank was getting under way the old national currency would continue to circulate. The Central China regime succeeded in having the Hua Hsing Bank discontinue its issue. But they got nowhere with the idea of ending the use of military yen, which the public disliked. The American government made representations in Tokyo about the proposed new bank. The Japanese Foreign Office replied that this was a matter pertaining to the "government" at Nanking, which felt that organization of the bank was a necessary part of that "government's" policy; and that Japan would give it every support, because maintenance of the national currency was helping to sustain Chungking and increase China's resistance to Japan.[16]

Japan formally recognized the Central China regime at the end of November 1940, eight months after its creation.[17] On December 20, the regime announced that the Central Reserve Bank would open January 6. The market effect of this announcement was considerable. The market expected the new notes to be liberally printed to raise revenue, and that the bank would try to substitute them for *fapi* and thus raid China's reserves. In the latter part of December 1940 the idea got abroad, aided unfortunately by circumstantial rumors from Chungking, that the Sino-British stabilization fund might cut off Shanghai in retaliation against the new currency. This forced the Fund to sell large amounts of foreign currency to check the deterioration. Again in January it had to sell heavily because of nervousness about the situation (see chap. XVI).

The new bank opened in Nanking on January 6, 1941, and at Shanghai on January 20. Its plan seemed moderate. It contained no provision for control of trade or exchange. There was no compulsion and no date set for eliminating national currency. All customs duties were to be paid in the new notes, but *fapi* also could be accepted. Reflecting Japanese disillusionment after their failures when trying to give the FRB notes in North China a value higher than *fapi*, the new notes were to be equivalent to *fapi* at par.

The Department of State instructed the Consul General in Shanghai to ask the American banks there not to do anything to facilitate the operation of the new bank. The non-Japanese banks in the International Settlement at Shanghai agreed not to accept the new notes.

Despite fears of some, the circulation of CRB notes did not at once attain much importance relative to national currency. The following data show the growth of circulation in 1941 (in millions of CRB$): January, 19; February, 24; March, 30; April, 39; May, 49; June, 71; July, 87; August, 105; September, 120; October, 151; November, 181; and December, 258. At the end of 1941 the circulation of *fapi* was C$15.8 billion, or more than 60 times that of CRB notes.

After the outbreak of the Pacific War, when Japan took over the international settlements and concessions, it became easier to push the use of puppet currencies. The public assumed that the Japanese could now succeed in their monetary moves, and these met little effective resistance. The following account is from the report of A. Bland Calder, American Commercial Attaché, who was interned at Shanghai until June 29, 1942:

> The new bank was able gradually to increase its circulation at first on a parity with *fapi* and, later, by means of propaganda with regard to the "inflationary character" of the *fapi* . . . and by restricting from time to time the amount of CRB notes which it would exchange daily at par for *fapi* to bring about or create in the open market a premium for CRB notes over fapi . . .
>
> June 25, 1942 . . . was set as the final date for "abolishment of *fapi*" and by that date the CRB notes had come into almost exclusive use in the Settlement south of Soochow Creek and in the Concession.
>
> Some observers felt that the methods employed by the Japanese sponsored and supervised Central Reserve Bank in thus bringing about this situation were tantamount to a swindling of the public. Observers in late June considered it likely that the authorities might soon declare it illegal to have *fapi* in one's possession, . . . thus to obtain still further amounts of *fapi* cheaply. But, up to June 29, 1942, the date of our departure, no such action had yet been taken. It was still only the use of *fapi* that was prohibited, not the possession of it. By early June 1942, the circulation of CRB notes had reached *yuan* 1 billion or more, as officially announced, and by various means its extension to interior areas was being furthered . . .
>
> American, British and Dutch banks at Shanghai were placed under Japanese supervisors very shortly after the outbreak of war, December 8, 1941, and later were turned over individually to Japanese banks for liquidation. Depositors were allowed to draw out a portion of their balances from time to time depending upon availability of cash assets and collections, but not to amounts greater than *yuan* 2,000 per month, per individual. Shanghai branches of Chinese national government (Chungking) banks, prior to December 8, 1941, had already curtailed their activities heavily and were operating only with skeleton staffs. The Central Bank of China and the Farmers Bank were ultimately turned over to Japanese banks for liquidation. It is understood that the Bank of China and the Bank of Communications were turned over to the Nanking authorities for such action. Local Chinese commercial banks were obliged to fall in line in observance of new regulations and to expect eventually closer supervision by the Finance Ministry of the Nanking "puppet" regime.[18]

After the Japanese take-over in December 1941, their propagandists spread the word that introduction of CRB notes as the sole money would bring an end to inflation and that " 'co-prosperity' would begin to be felt almost immediately." But instead rates for utilities were sharply boosted, price controls were ineffective, the Japanese were "pillaging . . . Shanghai and the interior for food and other supplies for Japan," and foreign trade was cut off. As a result in the first half of 1942 "it was plain that both Shanghai and its hinterland was taking probably the worst punishment in its economic history." [19] The deterioration in terms of CRB currency continued, and before long became much worse than in Free China. Table 26

TABLE 26. Comparison of note issue and prices in Central Reserve Bank currency and Chinese currency, 1941–1945

| Year | Growth of note issue in the period[a] (in per cent) | | Prices (based upon January to June 1937 = 1) | |
	CRB$	C$	CRB$, Shanghai	C$, Free China, average
1941	—	92	15.6[c]	19.8
1942	1,330[b]	127	44.7	66.2
1943	418	119	214	228
1944	630	152	2,490	755
1945 (to 8/31)	2,280	194	85,200	2,647

SOURCE: Appendixes B, Tables 48 and 57, and D, Tables 61 and 64. The Shanghai price figures are those of the China Institute of Economics, converted to the first half of 1937 as the base.

[a] Issue of the four government banks to mid-1942, and of the Central Bank thereafter.

[b] The Central Reserve Bank began operations in January 1941. The large expansion in 1942 largely reflects displacement of *fapi* after outbreak of the Pacific War.

[c] Prices were mainly in *fapi* until CRB$ took over during the spring of 1942.

compares the rate of growth of CRB issue and the rise of prices in Shanghai with corresponding data for Free China. In 1942–1943 prices at Shanghai rose somewhat less than in Free China. But thereafter, with CRB note issue growing much faster and with Japan's worsening position, the inflation in Central China reached the "galloping" stage.

No series of quotations of exchange rates between *fapi* and CRB currency is available. The two were roughly at par until March 1942. The Japanese authorities then began various actions designed to injure the position of *fapi*, namely, limitation of the amount exchangeable at the new bank to C$300 per person daily, and limiting those exchanges to 2,000 persons daily; segregation of bank accounts into CRB currency and *fapi* respectively; and discrimination against certain specified issues of notes of the Bank of China and the Farmers Bank, which caused the public to be doubtful about *fapi* in general. These measures resulted in creating a large demand for exchanges at the money shops, and hence a premium on CRB notes. On March 12, the new bank set a rate of CRB$77 for C$100. Then various suspensions and limitations upon conversion were announced, causing market rates of exchange to move against *fapi*. In May the bank announced daily increasing discounts against *fapi*, until on May 25 the rate was set at CRB$50 for C$100. Finally circulation of *fapi* was declared to be abolished from June 25.[20]

At about the end of 1943, with deterioration of Japan's position in the war, and as the inflation in occupied Central and South China moved faster than in Free China, *fapi* began getting the upper hand over CRB currency. By the latter part of 1944, the advantage of *fapi* was about 2–1; and by the spring of 1945, about 7–1. As the end of the war began to seem near, the value of CRB notes collapsed. After fighting ended on August 15, these notes continued to circulate in Central and South China because they were the only currency immediately available.

In September 1945, the value of CRB money fell to 250 or more per C$1. Prevalence of such rates was cited to justify setting a final exchange rate of 200–1 (see the preceding section on Puppet Currencies in North China). But market rates partly reflected a temporary scarcity of *fapi* in the liberated areas of Central and South China, and partly official indications of a policy detrimental to puppet money. The rate of 200–1 greatly overvalued *fapi*, since prices at Shanghai in September were about 30 times as high as average prices in Free China. Thus *fapi* flowed rapidly into the liberated areas, brought to a great extent by those coming from the Free China area. Holders of *fapi* had an enormous advantage in purchasing power, and as a result prices in terms of *fapi* in the liberated areas rose several-fold in the fall of 1945. Holders of CRB money, who mainly were loyal Chinese, suffered greatly from the adverse rate. Their bad treatment reacted strongly against the National Government, which many viewed as an exploiter of those who had borne the burden of the occupation. The communists were able to capitalize heavily upon the dissatisfaction.

JAPANESE MILITARY YEN

The Japanese invaders found problems in trying to finance their military costs by the use of Japanese yen notes and Bank of Chosen notes in North China, and by yen notes in Central China. These notes, flooding the market, promptly went to a discount in terms of *fapi*. This clashed with the propaganda that the Chinese government was incapable of running the country, and was about to collapse. Japan soon turned to issuance of puppet notes. But the army did not want to be wholly dependent upon civilian-run agencies; and the failures of the Central Reserve Bank delayed plans for similar operations in Central and South China.

Payments connected with the large-scale Japanese military operations in the Shanghai-Nanking region in the second half of 1937 were made largely in Japanese yen. At times the yen commanded a premium over *fapi* and at times a discount. When *fapi* exchange slumped beginning in March 1938, the yen slumped also, influenced by the plethora of supply and by psychological factors, even though it went to a premium over *fapi* which in the fall of 1938 was 4 to 15 per cent. The slump of yen in China made possible various arbitrage deals. Yen collected in Shanghai, at a discount compared with their parity of exchange in Japan, were taken to Japan by tourists and others who could convert them there into foreign currencies. These currencies in turn could be sold in Shanghai and the process repeated. Also yen were taken to Honolulu and sold there to persons of Japanese extraction for remittance to Japan. Another procedure was to buy Japanese goods with depreciated yen in Shanghai and export them to the South Seas, where the goods would realize foreign currencies. Insofar as the foreign currencies realized from such transactions were sold in Shanghai, they provided foreign exchange for China from the proceeds of Japanese exports and remittances to Japan.[21] Such transactions, however embarrassing to Japan, were probably not on a very large scale.

To summarize, the Japanese found themselves in an awkward situation in 1937–1938 resulting from: (1) flooding parts of China with ordinary yen and Bank of Chosen notes; (2) maintenance of the yen at a nominal parity of 14d., equivalent in 1938 to US$0.27½ to 29; (3) the fact that the Japanese found it hard to refuse to accept their own money in payment for Japanese goods sold in the occupied areas; and (4) the initial depreciation of yen in China, followed by the slump in the exchange value of *fapi*, which tended to carry the yen down with it in the Shanghai market.

With a view to remedying matters, the Japanese Army issued military yen (MY) or *gunpyo*, beginning late in 1937 after capture of Shanghai (Chinese city) and Nanking. The Army used the new notes to pay for such goods and labor as were not taken without payment. The occupying authorities also promoted circulation by requiring use of military yen in payment of railway fares and certain utilities. Further the use of these yen was required in payment for certain goods moved in or out of occupied areas. The currency was a forced issue, and naturally not popular with the people of the occupied areas, who tended to spend it as fast as they got it. As indicating the difficulties of pushing Japanese currency, a forced payment of MY700,000–800,000 for Chinese cotton at Hankow in February 1939 caused a drop in the MY-C$ rate from C$1.25 to below par, some yen being offered as low as C$0.70. It took restrictive and control measures, including buying of yen by Japanese banks, to restore the yen to a premium over *fapi*.[22]

The military yen was not popular with the puppets. The proposal early in 1940 of "Finance Minister" Chow Fu-hai, quoted in a preceding section of this chapter, referred to these yen as "forced into circulation," and urged their withdrawal, to be replaced by CRB notes. But the Japanese military would not have this. In December the compradore of the Hongkong and Shanghai Banking Corporation was quoted as stating, "Japan will not allow issue of larger denomination notes [of CRB currency] owing to competition with military yen," and that the Japanese and puppets had not yet reached an understanding about these yen. On December 19, Chow publicly stated, "With regard to the circulation of Japanese military notes which is in a special condition during the continuation of hostilities, the new legal tender will give mutual assistance so that both may be able to complete their respective tasks." The Japanese military consented reluctantly to issuance of CRB notes, which were bound to affect the position of military yen. But Wang Ching-wei's paper, on January 10, 1941, just after the new bank opened, urged that the Japanese permit its notes ultimately to control in the monetary field.[23]

In 1938–1940 military yen commanded a moderate premium of 5 to 15 per cent over *fapi*. But from mid-1940 the premium steadily grew to over 100 per cent early in 1941, because of relative moderation in issue of yen while the printing presses were busy putting out more and more *fapi*. When military yen began to appreciate considerably in terms of *fapi* in March 1941, the Japanese were worried. These yen were important as a means of payment for imports from Japan, and the relative depreciation of *fapi* raised the cost of these imports. A Japanese military spokesman said at Shanghai in a statement published on March 28:

> The recent sudden rise in the rate is abnormal and is caused by recent terrorism. The rate, in the opinion of the Japanese army, is too high for practical purposes and should be fixed at a reasonable level. *Fapi* not only are the Chungking currency but also the currency of the people of the occupied areas. Too much depreciation would cause anxiety to the Chinese population.

The cost of military yen did not appreciably exceed the high of March until the latter part of 1941. The available quotations of military yen are shown in Table 27.

During the war the Japanese authorities did not reveal the amount of issue of military yen, regarding that as a military secret. The circulation, according to postwar official figures, is shown in Table 27. But contemporary non-Japanese estimates were higher, for example, that the circulation at the beginning of 1940 was 200 million, and a year later 500 million, of

TABLE 27. Circulation, 1937–1945, and quotations, 1938–1941, of Japanese military yen

Circulation, 1937–1945		Quotations, 1938–1941 (cost in C$ of MY100)	
End of	Amount (millions of MY)	Period	
1937	1.4	1938, September	104–115
1938	36	1939, May 31	114
1939	151	1940, First day of	
1940	248	June	111
1941	244	July	114
1942	381	August	118
1943	407	September	129
1944	671	October	143
1945 (8/15)	2,299	November	160
1945 (8/31)	1,516	December	163
		1941, January	165–175
		February	172–183
		March	181–242
		April	205–229
		May	227–239
		June	214–232
		July	221–238
		August	236–250
		September	246–252
		October	251–450
		November	360–450

SOURCE: Circulation from *Statistical Yearbook of Finance and Economy of Japan*, Ministry of Finance, 1948, p. 823; Quotations from *Finance and Commerce, passim*, and Central Bank of China.

which latter sum about 70 per cent was in the lower Yangtze area and the rest divided between the areas of Hankow and Canton.[24] Some then believed that the Japanese military had no accurate record of issues. Figures of circulation of the various Japanese-sponsored currencies are given in appendix D, Tables 63 and 64. These figures show that the military yen was much less important in quantity issued than the FRB and CRB currencies.

After the outbreak of the Pacific War the Finance Ministry of the Nanking regime announced that from March 7, 1942, rates for military yen would no longer be quoted in *fapi* but only in CRB currency. Calder's report of November 16, 1942, to the Secretary of State thus described developments affecting military yen and CRB currency in the first half of 1942:

It is obvious that the Japanese authorities wished to go slow with the new currency since military yen already had such wide circulation in the lower Yangtsze region. It must be borne in mind also, that, even though *fapi* was abolished as legal tender in Shanghai and vicinity, the military yen still continued in use as almost the exclusive circulating medium in the Hongkew and Yangtszepoo areas of the International Settlement north of the Creek and still had general circulation in the lower Yangtsze region. It appears patent that the Japanese were in no great hurry to permit the Nanking regime to introduce the CRB notes since it would mean some relinquishment of economic control to the "puppet" government. The delay was also without doubt used as a check upon Nanking to insure the latter keeping in line more faithfully with Japanese dictates and controls. As a symbol of autonomy, therefore, it was not to be conferred upon Nanking too precipitately or too soon. The action was possibly held up until certain differences were settled. So, CRB notes circulated "alongside of" military yen and there was no indication in June, 1942, that there was any intention to retire military yen from circulation in favor of CRB notes. (The amount of military yen in circulation is not announced and is probably known only to the Japanese military authorities.) The Japanese controlled railways, power companies, steamship companies, bus companies and other utility enterprises operating in the interior in Kiangsu, Anhwei, and Chekiang Provinces, however, as of June 20, 1942, were instructed to accept CRB notes for fares and services instead of only military yen as hitherto. The rates were still in terms of military yen and patrons could either pay in that currency or in CRB notes at a rate of CRB yuan 100 to military yen 18.

After 1941 there was a much more rapid expansion of CRB notes than military yen. At the end of that year the circulation of the two was about equal. Until 1945 the expansion of military yen was relatively moderate. At the end of the war, in August, the maximum issue of CRB notes reached CRB$3.3 trillion, more than a thousand times the maximum for military yen (see appendix D, Tables 63 and 64).

COMMUNIST CURRENCY

During the silver-standard period the communist armies issued in 1930–1934 silver coins of C$1 and C$0.20, all bearing the hammer and sickle insignia, as well as copper coins. Also the "Chinese Workers and Peasants Soviet Government State Bank" in 1934 began issuing paper money. The various kinds of money were made in several provinces, using the crude machinery which was available. After the government nationalized silver in November 1935, the communists issued only paper money. In 1936 at their base in Shensi Province in the northwest they used an exchange rate of communist $1.21 for C$1. They also had a supply of *fapi* which they gained largely by seizure, and which they used to obtain goods from China beyond their base.[25]

Following the formation of the United Front early in 1937, the National Government gave financial support to the communist forces. The support, however, petered out as friction grew. The communists had to find their own money. This they did through issuance of paper currency in the regions of their control, through a variety of banks, eventually a dozen or more.[26]

As to conditions in 1942, I quote the following from a report of A. M. Lindsay, received in August 1942 at Chungking, following his extended stay in the communist-controlled region:

The currency seems to be well managed in the Shansi-Chahar-Hopei area. The local currency were originally issued against central government notes of which a 60% reserve was kept but as national currency depreciated most of this reserve was spent in buying gold and silver of which considerable quantities were available as the currency law of 1935 had never been applied in North China. It is claimed that the currency has now got 60% specie backing and that government expenditure has been kept within the yield of taxation. As a result the value of the local currency is considerably higher than national currency. The comparison cannot be made directly as there is no trade with the rear but at the end of 1941 when the rate between Chungking currency and the Japanese controlled North China currency was about 4 to one, the rate between the Shansi-Chahar-Hopei currency and the Japanese controlled currency varied between 1.5 and 2 to one. There is, of course, no regular market as both sides forbid the use of the other currency and the rate fluctuates greatly according to the balance of trade in different areas. In some places during the season of maximum exports from the country the value of the Shansi-Chahar-Hopei dollar has actually been higher than the Japanese controlled dollar. The government owned bank makes some attempt to smooth out the local and seasonal fluctuations but it is not very successful. Prices have risen a great deal and are still rising but this is at least partly due to the shortage of goods caused by the destruction during the Japanese offensive and the poor harvests caused by dry weather and, for imported goods, the increasing strictness of the Japanese blockade and the rapidly rising prices in the occupied areas.

The other areas seem to have been less successful in their currency management. In the autumn of 1941 the Southeast Shansi currency exchanged at 5 to 1 with the Japanese controlled currency and prices in Northwest Shansi are said to be several times higher than in Shansi-Chahar-Hopei.

Subsequent developments are thus described by Cho-yuan Cheng:

When the *Kang Pi* was first issued, it was used as local currencies and was therefore linked to the *Fa Pi* issued by the National Government. It was not until the second half of 1943 that the Chinese Communists began to discard the orthodox *Fa Pi*. It was first experimented in coast areas of Shantung Province; the *Fa Pi* was prohibited and driven to the Japanese occupied areas, in order to make the *Kang Pi* gradually independent. This practice was soon followed in Central Shantung, Southern Shantung and North Sea Area in the first half of 1944. By the end of 1944, the system of *Kang Pi* was formally established. At first, it was regulated that the values of *Fa Pi* and *Kang Pi* were equal. Later on, to promote the value of *Kang Pi*, it was regulated in 1944 that one dollar of *Fa Pi* equaled 20 cents of *Kang Pi;* in the spring of 1945, the rate was decreased to 4 cents of *Kang Pi* in exchange for one dollar of *Fa Pi* . . .

When the *Kang Pi* was first introduced, the bank-reserve, according to the Communists, was made up by commodities as well as the assets of factories and shops. When the *Kang Pi* was issued in northern Kiangsu Province, it was guaranteed that one dollar would be exchanged with one catty of wheat. Actually, there were scarcely any industry in the Communist occupied areas, and even ordinary commodities were in great shortage. So, this so-called material assurance for the

Communist currency was merely a deception. Nevertheless, it was in that period that the Communist monetary system began to take shape.[27]

An American intelligence report of 1945 states as follows:

The Border Region currency has a fair degree of stability within the issuing region. Since there is little trade between the various Border Regions, it is impossible to determine any accurate standard of value as between the various currencies. In general, however, it seems that currency of the Yenan area is less valuable than that of some of the other areas. As a matter of fact in all of the Border Regions money is of relatively minor importance, because wages and salaries are paid in millet or other commodities and taxes are collected in kind. Millet is in reality the standard of value in the northern areas and rice is probably the standard in the New 4th Army areas. According to National Government sources approximately $350,000,000 worth of this Communist currency had been issued by the end of 1943. All such currency is illegal in the eyes of the Chungking Government . . .

Prices have gone up considerably in all of the Communist areas and there is unquestionably currency inflation everywhere. Inflation seems to be the worst in the Shensi-Kansu-Ningsia Border Region but most observers agree that inflation is not as serious as in the Chungking area because salaries and wages are paid in kind to a very large extent and hence currency inflation matters very little.[28]

The same report (p. 2421) gives quotations of exchange rates, showing the cost of C$1 in terms of Shensi-Kansu-Ningsia currency (SKN$) as follows: 1937, SKN$1.21; February 1941, SKN$1.50; 1943, SKN$2.20; and 1944, official rate, SKN$8.00. The foreign journalists who visited Yenan in the spring of 1944 reported that they received SKN$8 for C$1. On March 16, 1944, the office of the American embassy at Sian reported an exchange rate of 12–1.[29]

XV. MONETARY MANAGEMENT IN THE FIRST YEAR

SILVER

American buying of China's silver was a major factor in strengthening China's financial position in the early part of the war.[1] The United States contracted to buy from China before the war 187 million ounces for a total price of US$94 million (actual deliveries were over 188 million). Those figures include the purchase of 62 million ounces at 45 cents per ounce on July 8, 1937, which was agreed before word of the outbreak of fighting on July 7 reached Washington. That purchase covered 50 million ounces held in the United States on which the Treasury had granted a credit of US$20 million, which was on a month-to-month basis because of American silver politics. The purchase also included 12 million ounces which China was holding at San Francisco. The agreement of July 8 also provided that the Federal Reserve Bank of New York would grant a credit of US$50 million against gold deposited by China. This credit was to be available until December 31, 1937, and was repeatedly extended during the war for half-yearly periods until terminated about 1943.

Immediately after fighting broke out in North China on July 7 the Central Bank began urgently to remove the silver reserves from Shanghai to safe places abroad. Every American and British ship leaving for other than Japanese ports was loaded with all that could be insured, usually a value of US$10 million per vessel. Before the fighting extended to Shanghai on August 13, all of the reserves of silver and gold that were there had been shipped to Hong Kong, London, San Francisco, and New York. Had this not been done, China would have suffered an almost mortal blow. It was not possible to remove the 40 million ounces held in North China (see chap. XIV), because of enemy operations in that area.

After the American purchase of July 8, further purchases became uncertain because of the American neutrality law, which restricted financial dealings with nations at "war," and because of isolationist sentiment against involvement in any hostilities. In the circumstances, China felt it unwise to press for further immediate sales of silver to the Treasury. But in the fall the need became urgent to convert silver reserves into usable foreign currencies. To have sold large amounts of silver on the markets of London and New York would have broken the price. So China appealed to Morgenthau, who was anxious to help China. He readily responded to the approach, no legal obstacle being found inasmuch as China and Japan technically were not at war. On November 3 the Treasury agreed to buy 10 million ounces at 45 cents, followed by weekly bids bringing the total to 50 million. On December 2 Ambassador C. T. Wang telegraphed from Washington that the Treasury would buy a further 50 million ounces at 45 cents, in semimonthly lots of 10 million each through February 15, 1938. These various purchases after July 8, 1937, were not made public until the spring of 1938. But the market realized, long before announcement, that the Treasury continued currently to buy.

With the outbreak of fighting, the government redoubled its efforts to collect gold and silver for the war chest — Madame Chiang Kai-shek took charge of a collecting station in the center of Hankow, and Madame Chou En-lai did the same duty across the river in Hanyang. The government badly needed foreign currency assets and paid good prices for the metals, even though the payments added to the supply of money. Anomalously, gold going out to be sold passed other gold coming in from Hong Kong for hoarding, which was about US$1 million in the first half of 1938. Much gold as well as silver continued to be hoarded in China. This was not surprising in view of the unhappy succession of emergencies, to meet which gold and silver hoardings were a valuable reserve.

China's total silver holdings as of August 1937, including monetary reserves, were estimated by the Bank of China and the Bank of Communications in the summer of 1938 at about C$1,200 million or about 900 million ounces. Deducting C$420 million shipped from China from August 1937 to August 1938, they estimated that there remained in China C$780 million or about 590 million ounces. Subsequent sales during the war were about 112 million ounces. On the basis of the above-mentioned estimate, the silver in China at the war's end was about 478 million ounces including the holdings of about 40 million ounces in North China which was mostly recovered after having fallen into enemy hands when the Pacific War broke out.[2]

After 1937 the Treasury continued buying China's silver. Three lots of 50 million ounces each, to be delivered in semimonthly installments of 10 million each, were bought with deliveries commencing in February, May, and July 1938. The price was US$0.45 per fine ounce for the first 20 million, and the Treasury then reduced the price to US$0.43, apparently in relation to the controversy with Mexico, the chief silver producer, about expropriation of American oil companies.[3] The Treasury abandoned for purchases after 1937 a requirement, imposed in 1935 at the time of the first purchases, that China use the proceeds exclusively for currency stabilization. That was to ensure that the deals were purely financial, and not for such objects as to buy military items.[4] The Treasury also waived two other earlier requirements: that China hold in silver 25 per cent of its note issue reserve, which was in line with what the United States was trying to do under a law of 1934; and that China issue silver coins.[5]

In the first year of fighting, the Treasury agreed to buy from China 312 million ounces, for a total price of US$138 million. Thereafter purchases were of lesser importance. In the fall of 1938 China sought to sell the remaining silver reserves of about 85 million ounces, all of which was in London except for 9 million in Hong Kong. But 65 million ounces were pledged to Dutch, French, and Swiss banks for credits, arranged when China was uncertain about further sales to the Treasury. The Treasury was unwilling to buy silver to facilitate paying debts to non-American creditors. The solution was for China to repay the credits from other funds, thus releasing the silver. It was then sold in the New York market, which the Treasury was supporting, except for 14 million ounces which the Treasury bought directly.

Those transactions disposed of most of the silver reserves held before the war. But more silver was gradually accumulated in the interior, and safely gotten out of China despite the risk of enemy interception. Details of China's sales according to official American and Chinese data are shown in appendix E, Table 65. Sales by years according to official Chinese data were as follows (figures in millions):

Year	Ounces of silver	Receipts in US$
1935	50.2	32.3
1936	75.6	34.0
1937 (to 7/10)	62.5	28.1
Total	188.3	94.4
1937 (after 7/10)	100.0	45.0
1938	208.7	90.2
1939	47.5	19.9
1940	5.1	1.8
1941	0.8	0.3
Total	362.1	157.2

Thus the grand total of official Chinese sales, 1935–1941, was 550 million ounces, for US$252 million.[6]

To recapitulate: China had about 372 million ounces of silver reserves when the fighting began, and collected about 53 million more. These 425 million ounces were sold to the Treasury for US$185 million. This conversion of silver into usable foreign currency was of enormous advantage to China, at a time when credits from her Western friends were not available. Illustrative of the difficulties which China might otherwise have met was the experience in disposing of silver in 1939. The American Treasury, because of congressional opposition to continued buying of foreign silver, first required China to agree to use the proceeds for purchases in the United States. At China's request, payment of American debts was also included. Then in June, when repeal of the Treasury's authority to buy silver passed the Senate, the Treasury was unwilling to buy 6 million ounces offered by China. When finally the conference committee rejected the repeal, the Treasury promptly purchased these 6 million ounces. Meanwhile, in view of the uncertainty, the Central Bank hedged the 6 million ounces by forward sales in the London market. Doubt whether the Treasury would continue to buy weakened the price in the free market, and the Treasury's eventual purchase reflected this fall. The 6 million ounces and further lots were bought at 35 cents, compared with 43 cents for the purchases begun in the spring of 1938.

The American silver-buying policy, adopted before the war to appease the silver interests and their inflation-minded allies, had unexpected results. Predictably, it drained silver reserves from China and brought acute deflation in 1933–1935. It forced China to abandon the historic silver standard and adopt a managed currency (see chap. XI). Without the American silver-buying policy there is considerable doubt whether China would have given up the silver standard in the mid-1930's. Had China been on this standard when Japan attacked, it would have been impossible to finance extended resistance without a monetary breakdown. As events turned out, the managed currency was a two-edged sword. It afforded means to finance a long and bitter resistance; but also it inevitably led to the inflation which was a major cause of the downfall of the government on the mainland. In *China and the Helping Hand*, I wrote: ". . . it is ironic and indeed frightening that an American policy promoted by special interests, and apparently when adopted of rather minor importance to the United States, changed world history in a way that could not have been foreseen." [7]

Holding the line, July 1937 to March 1938

The incident of July 7, 1937, looked serious from the start, and quickly shook confidence. The monetary authorities, however, could not assume it would lead to general warfare. Therefore, the Central Bank felt it essential to support exchange at the existing level. The Bank obtained an informal "gentlemen's agreement" with the banks, that they would confine exchange operations to "legitimate purposes" and to their normal customers. From July 7 to August 13 exchange support entailed a net cost equivalent to US$42 million. The incident also caused a shock to the Shanghai market for *fapi* government bonds. The 6 per cent Consolidated Bonds "A" fell from 87–88 and a yield of about 7.75 per cent in the week July 5–10, to

75½–82 in the next week with yields of 8 to 9 per cent. In the latter part of July the government pegged prices on about a 9 per cent basis, to avoid a financial panic. Also prices of China's foreign currency bonds slumped badly in London (see chap. VII).

When serious fighting broke out at Shanghai on the morning of Friday, August 13, the government declared a bank holiday, effective at 10:15 a.m., wisely rejecting the alternative suggestion of a moratorium on payments. The chief immediate problem was the inability of the banks to meet the public's demand for cash, because of general illiquidity.

During the hectic week end that followed, the government faced major decisions on monetary policy. These had to be threshed out while the International Settlement, where the banks were located, was at the verge of the battle, struck by several bombs and by innumerable stray missiles. The government's advisers, Cyril Rogers of the Bank of England who had been in China since September 1935, and was working primarily on plans to convert the Central Bank into a central reserve bank, Fenimore B. Lynch, Adviser to the Central Bank since 1929, and the writer as Financial Adviser to the government since 1929, submitted recommendations which were substantially adopted. Their memorandum of August 14 said:

Our present difficulties are no new ones in general experience and can be surmounted if sane and balanced action is taken. There is absolutely no reason why we should be stampeded into "breaking up the house" unnecessarily. The essential requirement is to keep the people calm by not cutting off their daily requirements for food and pocket money and to keep industry and trade going as far as possible.

The main decisions were:

1. To limit cash withdrawals from current accounts to 5 per cent per week, not to exceed C$150 — later amended to exempt accounts below C$300. Deposits made on and after August 18 were to be free of the restrictions. Fixed deposits were frozen to maturity, and if not renewed were subject to the same restrictions as current accounts. Currency could be withdrawn by special arrangement with the respective banks to meet payrolls or expenses related to military operations. Cashier's orders could be used for interbank settlement only. The government also authorized transfer money known as *wei wah*, that is, cash orders of commercial and native banks. These could be transferred only between Shanghai banks and could not be exchanged either for currency or to buy foreign exchange. Depositors with commercial accounts in local currency at commercial and native banks were allowed to draw *wei wah* from these accounts to meet business requirements, over and above withdrawals permitted in cash. Also *wei wah* could be used to pay customs duties daily up to 1,000 customs gold units (CGU)[8] for imports, and up to C$1,000 for exports. For a time *wei wah* were dis-

counted at up to 6 per cent but soon the discount fell to 1 per cent and for some months varied around 1 to 2 per cent.

2. To continue to support exchange at the prewar level. Allowing exchange to fall would have severely shocked confidence, the currency was if anything undervalued, and China had large reserves. Maintenance of all possible confidence in the government was deemed highly important in the critical early stage of fighting, in which the government sought to rally support internally and from friendly foreign powers. To strengthen the monetary situation the "gentlemen's agreement" of July was made more explicit, as embodied in a letter of August 15 from the Chairman of the Chinese Bankers' Association to the Chairman of the Foreign Bankers' Association, as follows:

> In order that the general policy in this market may be coordinated to the mutual benefit of all concerned I should be very grateful if you could kindly arrange with the members of your Association to cooperate with us in the following matters:
>
> (1) Not to open new accounts for Chinese depositors, nor to permit unusual additions to existing Chinese accounts;
>
> (2) To confine operations to dealings with member banks' own customers — particularly as regards "over counter" sales of exchange to Chinese;
>
> (3) Not to sell exchange to speculators.

The government rejected without much discussion the suggestion of exchange control — which the advisers described as "the worst possible thing to do." China, because of extraterritoriality and lack of jurisdiction, could not enforce its measures in the foreign settlements and concessions. Japan was in course of seizing the main ports, and overrunning rich areas. China could not control imports, nor could she force exporters to hand over the foreign currencies received. Also China lacked the administrative personnel to operate controls. But although at this stage exchange control was not seriously considered, the mention of it was the beginning of an issue that was later to cause a split both in China and among China's friends abroad (see chaps. XVI and XVII).

The government also firmly rejected schemes put forward in the early weeks of fighting to create a new and inconvertible currency for purely internal requirements to finance the war. The theory was that this would permit maintaining the national currency intact and without depreciation. Rumors that such schemes were under consideration disturbed confidence from time to time, as did rumors of exchange control. Schemes for a new currency then had considerable support in Nanking and Shanghai, and persisted during the war and after — eventually bearing fruit in the unfortunate gold *yuan* currency in 1948 whose rapid failure played an inglorious part in the collapse of Nationalist rule. Commenting on the subject of issuing a new currency, in a memorandum to Minister Kung on October 16, 1937, I said:

Such a scheme would shock confidence and would fail to maintain the value of the present legal tender notes and to conserve foreign currency reserves. Both kinds of currency would be equally available for purchase of goods and services, and the introduction of the new notes would tend to make the circulation relatively redundant. Consequently the present notes would tend to be presented for purchase of exchange, thus depleting the foreign currency reserve. The increase in the volume of the circulating medium would tend to cause a rise in the internal price level, regardless of whether due to increase in the one or the other form of currency. The new notes, being admittedly less good than the *fa pi*, would soon depreciate.

When the banks opened on Tuesday, August 17, money was very tight. Sales of US$42 million between July 7 and August 13 had already tightened the market, and now many wanted money for emergency needs. Hence little money was available for speculative buying of goods or for flight of capital. Instead, there were considerable sales of foreign currencies to raise local currency. Before the end of August the Central Bank was able to buy in the market the equivalent of US$4 million. The Bank maintained the level of exchange without cost for about the next two months.

In the latter part of October, however, the demand for foreign currencies increased. During the summer a study disclosed that a large demand for exchange would be met in the late fall and winter. Exchange covering exports already shipped had been sold in the market at the time of shipment. But exchange for imports had not been generally covered, imports being sold on three or four months' credit for distribution throughout the country, and remittances from outlying districts had not yet reached Shanghai. It was felt that this demand could be worked off in two or three months, and by February 1938 it had mostly dried up.

Whether the Central Bank should continue to sell forward exchange caused long and earnest debate behind the scenes. There was a legitimate demand for forward exchange for trade purposes. The decision in August was against unlimited forward business. But the Central Bank in October decided to provide to the members of the Foreign Exchange Bankers Association up to about C$5 million (about US$1.5 million) per month of change-overs at a cost of ⅛d. for sterling and ¼ cent in the rate for US dollars, that is, about 10 per cent per annum. These facilities were limited to £20,000 or US$100,000 per bank and £5,000 or US$25,000 per person. For the month of December 1937, the total amount of change-overs provided by the Central Bank was tripled. Nevertheless market rates for forward exchange tended to be weak because of uncertainties, and toward the end of the year the market discount for one month forward was as much as ⅜d. and ¾ cent for US dollars, equivalent to an interest cost of over 30 per cent per annum. The total amount of change-overs done by the Central Bank was equivalent to about US$15 million in the first year of the war, as shown below:

Year	Sterling	Dollars
1937 August	£60,000	US$4,650,000
September	—	
October	120,000	600,000
November	160,000	650,000
December	480,000	600,000
1938 January	200,000	450,000
February	—	—
March	215,000	—
April	270,000	—
May	210,000	—
June	170,000	—
Total	£1,885,000	US$6,950,000

The premise of exchange support was that money would be kept tight. In the early months the government was responsive to the urgings of the Central Bank and the advisers to keep money as tight as possible. The Liberty Loan, announced in mid-September, was promoted with patriotic fervor and pressures on the well-to-do to subscribe. It produced nearly C$200 million from the public, a good record. Sales of exchange up to March 12, 1938, took about C$400 million from the market. Total note issue of the four government banks grew only from C$1,407 million in mid-1937 to C$1,679 million on March 31, 1938.

But strong forces were working against tight money policy, and the situation was deteriorating. First was the government's urgent need for funds for the war and to assure essential economic activity at a time when tax revenue was falling drastically because of enemy seizures of ports and other productive areas. Also the government, pressed by advocates of all kinds of projects to increase production and struck by the backwardness of the rear areas as a war base, leaned toward a soft money policy. There was pressure for credits by business enterprises unable to get normal bank accommodation, and by banks wanting money to lend. In the fall of 1937 the government adopted a plan whereby the four government banks would act jointly in financial matters through a central office — the plan for changing the Central Bank into a Central Reserve Bank having been dropped because of the war. One measure adopted was to create "Rediscount Committees" in leading centers. These were to provide funds in the emergency to other banks and financial institutions to make loans on commodities, commercial paper, and government bonds. Early operations were restrained, and available data indicated that by January 1938, about C$18 million had been loaned, about two-thirds of which was at Hankow. Also about C$3 million had been loaned through special commissions for foreign trade, industry, mining, and agriculture. On June 4, 1938, Minister Kung announced that about C$50 million had been loaned including C$15 million at Chungking. At the end of November 1937 the arrangement came up for renewal whereby the commercial banks could get bank notes from the government banks by turning in 60 per cent silver and 40 per cent in approved securities. The Central Bank and the advisers saw the inflationary dangers and recommended against renewal, but without avail. They urged repeatedly that credit should not be allowed for unessential purposes. My judgment as expressed in a memorandum to the Finance Minister January 3, 1938, was, "Funds have been and are being made available too freely, with the result that free money is available for flight of capital." I urged a "really strict policy in the future," even though it would be unpopular and cause some hardship.

The growth of the money supply combined with shortage of goods and the public's fear of the future to bring about a steady rise of prices. In December the average was higher than in the first half-year by 18 per cent, and in March by 29 per cent. That was a creditable showing, when enemy forces were overrunning huge areas and pushing China's armies back into the interior. China's showing on prices compares favorably with the situation in England two years later, when prices rose by 37 per cent in the first nine months after outbreak of World War II.

China's currency meanwhile was becoming more and more overvalued at prewar rates of exchange. In all the circumstances, and with the future outlook so disturbing, an increase in the demand for foreign currencies was unavoidable. To add to the difficulties, the Japanese announced on February 15 their intention to open a puppet bank of issue in North China. Until then sales of exchange were tapering off from the peak in November. But this announcement reversed the trend, and was followed by heavy increase in capital flight and speculation, despite the "gentlemen's agreement."

Sales to support the market, up to the change of policy effective March 14, 1938, were:

1937	Millions of US$ (equivalent)
July 7–August 13	42
August 17–31	−4
September	1
October	4
November	28
December	18
1938	
January	10
February	12
March 1–12	10
Total	121

The government had spent further large amounts for war purchases abroad and debt service — about US$70 million and US$15 million, respectively, from mid-1937 to March 12 — and there were further foreign payments for the diplomatic service, etc. From a total of US$379 million in mid-1937, total foreign currency resources had fallen to less than half that figure early in 1938.

Clearly the drain of foreign currency funds for exchange support had to be curtailed. But when and how to change the policy presented grave difficulties. Internally, exchange maintenance upheld confidence in the face of Japan's surrounding Shanghai in November and capture of the capital, Nanking, in December. The unchanged rates symbolized China's strength. A break in rates would spur inflation and flight of money into goods and foreign currencies. In China people were more than usually exchange-minded, especially because of the long experience with variable rates under the silver standard. Any considerable fall of the value of silver currency tended to cause the marking up of prices of imported goods, in the first instance; and then of prices in general.[9] After adoption in 1935 of the managed currency system, people naturally took a similar view of the consequences of a fall in the exchange value of the currency. Externally, the maintenance of rates, like the resistance at Shanghai beyond what was advisable on purely military grounds, was viewed as a means to increase the chances of aid, and in particular rates were held in the fall of 1937 to show the Brussels conference, meeting about November 1 to consider Japan's aggression, that China was capable of holding out and worthy of aid.

Early in March a clue to possible action came when Japan announced that the new puppet bank would open in North China on March 10. Clearly the public would take this as justification of a drastic move.

THE EXCHANGE RATIONING SYSTEM

The situation called for a scheme allowing adjustment of rates, while keeping as much as possible the confidence dependent upon governmental support of the exchange market. The decision to act over the week end was taken on Friday March 11. During the series of almost continuous meetings that followed until Sunday morning, there was strong advocacy of trying a general exchange control. That policy was at first tentatively adopted, despite the objections of the advisers and some of the bankers. But it was realized, on further consideration, that it was quite impracticable for the government immediately to begin to pass upon a great mass of individual transactions, and that under the conditions that existed a general control was not workable. The solution that finally prevailed was a scheme of exchange rationing, devised mainly by Cyril Rogers and Tsuyee Pei, then Manager of the Foreign Department of the Bank of China. The plan was for the Central Bank to receive from the Finance Ministry lump-sum allotments for the market, and to ration the individual banks after submittal of weekly lists of their customers' needs. The Central Bank would apportion allotments having regard to the proportionate amounts of its exchange sales to the respective banks during the previous period of exchange support. Exchange would be supplied to the banks, and by them to their customers, at the former official rates.

Effective on Monday March 14 the government issued its mandate. This stated that the "gentlemen's agreement" had been successful in maintaining trade and confidence, but that the recent organization of the puppet bank had created a new situation. To meet this the government had adopted the following procedure:

(1) As from March 14, 1938, sales of foreign exchange shall be centralized through the Central Bank of China at the seat of the government. For convenience the Central Bank of China may establish a Forwarding Office in Hongkong.

(2) Banks desiring to purchase foreign exchange for legitimate requirements shall apply to the Head Office of the Central Bank of China or through its Forwarding Office at Hongkong in accordance with the procedure separately announced.

(3) After consideration of the applications, the Central Bank of China shall furnish foreign exchange at the existing level of rates.

Applications by banks were to be lodged with the Central Bank each Thursday at 10 a.m.; and on the following day at 10 a.m. the replies were to be communicated. Foreign currencies were to be delivered on the day of the replies. The banks were to report the disposal of the exchange granted, and forms for these reports were distributed.

On Saturday March 12, the last business day of exchange support, rates were at par: 14¼d. and US$0.29½. In the following week rates held fairly well in a nervous market, falling only to 13¾d. and US$0.28½ for cash transactions. When allotments of exchange were made available on Friday March 18 for the first time, the chief banks sold this exchange at par, less commission. It was reported that some banks of lesser standing followed the free market and sold at less favorable rates, but the Central Bank insisted that the benefits of the official rates be passed on to the customers and the banks subsequently assured that this was being done.

Applications at Shanghai in the first week under the new system were about double the amount granted. This condition inevitably led the public and the banks to increase their applications, hoping thus to enlarge the allotments received. Applications soon came to be several times larger than allotments, especially as the latter were gradually reduced. But this failed to move the authorities, who continued to fix the amounts allocated to the respective banks having regard to the amounts of exchange sold to each under the former system of free selling. The banks, being unable fully to meet their clients' needs from allotments, distributed what was available by giving the clients part of their needs based on the official rates and the rest at the free market rates.

For a short time some leading banks tried to keep all their transactions on the basis of the official rates. But they soon had to give up. Allotments could not possibly cover even the "legitimate" demand at these rates. The free market moved down as other banks and the public dealt at lower rates and exchange cover was diverted to the free market. Shanghai complained that the allotments were too small, some however saying that if the backlog of demand were met the allotments would meet current demand. Of course the Central Bank could not admit that reserves were not large enough for such liberality.

At the start, financial circles in Shanghai feared that the new policy was a move to decrease the importance of that city as the leading financial center, since basic policy was being made at Hankow and the Forwarding Office was located in Hong Kong at the Central Bank's office there. The use of Hong Kong was necessary because it had free communication with Shanghai, which Hankow did not. To reassure Shanghai and facilitate operations, the Central Bank early in April 1938 set up a Forwarding Office in Shanghai also. At the same time, effective April 20, the Bank required 100 per cent deposit in cash with applications, to reduce padding.

The practicability of restricting imports had been under consideration from the start of the war. But though the Maritime Customs Service remained intact in form, it was subject to Japanese pressure in the main ports that were occupied or blockaded. It was certain that the Japanese would not allow China to enforce trade restrictions imposed in the interest of the war effort. The exchange rationing measure of March 14, 1938, however, opened the possibility of enforcing trade restrictions via exchange allocations. Also things had shaken down so that the practicability of measures behind the fighting lines to reduce consumption of unnecessary imports could be considered.

On April 8, 1938, Rogers and I presented to Minister Kung a memorandum on the subject. This memorandum proposed a nationwide campaign to induce the public to reduce imports either by using less, going without, or substituting articles produced in the country. In any program of reducing imports, however, precautions had to be taken not to aggravate the rise in the price level. Imports might be divided into categories of essential, less essential, and unessential articles. Essential items would comprise a relatively short list of goods of larger consumption and would receive preference in allocation of exchange under the rationing system. This would help to keep down the prices. To facilitate study of the technical problems the Inspector General of Customs, Sir Frederick Maze, sent to Hankow at the request of the Minister two customs experts, G. E. Gilbert and Carl Neprud, in the middle of April.

A full analysis was made of the problem and of the chief possible courses of action, including a detailed study of China's imports. It was clear that the measures to be adopted would have to be as simple as possible. Any attempt at full control of import trade was clearly impracticable, both because it could not be made effective in the occupied areas, and because of difficulties of administration. A careful study of China's treaties indicated that China had the right to introduce a trade control in the circumstances; but it was decided to use other means and thus avoid this issue.

The plan adopted and put into effect about June 1, 1938, was based upon issuance to the banks, "For office use only, and not to be made public," a "List of goods to receive preference in banks' applications for foreign exchange." This list comprised the main necessities, for example, fibers, metals, machinery, chemicals, fuels, food, etc. The procedure as finally placed in effect provided for four categories:

(1) the preferred list;
(2) personal and other requirements;
(3) other more or less essential commodities;
(4) unessential commodities such as luxuries and semi-luxuries, and any other items considered not deserving of an allotment.

Forms were prepared whereby the bankers would submit to the Central Bank the names of their customers and the items and amounts applied for. This supplanted the system of reports previously introduced. In the first allocations, not over 10 per cent of the total allotment was given to the more *bona fide* items included in the third category, and thereafter this category was practically eliminated.

After careful consideration it was decided not to issue a prohibited list. Analysis of import trade showed that the items that could be classed as unessential amounted to less than 5 per cent of the total trade, and that little of this came to areas China could control. It was decided to let such of this trade as continued get exchange in the open market at less favorable rates. Minister Kung included with his opening address to the Economic Conference on June 1 an appeal to the public to abstain from the use of luxuries and to reduce their consumption of other goods, especially imports, to the extent possible. He urged a simpler life and avoidance of unnecessary expenditure, such as for building and furnishings. He further urged growing more food and avoiding use of imported food as far as practicable. He pointed out that this was a temporary measure caused by the emergency and not directed at the foreign exporting countries. Meanwhile by administrative procedure the Central Bank would reject applications for import of items deemed to be less essential.

Introduction of the restrictions of June 1938 was disturbing to the market, especially as it coincided with military reverses to the Chinese armies and rumors that the temporary capital might be moved from Hankow to Chungking or Kunming. Before the plan was put into effect there was some leakage, and it was rumored that the action was to be more stringent than it proved to be. In the first ten days of June the market was very weak, falling by nearly a fifth. There was nervousness about the new system. Formerly each bank distributed among its clients the sums of foreign exchange granted by the Central Bank. Now the bankers were to submit applications to the Central Bank for decision. This was taken to mean that certain parties might not receive exchange as theretofore. So importers who felt they might be excluded hurried to cover their exchange in the free market.

In the latter part of July, the government directed that no applications for foreign exchange be accepted for cargo imported into China after January 1, 1938, excepting special cases approved by the government. This measure, which was based on recommendations from the Central Bank at Shanghai after discussion with the foreign bankers, was intended to help to clear up the situation by dealing with the older transactions. Figures thereafter obtained from the banks indicated that the approximate total of such cargo was £500,000. This excluded consignment cargo, which was regarded as speculative and without exchange commitment.

Gradually the government reduced weekly allotments. In Shanghai there was complaint about not providing enough exchange for needs. But at Hankow and Chungking there was always an argument whether allotments should be cut faster, or even stopped. Reserves were shrinking and many felt that Shanghai, which was enemy-surrounded, was a hotbed of speculation and flight of capital. Nevertheless, a realization of the psychological importance of sustaining the currency as far as practicable prevailed, and the funds allocated were large enough to give some support to the market and to avoid a more abrupt drop in exchange.

Particulars of weekly applications and allotments, and allotments at Shanghai and outports, respectively, are shown in appendix F, Table 69. The approximate total allotted monthly in dollars and sterling was (equivalents in thousands):

Month	1938	1939
January		$100
February		65
March	US$7,800	78
April	6,600	55
May	4,600	55
June	3,500	70
July	1,450	—
August	1,175	—
September	800	—
October	370	—
November	230	—
December	220	—

The total allotted under this system in 1938–1939 was equivalent to about

US$28 million, of which about 85 per cent went to Shanghai and 15 per cent to outports. Besides about US$27 million as per the items tabulated above, about US$800,000 was allocated through a "special account" in a foreign bank. This was to provide for a limited allotment to Japanese banks for import of "legitimate" items, and was a measure of expediency adopted with the hope (which was realized) of preventing the Japanese who surrounded Shanghai from taking action to shut down the exchange market there.

There were some sharp breaks in exchange rates in March–June 1938, as shown below:

	Sterling (pence)		US$ (cents)	
1938	High	Low	High	Low
March	14.25	11.75	29.91	24.37
April	13.31	12.44	27.81	25.69
May	12.78	10.37	26.56	21.43
June	10.25	8.10	21.19	16.75

The system of exchange rationing, however, succeeded in effecting a transition to a less costly system and a lower level of rates without too great an undermining of confidence. Also the plan, announced as a means to combat Japanese currency schemes, proved a strong weapon against them, as explained in chapter XIV.

Not so tight money

While the government was working out application of the measures to readjust the level of exchange rates, there were developments tending toward too easy money and needlessly increased spending. These developments — in line with similar developments during the rest of the war — added to the difficulty of sustaining the value of the currency and of holding the reins to prevent galloping inflation.

The need to strengthen war-related production was inescapable. The modernization of China was progressing fast in 1937. But the accomplishments were largely along the seaboard and the Yangtze River, areas vulnerable to Japan's advance. As the government was forced back into the interior, its leaders faced the hard problem of resisting mechanized armies from a base which, in economic development, was only beginning to emerge from the middle ages. In the early months of the war over 600 factories, 120,000 tons of industrial equipment, and many stocks of finished goods were moved hurriedly from the seaboard to the interior. Some went directly to Szechwan Province in the distant west, while others went to the Central Yangtze region and later inland when Japan's armies drew near. Also 10,000 skilled workers were moved westward.[10] This transplanting of enterprises and much of the key personnel, often under air attack, was an epic affair. The government encouraged and supported it with transport facilities and credit.

Such emergency action was amply justified, not merely for defense but to add to the supply of essential goods for the civilian population and thus to check price rises. It was, however, understandable that with these emergency measures went a determination to modernize and improve the economy while fighting. An important indication of policy on spending was the declaration on "resistance and reconstruction," adopted by the Extraordinary National Congress of the Kuomintang at Hankow April 2, 1938. Pertinent parts are quoted in chapter IV on Fiscal Policy. The program called for "improving the people's livelihood," and for various major capital projects in agriculture, mining, industry, and communications.

On April 29, 1938, the Finance Ministry issued certain "Principles governing readjustment of local financial organizations," to develop agricultural and industrial production. Such organizations could "apply for one dollar and subsidiary notes from the Four Government Banks" in proportions of 60/40, on the security of property, commodities, commercial paper or securities. They were to put up at least 20 per cent in legal tender notes and not over 30 per cent in bonds. Besides interest they were to pay the printing cost of the notes. The circular telegram of the Ministry stated that the Rediscount Commissions and three commissions to readjust agriculture, industry and mining, and trade had been at work but "the tight monetary market in the interior has not been eased." "During the period of armed resistance . . . efforts should be directed not only towards the maintenance of China's rural economy but also towards the active improvement of it, thereby developing her agricultural productivity." [11]

Professor J. Lossing Buck, leading authority on China's agriculture, and who was then representing the American Treasury in China, in a letter of April 29 to me said, "I think there is no question that something must be done to relieve the acute shortage of currency for production purposes." China was no exception to the situation in underdeveloped countries where capital is scarce and interest rates high.

On May 4, 1938, I gave the Finance Minister a memorandum on the April 29 scheme. This recognized the need to provide adequate credit "to promote production of agricultural necessities and articles related to the war effort," but suggested that this could best be done through ordinary banks, notably the Farmers Bank, rather than through "local financial organizations" that were likely to be inexperienced and subject to local pressure and might even be financially irresponsible. Any such credit granted should be against actual production and be self-liquidating. Care was needed to avoid action that would be mainly inflationary, and "a stern policy of restricting credit to essentials is vital to China's interests." Moreover the emphasis on issuing one dollar and subsidiary bills was unfortunate. A legitimate borrower should have the credit in the form most convenient to him, in whatever denomination of bills he needs or in deposit credit. Besides the implication of issuing special currency for a special purpose would be disturbing to confidence (in the two weeks after April 29 the exchange market slumped by about 15 per cent). Finally the measure, I hoped, would be administered so as to avoid granting credit for other than ends essential to the war effort. In a letter of May 6 to an associate I said, "I fear that the scheme is urged by some who are not disinterested and who have frozen items to work off." Fortunately in actual practice, issuance of these one dollar and subsidiary notes did not prove to be an important direct factor in the inflation.

Despite rumors that the Economic Conference called for June 1, 1938, would take fundamental measures about currency policy, this conference took no such action. It did adopt a strong pronouncement for economy in private life, and especially in use of imported goods. This was helpful but the practical difficulty of getting imports had much more effect. During June a rumor spread that the government was issuing C$200 million of inconvertible currency, but this was firmly denied.

On June 20, 1938, Hsi Te-mou, manager of the Banking Department of the Central Bank, telegraphed to Hankow from Shanghai that he was unable to tighten the market because of (1) continuous remittances to Shanghai from other parts of China, including influx of money spent by the government, and (2) "loans and advances continuously made by the government to commercial banks." Despite frequent urging no clear distinction was ever made and enforced between, on the one hand, urgent war needs, and, on the other hand, projects and credits that could be postponed because of being unessential and needlessly promoting inflation. As the war progressed the temptation to spend money that could be gotten merely by printing proved too strong in far too many cases.

XVI. STABILIZATION OPERATIONS,
JUNE 1938 TO AUGUST 1941

Exchange rationing was recognized by the policy makers as an expedient, to permit a needed downward readjustment of exchange rates and to gain time to consider future monetary policy in a very difficult situation. China's military position was worsening, and the summer of 1938 saw removal of the temporary capital from Hankow to Chungking. China nevertheless was firmly resolved to fight on, and the end of the war was not in sight.

As the second year of fighting began, there were both debit and credit items in the economic and financial field. On the debit side, inflation was seriously under way. Average prices were up about 40 per cent, and the rate was likely to quicken. The budget deficit in the first year to June 30, 1938, was nearly 75 per cent. While cash transactions with the public, comprising sales of foreign currencies yielding C$499 million and sales of bonds yielding C$256 million, reduced to C$777 million or 37 per cent the figure of net deficit covered by inflationary credit to the government by the government banks, it was clear that such helpful offsets to inflation would not continue on so large a scale. The government was failing to give adequate attention to raising more revenue, and to control of spending and bank credit. Foreign exchange slumped in the first year to a low less than 60 per cent of the prewar level. Exchange support and purchase of war supplies was costly, and external assets dropped from US$379 million on June 30, 1937, to less than US$100 million a year later. It was certain that China could spare little foreign currency thereafter to support the market.

Yet the credit side showed some strong features. Despite disheartening defeats and loss of the main ports and centers of industry, China's economic and financial system though badly hurt was far from paralyzed. The decentralized and largely rural economy was resilient. The people showed remarkable vitality and ability to carry on despite suffering, and to frustrate enemy moves. Vitally important machinery and supplies and personnel had been moved to the interior from Shanghai and other vulnerable centers. The government's higher personnel, including that of the head offices of the four government banks, had moved inland.

Though the value of money had suffered badly, neither the price rise of about 40 per cent nor the even larger slump in exchange was calamitous. China's people as a whole were showing impressive trust in their currency.

The exchange rationing scheme had been adopted with minimum damage to confidence, letting rates slip gradually. Withdrawal of large amounts of money by heavy sales of exchange had been a major counterinflationary factor. The growth of note issue was not quite as bad as it seemed. Some notes were being substituted for silver coins. In the emergency many people were hoarding notes. Banks needed to hold larger reserves of notes against emergency. Also with banking facilities disrupted, a larger share of business was done with cash. Enemy efforts to drive *fapi* from North China and other occupied areas had been stymied. *Fapi* held a premium over puppet money. The American Treasury was buying China's silver on a big scale and thus helping to mobilize this major asset for use in expenditure abroad. Russia had granted a second credit of US$50 million for war purchases July 1, 1938. Just as Japan's ruthless campaign had brought defeats but had not broken China's power to resist force with force, so the financial front had yielded but was far from broken. China could not win alone and had to play for time, hoping for further financial support and eventual military aid.

Of special importance was the fact that the currency, at exchange rates in June 1938, was materially undervalued. Although average prices were up by about 40 per cent, the cost of foreign currencies had come close to doubling. The average cost of US$1 and £1 in June, 1937, was C$3.36 and C$16.60, respectively. At the lows of June 1938, the cost had risen to nearly C$6.00 and C$30.00, respectively. At times exchange rates outrun general prices in a free market at a time of severe inflation and uncertainty. It seemed highly probable that China could hold the new lower level of exchange for some time without serious cost by means of operations to stabilize the market. Early in June Tsuyee Pei of the Bank of China proposed such operations. T. V. Soong, head of the Bank of China, and I recommended the plan to Finance Minister Kung, and he agreed.

THE BEGINNING OF EXCHANGE STABILIZATION
BY MARKET OPERATIONS, JUNE 1938

The Bank of China arranged for the Hongkong and Shanghai Banking Corporation to share equally in providing funds for market operations, under Bank of China guarantee. The Hongkong Bank, as it was called, agreed to take the leading part in actual operations; and at times arranged with the Chartered Bank of India, Australia, and China to operate for it, to hide its hand. The Hongkong Bank had acted as regulator of the exchange market before the currency reform of 1935, and had close relations with the Bank of China. Tsuyee Pei and Cyril Rogers, who well understood China's monetary problems, had immediate supervision of operations.

Operations began June 14. On the preceding day rates had reached a low of 9⅛d. and US$0.16¾. The weakness was a result partly of Chinese military reverses leading to the loss of Kaifeng, and rumored removal of the capital from Hankow to Chungking. The first sales of exchange brought a prompt recovery of steadiness. The operation became known and helped to keep confidence. The market, however, underwent some vicissitudes. At the end of July the collapse of vital defenses on the Yangtze River near Kiukiang brought pressure on rates. It also became known that Rogers, who had gone to London to seek financial aid, had returned empty-handed. The ensuing pressure on rates led to a drop which was allowed to take rates down from 9d. to around 8d. where support was forthcoming.

The fall of Canton and Hankow on October 21 and 25 severely tested the operation. *Finance and Commerce* of Shanghai thus described what took place, in its issue of October 26:

Every fresh report of Chinese troops retreating sent timid people running into the market to buy sterling or U.S. dollars, but on discovering that sellers were still firm in offering 8d. or a fraction over, and that the market continued to receive the support it had been enjoying for so long, the demand for foreign currencies subsided as quickly as it came into being.

Influence "from a certain quarter," said this journal in its issue of November 2, "was exercised very skillfully and promptly"; and, "Throughout a week of intense outside excitement the exchange-market remained remarkably placid, to the astonishment of those who foretold a financial typhoon to follow the fall of Hankow . . . The net result of these carefully planned activities has been to maintain a remarkable degree of confidence on the market, in spite of most unfavorable influences elsewhere." The initial operation was costly, as the banks then sold the equivalent of about US$15 million. But, as the shock wore off, they were able to buy back as the speculators, seeing the strength of the support, sold the foreign currencies they had bought. By December 2, the sales of US$15 million were entirely covered. E. Kann, the well known financial authority of Shanghai, wrote in *Finance and Commerce* of December 28: "The management of China's currency since June was most skillfully handled, and the result of these endeavors can only be presumed a complete success." [1]

When the market weakened as the adverse news developed, Minister Kung was understandably worried about whether rates could be held without undue cost. Cash aid from abroad was not in sight, and reserves were shrinking dangerously. On October 23 I pointed out in a memorandum that "the currency is in a relatively favorable position," since exchange rates had fallen more than prices had risen. "In this critical time," I said, "people must not be allowed to think that China's national structure is breaking"; and, "To prevent this idea from gaining ground just now, the expenditure of a substantial amount of funds is fully justified." Rogers shared these views, and telegraphed to me on October 25: "If we do not hold the currency we 'let down' the Chinese people who have great faith in the Chinese dollar and hence in the government. We also sell out to puppets and give Japanese control over currency, financial system, et cetera, which otherwise they would not have in spite of all military successes." He said that Japanese banks were not actively buying foreign currencies.

On January 14, 1939, with governmental authorization I gave to the press at Chungking the following spokesman's statement, summing up operations to that date:

For several months past, it was authoritatively revealed today . . . by a person closely in touch with the Chinese financial situation, China has been conducting exchange stabilization operations. It is now learned that substantial funds have been earmarked to facilitate such operations on a scale that makes it possible to counter speculative or other activities unrelated to basic currency conditions.

It was pointed out that after the imposition in March of the exchange restrictions necessitated by the Japanese currency measures in North China, exchange was allowed to decline in an orderly manner so that the market might gradually be adjusted to a level in harmony with existing and prospective conditions. Such a level was attained early in June and the market has since shown a gratifying degree of stability . . .

In calling attention to the widespread confidence in the currency in all parts of the country . . . [the] informant stated that the action now taken materially strengthens the position of the currency and affords valuable means of minimizing fluctuations in the exchange value of the Chinese dollar. He further stated that all operations remain fully covered in foreign exchange.

This statement was timed to counteract possible effects on the exchange market of announcement the next day of suspension of payments on the foreign currency debt (see chap. VII).

Although there had been no net cost to the Bank of China as of early 1939, it soon became clear that the favorable technical situation that had made possible extended success was coming to an end. In late February exchange weakness developed. This was prompted by uncertainty and nervousness caused by enemy currency maneuvers in North China, and talk that the Japanese would set up a puppet currency in Central China. These developments forced substantial sales of exchange, and the Bank of China's operation began to go into the red.

For some time it had been clear to those of us concerned with the stabilization program that it called for larger external funds than China alone could supply. In the fall of 1938 there were negotiations with the Hongkong Bank and the Chartered Bank to provide a private credit of £3 million for stabilization. But these led to no result. The only credits which China got in the first 20 months were the purchase credits described in chapter VIII. These indirectly helped the currency, by lessening the need to spend shrinking assets abroad for purchases and thus freeing funds that could be used if desired for currency support. But the credits provided no funds in foreign currency directly available for that purpose. Meanwhile, the Bank of China's operation continued, in view of the hope for external aid, which soon materialized as described in the next section.

When the Bank of China's operation ended early in April, its net oversold position, after 10 months, was equivalent to US$6 million. In this period also the Central Bank had allotted about US$6 million under the rationing procedure, though by the spring of 1939 allotments had become only nominal. Thus the total cost of holding the currency for 10 months had been only about US$12 million. This was a very good record indeed. The operation had helped to sustain morale in the face of two grave defeats. The exchange market was kept orderly, within a range of about 8–9d. and US$0.15½–17, mostly around the lower figures. The prevention of panicky fluctuations in exchange at Shanghai, the main financial center, sustained a large degree of confidence in the currency and in the outlook, and thus tended to check the price rise throughout the country.

Nevertheless, questions were beginning to be raised at Chungking. Strong elements in the government disliked the idea of spending precious funds at Shanghai, which they viewed as a hotbed of enemy agents and speculators. The issue gradually became a bone of contention within the government, and from there the argument spread to the United States and Britain in connection with their later aid. But early in 1939 there was general agreement that the stabilization policy should be continued.

THE ANGLO-CHINESE STABILIZATION OPERATION,
APRIL TO AUGUST 1939

Although in the summer of 1938 London turned down the idea of supporting China's currency, they had not dropped the subject. On December 7, the British embassy at Washington told the State Department they thought of a possible currency credit of £3 million. They had not yet decided what to do, but said their action would be much influenced by whether Washington would "take parallel and simultaneous action." This the British felt would aid Chinese morale, lessen the chance of Japanese retaliation, and help preserve the Open Door. They believed that a currency credit was the best available way to help China. The United States, however, was about to grant the US$25 million purchase credit announced December 15, and did not deem cash aid feasible. After granting that credit Washington felt that the United States was thereby doing all it could for the time being, along with purchase of Chinese silver, both of which aided China's currency. Also the United States wanted to avoid anything looking like collusion to coerce Japan.[2]

A breakthrough to obtain foreign support for the currency, nevertheless, was near. The granting of the American purchase credit encouraged London to act in March 1939. While London was disposed to go ahead with the stabilization credit, they were concerned about whether to make it contingent on China's resuming payments on the foreign debt, suspended early in the year, and on giving effect to the Anglo-Japanese customs agreement.[3] The decision was to ask China to make a proposal for partial resumption of debt payments. As to the customs agreement, Ambassador Clark Kerr telegraphed from China on February 1 that he had misgivings about insisting upon implementation.[4]

Britain's decision to arrange the credit was influenced by the success of the stabilization operation above described. The example of the American purchase credit helped, along with the fact that the United States had acted without serious trouble with Japan. Ambassador Craigie in Tokyo favored going ahead, and was confident that the credit would not lead to war.

The agreements of March 10, 1939, set up a stabilization fund of £10 million (about US$47 million). At the last moment Rogers was able to get the British part raised from £3 to £5 millions. Half of the total fund was to be supplied by the Hongkong and Shanghai Banking Corporation and the Chartered Bank of India, Australia, and China, and half by the Bank of China and the Bank of Communications. The British government, subject to parliamentary approval which was duly obtained, was to guarantee the British banks against loss of principal and interest. The Chinese banks were to pay interest on the British contribution at the favorable rate of 2¾ per cent per annum. The fund was to be operated by a management committee of five, one from each bank together with a British subject acceptable to the British government and the British banks, to be appointed by China and to be the chairman. Cyril Rogers was named to this post.

The Chinese government gave several assurances. During the life of these agreements "the financial, economic and monetary policy of the Chinese Government will be designed to maintain the stability of the Chinese dollar in terms of sterling." To that end the government was to restrict its foreign exchange commitments to the greatest possible extent and not buy exchange in excess of immediate needs. All exchange was to be bought through one or more of the banks represented on the committee. The Chinese government banks were to cooperate in every way with the committee, and foreign exchange acquired in any manner and not required for immediate commitments was to be sold to the Fund at cost, so long as the Fund was not in excess of £10 million.[5]

China promptly made in London a proposal for partial resumption of debt service, which, in effect, was a *quid pro quo* for the credit, and negotiated in good faith but the negotiations finally had to be dropped (see chap. VII).

Britain still hoped for parallel American action in support of China's currency. Stanley K. Hornbeck, Director of the State Department's Far Eastern Office, who throughout took a penetrating and far-sighted view of the issues, raised broad questions of American policy in a memorandum of March 8. He asked:

> Ought we not concern ourselves more about the problem of seeing to it that Japan does not conquer China than about discouraging interference by Japan with American interests in China? . . .
> The British Government is at this moment taking a new step toward assisting China (currency loan). This Government has given the British Government an assurance that we would study possibilities of action here with a hope that we would be able to take some new and parallel step in the same direction. Is not the moment at hand when, if at all possible, we should be taking some such step?[6]

But Washington was not yet ready to think seriously about this.

Conditions in April, when the Anglo-Chinese fund began operations, were much less favorable to success than ten months earlier when the Bank of China's operation began. The currency, instead of being undervalued, was now overvalued. Exchange rates during those ten months changed little, and in April were about 8¼d. and US$0.16. At those rates the cost of buying sterling or dollars was about 75 per cent above the prewar cost. But average prices in April were 109 per cent above the prewar level. Prices had risen about 50 per cent during the ten months. With fresh currency constantly put out in the interior to meet the deficit, it was impossible to prevent some of it from coming to Shanghai and being used to buy exchange for imports, personal needs, and capital flight. Shanghai funds commanded in the interior a premium around 20 per cent in the spring of 1939, but still money flowed into Shanghai. The balance of payments was out of equilibrium at the existing level of exchange. In the spring the balance was normally adverse, and this time imports of cereals, raw cotton, yarn, and thread were unusually large because of the cheap exchange and the disturbed conditions.[7] The North China happenings described in the preceding chapters XIV and XV were damaging to confidence in the currency. And concretely the requirement from March 10, 1939, that exporters in North China hand over to the control the proceeds of leading exports reduced the market supply of export exchange. Also the Japanese controlled the Yangtze River, the chief outlet for exports from Central China.

In Free China the government was obliged to buy goods — tungsten, tin, tea, wood oil, and the like — to ship abroad as payment on purchase credits and barter deals with Russia, the United States, Britain, and Germany. These exports therefore did not add to the market supply of exchange. In Yunnan the provincial authorities, who were not under real control by Chungking, insisted on receiving foreign exchange from tin exports. The agencies buying the export goods had to pay locally prices sufficient to maintain production. The buying added to the deficit that had to be met by the printing press, and thus increased the inflation.

These formidable difficulties did not mean that the Fund's task was hopeless and should not have been undertaken. The success of the earlier operation had shown that, despite serious difficulties, an orderly exchange market could be maintained without unreasonable cost at proper levels of rates.

With the factors described working against the balancing of China's international payments, it was not surprising that the new Fund had to sell foreign currencies heavily almost from the start. Its managers realized the need to lower the rate, and soon after the Fund began operations they wanted the operators at Shanghai to lower it at the first opportunity. The British bank manager operating for the Fund at Shanghai, however, wished to wait, expecting that speculators could be squeezed at the end of April. The Fund's managers followed his judgment but the squeeze failed to eventuate.

Failure to adjust the rate promptly proved costly. Toward the end of April it became known that the Japanese were about to open the Hua Hsing Bank at Shanghai as a bank of issue. Announcement of its opening was a shock to confidence, and made it harder for the Fund's managers to act. On May 2 the Fund sold over £1 million, bringing total sales to £3.5 million. Since it could not long stand such a drain its managers on May 2 sought Chungking's approval to adjust the rates. Kung's reply authorized suspension of the Fund's sales, but foreshadowed issues of policy that persisted. He queried whether it would be better to reduce the drain by making some sales according to merit of the applications and rejecting doubtful applications. Sales based upon merit would have resembled the rationing scheme of 1938. While nominally keeping a fixed rate such sales would have been small, and the main market would have fallen away drastically. The Fund's managers did not at once adjust the rates, because pressure eased. The new bank opened May 10 and remained a threat, but never amounted to much.

Some of the drain was caused by Chinese government action. Various offices were paying out *fapi* at Hong Kong and to some extent at Shanghai for imports. The Finance Ministry always had inadequate control over the financial organs of other parts of the government. For example, in May 1939 the military contracted to pay Chinese dollars in Hong Kong for cloth costing about £200,000. Naturally this money was mostly sold there for foreign currencies. Minister Kung tried to stop such deals but was not wholly successful. Also the government kept such exchange as it got from private exports under the export control, and did not turn it over to the Fund in accordance with the assurances given the British government in March. Furthermore the Postal Remittances and Savings Bank, which was under the Ministry of Communications and not the Ministry of Finance, drew off for official use some of the overseas Chinese remittances. These remittances were equal in total to about US$100 million yearly, mainly via Hong Kong, and were a main item in the supply of exchange in the market. By the spring of 1939 the Central Bank had used up its assets abroad except for US$25 to 30 million which was needed for working capital. So the temptation to various official agencies was strong to lay hold on any available current foreign exchange.

Advices from Shanghai were that various banks, both Chinese and foreign, were selling exchange for other than "legitimate" needs. The Ministry of Finance pressed the Chinese banks. Similarly the British authorities took up the matter with British banks. On May 1 the American embassy at Chungking telegraphed to the Department of State a statement I gave them expressing the hope that the American banks would cooperate in every way to maintain the spirit of the 1937 gentlemen's agreement and thus help to sustain the Chinese currency. The Department passed this on in substance to the head offices of the American banks.[8] But in the absence of power to regulate the market effectively, or even at all, the desire of most of the various banks to do what competitors were doing was stronger than concern for China's interest, so things went on much as before.

From April to June London and the managers of the Fund pressed for some formula to let the Anglo-Japanese customs agreement come into effect. The Fund was badly hurt by the plethora of money in the market, some of which the agreement would have withdrawn. But no such action proved feasible.[9]

The drain of exchange continued. On June 6 Rogers telegraphed that he and his associates felt that rates should be adjusted without further delay. In advising Kung's concurrence I telegraphed:

He asks whether it would be better to adjust quickly to new level to avoid uncertainty of extended period of adjustment.

I am too remote to offer specific advice but in principle suggest new level be conservatively chosen so that it can be held for some time.

On June 7 the Fund suspended support. When it again intervened after three days it was able to restore stability at small cost around 6½d. and US$0.12¾, a drop of about 20 per cent. On June 11 Kung telegraphed to the Chinese embassies at Washington, London, and Paris an explanation of the situation and the reasons for adjusting rates. This was to be communicated to the respective governments. This message summarized the explanation given in a press statement which stressed the need to reduce the adverse balance of payments, and also Japanese interference with trade and the currency, and stated:

Reduction of the rate was not expected by the market and caused some ill-considered comment, but advices indicate that the adjustment is being satisfactorily made and that there is no cause for concern.

The government is taking measures to curtail non-essential imports, encourage exports, contract credit, reduce spending to war necessities and further to consolidate the organization of the government.

By June 12 there was good prospect for temporary stability around the new level, apart from shocks from other than economic causes. The large sales of exchange during April and May had withdrawn a large amount of Chinese currency from the market, and its tightness was shown by the rise of call money rates. There was reason to think that the Fund could buy back substantially during the remainder of June.

Events at Tientsin, however, swiftly changed the situation. On June 13, as described in chapter XIV, the Japanese suddenly blockaded the Tientsin foreign concessions. At once Shanghai began to worry whether deposits in Chinese banks in the International Settlement were safe. This brought on simultaneously a banking and an exchange crisis. People hurried to take money out of the banks, to buy foreign exchange and goods. The banks were strained and a heavy drain on the Fund began. The situation was made worse because it came so soon after the opening at Shanghai of the Hua Hsing Bank on May 10.

On June 20 the situation became so bad that Kung instructed the government banks at Shanghai to stop loans to other banks, in order to tighten the money market. Wednesday June 21 was a holiday because of the Dragon Boat festival. On that day Soong, head of the Bank of China, and Rogers telegraphed from Hong Kong proposing a bank holiday of two or three days to give time to devise emergency measures. But Kung feared this would be too much of a shock. Instead, emergency restrictions on deposit withdrawals were hurriedly drawn and telegraphed to Shanghai, effective June 22.

As from June 22 in Shanghai, withdrawals other than for payrolls and official use were to be limited to C$500 per person per week. Larger amounts could be withdrawn only in *wei wah* currency, which could not be converted into cash but was only transferable between banks. The order did not apply to transfers of bank funds to the interior. In announcing this measure, the government spokesman stated that "this action was deemed necessary as a temporary measure to check speculation in connection with adjustment of the economic situation to the lower level of rates of exchange." The government also requested the American, British, and French embassies to press the respective foreign banks not to accept deposit of money withdrawn from Chinese banks.

This order made the Shanghai money market very tight. *Wei wah* money went to a discount of over 10 per cent. Exchange rates became firm. Various banks were obliged to sell foreign currencies to realize funds to meet their local obligations in Shanghai. The Fund recouped a substantial amount of exchange during the latter part of June.

The benefit from the June 22 restriction of deposit withdrawals, however, was short-lived. This measure was hastily drawn and not as tight as the Fund's managers and I had urged. It did not sufficiently check the flow of money into the market. It had been intended to limit withdrawals per person to C$300 weekly. But somehow the figure of C$500 was announced and it became too late to change it. Most depositors withdrew the maximum. Also worry grew about the Fund's ability to maintain rates.

On June 27, 1939, the government decided to continue the policy of exchange support, and to introduce as soon as possible measures that were being prepared to curtail imports and encourage exports and to give effect to rationing of exchange. These measures, announced July 3, applied to all China, but could have only nominal effect in the occupied areas and the international settlements and concessions. The announcement made clear that these measures would not affect the policy of the Fund. Importers of essential goods were to apply to an Exchange Examination Committee at Chungking giving particulars of the proposed importation. If approved the exchange would be granted at the old official rates, but the applicant was to pay a charge equal to the difference between these rates and rates to be announced from time to time by the Bank of China and the Bank of Communications. Similarly an allowance was to be given to exporters. The rates announced were 7d. and US$0.13⅝, which were near the actual market.[10]

The government issued a lengthy list of prohibited imports. For reasons explained in chapter XV, it was deemed unwise to issue such a list earlier. Now it was felt that such action would have psychological value even though the amount of the items imported into the ports of Free China was not relatively very important. The Inspector General of Customs was instructed for the record to apply the restrictions at all ports, but as anticipated he replied that the Japanese would not permit him to do so in the occupied areas.

These measures nominally applied to all China. But the Central Bank office at Shanghai was told confidentially that while importers in the occupied areas could apply, it was not expected that they would receive anything. Statistical studies of Free China's trade had shown that the figures involved were not relatively large, and that it was quite feasible to provide from exports enough to cover such essential imports as could move. But in actual practice the measures led to granting of relatively little exchange in Free China. The committee in charge devised a procedure calculated to discourage imports. In a letter of July 25 to Rogers, I wrote:

I put it squarely up to them as to whether they wished to facilitate imports of needed goods in order to see that the country has them, and at prices that will tend to hold back inflation; or merely to have a nice appearing system under which little business would be done. I suspect that they are afraid of being blamed in case their system actually leads to the paying out of any exchange.

I shall have a talk with Dr. Kung. The Generalissimo's statement . . . indicates that he wishes the system to work.

Also I sense an intention not to make full use of the Customs people. Narrow nationalism seems to be growing and it might well turn anti-foreign. It should be closely watched.

As to exports, all exchange was to be sold to the two banks except that, in view of purchase credits and barter agreements, wood oil, tea, bristles, and mineral products would continue to be handled primarily by government trading organizations.

These trade measures, however, did not help the exchange market at Shanghai. Rather they added to the nervousness, as it was rumored that Shanghai would be excluded from the import exchange system.

As money began trickling into the market, the drain on the Fund began again on June 30. The suspicion that the Fund might be forced to suspend support impaired confidence that the market could be held, and thus promoted the movement to buy exchange. By July 12 the Fund was nearly exhausted, but the Bank of China and Bank of Communications put up £500,000 additional. The managers of the Fund felt that they could obtain a squeeze of speculators if they could hold out to the end of July. Speculators were heavily overbought in foreign currencies, and sales of exchange had taken a large amount of local currency off the market. The managers of the Fund hoped also that China would be able to announce partial resumption of debt service. That would have added to confidence and might have turned the tide. They hoped that the Central Bank would provide additional funds.

Kung was in a difficult position. The Central Bank had only about US$25 million on hand in foreign currencies. The Bank of China and the Bank of Communications could contribute little more. The Japanese were steadily tightening their economic control on occupied areas — on July 1 they announced that from July 10 the puppet bank in North China would take over the foreign exchange proceeds of all exports instead of only 12 major items as before. The using up of the equivalent of about US$43 million in market operations in the first three months of the Anglo-Chinese fund naturally made Kung apprehensive as to future prospects. The British would not put up further funds, negotiations for French aid had stalled,[11] and there was no indication of cash aid from the United States. Kung's decision was that he could provide no further funds for market operations. He had been doubtful about the wisdom of putting up the £500,000 on July 12. He also felt that the worsening of the situation made it impossible to proceed with the debt negotiations. Where could China get the money to pay?

By July 17 the Fund was practically gone. On the 18th it was out of the market. The Fund's approximate net sales by months were: April, £2,000,000; May, £4,600,000; June, £3,100,000; and July, £1,000,000 — total £10,700,000. To the original £10,000,000 the Bank of China had added £300,000 June 28, and, with the Bank of Communications, £500,000 July 12.

With support withdrawn, rates fell on July 18 from the previous level of 6%₁₆d. and US$0.12¾ to 5¼d. and US$0.10¼, a break of about 20 per cent. By August 11 the drop was 50 per cent — to 3¼d. and US$0.06⅝₁₆. *Wei wah* money went to a discount of 20–25 per cent. Chinese foreign currency bonds dropped by about 15 per cent in London.

What was the effect on prices? Representative indexes are shown in Table 28. In the six months to June 1939, the average rise of these indexes

TABLE 28. Indexes of price rise in 1939 (based on January–June 1937 = 100, except that column 5 is based on July 1936–June 1937 = 100)

Year	Retail prices, average in Free China	Shanghai		Chungking	
		Retail	Wholesale	Retail	Wholesale
1938					
December	176	166	135	157	160
1939					
January	190	171	139	165	166
February	195	174	143	171	170
March	202	176	149	173	174
April	209	178	150	179	178
May	217	182	152	187	187
June	226	184	164	191	197
July	236	195	169	201	200
August	246	207	208	207	225
September	276	237	253	237	255
October	288	241	274	249	272
November	303	251	283	269	300
December	323	272	318	282	316

SOURCE: Columns 1, 2, and 4 from Farmers Bank of China; column 3 from China Institute of Economics, with figures converted to the base of January–June 1937 from 1936; column 5 from Nankai University Statistical Service.

was 21.1 per cent. But in the following half year the rise was 58.5 per cent. Wholesale prices in Shanghai, which were the most sensitive to changes in exchange rates, almost doubled. Other factors were involved in the rise: first, the banking crisis brought on by Japanese measures at Tientsin; and, second, outbreak of war in Europe September 1. But there seems no room for doubt that the panicky fall in the exchange value of the currency in July and August caused a shock to confidence that speeded the price rise and caused widespread flight of capital into foreign exchange and goods.

Psychologically China's inability in the summer of 1939 to maintain the value of her money in foreign exchange was a hard blow to morale, and a severe defeat on the financial front. It raised doubts at home and abroad about how long China could hold out. Likewise, it encouraged the Japanese, who had been floundering in a morass of problems despite their military victories and wondering how they could ever end the "China incident." It led them to intensify their currency measures in North China. In July 1939, for the first time *fapi* went to a discount below FRB notes, though it recovered a premium in the fall. Morale in China also was affected by the Anglo-Japanese talks at Tokyo on the Tientsin issues (see chap. XIV). Press reports raised doubts whether the British would feel called upon to yield too much to Japanese pressure, though finally they held out well, considering the difficulties. But, strikingly, China's troubles were paralleled by a slump in Japanese bonds and currency. When Chinese bonds fell by about 15 per cent at London, Japanese foreign issues, which were still receiving service but yet were quoted at about the same level as Chinese bonds, dropped by about the same proportion. Similarly the Japanese military yen slumped along with the Chinese currency, dropping by August 10 to about US$0.07 to 0.08 despite the yen's nominal parity of about US$0.27. These yen increased their premium over Chinese money after the slump. Yet by August 10 that premium at Shanghai was only 10 per cent for small denominations and 20 per cent for large. In Tientsin on August 10 Chinese money had a 1 per cent premium over FRB notes. Despite the shock of the slump in exchange, confidence in the national currency was by no means gone.

Whenever China's currency had a severe setback someone proposed a new currency. This time was no exception, and the thought was to provide a new currency for the occupied areas and thus free the national currency from the influence of wicked men there. Fortunately the serious elements in Chungking realized the nonsense involved in that scheme. But the idea was sufficiently current to lead me to submit a memorandum of August 17 pointing out the obvious weakness of the project, and stressing that the available resources and effort were better used in behalf of the existing currency.

After the Anglo-Chinese Fund's breakdown in July 1939, "Commentator" made some penetrating observations in the *China Mail* of Hong Kong, as reported by *Transocean News Service*, July 27. He said that the Chinese financial authorities have long wished that they could allow convertibility into foreign exchange for "legal purposes" only, because a free market was open to Japan to convert confiscated currency or seized customs receipts. But he said that China's "only available means" to support the currency was to maintain its convertibility in a free market. He went on to say that, "Most of the big demand which made the crisis acute originated from the flight of capital and speculation in Chinese quarters," rather than from Japanese action. China, he believed, should have a greater realization of the threat to survival which aggravation of the financial crisis would present. It was in the interest of the British, American, and French governments, he said, to give larger financial support to China, since a breakdown of China's currency would cause Japan to intensify hostility to the West.

Reviewing the new situation I said in a memorandum of August 17, 1939:

Though the Chinese dollar has suffered a serious shock it is far from lost. If it can be held near (and preferably a bit above) the present level (3½d. and US$0.06½) the more serious consequences will be postponed and can in part be avoided . . .

At or near the present level of exchange it is possible to maintain stability for an extended time with a fund of say £10 to 15 million or say US$50 to 75 million, without any considerable portion passing to Japanese hands. The risk of this latter is far less than the risk of letting the currency go . . .

Exchange can only be held with external support. A new scheme can avoid faults of the former:

A. The fund should be adequate.

B. The Chinese banks should be brought under strict discipline so that money could be more effectively tightened.

C. Chinese and foreign banks should agree to sell exchange only for "legitimate" needs.

D. The Stabilization Committee should not include representatives of any commercial bank.

E. Renewed efforts should be made to obtain the physical setting aside of a fair part of pledged revenues collected in the occupied areas in order to withdraw such funds from the market (but such efforts are not likely to succeed).

F. The Chinese Government should undertake carefully to restrict expenditures for barter and other purchases in the occupied areas; and capital outlays whose benefits are not to be realized at an early date in Government-controlled areas.

G. On such a basis, the risk of incidental benefit to the Japanese need not deter the Chinese Government from support of the open market rate.

H. There should be some form of American-British-French cooperation.

Effective measures are possible only with positive international support involving actual cooperation in practice. Such support obviously raises difficult problems for the friendly Governments, since it would be likely to lead to direct collision with Japan and might precipitate further Japanese action against the western powers, including further action against the concessions. The friendly Governments, however, have already arrived at such a state of conflict with Japan that they have a choice between allowing matters to drift, with the financial breakdown of China which will involve for an indefinite time Japanese control of the financial system centering at Shanghai and expulsion from China of the greater part of western economic and cultural interests; and giving positive aid to China where it is most needed, at present for support of the currency, coupled with measures against Japan such as retaliation for illegal acts already done against their interests.

It was clear that China had used up her resources to such an extent that she could no longer fight on the financial front on the scale of the previous two years without more aid from friendly powers. Accordingly on July 27 the government telegraphed communications to them through the Chinese embassies in London, Paris, and Washington. These telegrams, which I helped to prepare, explained what had happened to the currency, mentioned the trade control measures adopted to shore up the currency in Free China, and pointed out the danger of extreme currency depreciation. The messages said that China no longer had the resources needed to support her currency, and that "China most earnestly requests the friendly foreign governments individually or collectively . . . to aid in maintaining the value of the Chinese dollar in the common interest." The drop in rates, said the message, "discourages imports and outward remittances and stimulates exports," hence further support should not be so costly. China was ready to discuss arrangements to "avoid difficulties encountered in the past."

While these messages implied continuation of the policy of stabilization operations in a free market, other ideas were developing in high quarters. Finance Minister Kung had growing misgivings about that policy. Being understandably worried about the low level to which reserves abroad had fallen, he felt not only that China could not afford to pay out large sums for support of the exchange market at Shanghai, but that currency support helped the enemy and the speculators. On several earlier occasions he had shown a partiality for attempting exchange control. That Generalissimo Chiang was being won over to Kung's views appeared from a speech made public July 24. He stated that the government "has already devised a sounder and more rational method of control" and said:

The government will certainly maintain the value of our national currency, supply foreign exchange for the purpose of legitimate transactions, and take appropriate measures to meet the situation . . . As far as the concessions are concerned, I have never been in favour of indiscriminate supply of foreign exchange to those who do business there, for this exposes our wartime currency to the injurious manoeuvres of enemy-actuated and unprincipled speculators. In the interior, however, the government will unreservedly maintain the stability of the national currency and its exchange rate . . . Likewise the circulation of national currency in the "occupied areas" will unquestionably be maintained . . .
. . . The method of managing foreign exchange in Shanghai in the past was not only of no advantage to Chinese merchants but also tantamount to bolstering up the enemy and puppet currency systems. If no change were made in this matter, we should be furnishing the Japanese with an ever more convenient instrument wherewith to work the destruction of the economic foundation of Resistance.[12]

Nevertheless the Generalissimo, with his characteristic courage and tenacity, went on to say what had happened would not be allowed to impair China's continuing struggle. He called upon the people to redouble their efforts. In a statement of August 12 to the people of Shanghai on the occasion of the second anniversary of the outbreak of fighting there he said:

It must not be forgotten that the fluctuation in the exchange market was entirely caused by the underhand methods of the Japanese and their puppets.[13] It has not affected the position of the legal tender in the least. Inasmuch as the relation between the national currency and foreign exchange entirely concerns foreign trade and inasmuch as the China-at-war is self-sufficient in the fundamentals of livelihood such as food, clothing, and shelter, the fluctuation in the exchange value of the dollar cannot fundamentally affect the national economy; neither can it affect the value of the dollar. Furthermore, the credit of the national currency is built on the entire resources of the country and on the inseparable relation between the citizens and the state. Consequently, the legal tender is backed by unlimited reserves and credit because China has unlimited underground wealth and resources. Now that the people are confident of victory and of a bright national future, there is no reason to expect them to lose confidence in the legal tender just because of a momentary fluctuation in the foreign exchange.[14]

Reflecting these other views, additional messages were sent to London about August 1 about which neither Rogers nor I were consulted, and of which I learned only from publication of the official British records. These messages suggested that in fresh operations either the Fund should operate with more control of transactions or that China supply exchange for needed imports at the rate of 7d. — the market then being but half to two-thirds of that figure. Probably these messages discouraged British aid, for on August 29 Lord Halifax told Ambassador Quo that there was little prospect of further British contribution to the Fund.[15]

In appraising the situation on the eve of World War II, Ambassador Johnson said in a report of August 13, 1939:

Financially the Chinese Government is practically at the end of its domestic financial resources. The small fund advanced by Great Britain for use as a stabilization fund to maintain exchange has been exhausted in the attempt to maintain Chinese currency in the occupied areas. Efforts by the Chinese Ministry of Finance to obtain French and American participation in this method of supporting the Chinese national currency have failed. The result is that the Chinese Government has, to all intents and purposes, abandoned the Chinese dollar in the occupied areas and Chinese economists and financiers are discouraged, feeling that such abandonment will react seriously upon the loyalty of Chinese in the occupied areas, compel them to accept Japanese sponsored currency for their products and thus help to establish that currency upon exchange derived from the sale of Chinese products shipped abroad.

He said, however, that the American notice to Japan on July 26, 1939, of intention to end the commercial treaty of 1911, helped China's morale. That action cleared the way for possible American sanctions against

Japan. Johnson said, in a telegram of August 21, that "economic assistance particularly in the support of Chinese currency would affect powerfully the outcome of the struggle." [16]

Appraising with the benefit of hindsight the Anglo-Chinese stabilization operation of April–July 1939, I said in *China and the Helping Hand:*

. . . it is clear that the Fund should have promptly adjusted rates to a lower level. At lower rates, sale of a given sum of foreign currency would have withdrawn more national currency, for example, a third more at 6d. than at 8d. A readjustment, if not done at the start, in April, should have been done early in May, when the Fund sought and received from the government authority to do it, since by the end of May nearly two-thirds of the Fund's resources had been sold. Of course there were strong objections to either date, and British opinion would have been surprised and critical of a change of rates so early in the game. But the result of postponement proved worse than what would have then happened. At lower levels the eventual cost of support would have been less, and lower rates would have checked imports and brought a better equilibrium in the balance of payments. The American Commercial Attaché at Shanghai reported on August 11 that importers and distributors were uncertain what to do about marking up prices due to the drop of about 50 per cent in exchange, since "a proportionate increase would virtually kill business in most imported commodities." At a level where technical factors were on China's side, the Fund might have retained an effective balance for an extended time and not run out of money after a little over three months. That would have blunted later criticism of the stabilization policy in Chungking. The Fund thus might have kept going until — what could not then have been foreseen — the onset of war in Europe permitted the Fund to recoup much of what it had spent.[17]

Exchange Vicissitudes After Outbreak of World War II

Hitler's march into Poland on September 1, 1939, had prompt financial repercussions upon China. The previous drop of 50 per cent in exchange rates from July 18 to August 11 reflected extreme pessimism. The low level of 3¼d. in terms of sterling was not to be broken decisively for about two years, but that statement must be qualified because at the onset of the European war a few weeks later sterling fell from US$4.68 to under US$4.00. In terms of dollars, the August low of US$0.06⅕₆ was not broken until the spring of 1940; and the rate fell only briefly below US$0.05 in the next two years. Clearly the drop in rates in the summer of 1939 led to undervaluation of China's currency in foreign exchange. At the low of August, exchange was at less than 25 per cent of the 1937 level. But, with average price indexes in August at 2.46 times the prewar level, the buying power of money was 40 to 45 per cent of prewar. This undervaluation was insurance against the likelihood of any considerable sustained further drop in rates for some time. The technical situation favored recovery.

No one, however, could have predicted the spectacular recovery of rates and the rebuilding of the Fund from market purchases of exchange that took place after outbreak of war in Europe, September 1, 1939. Even before fighting began in Europe, people started to repatriate their money to China. They anticipated a fall in the value of sterling and other European monies. Sterling rates fell from an average of US$4.68 in July and US$4.61 in August to about US$4.00 in September. Holders also feared that exchange restrictions might tie up their money abroad indefinitely. Funds were brought back from the United States as well as Europe. Overseas Chinese also sent funds to China, from fear that foreign restrictions would tighten as the war progressed. The trade balance improved. Imports fell off because of restrictions and shortages and the hazards to trade caused by the war at sea. At the same time prices of China's exports tended to rise because of the world-wide demand for goods. Speculators who had overbought in foreign currencies hurried to cover their positions.

On exchange rates in China the impact was sharp. In the first few days of September rates rose by 20 per cent as a result of speculative covering. The Fund would have intervened to check so sharp a rise, but for several days had no means of doing so because of cable censorship at Hong Kong. Rates soon dropped back toward the former level around 3½d. and US$0.06½. But from that point rates began a rise that carried them to 5⅞d. and US$0.09¹¹⁄₁₆ about November 1. These peak rates showed a rise of about 80 per cent for sterling and nearly 55 per cent for dollars from the August lows. Thereafter rates drifted lower, until they leveled out in the spring of 1940. Appendix C, Table 59, and the graph at the front of this book show the course of rates.

These conditions enabled the Fund to recoup much of its loss of exchange and, while doing so, to avoid a disorderly upward movement of rates. The Fund was known to be in the market. Press reports stated that it had bought back £1 million in the first week or two of war, and £2 million by the middle of October, those being guesses by persons close to the market. The guesses were under the actual amount. By the end of 1939 the Fund had restored its holdings to about £4.2 million, thus having bought back about 40 per cent of what it had sold up to the summer of 1939.

There was, however, no assurance that these holdings would enable the Fund to perform its function for an extended time. In the first year of fighting to mid-1938 China covered more than 60 per cent of her costs by noninflationary income. But in 1939 the figure fell to less than a fourth. Note issue grew 40 per cent in 1938 and 86 per cent in 1939, and in those years average prices rose 49 and 83 per cent, respectively. The pace of deterioration was quickening. The rate of rise was steeper after the shock to confidence caused by the exchange slump in the summer, and also because of shortages resulting from the European war. In the exchange market China had a breathing spell, but this could not continue indefinitely.

Pressure on the Fund began at the end of February 1940. The continuing inflation suggested not defending the level too aggressively, and rates at about 4d. and US$0.07 were above the lows of the previous summer. The Fund's managers, however, felt in the spring of 1940 that it was important to avoid weakening of exchange and possible market disorder in view of the impending establishment of the Central China regime under Wang Ching-wei, which the Japanese set up about April 1. Adding to the nervousness were various acts of terrorism in Shanghai, including the kidnaping of a prominent banker and his family, for whose ransom payments of C$2 million in cash and C$3,600,000 in securities were handed over to the Yokohama Specie Bank. Other bankers got threats of like treatment if they did not sign declarations of "voluntary cooperation" with the Japanese. A further factor was the announcement February 6 by the Japanese Finance Minister that the proposed new "Central Government of China" would establish a bank of issue at Shanghai. Also sales were heavy in the middle of March on conclusion of peace between Russia and Finland. Nevertheless the Fund effected a squeeze of speculators at the end of March and bought back a substantial amount of foreign exchange.

Early in April, however, pressure began again after establishment of the puppet regime. Also there were rumors that the Fund was running low on assets. Certain foreign and Chinese banks did not cooperate and lent themselves to speculative operations. The cooperation of both foreign and Chinese banks in support of China's foreign exchange policy left much to be desired at Shanghai, where China lacked jurisdiction and market controls were not feasible. In March 1940 the Chinese government sent communications to the American, British, and French governments urging them to do what they could to keep the respective foreign banks in line. After a visit to Shanghai in February 1940, I commented as follows in a letter of March 14 to Stanley K. Hornbeck of the State Department, with the hope that Washington might do something informally:

It has been necessary to rely upon voluntary cooperation, and this has been made more difficult because of the lack of mutual confidence among the managers of some of the foreign institutions at Shanghai. The feeling has been most noticeable between the American and British banks. Some of the latter have inclined to assume a position of superiority, which is naturally resented; and the American banks feel that there has not been enough mutual consultation. The American banks also resented the unfortunate episode last June at the time when market support was temporarily withdrawn, when one of the control banks bought exchange from the American Express Co. though it knew that support was temporarily withdrawn. The control bank could not properly have stated that the control was not selling, because the control's operations must be kept confidential; but as a matter of ethics it should have declined to buy . . . Besides, a non-control British bank was buying heavily for speculation, for which it was strongly taken to task by London . . .

At times, the banks have intimated that they are entitled to engage in any lawful activities because it is their business to make a profit. In the narrow sense this is perfectly true; but it remains equally true that there is a broad American interest in maintenance of the Chinese currency, which is of vital importance in the situation here. Pursuit of a little more profit by banks, through speculative operations at the expense of the currency, is a shortsighted policy. Regardless of the merits of the charges and countercharges it is clear that the maximum cooperation of all foreign institutions to do what they can to limit their operations to "legitimate" business is in the general interest.

This episode of June 1939, between American and British banks, showed an unsatisfactory aspect of having private banks act officially in the operation, with information not available to competitors.[18] But, as conditions were at this stage, no better arrangement seemed feasible. In May the Chinese government set up an informal Foreign Bankers Consultative Committee at Shanghai. But this led to no very useful result, partly because the arrangements were not well handled on the Chinese side.

The Fund hoped for a squeeze at the end of April. But in the latter part of the month, in spite of the contribution of an additional £500,000 by the Bank of China, the Fund lacked the resources for the aggressive selling of foreign currencies that would have brought off the squeeze. Sensing the situation, speculators changed over their positions from April to May at an interest cost equivalent to 50 per cent per annum. During April there were negotiations to add to the resources for stabilization. But before the arrangements were agreed the Fund once more was about exhausted.

One factor in the month-end difficulties was release of a telegram which the American Information Committee of Shanghai, composed of prominent Americans, sent to Secretary Hull on April 30 appealing for support of China's currency to frustrate Japan's attacks on the currency and bolster China's morale. Press reports of this well-intentioned message stated it was based upon reliable reports that the Fund was nearing exhaustion. So the immediate effect was to add to the pressure.

On May 2 the Fund withdrew support and let the exchange drop. The desirability of a lower level was shown by the continuing rise of prices, as well as the usual spring import demand. The Fund, however, was fairly confident because the large amounts of exchange sold had tightened the market, and it felt that the tightness would prevent runaway rates. In three days to May 4 rates fell by about a fourth to new lows — sterling from about 4¼d. to 3⅟₁₆d., and dollars from about US$0.06 to US$0.04½. But from these levels rates recovered irregularly, for technical reasons described below, and by July were close to the level of April.

MOVES TO OBTAIN MORE FUNDS FOR CURRENCY SUPPORT

In October–November 1939, I visited New York and Washington on Chinese legal business concerning China's attempt, eventually unsuccessful, to recover on a claim against assets in the United States of the former

Russo-Asiatic Bank, which failed in the 1920's while holding Chinese loan funds. I had no negotiating mission, but thought it useful informally to explain China's needs to the State and Treasury Departments in a personal capacity. High officials favored support of China's cause, and on November 12 I wrote to Rogers in China: "Events in Europe and/or Asia are likely to modify opinion toward support of a more active policy."

In a talk with Secretary Hull about the middle of November, I explained that China's most vulnerable spot was probably finance. Time was not all on China's side because of the risk that the "inflationary spiral" would develop at some future time, unless the rate of deterioration of the finances could be checked. In a memorandum of November 16, informally requested by the State Department, I explained that "if a reasonable degree of continuing confidence in the currency can be maintained through avoidance of any unduly acute and sudden rises in the cost of living, the situation can be prolonged for a very considerable period." I stressed that the maintenance of the circulation of the Chinese currency in the occupied areas and foreign concessions was important, both for political reasons and to prevent it from being forced back into the free areas with consequent inflationary effects there. I stated, "China in the fairly near future will need support for the public finances in order to avoid the risk of serious consequences from the wear and tear that are unavoidable as time goes on." Hull was keenly interested and sympathetic but could promise nothing.

Also, in talking with Secretary Morgenthau, I explained China's need for cash funds to maintain an orderly foreign exchange market. He stated his great sympathy for China — which he had manifested in a practical way by buying silver and supporting the grant of credits during the hostilities. But he made it clear that he was not then in position to provide any cash aid. In the Treasury also I discussed with Harry D. White procedure and policy in the event of later American aid. In a memorandum of November 16 I suggested an American-British-Chinese Committee for cooperation in management, not to include any representative of a commercial bank. I pointed out that China's currency was then undervalued and could probably be held for some time; but that it should not be held at a level that would "involve undue cost and encourage an adverse balance of payments." White did not heed this advice when rates were set under the eventual exchange control scheme of 1941, although a joint operating agency was then set up (see chap. XVII).

The State Department asked me to develop further what might be involved in cash support of the Chinese currency, so as to be in position to act as intelligently as possible if this should later become practicable. They wanted to know the approximate cost of currency management during the various phases of China's exchange policy; what resources would be necessary, beside China's available funds, to assure support of the currency at a reasonable level for one or two years; and what means China might have for guarantee of payment. Also they were interested in the relation of the Japanese to the problem, the possibility that they might in the future attack the Chinese currency, and how such action might be counteracted.

In replying, I explained in a full memorandum of December 22 the history of operations to date, including the success of the Bank of China's operation and the reasons for the difficulties met by the Anglo-Chinese Fund in the summer of 1939. Had that Fund been a little larger, it could have held the situation. I thought that the currency could be held at a reasonable level for a year or two with US$75 million, but it would be well to have on call a further US$25 million. As to the Japanese, I felt that they needed for military and civil costs most of the moneys coming into their hands, and that their operations did not pose a serious threat of buying exchange. China's debt was relatively small, and if China "can be reconstructed" repayment should not offer serious difficulty. Finally I stressed that currency support would help to check Japanese moves against the Open Door, as well as strengthen China's resistance.

Records now available show why the State Department had asked me to comment on the subject. Hornbeck and his colleagues gave Hull an important memorandum of December 29 on future action in the Far East. This memorandum said, ". . . at the present time the extension of aid to China appears to hold more of promise toward protecting the interests of this country in the Far East than does the adoption of economic measures against Japan." It urged "further substantial credits to China" by the Export-Import Bank. The memorandum stressed the importance of maintaining the "external and internal value of the currency," the circulation of which in Shanghai and the surrounding enemy-controlled areas was "the main obstacle" to Japanese monopolization of the trade there through creation of puppet currency and introduction of controls of trade and exchange. Collapse of China's currency would be a serious blow to morale. The memorandum recommended that Secretary Hull approach the Secretary of the Treasury about the possibility of seeking approval of Congress for use of perhaps US$50 million of the Stabilization Fund to aid China.[19]

Hull received these recommendations favorably, and on March 6, 1940, Hornbeck called on Morgenthau on his behalf. Hornbeck's memorandum of the talk explained that the State Department

. . . was neither recommending nor asking any course of action but that my mission was purely exploratory. I made mention of the fact that Dr. Arthur Young, when here last fall, had talked to us to the effect that in his estimate China's currency might need support in the spring of 1940; I said that one at least of our officers feels strongly that such will probably be the case; and I said I believed that Dr. Young had talked with Mr. Morgenthau.

Morgenthau said that at that time he had not been in position to give the matter serious consideration, but that the Treasury would go into the subject and was sympathetic to aid to China. Hornbeck then talked with Harry D. White, asking whether use of the Stabilization Fund would be feasible and useful from the standpoint of financial aid to China, and referred to political effect in the Far East. White stated that the Treasury had felt that it should not study the problem unless the State Department so suggested. Hornbeck thought that the Secretary of State would not be ready to commit himself until he learned whether the Treasury thought that action would be practicable. Hornbeck gave White for his information a copy of the memorandum of December 22, 1939, which I had prepared at the request of the Department of State.[20]

At this juncture the Export-Import Bank announced on March 7 a loan of US$20 million to China to finance exports, to be repaid out of shipment of tin and other metals.

On April 11, 1940, Hornbeck wrote to Morgenthau quoting views I had communicated through the embassy at Chungking, to the effect that

. . . although the Chinese Stabilization Fund may be able to cope with the debit balance of payments growing out of the seasonal demand for imports which extends to early summer, the Chinese Stabilization Fund does not possess reserves adequate to protect the currency against such adverse developments as further attacks upon the currency by the Japanese, the creation of a new "central government," serious military reverses, or further repressive action by the Japanese military forces against foreign settlements and concessions in China.[21]

Morgenthau favored aid to China, but wished to provide it by credits for specific purchases rather than for direct currency support. Also he lacked confidence in the Chinese leaders other than K. P. Chen. On April 30 he rejected the State Department's approach, saying that he would need congressional authorization to use the Stabilization Fund to help China and that he did not think it appropriate to seek such permission at that time. His reference was to a letter to Senator Vandenberg made public October 25, 1939, in which he repeated a statement made some time earlier to the Senate Banking and Currency Committee: "Senators, if there is a war in any foreign country, before we would use the Stabilization Fund or any money in the Treasury to assist any country in prosecuting that war, I would come up before the proper committee and ask for guidance." [22]

Morgenthau's rejection coincided with the Fund's withdrawal of support on May 2 because of lack of resources (discussed earlier in this chapter). White's Division of Monetary Research advised the Secretary on May 10 that the break in exchange probably gave the Japanese and their puppet regime "an important victory in the currency war." At this time White and his staff sympathized more than Morgenthau with the State Department's approach.[23]

With the Fund about gone, and foreign currency reserves down to working balances of about US$25 million, the weakness of exchange in the spring of 1940 was disheartening to China. Nevertheless, efforts were made to mobilize further resources in China. On May 6 it was announced that the Fund's resources had been strengthened. The new arrangement (Fund B) was that the Hongkong Bank, the Bank of China, and the Bank of Communications would provide a total sum equivalent to about US$10 million. The Bank of China guaranteed the Hongkong Bank against loss, together with payment of interest at 2¾ per cent per annum on sums that the latter might advance. Fund B was not to operate until the older Fund had been exhausted. A subcommittee of the Hong Kong Committee was to operate Fund B. That Fund, as it turned out, was never used. Its announcement added to confidence, but, more important, events in Europe once more played into the Fund's hands. Hitler's drive into the Low Countries and France brought a fresh repatriation of money to China. These sales of foreign currencies came soon after the Fund's large sales about the first of May had already tightened the market. Rates recovered in the second half of May, and the Fund was able to buy back about £2 million.

Despite the replenishment, resources equivalent to about US$20 million were not enough for facing the dangers ahead. The time had come for a further effort to strengthen China's resources. Generalissimo Chiang was worried, and on May 11 called me in to discuss the problems. I stressed the need for both internal and external measures to deal with the inexorable rise of prices. As to internal measures, I repeated earlier recommendations on fiscal policy and bank credit, and urged measures against hoarding of necessities, and if feasible temporary suspension of conscription during the coming harvest to help to offset poor crops. As to external measures, clearly there was need to add to the funds for currency support. The Generalissimo asked me to draft for him a message to President Roosevelt.

This message, presented May 31, stated that China was taking action to control expenditures and credit, and urged the need of "supporting the Chinese currency by a cash loan or by other effective means which your financial experts may suggest." Chiang was ready to send a representative to negotiate at Washington. Also in a separate message he asked whether China could use in cash, instead of for purchases, part of the credit of US$20 million granted April 20.[24] Chiang, Kung, and I talked with Ambassador Johnson, who strongly supported the proposals. Johnson stated that the United States had "to a large extent benefited by the efforts of others," and said that it seemed to him that "it should be found possible in some way to make a contribution to this existing fund for the purpose of aiding American commerce and objectives in China." He felt that if the currency collapsed the results would be serious.[25]

The State Department was favorable to China's proposal, and on June 3 Hornbeck and his colleagues told Secretary Hull that they felt that the temper of American opinion had changed so that Morgenthau could get congressional authority for currency aid to China. A currency credit, they believed, "would seem to have more to commend it than any other move of this character which we might make"; and they proposed that Hull try to get the President to talk to Morgenthau.[26] Ambassador Hu reported on June 4 that he learned that the President told Hull that the United States should plan more aid to China.

Even though the United States had not replied to China's proposal to send a representative to Washington, T. V. Soong and I left for the United States June 15. He proposed to Morgenthau on July 12 a credit of US$50 million, and also credits for military and other purchases.[27] He gave the Treasury at their request on July 27 a memorandum in support of the currency proposal. The memorandum described stabilization operations to date, the need to continue them, and dealt with the objections raised against the program. The first objection was that the Japanese could acquire foreign exchange in the market. But, it was explained, the indications were that they had not been able to get very much and that whatever they got was a small price to pay for the integrity of the Chinese currency. As to the objection that capital flight was promoted, the memorandum explained that maintenance of stability of rates tended to check such flight. As to the argument that maintenance of exchange encouraged import of nonessentials, the memorandum stated that on the contrary the problem was that essential imports were so heavy owing to the distressed condition of the occupied areas. The memorandum dismissed exchange control as impracticable. It argued strongly for a new Stabilization Fund since the total of only about US$20 million, available in the old Fund plus Fund B, was clearly inadequate. Operation of the proposed new Fund, it was suggested, should be coordinated closely with that of the existing Funds through an American-British-Chinese committee. The memorandum admitted that the Chinese government had not been united on the merits of undertaking stabilization, but stated that the government now accepted the principle. Assistance to China was vitally important, Soong declared, and support of the Chinese currency was the most effective way in which the United States could concretely aid China.

While Soong and I were preparing the memorandum Dr. Ludwig Rajchman, who was then advising Soong on general and political matters, suggested showing the draft to Frederick V. Field. Field was then a writer for communist and communist-front periodicals, although Soong and I did not know it. Rajchman is understood to have been connected with the Communist regime in Poland after 1945, and later with UNICEF. Field read the draft and proposed some changes which were minor but helpful. It is thus possible that valuable inside information about China's finances went to the Chinese communists.[28]

The Treasury meanwhile continued to be skeptical about currency support. A memorandum of July 1, drafted in White's office and which Morgenthau gave the President, referred to Soong's and my previous efforts in behalf of currency support, and stated that Soong would probably seek aid by the American Stabilization Fund. The Treasury felt that such use of that Fund was beyond its scope. Exchange rates could be held for a year or so for US$25–100 million, but "if the United States is willing to extend that much aid, it can be extended for more effective purposes than an attempted stabilization of the currency." The risks, in an area outside China's control, would outweigh the advantages. Reflecting Morgenthau's lack of confidence in Chinese leaders other than Chen, the memorandum indicated doubt about Soong's support of "continued resistance to Japan" — a surprising and quite unwarranted allegation.[29]

The issue of further aid for currency support dragged along through the summer and fall of 1940. The war in Europe was at a critical stage, with Britain's fate in the balance, and American attention was primarily focused there. Japanese threats forced Britain temporarily to close the Burma Road from July to October. Meanwhile, China's situation was worsening, and Generalissimo Chiang pled for further and larger-scale foreign aid as vital to China's continued resistance. Ambassador Johnson eloquently backed his urging. Toward the end of November, the prospective Japanese recognition of the puppet regime of Wang Ching-wei at Nanking posed an additional threat to morale. Roosevelt decided to act at once, Britain followed suit, and finally American and British credits totaling US$100 million and £10 million were announced about December 1. Half of these were for currency support and half for purchases.[30]

The granting of these credits for currency support brought to a head issues that had long been smoldering about monetary policy in China and in particular about exchange control.

The alternative of exchange control

From the start of the war, the use of exchange control was in the background as an alternative to free market operations. Finance Minister Kung never gave more than half-hearted support to the latter policy, and influenced Generalissimo Chiang toward his views.

On May 31, 1940, when Ambassador Hu Shih talked with President Roosevelt about further support for China's currency, Hu reported that the President spoke at length about the German system of control. Kung inquired, and Hu clarified his report by saying that the President had indicated that he realized that such a system was not feasible for China. That exchange of messages led me to submit to Kung on June 4 the following comment on application of exchange control under existing conditions:

(1) Such a control presumes effective jurisdiction throughout the area where the currency circulates. At present, however, China does not have control in the internationally-governed and the occupied areas, and notably in the Shanghai market which is the focus of the forces that determine the exchange value of the Chinese currency. Nine-tenths of the foreign trade passes through these areas, and a very large share of the currency circulates there. In the countries where such controls are feasible all or at least the greater part of exchange transactions are brought under regulation; whereas in China only a very small part could be so regulated.

(2) As of July 1, 1939, the Chinese Government introduced a system of import and export exchange control, similar to systems employed elsewhere. While the procedure does not exclude the occupied areas, it has not in practice applied thereto. The system has since operated on a limited scale, but without any very positive effects. First, the majority of import and export trade is for Government account, i.e., import of gasoline and other essential commodities, and export of wood oil et cetera under the various commodity credit agreements. Second, the procedure for granting import exchange has not been very workable; and the rates at which export exchange has had to be delivered have been so unfavorable as to promote evasion.

(3) The attempt to set up the usual type of exchange control at Shanghai may be considered either: (a) as a complete substitute for the system of exchange support that has obtained since June 1938; or (b) as a supplement to the present system.

In case of (a), the immediate effect would be a very severe shock to confidence in the value of the Chinese dollar, a break in rates and a further sharp rise in the price level. The fact that certain exchange would be allotted to applicants would be almost entirely ignored, as was done a year ago when the system of import and export control effective July 1, 1939, was announced. The general public reaction would be that the Chinese Government had abandoned the dollar to its fate, and the economic and political consequences might even be fatally to weaken Chinese resistance. Course (a) would be suicidal.

Technically the scheme would be impracticable. Exchange would be sold for approved purposes at rates above the market (as is done now in special cases), to meet a small part of the demand. But there is no way in which the control could obtain any considerable current supply of exchange at the official rates, because it could not force people to turn over their exchange to it. And if it bought at market rates a constant and large loss would be incurred. So when the supply of exchange set aside for sale by the control had been sold, there would be no chance to recoup.

In case of (b) all that would be necessary would be to expand operations under the July 1, 1939, procedure, provided that some amendments were made so that the procedure would become more workable. But the advantage of giving exchange at specially favorable rates to certain importers in the occupied areas, e.g. at Shanghai, is doubtful; and the practical problems that would arise would be considerable. Either a limited number of commodities (or of firms) would be specially favored; or a percentage of exchange would be granted, on lines similar to the allotment system in 1938; or there would be some combination of the two, also as in 1938. Very difficult questions likewise would arise with regard to treatment of Japanese interests.

Under present international conditions, an attempt to extend such a system to the occupied areas, even as a supplement to the present system, would seem clearly unwise. It is much better to maintain and strengthen the present system of supporting the exchange market, despite the difficulties encountered.

A few days after this memorandum was presented, T. V. Soong and I left for Washington to seek aid. Before departure Soong got authority to seek funds for market support on the lines of the policy then being followed. He told the American Treasury in a memorandum of July 27, "Hard experience has finally convinced the Government of the necessity of stabilizing the currency, and has demonstrated the impossibility of establishing exchange control in the areas where the Government cannot regulate import and export trade."

The appearance then that the policy of market support had won out proved illusory. The issue between that policy and exchange control was only dormant for the time being. After the United States and Britain granted large credits for currency support, the question arose how China's currency should be supported. Let us now look at the issues in the controversy.

THE CONTROVERSY: PRO'S AND CON'S

Inflation and a falling exchange value of China's currency were inevitable. The problem was how best to control them and lessen their bad effects. First, it was important that the exchange market be orderly. An orderly market with a steady exchange value of the currency sustained confidence in China and her future, made people more ready to accept *fapi*, and thus helped to make possible continuing reliance upon note issue to cover the major part of war costs. On the other hand, disorderly fluctuations of exchange with falling value of the currency led people to spend money faster rather than hold it, and the speeded rate of turn-over magnified the effects of growing note issue. A disorderly market encouraged flight of capital abroad, speculative buying of exchange and commodities, and hoarding.

A steady market encouraged remittances by overseas Chinese. For years these had been a major supply of exchange and a support for the currency. In 1938 they were equal to about US$100 million. Whenever rates varied widely, remittances tended to be held back.

The stabilization operators could step in to meet temporary strains, such as those caused by military defeat, enemy action against the currency, or events abroad. Also the operators could help to even out seasonal fluctuations such as those from reduced exports in the first part of the year. And when rates had to be allowed to drop, they could maintain an orderly market at a new lower level.

Especially important was the fact that maintenance of the value of the currency in a free market checked enemy currency schemes and retarded exploitation of the conquests. On the map Japan had overrun huge parts of China. But actually what Japan had captured were cities along the chief lines of communication and some coastal ports. The vast inland areas away from these cities and ports were mostly held by guerrillas. They used *fapi* and depended largely upon financial support by the Chinese government in *fapi*. Hence exports from this hinterland, even though sold through occupied ports, had to be ultimately paid for in Chinese currency. Maintenance of its value in the free markets of Shanghai and Tientsin thus was closely related to maintaining its use in the adjacent Chinese-controlled regions. That situation forced the Japanese to acquire national currency, often by sale of foreign currencies, in order to pay for Chinese exports. We have seen in a preceding section how maintenance of the currency in a free market in North China proved a strong weapon in holding back the Japanese attempt to substitute, first there and later in Central and South China, new currencies maintained by control of trade and exchange. That policy frustrated enemy schemes of economic exploitation for a good part of the time prior to Pearl Harbor. Moreover, the promotion of trade in terms of *fapi* between the seized ports and the free or occasionally occupied regions helped to supply the hinterland with needed goods, and even with strategic items, since many Japanese and puppet officials were venal. Non-Japanese foreign interests gained, because the policy followed prevented until the Pacific War the extension of Japanese controls of trade and exchange to Central and South China.

Furthermore, if the Japanese had been able to push circulation of their notes successfully, China would have had to spread her inflated note issues over only the shrinking area of Free China; whereas by 1941 something like a third of the national currency circulated in the concessions and the occupied areas. Thus maintenance of the position of national currency in these areas tended to hold back inflation.

Support of China's currency maintained it as a symbol of national unity, and showed to all at home and abroad that China despite Japan's pressure remained a going concern. It bolstered over-all confidence and the will to resist, and politically was of first importance. Externally, currency support enhanced the chances of aid. If demoralized markets for the currency persisted, China's friends might feel that the situation was beyond help from abroad.

There were disadvantages as well. With inflation proceeding inexorably, market support had to be a rear-guard action. It could make the retreat orderly. But it was a series of holding operations, and could not in itself turn the tide of war on the financial front. It was not an easy art to weigh the exchange value of the currency as against its internal buying power, and to retreat to a lower level when pressure became too great. When rates had to be changed the right conjuncture had to be sought, and if there was delay the cost of support at an uneconomic level mounted. Mistakes were unavoidable.

Operations were costly. After a year of fighting, the government and Central Bank could not spare much foreign currency. The Bank of China and Bank of Communications could offer at times some relatively small contributions. But apart from these sources and from foreign aid, the only other support had to come from whatever exchange the Fund's operators could buy skillfully when the market was strong, without disturbing rates. It was hardly surprising that any sizable sales for market support should pain the Finance Minister, and lead him to worry whether foreign currency assets were going down a rat hole.

Apart from cost, far and away the main objection was that market support benefited mostly the enemy and speculators. *Prima facie* it was not unreasonable to query the wisdom of freely selling limited and precious reserves in an enemy-surrounded and notoriously speculative market, Shanghai. What truth was there in the persistent charge that the Japanese were using the free market on a large scale to buy foreign exchange and raid China's precious reserves?[31] At the time we made every effort to find the facts, but of course we had no access to Japan's financial secrets. A member of the Japanese embassy told American Consul Horace H. Smith about May 1, 1939, that since about September 1938, the Yokohama Specie Bank had been converting *fapi* funds (apparently customs collections) into foreign exchange "as rapidly as this could be done without disturbing the market," and because there seemed little likelihood that the customs agreement would be implemented in the near future.

Rogers reported this to me in a letter of April 9, 1939. On the other hand we had evidence that reassured us as to major policy. The above-quoted report from Consul Smith also stated that the Peiping "Provisional Government" and the Nanking "Reformed Government" were receiving substantial customs revenue. On October 26, 1938, Rogers telegraphed to me from Shanghai that "Japanese banks do not seem in," referring to the heavy buying of exchange that accompanied the fall of Hankow and Canton. His judgment is supported by information since available that on October 29, 1938, a shipment of about US$1.6 million of gold was sent from Japan to Shanghai, presumably to buy *fapi* for Japanese requirements.[32] From time to time we had banking reports that Japanese banks were sellers rather than buyers of exchange.

In any event, we knew that in the first ten months to April 1939 the net cost of exchange support had been about US$12 million. That clearly showed that enemy operations, whatever they were, had caused on balance no serious disturbance. For the whole three-year period of exchange support up to the summer of 1941, the best evidence we could get, including the views of the banks operating for the Fund who were close to the market, was that Japanese buying of exchange was not a persisting important factor. The Japanese found it hard to get enough currencies to spend in China. They had to sustain up toward a million troops; and to finance collaborating regimes, business operations, and purchase of goods needed in Japan. To meet these needs they had to rely partly on *fapi*, since support of *fapi* at Shanghai and in North China was making it hard to push the issue of puppet and military yen notes as they wished. They could of course have bought foreign currencies with the *fapi* they got, but these other needs seemed mostly to have priority.

In mid-1939 about half the national currency was circulating and otherwise held in the occupied areas, according to estimates of the American Commercial Attaché at Shanghai. Total issue was C$2,700 million for the government banks, plus about C$500 million for other banks in Free China, a total of about C$3,200 million. FRB issue was FRB$264 million and the attaché estimated Japanese yen and military yen at Y200 million.[33] Thus in China (except Manchuria) the total of enemy-sponsored issues in mid-1939 was perhaps 15 per cent of total circulation, and 30 per cent of circulation in the occupied areas. After Pearl Harbor the Japanese took over the foreign-controlled areas of Shanghai and Tientsin. That made it easier to push puppet notes and military yen. The resulting displacement of *fapi*, forcing it back into Free China, was a factor in the faster pace of inflation after 1941.

Regardless of China's support of Shanghai exchange, the Japanese had the means of getting money by reason of their control of the taxing power (which apart from customs they never succeeded in organizing very effectively). Also they had the means of getting export goods. The strenuous efforts to substitute puppet notes for *fapi* showed that the Japanese authorities did not feel that the *fapi* policy was helping them. Of course Japanese business men, like Chinese and foreigners, benefited from orderly markets. Many civilian Japanese including some officials opposed the Japanese currency moves in China.

Such evidence as I have been able to get from Japanese sources since the war confirms the above analysis. I talked in Tokyo in 1958 with Japanese bankers who operated in China during the war. I could not get concrete figures, which they think no longer exist. Their recollection is that most of the *fapi* obtained went for military and civilian needs in China, rather than for exchange.

What about speculation and capital flight? In a free market with inflation rampant, these were bound to occur. But these evils were less in an orderly market than when rates swung widely without control. Speculators were sometimes squeezed and their operations made costly. They paid an interest cost reflected in the difference between rates for spot and forward exchange, and that cost would be lost to them if rates did not fall. In any event flight of capital and speculation could not be prevented, since, as previously explained, there could have been no effective system of trade and exchange control.

Moreover exchange sales, even for capital flight, tended to check the inflation. Payment for them withdrew money from the market, thus lessening the need for fresh issues. Of course it was hard to defend outright capital flight. Especially was this the case with regard to foreign aid funds, since even incidental benefit to speculators and flighters is politically vulnerable, whatever the absolute benefits. So it had to be argued, rightly I believe, that capital flight was an incidental and admitted evil, greatly offset by other benefits. The situation was made no better because the speculators and flighters were so largely Chinese, including officials, who were sending abroad whatever funds they could convert. Japanese bankers then in China with whom I talked in 1958 in Tokyo thought that the chief buyers in 1938–1941 were Chinese, including insiders. This aspect of the war period was least creditable to China.

I felt at the time and still feel that the advantages in this period of trying to maintain an orderly free exchange market at Shanghai and to hold on at Tientsin far outweighed the disadvantages.[34] But there were three important requisites of maximizing the advantages:

The first was a will on the government's part to sustain the market and follow the policies indicated to that end. Here there were divided counsels and lack of firm action in keeping in hand the military and civil branches and organizing the economy for war. Nevertheless, until the summer of 1941 the government did follow, though not whole-heartedly, the policy of exchange support with periodic adjustment of rates.

The second requisite was possession of sufficient holdings of available foreign currencies. During most of the period China was handicapped by lack of funds. On the whole China provided for exchange support from her relatively meager resources as much as could properly be spared. On some occasions, I feel in retrospect, I pressed too hard for more generous allocations, and with the perspective of 25 years I feel that Minister Kung spared about as much as he reasonably could. The only foreign credit for market operations was the British credit of £5 million in 1939. The United States was never ready to provide any funds for this purpose. If China had had the foreign exchange resources to keep on supporting exchange rates in a free market, though at flexible rates, and buying up a certain amount of *fapi*, such action if coupled with a reasonably tight money policy could have kept inflation within safer limits and maintained a larger degree of confidence. The cost of such a policy, *at proper rates of exchange*, would not have been too great, considering that it might have materially checked the deterioration.

The third requisite, as suggested in the preceding paragraphs, was the adjustment of exchange rates to a lower level from time to time, after price rises showed that the currency had become materially overvalued. Experience shows that some overvaluation and some lag in making adjustments work in favor of retarding inflation. In actual conduct of operations in China in this period, however, there was too much tolerance of overvaluation and too much lag.

Whatever benefit the enemy, speculators, and flighters may have gained was a price that had to be paid for a greater gain, the integrity of China's currency and the checking of inflation. Many of China's high officials never appreciated that, while they were using the printing presses to pour out billions of *fapi* to finance the war, the stabilization operators were steadying the currency and helping to give it a value throughout the whole country so that Chungking could continue to rely heavily upon this method of finance — which it had to do in default of adequate other revenues. *Without the stabilization operations of 1938-1941, there is grave doubt whether China could have avoided financial collapse during the war, perhaps even before Pearl Harbor.*

HOW SHOULD THE NEW CURRENCY CREDITS BE USED?

The American credit of US$50 million announced November 30, 1940, and the British credit of £5 million announced December 10, were hurried gestures designed to sustain China's morale at a critical time. Japan was in course of recognizing the puppet regime at Nanking; and in Europe the issue of survival of the free nations hung in the balance. The American credit was "for purposes of monetary protection and management as between American and Chinese currencies." But Washington had not decided what that meant. London had more definite views on what China's monetary policy should be, but there were delicate questions about the position of sterling.

Moreover, in China there were differences about policy, largely reflecting differences within China's leading family, mainly between Finance Minister Kung and Madame Kung and her brother T. V. Soong who was Finance Minister up to the fall of 1933 and in 1940 was head of the Bank of China. The controversy on the Chinese side involved delicate issues for me in 1938-1941, since as Financial Adviser it was my responsibility to handle stabilization matters at Chungking. My experience and judgment led me to feel that exchange control would be a failure under existing conditions, and that the effort to maintain an orderly free market at Shanghai was the best available policy. Viewing the Chinese government and people as my client, I tried not to be regarded as anybody's "man," and to avoid being embroiled in internal political or personal differences. I feel that on the whole I was able to keep the confidence of both sides, despite numerous arguments. Once Soong told me that he knew I kept his secrets, and that Kung knew also that I kept Kung's.

American-British negotiations about wartime aid delayed the preparation of a Treasury draft of an agreement. It was finally given to Soong on December 26. The draft proposed creating the Stabilization Board of China, with three Chinese members of whom one would be chairman, and with one British and one American member appointed by China upon nomination by the respective governments. Besides the American contribution of US$50 million and the British equivalent to about US$20 million, China would provide a sum eventually set at US$20 million. With the balance remaining in the Anglo-Chinese Fund, the Board's total assets would be about US$100 million. Interest on American funds used would be 1½ per cent per annum. China would repay on 30 days' notice any of these dollars used. The draft stated that the funds would be used "exclusively for the purpose of stabilizing the value of the Chinese *yuan* with respect to the United States dollar and other foreign currencies," but gave no indication of the policy to be followed. Morgenthau, however, put in the draft a provision that China would not draw more than US$5 million monthly (cumulative) without his prior consent. That was to assure that the money would last at least 10 months. Also a draft letter to accompany the agreement proposed that China set up an agency with power and authority to manage and control all the foreign exchange assets of China, other than those held in the stabilization fund. Such agency would have authority to set up a system of exchange control, and to require citizens of China to turn over for fair compensation their foreign exchange assets including gold and silver. China was to undertake that its financial and economic policies would be designed to achieve exchange stabilization. The lending countries could end the agreements upon a month's notice, whereupon repayment by China would become due.

The American draft was subsequently signed with no important change, except removal of the limitation of US$5 million monthly. Soong at once objected to that clause, and Chiang instructed him not to accept it. Apart from the fact that it would have deprived the managers of the Fund of flexibility and tempted speculators to raid the Fund if the limitation became known (as it probably would have), Chiang rejected the idea of such "strings" that would limit China's freedom of action. Finally Morgenthau yielded the point.

While negotiations proceeded, the argument of policy went on within each of the three governments. The issue was between support of *fapi* in a free market and some form of exchange control. Inclined to the former, on the Chinese side, were most financial interests both Chinese and foreign, T. V. Soong, and advisers Young and Rogers; the American State Department; and, in Britain, most but not all of the government. Inclined to exchange control were the American Treasury; in Britain, J. M. Keynes and others, although later they abandoned the idea; and in China Generalissimo Chiang and Finance Minister Kung. It was the American Treasury that carried the greatest weight, because of their provision of the largest part of the money and the dependence on them of Britain as well as China.

The idea of "external exchange control" was proposed to get around China's lack of jurisdiction in the internationally controlled settlements and concessions and the Japanese-occupied areas. The plan was to control the transfer of funds in the United States and Britain. That involved "freezing," and was the plan finally adopted in July 1941. It was clear that such control would be needed if the Japanese made it impossible for a free market to continue at Shanghai, or in case of a Pacific War. The issue was whether to continue meanwhile the *status quo*.

British wartime monetary control of sterling posed difficult technical problems in view of the fact that sterling was mostly inconvertible into dollars, but was freely traded in China, Hong Kong, and Japan. London wanted to avoid leakage of sterling via the uncontrolled area, and thought of arranging payments agreements with both China and Japan. To help in dealing with these problems, Rogers came to Washington at Soong's request, and then went on to London. After discussions there, and exchanges of telegrams between Soong and Rogers, Lord Keynes and others in London who had been seeking some plan for external exchange control for China concurred with the view that Soong, Rogers, and I had held all along, that an attempt to operate such a plan involved serious risks.

In January the State Department thought of telegraphing to Chungking that it felt that China's policy as to foreign exchange was generally right, and that exchange control was not feasible. London was then contemplating a message on those lines. But the American Treasury objected, saying that they wanted to wait the return from China of Laughlin Currie, who was there in February to look into the situation on the ground. In the latter part of 1940 the State Department was in close touch with the British and inclined to a joint effort to devise a plan. But the Treasury was not disposed to work closely in this matter either with the State Department, the British, or China's representatives in Washington. White commented that the problem of China's currency "is the really most difficult monetary job there is in the world, because it is the only country which has so many currencies operating in areas over which it doesn't have complete control." [35] But although Rogers and I had been dealing with the problem for three and a half years, the Treasury people were never ready to discuss with us the issues and what should be done.

Meanwhile Chungking was getting the idea that both the American and British governments favored exchange control. Kung telegraphed to Soong December 9 that he favored action to prevent the enemy and speculators from buying exchange, apportioning it for "legitimate" purposes, and adopting long-term stabilization. The latter foreshadowed the policy, in 1942–1945, of maintaining fixed official rates regardless of rapidly rising prices. On January 27 Chiang told British Ambassador Clark Kerr that he opposed currency support at Shanghai, and Kung amplified the views in a memorandum.[36] London was then busy with working out its policy about China's currency. On February 19 the British embassy told the State and Treasury departments that they had instructed the Ambassador to inform the Generalissimo that,

> We should consider it a fatal mistake to reverse the policy of supporting FA-PI unless and until some other constructive policy can be adopted in its place. We doubt if such constructive policy can comprise exchange control in China, which would not be effectively administered under existing conditions in China.[37]

The memorandum for the Generalissimo stressed the importance of convertibility in a free market, which was a main factor in causing the people to prefer *fapi* to puppet money. To abandon support at Shanghai would encourage the Japanese to push their currencies and gain full economic control of the occupied areas. Any advantages to Japan from the free market, it was argued, were insignificant compared with the advantages to China.

China's reply of February 26 stated that the government "is fully aware of the importance of the Shanghai market," but "must follow a policy in respect to the value of the National Currency (*Fapi*) as a whole." The reply continued:

> It is therefore the intention of the Chinese Government to immediately develop a free exchange market in Chungking, and the Chinese Government feels strongly that all requirements for foreign exchange for legitimate demand should be fully met regardless of location of applicant . . .
>
> There has never been any thought on the part of the Chinese Government to abandon the Shanghai market nor to impair the convertibility of the Chinese Dollar.

In line with the thought that another market should be available, because of the threat to Shanghai, the government announced on March 1 the opening of an exchange market at Chungking.

Because Washington was puzzled about what to do, early in 1941 Laughlin Currie, a presidential assistant, was sent to China to investigate and report. He returned early in March. At Chungking he discussed at length with the

Generalissimo the wisdom of continuing exchange support at Shanghai. He thought that the only weighty advantage of that policy was the need to avoid a huge flow of currency from the occupied areas to Free China. He said:

If the British and American Governments can be persuaded to block private Chinese balances abroad, the chief disadvantage of supporting the black market, namely the opportunity it affords for private capital export, will be removed.

Support of exchange at Shanghai, he said, "should not be discontinued for the present." But because of Shanghai's vulnerability "an open market in exchange should be gradually developed at Chungking" (see above). He favored freezing and would

. . . urge the United States and British Governments to freeze private Chinese balances. Such action would greatly restrict the possibility of further export of Chinese capital. It would permit the foreign exchange resulting from current exports and from remittances of overseas Chinese to be applied exclusively to purchasing needed imports and meeting other expenditures abroad. Finally, such action would pave the way for eventual action by the Chinese Government to compel its nationals to surrender their previously exported capital for fapi.[38]

The term capital flight imports the idea of something wholly evil. But Currie and many others overlooked one effect that capital flight was then having in China. Apart from protecting the flighters' assets, it withdrew *fapi* from the market and tended to check inflation, especially when the exchange market was kept orderly. Also generally overlooked was the fact that surrender of foreign exchange against payment in *fapi* would add to inflation, because such *fapi* would tend to seek refuge in buying commodities for hoarding — a procedure which the government showed little ability or disposition to control. There was, however, in China some realization of this situation — the influential *Ta Kung Pao* of Chungking commented on September 11 that taking over foreign holdings "requires the issue of more bank notes which may in turn usher in vicious inflation" (translated). Eventually no way was found to take over Chinese assets abroad because banks could not be forced to disclose the names of holders.

At length on April 25, 1941, the agreements were signed. The Sino-British agreement paralleled the Sino-American. Neither specified the nature of operations. The Sino-American agreement referred to "the purpose of stabilizing the exchange value of the Chinese yuan with reference to the United States dollar." The Sino-British agreement referred to "the purpose of checking undue fluctuations in the Chinese dollar in relation to sterling."

It soon appeared that Kung and Chiang did not like the terms of the agreements Soong had negotiated. On August 18 A. Manuel Fox, who became the American member of the Stabilization Board, reported this to the Treasury.[39] Two months later the American embassy at Chungking reported that an informant (not this writer) said that Kung objected to "the severity of the language employed," some of which suggested drafting by "some expert mortgage attorney in Washington." He and the Generalissimo were "astounded to learn that Mr. T. V. Soong would sign such an agreement." The British agreement, however, was not so objectionable. They hesitated to send the agreements to the Legislative Yuan for fear it would reject them. Early in 1942 Fox again reported, "Both the Generalissimo and the Kungs have expressed dissatisfaction with the agreement, claiming that the terms were too one-sided and smacked of a colonial agreement." For example, the United States could cancel on one month's notice but China could not.[40] These thoughts forecast China's termination of the agreements in 1944 (see chap. XVIII).

ISSUES AND THEIR REPERCUSSIONS, JUNE 1940 TO JULY 1941

Knowledge that Soong was negotiating for currency support helped to prevent wide movement of exchange rates during the second half of 1940. Roosevelt's announcement on November 30 of the US$50 million credit for "monetary protection and management as between the American and Chinese currencies," followed by the British announcement on December 10 of the currency credit of £5 million, strengthened confidence. But uncertainty about the monetary policy to be followed affected the market. In Shanghai the view spread, by China's unexcelled rumor system, that the fresh funds would be used only in Free China. There was fear that Chungking would cut off Shanghai in retaliation against the new puppet currency slated for issue January 6, 1941. On Sunday December 22, the Chinese press published details of a scheme said to be receiving serious consideration in Chungking. The scheme was to lower exchange rates at Shanghai and redeem the national currency circulating in occupied areas in proposed "War-time exchange certificates," based upon the funds to be received from the United States and England. The certificates were to be available at higher rates of exchange in Free China. The purported object was to check the price rise in the interior and prevent the Japanese and puppets from raiding the exchange reserves.

It was not clear how far the scheme had official support, but its publication was disturbing. Of course any such scheme would have cleared the way for general use of puppet notes in the occupied areas, including purchase of goods which could be shipped abroad to acquire foreign currencies. Its political effects would have been disastrous by attacking the sense of unity which use of national currency promoted all over China. A memorandum of comment from Chinese sources sent to us at Washington at the time said:

The fact that the Japanese have occupied only certain points and lines of communications after more than three years of life and death struggle and have failed completely to consolidate their economic position in these areas, is a credit to the sound war-time currency policy which has been responsible for the continued loyalty and support of the unfortunate millions and for the continued supply and activity of the guerrillas.

Referring to the "disturbing psychological repercussions," it said:

The complete loss of confidence will operate itself in a wild scramble for foreign exchange and in a competitive hoarding of whatever goods that can be had, leading to economic and political consequences far too unpleasant to imagine.

Because of this and other rumors from Chungking the Shanghai exchange market became demoralized on December 23. Rates broke sharply. But the Fund intervened and restored steadiness at the cost of considerable sales of foreign exchange. Besides the rumors as to future policy, China's currency was becoming overvalued in foreign exchange. Soong and I telegraphed our view that in this situation it seemed better not to defend the level too stubbornly. The managers of the Fund replied that they intended to put on a brake if the market tended to run away. But they stated their dilemma. Steady rates, if they became taken for granted, no longer had much positive influence on the general price level. But lowering of rates would tend to provoke faster increase.

The Anglo-Chinese Fund closed 1940 with a balance of nearly £2.5 million, equivalent to about US$10 million. The supplementary Fund B remained unused with its balance equal to about the same total. The net cost of market support in 1940 was about £2 million, or say US$8 million. This included £500,000 which the Bank of China helpfully put up in the spring, when the Fund was under pressure.

In mid-January 1941 China's exchange market again turned weak. In a few days the Fund sold over £1 million. The demand seemed to be mostly to cover imports of rice and cotton, which were scarce because of Japanese seizures of these products in the interior. On January 17 the Fund withdrew support. The drop in rates, however, did not prove serious, being under 10 per cent. There followed an irregular rise toward the former level, without the Fund's intervention. This reflected reluctance to buy foreign currencies, because of talk that the United States might freeze balances held by residents of China. For some time rates stayed on a fairly even keel despite the seasonal import demand and growing inflation.

On March 1 the Ministry of Finance at Chungking announced, as mentioned, that "the Government is intending to increase the facilities of the exchange market in Chungking," and that the Central Bank "has received instructions from the Ministry of Finance and, under the direction and scrutiny thereof, will resume market operations in the buying and selling of foreign exchange to meet all requirements for legitimate purposes." The Bank's instructions said that as from March 3 it was "to *freely* sell foreign exchange *subject to control by the Ministry of Finance*, at your Head Office and branches at prevailing rates" (emphasis added). At Chungking, however, dealings in exchange were relatively small. In the first two months the Central Bank sold less than US$200,000 under the new policy. So the over-all result of Chungking's action was to make little change.

Shanghai's first reaction was to associate the new move with Currie's visit. He had in fact recommended developing an open market in Chungking in view of Shanghai's vulnerability, though he felt that supporting operations at Shanghai should continue for the time being. Shanghai feared that Chungking's announcement presaged abandonment of support of its free market, and rates turned weak. But the Fund sold some foreign currencies at Shanghai after the Chungking announcement, to show an unchanged policy. Also talk of freezing checked any large flight from the currency. From mid-January to mid-March support cost only £200,000 (US$800,000).

While these events were taking place, China's currency was becoming seriously overvalued. In the two years from mid-1939 to mid-1941 prices rose inexorably, but fortunately with no clear tendency to accelerate.[41] Despite the cumulative effect of the rise, exchange rates lagged. The lows in August 1939, before sterling exchange dropped from about US$4.60 to US$4.03½, were 3.22d. and US$0.0625; and in June 1941, 3.28d. and US$0.0534 (see appendix C, Table 59, and the graph at the beginning of the book). At the latter rates, averaging the levels of dollars and sterling, national currency stood at about a fifth of the 1937 level; whereas the buying power of money was down to around a tenth. The steadiness of exchange rates resulted partly from the buoying effect of China's Washington negotiations. Also it resulted partly from the growing fear that freezing might tie up money abroad. This dampened capital flight and brought some repatriation of funds. The Fund had little occasion to operate in the market after January 1941. It was able to hand over to the new Stabilization Board in the summer of 1941 funds equivalent to about US$5 million. Meanwhile in the spring of 1941 Fund B, which had never been used, was wound up.

XVII. FREEZING AND EXCHANGE CONTROL, JULY TO DECEMBER 1941

THE ADOPTION OF FREEZING, JULY 26, 1941

The possibility of freezing Chinese assets in the United States, to help China to get control of them for the war effort, was discussed by the Treasury and State departments as early as May 1940. That was a few weeks after American freezing policy began, with freezing Norwegian and Danish assets on April 10 following Hitler's invasion. Freezing was thereafter extended to other invaded countries, and on June 14, 1941, to Germany and Italy.[1] In May 1940, the State Department felt that the disadvantages of freezing Chinese assets would outweigh the advantages. In December the Treasury proposed freezing *all* foreign funds in the United States. But Secretary Hull objected, seeing that Treasury operation of the controls would inject the Treasury far into handling delicate issues of foreign affairs.[2]

The idea that freezing Chinese funds would permit an exchange control in a way otherwise unattainable introduced a new element into discussion of China's monetary problems, as noted in chapter XVI. Possible freezing of Japanese assets also began to be discussed. After Currie in his report of March 15, 1941, recommended freezing Chinese assets, the issues became active.[3] In a memorandum of March 31, I concluded that a scheme based upon freezing would have serious loopholes and be hard to work well; that it should not be tried unless the situation became "quite untenable"; and that "the question arises whether the hurt done to Japan by restrictions imposed by the United States under a general control would offset the certain injury to China." The State Department apparently shared that view. George Luthringer of the Economic Adviser's Office stated in a memorandum of April 12 that the "disadvantage of freezing Chinese funds at this time would probably exceed the gains," especially if Japanese assets were not frozen at the same time.[4]

When Currie returned from Chungking in March, he brought with him what he described as "a strongly written appeal" from Chiang to Roosevelt urging the freezing of Chinese assets. Roosevelt sent Chiang's letter to the Treasury, which decided to delay consideration until the signing of the stabilization agreements, which took place April 25.[5] Meanwhile, the State Department had no knowledge of the Generalissimo's letter.[6]

The freezing of German and Italian assets on June 14, 1941, brought nearer like action about Japan. The State Department had been holding off, preferring aid to China to sanctions against Japan. But on July 14 Japan forced the Vichy government of France to yield bases in Indochina. This overt aggression, threatening the rest of Southeast Asia, overcame the State Department's reluctance to impose sanctions. Five days later Acting Secretary of State Sumner Welles, following Cabinet approval, asked that the necessary papers be drawn by Monday, July 21, to freeze both Japanese and Chinese assets, to prohibit or restrict imports of silk from Japan, and to restrict export of petroleum products to Japan. On July 21, also, Fox telegraphed to Morgenthau from Hong Kong, just after his visit to Shanghai, "unhesitatingly" recommending "that all Chinese funds in the United States be frozen, that simultaneous action be taken by both the American and British Governments and that a satisfactory organization be established for unfreezing Chinese funds." [7]

Roosevelt announced on July 26 the freezing of both Japanese and Chinese assets in the United States. Executive Order 8389 (as amended) brought under control, as to Japan, all financial and trade transactions with the United States involving Japanese interests. As to China the announcement said:

At the specific request of Generalissimo Chiang Kai-shek and for the purpose of helping the Chinese Government, the President has, at the same time, extended freezing control to Chinese assets in the United States. The administration of the licensing system with respect to Chinese assets will be conducted with a view to strengthening the foreign trade and exchange position of the Chinese Government. The inclusion of China in the Executive Order, in accordance with the wishes of the Chinese Government, is a continuation of this Government's policy of assisting China.

The American action was accompanied by similar action by Britain and The Netherlands. Japan retaliated with its own freezing. Also from August 1 the United States subjected oil exports to Japan to licensing control.

The American policy as to Japanese trade was first intended to be flexible, allowing limited transactions and cutting oil shipments to the level of 1935–1936, except for embargoing high-octane gasoline. But Japan gave no sign of stopping her aggression in Southeast Asia, and the American action became in effect an economic blockade.

As of June 14, 1941, the date of freezing German and Italian assets, a Treasury census showed Chinese assets of US$356 million, Hong Kong assets of US$84 million, and Japanese assets of US$161 million. These figures indicate roughly the amounts frozen six weeks later. Details are given in appendix F, Table 70.

The Treasury administered the freezing through its Foreign Funds Control, and issued General Licenses for trade and other transactions with China. Operations in China were handled through Appointed Banks, originally 14 and later expanded to 26, comprising the chief Chinese and non-Axis foreign banks in China. The banks were later described as "banks cooperating with the Stabilization Board of China and buying and selling foreign exchange with the permission of, and subject to the conditions prescribed by, such Board." These banks were to apply to the Stabilization Board for exchange to cover "legitimate imports" by their clients, and the Board would notify them whether it approved. No exchange was to be used for imports prohibited by China. Merchants receiving exchange from these banks were required to sell to them at official rates the proceeds of their exports, or set them off.[8]

THE STABILIZATION BOARD OF CHINA TAKES OVER

The Stabilization Board, with resources equivalent to nearly US$100 million, was constituted in the summer of 1941 with five members: K. P. Chen, Chairman; Te-mou Hsi of the Central Bank; Tsu-yee Pei of the Bank of China; A. Manuel Fox, nominated by the American Treasury; and Edmund (later Sir Edmund) Hall-Patch, nominated by the British Treasury. Fox died suddenly in Chungking in the spring of 1942. His alternate, William H. Taylor, was captured by the Japanese at Hong Kong, and Fox's work was taken over by Solomon Adler of the Treasury, as acting alternate member. Morgenthau suggested that K. P. Chen be head of the Board, and the Generalissimo and Kung agreed. But apart from any question about Chen personally, whom they might have named in any case, they were unhappy about what they regarded as interference in China's internal affairs. The Secretary-General was Chao-ting Chi, a secretary to Minister Kung. After the communist take-over in 1949, Chi received an important post with the seized Bank of China. During my association with him in 1941–1945 I saw no indication of disloyalty.

On August 6 Finance Minister Kung sent an instruction to the Board which stressed the importance of maintaining confidence in national currency and said:

2. Since in the past the system of government allotment of exchange was not used in the operation of the stabilization fund, the manager of the fund was not able to prevent both the enemy and speculators from getting ahold of China's exchange resources and stop the flight of capital; hence the fluctuations in the exchange market were often great and serious consequences followed.

Attention therefore must now be directed to the objective of preventing flight of capital and making it impossible for the enemy and speculators to get hold of our exchange resources so that the resources of the stabilization fund will not be squandered but will be effectively used.

3. In case when legitimate businessmen, for proper use, request to buy foreign exchange, the request should be carefully considered so that such demand can be properly supplied.

In reporting this to the State Department Ambassador Gauss said: "Apparently Board is to be merely rubber stamp Ministry." [9]

An immediate problem was the setting of official rates. This, as explained in chapter XVI, involved the difficult problem of the existing overvaluation of the currency. In a memorandum of August 9 for Minister Kung I called attention to this overvaluation, urging that the disadvantages of an overvalued currency should be weighed:

A. Sales of exchange for currency stabilization or to support China's public finances . . . will not withdraw as large a sum from the circulation as if the rate of exchange were lower. B. Discouragement of overseas remittances . . . C. Discouragement of exports. D. Increased difficulties to philanthropic and missionary institutions whose income is in foreign currency . . . E. Overvalued exchange tends to cause over-importing and an adverse balance of payments. F. Building up a false and artificial situation, which later will have to be corrected in order to effect a proper economic adjustment between China's economy and the economies of other countries.

This memorandum pointed out that the old official rates of 14½d. and US$0.30 were obsolete, and that the system of adjusting foreign trade rates, which then were 4½d. and US$0.07½, had proved inflexible in practice. The plan whereby the Central Bank was selling exchange for imports since March 1941 based on open market rates had proved more flexible. The memorandum continued:

. . . any rate that long remains fixed will soon be too high, since we must anticipate the continuing fall in the internal value of *fapi* until reconstruction is in sight.

To minimize these disadvantages there must be provision for flexible adjustment of rates. The first official rates could hardly be below the Shanghai market — say 4¾ [cents] and 2⅞ [d.]. Adjustment of rates could be left to the Stabilization Board, which could be guided by the open market as long as this is fairly broad. If and when the market is not a useful guide, the other pertinent considerations, chief of which is the internal price level, can be more relied upon . . .

It is very important to allow a limited free market and to leave an outlet abroad. The damming up of funds within China will intensify the price rise, not only by stopping the offtake of certain amounts of *fapi* but also because the confidence of the public is bound to be affected if they know that they cannot obtain foreign exchange when they want it — even though they may not at the time want it. With all the difficulty which the Government has in getting back *fapi* by taxation and borrowing funds from the public, once *fapi* are put in circulation, it is important to draw upon foreign financial help to sustain the internal value of *fapi* and to use foreign exchange resources as a substitute for *fapi* when practicable, and thus to check the rate of increase of note issue. To do these things some sort of market has to be allowed. Clearly sales by the Stabilization Board are helpful in sucking up *fapi*, if done without too much strengthening of rates.

Effective August 18, 1941, the Stabilization Board announced its official rates, 3⁵⁄₃₂d. and US$0.05⁵⁄₁₆. On August 16 (Saturday) the market had closed at 2²⁷⁄₃₂d. and US$0.04¾. So the official rates were about 10 per cent above the free market, despite the existence of considerable overvaluation. The rates chosen were the average rates of July, a basis said to have been suggested by Harry D. White. Early in July Morganthau had turned over to him full responsibility for handling China stabilization affairs.[10]

EXCHANGE AND TRADE CONTROL, AUGUST TO DECEMBER, 1941

As from August 18 the Board began receiving applications for exchange at official rates. The market's big questions were how the Board would interpret "legitimate imports" and when they would act. The Board set up its main office at Hong Kong, which had communications with both Shanghai and Chungking. With no office yet established at Shanghai, applicants made a trek in force to Hong Kong to press their claims for favorable action. The Board had not prepared for a smooth transition from the old arrangements, and lacked a staff, offices, codes, and above all familiarity with the problems at first hand. It was at once swamped with work, and had to improvise means to deal with it. Hurriedly the Board made arrangements to pass upon a multitude of applications.

The Board at once began to prepare a program of permitted imports. Fox favored encouraging essential imports to Shanghai, because it not only met the needs of Chinese in an important part of the internationally controlled area and adjacent occupied regions, but because part of the goods flowed into Free China. Cochran of the Treasury visited Shanghai in October, and took a similar view. Fox reported to the Treasury in November that much of Shanghai's output reached the interior, including 65 per cent of the textiles, 45 per cent of the knitted goods, and 35 per cent of machines and machine tools. But Chungking did not relish the thought of nourishing that hotbed of speculators, Japanese, and puppets. The People's Political Council criticized the Board in November for support of Shanghai and for staying at Hong Kong rather than Chungking.[11]

Meanwhile Shanghai was becoming more and more critical, despite the Board's generous allotments of exchange. The sale of these allotments tended to tighten the market and to check an immediate large drop in free rates. But soon the free market began to fall away further from the official rates of the Board. By October comments were that the Board's work was a "virtual failure . . . due to the yuan not being stabilized," and that "Shanghai is becoming heartily sick at the mere mention of the name of the Stabilization Board." [12] The next section deals with the repercussions on exchange rates and general prices.

The study of how to control trade was actively pressed both at Chungking and at Hong Kong. The Board when it began operations August 18 had no program of how to restrict unnecessary imports and items that might benefit the enemy. Kung summoned G. E. Gilbert of the Customs, and later his colleague Carl Neprud, to work on this with the Finance Ministry. The first fruit of the studies and of the Board's work at Hong Kong was revision of the prohibited list of imports and preparation of a program of restriction of other items. This enabled the Board to prepare a monthly program of permitted trade. In Chungking we also tried to devise means to stop shipment to China of unwanted items prior to export from the United States, the British Empire, and the Dutch possessions. About two-thirds of China's imports were from those areas. On September 12 Neprud and I proposed to Kung that these countries be asked to allow shipment to China of only items covered by Chinese import licenses, since the Board naturally would provide exchange only for such items. This was taken up with the Board, which did not then act but two months later adopted a similar plan based on proposals by the American Treasury. Meanwhile the British helped on August 23 by placing under license all shipments to China other than via the Burma Road.

The Board sold about US$10 million worth of exchange in the first six weeks, and rejected applications for half as much more. In the first two and a half months from August 18 to the first part of November the Board sold US$13.3 million and £1.87 million — a total equivalent to about US$21 million or say US$8 million monthly. They granted 56 and 78 per cent, respectively, of dollar and sterling applications. By December 1, 1941, the Board had sold about US$15 million and £2 million, a total equivalent to about US$23 million. The dollar sales came out of the Chinese contribution of US$20 million. The American contribution of US$50 million had not been touched. But the sterling sales came from the British contribution of £5 million. Thus for three and a half months the Board's average cost was about US$6.5 million per month. For the future Fox expected a net drain on the Fund of perhaps US$5 million monthly.[13]

In an economy subject to full and efficient controls a good part of the benefits of importing goods at cheap exchange rates could have been passed on to the consumer. The Board made efforts to that end. It required importers at Shanghai to undertake "not to deal with groups whose interests were inimical to China"; to keep prices at a "reasonable level"; and to sell a volume at least equal to that for which exchange was granted.[14] In October the Board issued a statement that a necessary counterpart to its continuing to provide exchange for needed imports into Shanghai was "a loyal effort on the part of the beneficiaries of this exchange to ensure that the imports thus financed are passed into immediate consumption at prices commensurate with their cost on arrival in Shanghai." In November the Shanghai Municipal Council set up controls. They arranged with the Board for regular imports of rice, flour, vegetable oils, and coal, to be sold at controlled prices based on the official rates of exchange. The Board undertook to provide over US$4 million monthly for four months for essential imports to Shanghai. These measures put such fear into hoarders at Shanghai that in November many unloaded stocks and consumers gained. But there were no such effective controls in Free China, the guerrilla regions, and the areas ruled by the Japanese and puppets. So, except for the internationally controlled part of Shanghai and the area immediately tributary thereto, the benefits of cheap exchange went mainly to various dealers and middlemen rather than to the ultimate consumer.

The Board soon realized that it would be hard to get current receipts of foreign currencies to cover much of its sales. Most of the exports from Free China were pledged to pay for the purchase credits granted by the United States, Great Britain, and Russia. The tightening Japanese controls collared most exports from North China, and were extending to the rest of the occupied regions. Overseas Chinese remittances were normally of the order of US$100 million yearly and were still large. But freezing raised doubts about transfer to the beneficiary of foreign currency drafts remitted to China or their proceeds. American freezing controls interfered with remittances to China by Chinese in the United States. And Chinese remitters overseas hesitated to send Chinese currency drafts which would be some time en route, being well aware of the accelerating depreciation of the currency, described in the next section. Yet some remittances continued and Kung told the Board on October 20 that the Central Bank would credit to the Board all such funds that it received.

The basic difficulty of the Board in seeking from the market cover for its sales was, of course, the great overvaluation of *fapi* at the official rates. After the freezing, prices of export goods in China rose rapidly along with other prices. The black market for exchange reflected this rise. Many exporters evaded the control by linking their deals with importers, sometimes with the aid of unappointed banks. Others used exports for flight of capital leaving the proceeds abroad. A leading Shanghai bank reported about November 1 that most exports were being handled in these two ways, and that practically no export exchange was being sold at official rates since prices of export goods were too high to allow this to be done at a profit. On November 30, the Board notified the appointed banks that all applicants for foreign exchange must agree to sell to such banks on the basis of official rates all foreign currencies coming into their hands, on penalty of denying exchange to such applicants. Despite all the Board could do, its total receipts of foreign currencies from exports were only equivalent to US$106,500 from August 18, 1941, to January 12, 1942. That was less than ½ per cent of the Board's total sales in the period. Total exchange acquired by the Board was perhaps 10 per cent of sales.[15]

In Washington the Treasury, like the Board in China, was not happy about the way the plan was working. Besides the troubles described, many of the goods shipped from the United States to occupied China under the

Board's procedures were apparently finding their way to Japan. A memorandum from White to Morgenthau stated:

Repeated instances of Japanese interests in China being the beneficiaries of exports to Shanghai have been received and there is reason to believe that a large percentage of the approximately [US] $10 million worth of goods shipped from the United States to Occupied China since freezing orders were issued, found their way to Japan proper.[16]

This came with strange grace from an agency that had persistently argued that the former policy helped the enemy.

The Treasury proposed that all Sino-American trade be cleared with the Board or its agents. The aim of the plan was to aid China in control of imports and to assure that the proceeds of exports to the United States would go to the Board. This plan also allowed remittances to China (except Manchuria) so long as the dollars remitted were made available to the Board. Exports from China to the United States had to have a consular invoice showing that the proceeds would go to the Board. H. Merle Cochran of the Treasury took the plan to China in October.

Cochran's visit was primarily to help to straighten out the trouble into which the stabilization program had gotten. But it also had some relation to the proposal of a joint American-British economic mission to China, which the Generalissimo suggested to Currie in February. For some months this idea was in abeyance. But in July the British told the State Department that they proposed to send to China Sir Otto Niemeyer, a director of the Bank of England, who had had wide experience in similar missions to other countries. Ambassador Gauss was skeptical about what such a mission could do, and his expectation that it might lead to a request for further large American aid was proven right in November. Washington considered having Fox work with Sir Otto, but the Treasury finally decided to send Cochran. The decision was that Cochran would not formally join in an economic mission, but would informally collaborate with Sir Otto during a brief visit. Sir Otto and Cochran arrived in Hong Kong early in October and shortly afterward went to Chungking. Cochran also visited Shanghai.[17]

The new plan for clearing all trade with the Board or its agents was approved by the Chinese government and the Board, and was announced in China and in Washington on November 12. Great Britain and The Netherlands took similar action at about the same time. Also the authorities of Hong Kong, which had a key position as regards China's currency problems, took action to help the Board control transactions in Chinese currency. They forbade such transactions except at official rates through authorized dealers, in accord with the Board; required registration of large holdings; and restricted import and export of Chinese currency. Hong Kong meanwhile had entered the sterling area on August 2, thus at last becoming tied in with the over-all British system of controls.

Because Pearl Harbor supervened within a month of the new measures there was little time to see their effect. The new controls would have shrunk the black market through control of export to China of unwanted goods from the chief areas of supply abroad. The black market no longer could have been used to buy exchange to pay for such goods. The controls also would have collared the proceeds of overseas Chinese remittances and of such Chinese exports as moved to the controlled countries. But, as inflation went merrily ahead, both remittances and exports at exchange rates yielding a fixed amount of national currency were discouraged. Exports to these countries under this procedure would soon have stopped unless rates were adjusted or means found to subsidize exports. In practice the result of the various measures adopted would have been to divert trade to Japan, and to strengthen Japanese and puppet measures of trade control and the pushing of puppet currency to displace national currency.

REPERCUSSIONS IN CHINA, PRICES, AND THE BLACK MARKET, APRIL TO DECEMBER 1941

In the year prior to freezing on July 26, 1941, the exchange market was strikingly steady, although general prices more than doubled. The steadiness was largely a result of fear of freezing and of possible war in the Pacific. Formerly, said *Finance and Commerce* of Shanghai[18] on April 16, war talk had brought buying of foreign currencies; but now,

Those days are gone. Any indication of further and more serious trouble in the Far East now brings with it a disposition to call money home from its far distant resting places, while the going is good.

Thus a large overvaluation of the currency was building up, presaging difficulties for the future.

Announcement of the stabilization agreements on April 25, 1941, did not greatly stir the market. The opposition in important circles in Chungking, and by the communists, to support of the free market at Shanghai was widely known. But *Finance and Commerce* of May 14 said (page 482) the market reaction was that "it would be exceedingly stupid to bring a huge stabilization fund into being in order to see the dollar grow weaker and weaker." In the issue of May 21 (page 509) it strikingly forecast the course of events:

If the stabilization fund is to be used on the basis of providing official allotments of exchange under permit, it will merely have the effect of establishing a one-way traffic. Merchants, and others with legitimate claims, will apply for exchange at the official rates, but all exchange which has to be sold will naturally be sold on the "black" market, which will continue as before. The stabilization fund will feed and to a certain extent encourage the import trade, but it will do so (if it is active) at the cost of a gradual depletion of its resources.

The writer saw the desirability of keeping exchange sold from "going into undesirable channels," but saw no way to solve the problem.

The London *Economist*, commenting on the situation after conclusion of the stabilization agreements, analyzed the difficulty of China's monetary problems. The *Economist* believed that exchange control, which was hard enough to run in Britain, "would create a nightmare of difficulties in a country such as China." The currency had a strong hold on "the loyalty and confidence of the Chinese population — even in the occupied parts of China"; and its "resistance . . . to the heavy odds against which it has had to contend has been unexpectedly tenacious and successful." The risks of maintaining a free market "must be accepted in the cause of upholding Chinese confidence in the *yuan*," and of forestalling Japanese efforts to oust Chinese currency.[19]

Fox, after arrival in China in June, made statements urging fiscal reforms, but naturally was not in position to say much about monetary policy. His visit to Shanghai about July 1 gave rise to some uncertainty in the market, because of his reported queries as to the effect of withdrawing support. *Finance and Commerce* of July 9 (page 39) quoted the Chinese press as reporting that Fox had "found adequate methods of improving the 'black' foreign exchange market here"; and commented that if so he "is an extremely fast worker," to solve in a week "a problem which has been worrying Shanghai banking circles for years past." There was some suspicion that he had in mind freezing. The Yokohama Specie Bank was reported to have sold US$1.5 million or more, and other banks also were reported to have sold foreign currencies, because of fear of freezing.[20]

The freezing caused nervousness in the exchange market. From a level of $3\frac{1}{4}$d. and US0.05^{11}\!/_{32}$ on July 25, just before the freezing, rates fell about 10 per cent to $2^{27}\!/_{32}$d. and US0.04\frac{3}{4}$ to August 18 when the official rates ($3\frac{5}{32}$d. and US0.05\frac{5}{16}$) took effect. Thereupon the free market came under a ban, and on September 6 publication of rates ceased at the Board's request. The free market was commonly called the black market, but more accurately it was a gray market. The government had no way to stop it in areas outside its control, and in Free China made no serious effort to stop it or to penalize those using it. *Reuter's News Service* reported from Shanghai on August 18, "The official rate applies only to merchants able to obtain permits under the freezing regulations," and, "Bankers said that the black market dealings would continue . . . on account of the fact that many would not be able to obtain permits."

For a time free exchange rates stayed fairly steady around the levels of August 18. The freezing reduced the demand for exchange. Also the Board's sales equivalent to about US$10 million in the first six weeks tightened money. But about the end of September the market broke badly. Linking of export-import deals began through unlicensed banks, thus reducing the supply of exchange offered. The advent of the Tojo government in Japan hurt confidence. Freezing checked the sale of foreign currencies that might have been repatriated because of fear of a general war. From a level of about 2¾d. and US$0.04¾ at the end of September, rates broke to about 1⅞d. and US$0.03¹⁄₁₆ by mid-October. After some recovery they slumped again, to 1⁹⁄₁₆d. and US$0.02⅝ on November 5. Those rates represented a drop of nearly half in a few weeks. The panic amounted almost to a flight from the currency. The disorder worsened when a *United Press* dispatch of October 14 from Washington stated that "informed sources" doubted that the Board would intervene to bolster the currency at Shanghai. There was special demand for dollar notes. These were quoted at 40 to 1 in early November — the method of quotation shifting from the value of C$1 in dollars to so many *fapi* per dollar. Despite various proposals, including mine, the Board declined to operate in the market to steady the rates with a view to stabilizing the situation, but finally acquiesced in the Bank of China supporting *fapi* in the note market at Hong Kong.

Announcement of freezing at once started a spurt of prices. *Reuter's News Service* reported from Shanghai on July 28 that already prices of essential foodstuffs and commodities had risen by 10 to 15 per cent. Those seeking to protect their money against inflation turned from exchange to commodities and real estate. Activity in commodities became feverish. Cotton yarn prices rose 40 per cent at Shanghai in the first two months. Sugar rose 140 per cent at Shanghai in November. There was immediate strong demand to remit funds to the interior for commodity speculation. Within a week the rates for inland remittances from Shanghai to Chungking, which had ruled at over C$1,300 in Chungking funds for C$1,000 at Shanghai, fell to C$1,130 (see appendix C, Table 60). The course of prices in Shanghai and Free China in this period is shown in Table 29.

Allowing for any imperfections in the data and their comparability, it is clear that the rate of price rise became much faster in the second half of 1941. It is not possible, of course, to isolate precisely the factors causing the accelerated rise in this period. Apparently the acceleration was not caused by a growing proportion of governmental expenditures covered by credit. There was no identifiable increase in the proportion of expenditures covered by inflationary credit in the second half of 1941 as compared with 1940.[21] The total circulation of the four government banks in the four half-yearly periods listed in Table 29 grew respectively by 40, 36, 36, and 41 per cent. Certainly the turn-over of money became faster in June–December 1941, reflecting impaired confidence. It seems clear that policy concerning currency and exchange was a major factor in the faster deterioration, although the advent of the Tojo government in Japan, war fears, and the growing scarcity of shipping were also factors affecting the course of prices in this period.

TABLE 29. Indexes of prices, June to December 1941 (prewar = 1), and comparison with preceding rates of rise

				Shanghai	
				Wholesale	
	Average in Free China, retail				China
			Retail,	Central	Institute
	Including	Omitting	Farmers	Bank of	of
Period	Shanghai	Shanghai	Bank index	China index	Economics index
June	10.5	—	7.36	8.91	8.03
July	11.5	—	7.41	9.15	8.40
August	12.6	13.0	8.08	10.1	9.50
September	14.1	14.6	8.89	10.5	10.6
October	16.0	16.5	10.0	12.0	11.8
November	—	18.1	a	14.6	15.1
December	—	19.8	a	16.0	15.6
Percentage increases					
December 1939–June 1940	51		43	49	42
June–December 1940	49		32	42	16
December 1940–June 1941	45		43	36	54
June–December 1941	88[b]		a	79	94

SOURCE: See appendix B, Tables 48 and 57.

[a] Data not available because of the outbreak of the Pacific War.

[b] Omitting Shanghai from the figure for December 1941.

COMPARATIVE COSTS OF THE STABILIZATION
OPERATIONS AND EXCHANGE CONTROL

The exchange control proved a far more costly way to aid China than had the policy of free market support from mid-1938 to mid-1941. The total cost of US$23 million (equivalent) in three and a half months up to Pearl Harbor averaged over US$6 million monthly. Fox's estimate in November of a future net monthly cost of about US$5 million was based upon the expectation of several million monthly from exports and overseas remittances. The fact that the Board only received perhaps 10 per cent of the cost from these sources to December 1, and only US$106,500 from exports up to January 12, 1942, showed that such an estimate was not realistic unless rates of exchange could be kept in harmony with internal prices.[22] How difficult it proved to be to change rates is shown by the fact that the official rates, equivalent to C$18.82 per US$1 from August 18, 1941, and changed to 20 to 1 as of July 10, 1942, were not further changed until February 1946, when the rate became 2,020 to 1. Maintenance of those wartime rates was possible only by virtue of various derogations and exceptions (see chap. XVIII).

The previous stabilization operations covering three years and two months from June 1938, to August 1941, involved the following approximate costs:

	US$, millions (equivalent)
Bank of China net sales June 14, 1939, to April 10, 1939, taken over by the Anglo-Chinese fund	6
Ministry of Finance, allotments of exchange to the market, June 14, 1938, until termination of allotments, June 30, 1939	6
Anglo-Chinese fund, net sales, April 10, 1939, to August 18, 1941, less Bank of China net sales taken over	34
Total	46

These costs averaged about US$1.2 million monthly for the whole period. But the Board, in only three and a half months, spent nearly half what the former operations cost in 38 months. The Board's average monthly net cost of US$5 to 6 million was four to five times the former average figure of US$1.2 million.

APPRAISAL

The consequences of the decision as to how China's currency should be supported went far beyond the field of finance. It was a crucial step in the events that led to Pearl Harbor. In *China and the Helping Hand*, pages 203–205, I thus appraised the interrelated financial and other consequences:

The freezing and resulting controls of trade and foreign exchange had far-reaching effects upon China, Japan, and the Western world. In China the measures were financially upsetting. Withdrawal of support of free market rates hurt confidence in the currency and led to a faster price rise. The measures indeed curtailed speculation in exchange, but diverted speculation to the buying and hoarding of goods — which was more damaging to China. Sales of exchange at the fixed bargain rates gave inordinate profits to importers, who sold the imports mostly at inflated prices. . . . And it was ironic that the creation with American backing of a system of overvalued exchange rates, whose operation was bound to be inflexible, set the scene for the costly financing of American military outlay in China after 1941. China's insistence upon payment in dollars, at the fixed rate of 20 to 1, for steadily depreciating Chinese currency led to serious Sino-American friction during the Pacific War . . .

The main advantage of the measures was to give the American Treasury, and also China's leaders, a superficially plausible defense against the charge that aid to China was being "poured down a rat hole" or going to the enemy (though the working of the new policy probably helped the enemy more than had the former policy). With dollars allocated to pay for specific imports, the "end-use" could be accounted for, and sales of exchange could be shown to be "legitimate."* In view of the financial detriment, an argument in behalf of the new stabilization policy must rest on grounds of American political expediency, as judged by the Treasury. By indicating that it favored exchange control, the Treasury at once gained the support of those leaders in China who already were so inclined. The Treasury thus overrode the views of those operating and supporting the former policy in China and of its backers in the State Department, and the considered financial opinion of the British government.

The freezing of China's assets had no necessary connection with the freezing of Japanese assets. Rather, it was done at China's request, and because it was needed for operation of the plan to control China's exchange. To have frozen Chinese assets alone would have seemed anomalous, coming a few weeks after the freezing of German and Italian assets. Thus the Chinese request and the plan of exchange control for China were intangible elements in the situation that led to the freezing of Japanese assets.

As to the effect of the freezing and trade controls on Japan, the die had been cast by Japan's fateful decision of July 2, 1941, after Hitler's attack on Russia, to embark upon a southward expansion regardless of opposition. The freezing on July 26, Hornbeck has pointed out, "was only one of many indications that we did not intend to withdraw or be ousted."[23] Freezing, however, was done at about the same time by the United States, Britain, and the Netherlands. It thus may well have worked to cause Japan to attack all three of her chief Western opponents at once on December 7/8, 1941. Had Japan proceeded piecemeal against Thailand, the Dutch Indies, and the British colonies, such aggression probably would soon have brought the United States into the war. But not with the promptness and unity and fervor caused by the surprise attack at Pearl Harbor.

On the very eve of Pearl Harbor I summed up my views on the new monetary policy in a letter to Mrs. Young. I said: "If a Pacific war comes, the harm that has been done will be lost sight of; but if there is no war for a few months the effects of the policy are likely to become more clear. The Board have a bear by the tail. They will have to keep on putting out millions of U.S. dollars month after month unless they abandon Shanghai . . . which would be the effect of stopping. We were blamed for the cost of our former policy; but it will be nothing compared with the cost of the new one if there is no war or if Shanghai is not abandoned."[24]

---

* Analogous to the Treasury policy of 1941 is a practice which has been used generally in providing American postwar aid. The United States commonly requires the aided countries to submit for approval import programs, listing the imports from the United States and elsewhere that are to be paid for by aid dollars and sold to raise local currency for the aid programs. To authorize and control this trade, which sometimes is a large part of the aided country's imports, the United States maintains an elaborate and costly organization. These imports are not the goods used for specific aid projects, yet the organization checks their "end-use." The justification put forward for this costly and obstructive procedure, which is inconsistent with American advocacy of free enterprise and the ending of foreign trade and exchange controls, is that some members of Congress and others want that information — which actually has little real importance. See my letter to the New York *Times*, February 5, 1961.

XVIII. MONETARY MANAGEMENT DURING THE PACIFIC WAR: INFLATION, AMERICAN MILITARY OUTLAY, AND THE RATE OF EXCHANGE

The outbreak of the Pacific War brought about a radically different monetary situation. Shanghai's broad market for trade and foreign exchange abruptly ended with Japanese seizure of the international areas on December 8. In Free China it became difficult to brake inflation by supporting the currency in a free market and withdrawing *fapi* by sales of exchange. Apart from the government's unwillingness to continue that policy after August 1941, the freezing made it hard to transfer funds abroad from one owner to another; under exchange control, exchange could be granted only to a limited extent and for approved purposes, while official rates that became more and more overvalued made this a costly use of foreign funds; and in any event the demand for exchange was limited by the tight blockade of trade and the general poverty of underdeveloped Free China.

The Stabilization Board's problems were transformed. Import transactions practically stopped as Japan overran Southeast Asia and cut the Burma Road. The tenuous air route over the Hump, which became China's chief communication with the outside world, had to be used for military items and not for commercial imports. Export trade was mainly in strategic goods bought and shipped by the government to repay credits from the United States, Britain, and Russia. These could move in planes that otherwise would have been almost empty on the return trip to India. Private exports could not move at the official rates, and toward the war's end private exporters were authorized to retain abroad the proceeds from exports, for purchase of essential imports. The meeting of personal needs for foreign currencies came to the fore. Before December 8 the Board was on a one-way street, and faced the exhaustion of its funds within a matter of months if the former rate of use substantially continued, as then seemed likely. Now this problem no longer threatened. Pressure subsided, and the Board was not very busy.

The main exchange market became that for dollar notes. Because of the growing overvaluation of *fapi* at official rates, the American forces from the latter part of 1942 were paid in these notes with the government's acquiescence. Payment in *fapi* obtained at the official rate had fallen increasingly short of what they wanted to spend in China, and payment in dollar notes avoided a serious morale problem. Soon foreign embassies began to sell notes. The supply of dollar notes grew as more and more American forces reached China. Existence of this market troubled the government, and high officials denounced it from time to time. But the transactions were not made illegal, and there was no real effort to suppress them. As the quantity of dollar notes in China grew, there was fear that they might become a general circulating medium and so promote a faster depreciation of *fapi*. Fortunately this did not result. The American notes were largely hoarded. The chief markets were at Kunming and Chungking and rates were highly volatile. The range of rates for these notes was (in C$ per US$1): *1942*, 26 to 50; *1943*, 44 to 98; *1944*, 86 to 680; *1945* (January to August), 470 to 3,250; and *1945* (August to December), 650 to 1,830. Monthly rates are shown in appendix C, Table 59. There was also a considerable market for Indian rupees at Kunming.

There was little trading in drafts or telegraphic transfers. A limited market for dollar drafts developed from June 1944, when the government allowed the United Clearing Board to sell dollars to raise funds for the work of American philanthropic agencies in China. In the first month the rate for the Board's drafts averaged C$82 per US$1, compared with a range of C$185 to 198 for notes. The latter were in greater demand because of ready transferability and use in an emergency. A considerable demand for the drafts gradually developed, and the disparity decreased between their yield and that of dollar notes. After the war the rates for drafts and notes came fairly close together (see appendix C, Table 59).

With China's international economic relations at a minimum, there were two major monetary problems, which were closely related. First was the inexorable inflation, aggravated by American military outlay. Second was the rate of exchange. During the war both problems were especially important in relation to American financial and military aid to China. And the extreme overvaluation of *fapi* which developed was building up difficulties for after the war.

INFLATION AND THE RISK OF MONETARY COLLAPSE

The new situation after 1941, with China at last having strong allies, did not bring any lifting of inflationary pressures. On the contrary, there were reasons to fear greater stress. The tightened blockade further cut the supply of goods, and the psychological effect of this and of early Allied defeats was an important factor affecting prices. The prospect was for greater spending of *fapi* as the war in China was stepped up with American aid. There was little chance of materially changing the dependence upon inflation to finance the greater part of war costs.

The constant danger after 1941 was that inflation would accelerate to the point of collapse. The closest precedents for the situation in China were some of the European inflations, under managed currency systems, at the time of World War I. Of course, the circumstances of inflations vary widely, and each is a separate case. The precedents, for what they were worth, were not encouraging. China already by December 1941 had fought alone for four years and a half, a period longer than the duration of World War I. The prospect was for several more years of fighting. I was acutely aware of the danger, because as the Economic Adviser of the State Department in the 1920's I handled matters concerning the relation of the United States to the European inflations that had gone to the stage of collapse, and I was in Germany at the end of its catastrophic experience. In a memorandum of August 25, 1942, for the Finance Minister, I described what happened under hyperinflation, comparing the inflation in China in 1937–1942 with European inflations of similar length, and setting forth the further course of those inflations that progressed to hyperinflation.[1] While warning of the risk that this might develop in China, I explained, "No one can say whether this stage will be reached in a given situation, or if so when, since financial, economic and international conditions always vary." This memorandum included detailed proposals to check inflation. On several later occasions, I called attention to the grave financial, economic, social, and political dangers that extreme inflation might bring to China and urged detailed recommendations for remedial action (see chap. IV).

There were some plus factors in China which encouraged in 1942 the hope that China could pull through without monetary collapse. The largely rural economy was resilient, and much of it was a subsistence economy. In 1941 China began to raise large revenues in kind, from the system of taxation and borrowing of grains, largely used to feed the army (see chap. III). The public retained a relatively large degree of confidence in the currency, and the rate of rise of prices after four or five years was less than in some previous inflations (see appendix B, Table 58). China's people seemed able to adjust to a medium of exchange that was depreciating on the average by about 10 per cent per month, although money was losing its position as a standard of value for other than relatively short periods. Finally, despite the bad military news for some time after Pearl Harbor, it was clear that China had strong friends and a good hope of being on the winning side.

The American and British credits of US$500 million and £50 million announced early in 1942 were intended mainly to shore up China's weakening structure, and helped to sustain confidence. The preamble of the Sino-American agreement stated as the first aim, "helping China to . . . strengthen its currency, monetary, banking and economic system." Some high Chinese officials viewed the main benefit of the credits as strengthening the currency by putting large reserves behind it. Undoubtedly the presence of reserves had some effect in bolstering confidence, but there is no reason to think that this effect was considerable or lasting. The reserves were primarily needed for postwar readjustments. The use of those large credits to allow the sale in China of dollar-backed securities proved of little benefit (see chap. VI). More important was the sale of gold in 1943–1945, although the American Treasury's foot-dragging under the direction of Harry D. White prevented the benefit to China that otherwise could have been realized (see chap. XIX).

Until 1942 prices rose at an accelerated rate (see appendix B, Table 48, and the graph at the front of the book). But fortunately in 1942–1944 the rate of rise, while still dangerous, tended to stabilize, being 235, 245, and 231 per cent, respectively, in the three years. There were some periods of a few months when the increase was faster, but these were offset by periods of slackening (see appendix B, Table 49). Late in 1944 the pace definitely began to quicken, and the increase in the first eight months of 1945 was 251 per cent. At this stage there was a serious risk of hyperinflation. The war's ending checked what otherwise would have become a very serious situation.

TABLE 30. Indexes of official and market exchange rates compared with indexes of prices, 1937–1945

December	Official rate for US$	Official rates with supplements	Average market exchange rate for US$ (June 1937 = 1)	Average retail prices (January–June 1937 = 1)
1937	1.00	—	1.01	1.18
1938	1.00	—	1.82	1.76
1939	1.00	—	3.98	3.23
1940	1.00	—	5.23	7.24
1941	5.60 (from August 18)	—	8.65 (November)	19.77
1942	5.95 (from July 10)	—	14.5	66.2
1943	5.95	8.93[a]	25	228
1944	5.95	11.90[b]	170	755
1945 (July)	5.95	11.90	870	2,593
1945 (December)	5.95	11.90	392	2,491

SOURCE: Exchange rates are indexes of averages of high and low rates, from the Central Bank; prices are the average retail prices in cities of Free China, from the Farmers Bank. See appendix B, Table 48, and appendix C, Table 59.

[a] The government authorized a 50 per cent exchange supplement as from April 13, 1943, for foreign embassies and consulates and from May 1 extended it to relief and philanthropic agencies. For famine relief contributions the supplement was 100 per cent.

[b] The exchange supplement was generalized at 100 per cent from January 20, 1944.

INFLATION AND OVERVALUATION IN EXCHANGE RATES

In chapter XII I described the foreign exchange policies and the changes in official rates during the war. To summarize for the period of the Pacific War: The official rates set as from August 18, 1941, C$18.82 to US$1, were changed to C$20 to US$1 in July 1942. There were supplements of 50 per cent and 100 per cent in the *fapi* outturn from sale of foreign currencies from April 1943 and January 1944, respectively. These supplements were first restricted but later substantially generalized. They were not considered changes in the official rates.

The measurement of the overvaluation and undervaluation is not easy. Table 30 compares indexes of official and market exchange rates with indexes of prices in China in 1937–1945. And Table 31 shows the purchasing

TABLE 31. Purchasing power parities of Chinese currency and dollars, 1937–1947

	Prices in		Exchange rates[a]		Purchasing power parity[b]		
Period	China	United States	In cents, U.S. currency	In fapi per dollar	In cents, U.S. currency	In fapi per dollar	Coefficient o overvaluation[c]
1937, January–June	1.00	1.00	29.75	3.36	29.75	3.36	—
July	1.04	1.00	29.66	3.37	28.50	3.51	1.04
December	1.18	1.00	29.57	3.38	25.20	3.98	1.17
1938, December	1.76	1.02	16.35	6.12	17.20	5.80	0.95
1939, December	3.23	1.04	7.47	13.4	9.60	10.40	0.78
1940, December	7.24	1.05	5.69	17.6	4.31	23.20	1.32
1941, December	19.77	1.12	3.44	29[d]	1.68	59.50	2.05
1942, December	66.2	1.25	—	49	—	178	3.64
1943, December	228	1.29	—	84	—	595	7.08
1944, December	755	1.32	—	570	—	1,920	3.37
1945, July	2,593	1.34	—	2,925	—	6,500	2.22
1945, December	2,491	1.35	—	1,318	—	6,200	4.70
1946, December	8,613	1.59	—	5,896	—	18,200	3.08
1947, December	129,348	1.74	—	144,287	—	250,000	1.73

SOURCE: For 1937–1945, indexes of average retail prices, of the Farmers Bank (see appendix B, Table 48); for 1946 and 1947, indexes of wholesale prices at Nanking, of the University of Nanking; indexes of American prices from the Bureau of Labor Statistics. Exchange rates are from the Central Bank, except that those for 1946 and 1947 are from Wei-ya Chang, *The Money and Finance of China*, p. 223.
a Rates were quoted in cents U.S. currency per C$1 through 1941, and thereafter in C$ per US$1. The rates are averages of high and low monthly rates in the periods shown.
b The formula for calculating purchasing power parity is:
  1. For rates quoted in cents U.S. currency per C$1:

  Prewar exchange rate $\times$ index of American prices

  Index of Chinese prices
  2. For rates quoted in C$ per US$1:

  Prewar exchange rate $\times$ index of Chinese prices

  Index of American prices
c Ratio of purchasing power parity in Chinese currency per dollar to the then current exchange rate.
d November 1941.

power parities of *fapi* and dollars. The graph at the front of the book shows the rates of rise of prices and exchange rates.

For roughly the first year of the war, *fapi* were overvalued in foreign exchange. From mid-1938 to mid-1940, *fapi* tended to be undervalued most of the time. Thereafter the lag in the movement of exchange rates became conspicuous, when despite constantly rising prices rates of exchange did not change much for a year. This was largely caused by technical factors, especially repatriation of capital and fear of freezing of assets abroad, which took place in July 1941. After outbreak of the Pacific War, when China's economy was cut off from the rest of the world, free market rates depended mainly upon conditions within the country, and were little affected by the play of international economic forces. The degree of over-valuation increased greatly, reaching a peak coefficient of about seven in 1943. The market was narrow and rates for notes fluctuated widely.

Deductions from the calculation of purchasing power parities, such as that in Table 31, have to be qualified. In normal free markets exchange rates tend to reflect relative prices in a given country and abroad. But index numbers of different countries are based upon different items, including local items not entering into foreign trade, and cannot be precisely com-pared; the price levels in the base period may not have been fully adjusted to exchange rates; and exchange rates may be affected for considerable periods by abnormal factors of speculation or capital movement. Further-more, and specially important in this instance, allowance must be made for obstacles to free economic interchange.

With China blockaded, and because of wartime controls of financial transactions and trade, there could be no close tie between *fapi* and foreign currencies. And dollar notes were being pressed on a market where elas-ticity of demand was limited by general lack of purchasing power for them, unfamiliarity with them, and uncertainty as to when they would have much use other than for hoarding. The rapid rise in exchange rates for dollars was most disturbing. But the rise fell far short of keeping pace with the rise of internal prices. The coefficient of overvaluation, per Table 31, was more than seven in 1943, but fell thereafter. If exchange rates in China had risen as much as average prices, allowing for a one-third rise in American prices in the period, rates at the war's end would have been of the order of 6,000 to 1. But in July 1945 they ranged from 2,600 to 3,250 to 1, and in August from 1,100 to 2,750 to 1.

Those who got and held dollars in this period were getting a great bargain. The relative cheapness of dollars put a premium upon flight of capital. Many Chinese of means profited by accumulating dollars at these rates. The total of private Chinese funds held in the United States at the end of the war was about US$300 million, compared with about US$189 million frozen in 1941 (see appendix F, Table 70). Holders could not have so added to funds abroad except at bargain rates.

Maintenance of the official rate became a fetish, to be stubbornly de-fended. The main argument for the policy was that to reduce the parity of *fapi* would spur inflation. But for the officials chiefly concerned there was also involved the issue of face, and a feeling that prestige was gained by stubbornly saying that *fapi* were worth a 20th of a dollar regardless of the reality. Finally, the more the United States and others paid for *fapi*, the greater the reserves China would command for postwar reconstruction and development.

Several times during the war I drew the attention of the Chinese government to the consequences of the extreme overvaluation of *fapi*, but the issues became so sensitive that it was hard to discuss them in high quarters. A memorandum of February 23, 1942, pointed out some of the disadvantages. Sale of the foreign currency loans, then being considered (see chap. VI), would bring in less currency per unit sold. The small equivalent in local currency of interest and principal payments on such loans would discourage subscription. Buyers of exchange especially for personal needs would get an undue advantage. Remittances to China by overseas Chinese and for philanthropic purposes would provide less benefit to China. "In general, overvalued rates build up a false and artificial situation, which later will have to be corrected at great cost in order to place the national economy on a sound basis and to effect a proper adjustment with the economies of other countries." The obtaining of the large American and British credits of 1942, I stated, offered an opportunity to readjust the official rates under favorable conditions and it would be harder to change them later on. Again in a memorandum of November 24, 1942, I brought up the subject with special reference to the bearing of the out-of-line position of official rates upon sale of the U.S. Dollar Savings Certificates and Bonds, and the problem of American army outlay in China. By that time it was pretty clear that there was little chance of changing the official rate, and I recommended meeting the situation by using special rates and subsidies and by acquiescing in use of the free market for exchange. Similar recommendations on later occasions stressed that the further internal and external value of *fapi* get out of line, the more drastic the readjustment that would have to occur.

An exchange supplement of 50 per cent was first granted as from April 13, 1943, for foreign embassies and consulates. It was extended to relief and philanthropic agencies as from May 1, 1943, and a supplement of 100 per cent granted for famine relief contributions. Supplements were generalized at 100 per cent as from January 20, 1944. The supplements fell far short of allowing for the rise of prices. When the first official rate of C$18.82 per dollar was set in August 1941 under the exchange control, it considerably overvalued *fapi*, as we have seen (chap. XVII). The adjustment of about 6 per cent to the round figure of C$20 per dollar as of July 10, 1942, made only a nominal change, since average retail prices meanwhile had risen more than three-fold (see appendix B, Table 48). At the time of the 50 per cent supplement of April 1943, average prices were at nearly eight times the level of August 1941; and about 20 times higher at the time of the 100 per cent supplement in January 1944.

During the war it was common to regard the free market rates for dollars as a correct indication of the true value of *fapi*. The continuing slump in value was something all could see, and at times was panicky and a shock to confidence in the currency. What was not generally realized was that over-all the slump fell far short of measuring the depreciation of *fapi*. The low buying power of dollars in China was particularly noticeable in Shanghai after the end of the war. This situation greatly added to the difficulties of postwar adjustment of the divergent internal and external values of *fapi*. When postwar rates of exchange were set for the purposes of exchange control, they were in line with the free market. But they did not prove to be equilibrium rates, because they put too high a value upon *fapi*, thus making it hard to bring the balance of payments into equilibrium. Also there was a continuing acute rise in prices. The result, complicated by serious difficulties internally and internationally, was a heavy drain of foreign currencies, which it proved impracticable to check by successive devaluations in line with the rise of prices.

THE END OF THE CUSTOMS GOLD UNIT

One unfortunate by-product of the defense of the 20 to 1 rate was the end, for practical purposes, of the customs gold unit (CGU) that had been created in 1930 to preserve the real yield of import duties in the face of the slump of silver.[2] Early in 1942 the question arose of using the stock of about 100 million unissued CGU notes. Only a small part of the original issue had been used, to facilitate customs payments before the war, and the notes had never had general circulation. The reasons for the proposal and just what was proposed were not at first clear.

In a memorandum of March 18 I urged that the CGU notes should not be used unless necessary; that if used they be surcharged with values in national currency as is often done with postage stamps; that the several denominations not be given any consistent relation to the existing currency, to avoid any suggestion that a new currency was being issued; and that it was premature to try to fix any relation between the existing currency and CGU, that is, gold. I said:

> It is desirable to retain the CGU as an already existing unit. When the control of ports is restored to China, it may well be desirable to retain the CGU as an independent unit for duty payment, and also it may even be used for other purposes in the period of reconstruction and while the finances are being stabilized. After the war of 1914–18, France collected customs in terms of gold while its currency was fluctuating in value.

K. K. Kwok and T. M. Hsi of the Central Bank made similar recommendations.

On March 31, 1942, the Ministry of Finance issued the following order to the Customs:

The Customs Gold Unit was defined in January 1930 as containing 60.1866 centigrammes of pure gold, being equivalent to US$0.40 or 19.7265 pence. With a view to meeting actual requirements, it is hereby ruled that beginning from the 1st April 1942, the above-mentioned Customs Gold Unit is to contain 88.8671 centigrammes of pure gold and to be equivalent to legal tender $20.

The American devaluation of 1934 had raised the CGU equivalent from US$0.40 to US$0.6773. The effect of this 1942 measure was to give the CGU a nominal value equal to US$1 after the 20 to 1 rate was set as from July 10, 1942, but actually to tie CGU to *fapi*.

The CGU notes were thereupon issued at the rate of CGU1 for C$20. Thus in effect they became larger denominations of currency. The apparent aim was to bolster the currency by suggesting a fixed link to dollars. But actually issuance of CGU notes caused some disturbance, because of fear that the government was putting out a new currency in place of *fapi*. There were reports of temporary effect in raising prices. Fortunately these difficulties did not become serious. More serious, however, was the practical abolition of a unit that could have been of great value later during currency depreciation, by aiding collection of customs and other revenues in terms of a relatively stable unit. It was discouraging to see an important prewar reform go by the board, in this case quite needlessly.

Financing American military outlay

Both for China and the United States the financing of *fapi* outlay for American military activities in China became a major problem. The American demand for *fapi* grew rapidly after outbreak of the Pacific War: for General Chennault's Flying Tigers, and the Fourteenth Air Force into which they were merged in mid-1942; for Lieutenant General Stilwell and his staff, and American training and support of Chinese troops; for the air route over the "Hump"; and for the B-29 bombing operation from West China. The Americans had to live mostly off the country, since only a limited amount of the most urgent military items could come over the Hump. Provision of *fapi* for these activities I called the "inward transfer problem." This was the reverse of the usual text-book transfer problem involving the finding of foreign currencies. The inward transfer problem also confronted the Allies elsewhere, especially in raising local currencies in the Middle East. Since the war it has become more commonplace, in areas where the need for local currencies, in connection with external aid, is great relative to a country's production and foreign trade, as in South Korea, Laos, and South Vietnam.

With the budget already seriously in deficit, the additional demand for *fapi* for the Americans could be met only by running the printing presses harder. Payment in dollars piling up in the United States could not, in itself, greatly check the deterioration. It was necessary to decide not only how China and the United States should share the costs entailed by American military activity, but also the rate at which dollars would be paid to cover the American share. Underlying was the weighing of military gains expected from a given project against the harm to China from faster inflation. Serious friction resulted from dealing with these issues.

The eventual arrangement for division of costs involved American payment in dollars for building and improving various airports, building roads, and transport. China, as reverse lend-lease, paid for lodging and food for the American forces. Reverse lend-lease is discussed in the next section; and further details of China's payments and advances relating to American military operations are shown in chapter II.[3]

The American forces obtained the *fapi* needed in three ways:

1. From the latter part of 1941 to January 1944, they bought *fapi* from the Central Bank for dollars at the official rate. Payments were US$1,400 in 1941, US$1 million in 1942, US$110 million in 1943, and US$26 million in January 1944. The total was US$137 million.[4]

2. From the fall of 1942, American personnel in China were paid in dollar notes, which they could sell in the free market. Figures of the total thus paid are not available. Through January 1944 it was US$6 million, and thereafter it must have been much more.

3. When early in 1944 the American government balked at paying 20 to 1 for further needs of *fapi*, China made advances of *fapi* pending settlement. The two settlements for outlays of 1944 covered C$15.5 billion for the first three quarters and C$8.0 billion for the last quarter — for which the United States paid US$210 million and US$45 million, respectively. For outlay in 1945 China and the United States agreed in April 1946 that the total figure was C$103.8 billion. The amounts by successive quarters were: C$14.1 billion, C$44.4 billion, C$41.8 billion, and C$3.5 billion. China wanted to obtain dollars for these advances and arranged a negotiating mission at Washington. But finally China's claim was set off against surplus American property handed over to China, by an agreement of August 31, 1946.

So long as American military outlay in China was small, the rising dollar cost of items paid for in *fapi* did not raise an acute issue. But, as outlay grew and prices steadily rose, friction grew over China's insistence on selling *fapi* only at the official rate. On November 2, 1943, I wrote in my diary: "If not fixed up, there will be feeling in the U.S. that the U.S. is being exploited. Many army personnel are sore and go home and talk." On December 27 I noted that it was a common view among GI's that China "made a profit" of the difference between 20 to 1 and the much higher free rate. And on February 18, 1944, I noted, after an effort on behalf of a more conciliatory attitude by China: "It is hard to argue or explain in conflict with views expressed. The point that a cost of US$80 for a simple chair is unreasonable, and greatly hurts China in the U.S., is missed." At this stage, with average prices 25 times those of July 1942 when the rate of 20 to 1 which even then much overvalued *fapi* was fixed, General Clay figured that at 20 to 1 the cost of the American program in China in 1944 might be a billion dollars.[5]

During 1943 discussions went on between the Chinese and American authorities about how to cover American costs in China. There were several proposals: To raise the official rate, for example, from 20 to 1 to 100 to 1; to give the American government a special rate; to sell gold or American currency to raise funds; to arrange advances of Chinese currency as reverse lend-lease or as a loan for later settlement; or some combination of these. But negotiations got nowhere, and meanwhile the problem got worse. Both in China and the United States the American authorities became more and more irritated. Treasury attaché Solomon Adler, telegraphing from Chungking on December 10, 1943, recommended "assuring China of some reasonable accumulations of U.S. dollar resources," but pointed out that costs were 8 to 10 times those for comparable services and facilities in the United States. He favored "lighting a fire under those persons inclined to be evasive and non-cooperative and desirous of continuing to exploit the situation for the purpose of accumulating large reserves of U.S. dollars out of our expenditures for the war effort." The Treasury's reply instructed him to tell Minister Kung that paying 20 to 1 for *fapi* could not be justified, and that they wanted 100 to 1. Ambassador Gauss told the Generalissimo on December 23 that the artificial exchange rate "might cause severe criticism that the American Government and Army are being exploited." The Generalissimo refused to alter the 20 to 1 rate, saying that "both the economic and military collapse of China would result from a failure to support the currency." But he said that Kung could discuss other ways to deal with the problem, such as by reverse lend-lease, which Gauss had suggested.[6]

The issue became more acute because of the plans to mount the B-29 operation at Chengtu in West China, hoping to bomb Japan. Construction of the bases called for huge *fapi* costs. The American authorities estimated total needs of C$24 billion for the four months beginning in February 1944, but fortunately the actual costs were less — that figure approximating total outlay in all of that year. The costs could only be met by flying in additional notes. On January 26 Minister Kung sent word to Morgenthau that the cost of the fields would entail 60 to 150 plane loads of notes, depending upon whether of C$50 or C$20 denomination. Ambassador Clarence E. Gauss after discussion with army HQ, telegraphed to Washington on February 24, 1944, his concern about the serious impact on China of the plans. He asked: "What will be the effect upon China's already tottering economy (and upon internal political situation) of the huge expenditures planned, the doubling of the rate of note issue, the inevitable spiraling of prices, the dislocation of farm labor?" He queried whether the program was necessary and advisable militarily, and wondered whether the United States was ready to take the risks and responsibility. The State and Treasury Departments questioned the wisdom of subjecting China to such a strain, and the War Department reduced some of its plans. Building the bases began in January. Over 300,000 conscripted laborers plus 75,000 contract workers were engaged in the work, largely done by hand.[7]

The fears on economic and financial grounds unhappily were justified, as the note expansion and pressure for supplies had a sharp effect on prices and exchange. At Chengtu the three price indexes showed a rise in February of 33, 34, and 39 per cent over January. The Chengtu cost-of-living index of the University of Nanking almost tripled in the six months to June 1944,

TABLE 32. Course of prices and exchange at the time of building the Chengtu air bases, November 1943 to June 1944

Period	Monthly increase of		Range of rice price per double shih tou (about 15 kg) at Chengtu	Free market average rate for US$ notes at Chungking
	Average retail prices in Free China	Cost of living in Chengtu (per cent)		
1943				
November	9	7	C$300 to 320	82
December	7	15	310 to 430	85
1944				
January	9	23	430 to 700	100[a]
February	16	33	730 to 820	215
March	13	11	720 to 780	247
April	11	15	820 to 1,080	220
May	11	27	1,050 to 1,430[b]	196
June	12	10	—	192

SOURCE: Average prices from the Farmers Bank, Chengtu data from the University of Nanking, and exchange rates from the Central Bank.

[a] Approximate.

[b] May 1 to 16 only.

and rice prices increased about four-fold. Table 32 shows the chief figures for this period. At the same time the market for dollar notes had one of its sharpest rises. From a range of 86 to 110 in January, it rose to 195 February 8 and as high as 245 later in the month. The chief cause was adjustment to the outpouring of notes. But also the speculators acted on rumors that the United States was asking for a rate of 100 to 1. Kung maintained throughout that talk of a 100 to 1 rate was dangerous to confidence. On one April day in Chungking money became so short that the Central Bank had to suspend payments for three hours, until money could be rushed to it from a Chungking printing plant with the ink still fresh. At about the same time in Kweilin the Bank almost ran out of money and had to send a plane urgently to Kunming for more. In my judgment, which is sustained by military analysts writing after the war, any military and other benefits to China from the B-29 operation were much more than offset by the financial damage and the aggravation of inflation. The local grievances caused by the operation helped to soften up the area for later communist penetration. This instance is a warning against imposing too heavy military burdens on less developed countries.

The argument about rates between dollars and *fapi* continued through most of 1944. The American negotiators let matters drag along, because early in the year China began advancing funds in *fapi* subject to later settlement and the Americans wished to avoid an *impasse* that might hold up work on the air bases. The issues came to a head when Minister Kung came to the United States in June for the Bretton Woods conference on postwar monetary plans. Direct talks finally brought a settlement, after hard bargaining. China agreed on November 25 to take US$185 million in full settlement to September 30, besides US$25 million already paid. Payment of US$210 million for costs of C$15.5 billion worked out at a rate of 74 to 1. For the first nine months of 1944 the average market rate was about 200 to 1. But, as shown in Table 31, China's currency was overvalued more than three-fold at the end of 1944 on the basis of current prices and the free market exchange rate. So the deal was highly favorable to China. On January 17, 1945, Morgenthau formally confirmed the arrangement and turned over the money.[8]

For the fourth quarter of 1944 the settlement was easy. China's services to the American forces were on a smaller scale than in the previous quarter, for which the United States paid US$60 million. For costs of about C$8 billion in the fourth quarter the United States paid US$45 million. That worked out at 178 to 1, compared to an average market rate of about 400 to 1, which latter much overvalued *fapi*, as noted above. That was the last cash settlement. China's costs for American account in 1945 were agreed in April 1946 to have been C$103.8 billion, which was set off against surplus American property.[9] Unfortunately disposal of this and other such property acquired after the war was not handled effectively, and China gained little benefit.

Total American payments to acquire *fapi* in 1941–1945 for military operations in China were US$392 million: to buy *fapi* at the official rates through January 1944, US$137 million, plus the sums of US$210 million and US$45 million mentioned above. It is ironic that the system of exchange control, with inevitable overvalued exchange rates for *fapi*, which the Treasury had such a large part in devising in 1941 (see chaps. XVI and XVII), contributed to so much additional cost to the United States.

REVERSE LEND-LEASE

The Lend-Lease Act of March 11, 1941, provided that a country receiving lend-lease aid might reciprocate by "payment or repayment in kind or property, or any other direct or indirect benefit which the President deems satisfactory" (Article 3b). This came to be known as reverse lend-lease. On June 2, 1942, the United States and China signed a mutual aid agreement, Article II of which stated that China "will provide such articles, services, facilities or information as it may be in a position to supply." [10]

In May 1943, the State Department proposed an agreement in broad terms for China to provide materials, services, and Chinese currency to American forces in China. How this would be done was to be worked out in specific agreements. As to finance the United States would pay in dollars at the official rate for an agreed part of the *fapi*, the remainder to be credited as reverse lend-lease.[11] That, however, involved setting a rate of exchange, and negotiations lagged.

Since the latter part of 1942 China had been paying for food and lodging for American forces in China, and also for building and improving various airports. The United States was paying for barracks, administration buildings, and transportation. But the United States undertook to pay in dollars for the Chengtu airfields that were built early in 1944. Up to then China had spent about C$2.5 billion for airfields, and in mid-1944 was paying about C$200 million monthly for food and lodging of American forces. The amount paid by China for this food and lodging in 1945, when prices were much higher, was about C$25 billion.[12]

In a memorandum of November 27, 1943, I urged:

Early conclusion of a reverse lease-lend arrangement to cover American military and other official expenditures in China, on a basis consistent with China's capacity, that would remove the basis for existing criticism of financial transactions between the two Governments. In the long run, such action would strengthen the possibility of China getting in future the financial help that will be needed from the United States . . . At present the British Government, as indicated in its recent announcement, is anxious that the American public realize the extent of reverse lease-lend.

Soon after this the Chinese government indicated readiness to sign the draft agreement. But by then the argument on exchange rates had become hot. Kung was ready to provide *fapi* at 40 to 1 or perhaps in some cases at 60 to 1, the excess over 20 to 1 to be credited as reverse lend-lease. He also was ready to pay for food and lodging of American forces, and for land for airfields. But, since the American government was insisting upon a much better rate of exchange, it did not want to sign an agreement in broad terms until there could be a concrete understanding about how China would implement it. So nothing was done at that time. Again in the spring of 1945 the embassy and military authorities in China wanted to make an agreement. But Washington decided against it, fearing China would want to insist on valuing deliveries at exchange rates out of line with the buying power of *fapi*.[13]

No reverse lend-lease agreement ever was made. Nor was there an agreement on the value to be given to China's deliveries of goods, services, and money. The only specific item, but an important one, which the American records show was US$3,672,000, being the value of P-40 fighter planes which China bought in 1941 for the Flying Tigers, and which were turned over to the United States in 1942 when that group was merged into the 14th Air Force.[14] The American obligation to China was canceled as part of the agreement announced August 31, 1946, whereby China acquired American surplus property in China and the Western Pacific area.[15] The 21st Lend-Lease Report to Congress of September 30, 1945, just after the war ended, said that China's great contribution was its stand against Japan, which "made insignificant any material contribution measured in dollars" (page 31).

THE CURRENCY SQUEEZE: NONMILITARY TRANSACTIONS

The fixed exchange rates caught in a squeeze those who had to sell foreign exchange in connection with nonmilitary activities in China. Correspondingly, it greatly favored those wanting foreign exchange who could buy it for *fapi* at those rates.

Missionary and philanthropic activities in China largely moved headquarters to Free China during the war. Their 1943 remittances to China were thus estimated in the latter part of 1942 by D. W. Edwards, Director for China of United China Relief (in millions of US$): relief funds, 7.7; and missions and education, Protestant, 4.5, Catholic, 2.0; making a total of 14.2. British and Canadian support of relief and education was estimated to be about US$2.7 million (equivalent), making a total of about US$17 million for 1943.

Foreign gifts could not possibly rise to keep pace with the price rise of about 10 per cent monthly while exchange continued at 20 to 1. From many quarters came appeals to the government to do something. Agencies were planning wholesale cuts of staff, or to close. On March 2, 1943, after a visit to Chengtu where various foreign-sponsored educational and missionary activities centered, I recommended urgent action by the government. Some home offices were holding back remittances, awaiting a better rate, and most institutions at Chengtu could not carry on more than two to four months even by using all their reserves. My report said that many were selling furniture, clothing, and other belongings to provide a minimum living:

> The case was cited . . . of a family dependent upon an annual salary of Canadian dollars 1,700 — for which the exchange is about 16.66. At present prices . . . their salary would buy only fuel for minimum heating through the winter and for the kitchen stove — leaving nothing for food and other necessities.

For some time Kung made available governmental contributions to supplement the funds of some activities, but this was not made general.

Finally the government granted from April 13, 1943, an exchange supplement of 50 per cent, as mentioned. This went first to embassies and consulates, but from May 1 was extended to "all cultural, missionary and philanthropic institutions." For famine relief, the supplement was 100 per cent. But the supplement did not apply to nonofficial foreigners until November. There were not relatively many of these, as only a few foreign business men stayed in Free China. The largest group was the press. Those who could get foreign currency notes used the free market. That market was not illegal, but because of my position I did not use it. In December 1943, to meet living costs, I sold for C$110,000 one of my two radios that originally had cost US$225 in 1939. At 20 to 1 the *fapi* price equaled US$5,500! On the same day I paid C$330 (equal to US$16.50) for the labor of half-soling a pair of shoes, using soles I brought from Calcutta.

The supplement was increased to 100 per cent as from January 20, 1944, and generalized. But this was far from enough. The National War Fund in the United States refused in April to make any grant to China unless the situation could be ameliorated. That led to permission to use the free market. After a procedure consistent with the American freezing regulations was devised, the various missionary and philanthropic groups combined to set up the United Clearing Board, to avoid competitive selling. Also the British embassy arranged to sell sterling in the free market for its needs, and this opened the way for others.

Remittances by Chinese abroad to dependents in China gave rise to much controversy. Formerly these remittances were of the order of US$100 million yearly, but with enemy occupation of Southeast Asia, the Dutch East Indies, and the Philippines, the amount was much reduced. Most recipients lived in occupied areas, but often funds could be gotten to them by devious ways. Their need was acute, especially because of the bad economic situation in these areas and in particular in the Canton region. The Bank of China handled much of this business, and pressed for a better rate. This pressure was generally believed to have been a factor in displacement of Soong by Kung as head of that bank. Not until November 1943, was the 50 per cent supplement extended to overseas Chinese remittances, when it was generalized for all foreigners, followed by the generalized 100 per cent supplement in January 1944.

Export trade consisted mostly of strategic goods bought with *fapi* by official Chinese agencies, for shipment to make payments on the purchase credits granted by the United States, Britain, and Russia. For this trade the official rates were no obstacle. But the United States needed from China additional strategic goods, such as tin and tungsten. From 1941 through June 1944, the Foreign Economic Administration paid a high cost to buy them on a 20 to 1 basis, paying out US$48 million.[16] Also they bought some of these goods with gold. Tin cost C$600,000 per ton in Yunnan in April 1944, or at 20 to 1 over 25 times the price in the United States which was US$1,100. The retail price level in Kunming was then 688 times the prewar level, but the free market exchange rate averaging 220 to 1 was about 67 times the prewar level. With such a disparity private exporters could not do business even at free market rates. By regulations of December 16, 1944, the government allowed private exports to retain abroad the proceeds of shipments, to buy goods needed by China.

The almost unbelievable cheapness of dollars at 20 to 1 created difficulties of a different sort for the government *vis-à-vis* those wishing to buy dollars. A strong demand soon developed from business men, students, and others who sought a more comfortable life abroad at small real cost. Many abused the privilege. A number of English language secretaries, including mine, left — despite the shortage of such talent in China. Late in 1943, 660 students qualified to study abroad. Finally the Generalissimo learned of the situation and put a temporary stop to it. Also many doctors went abroad to "study," despite the acute lack of medical facilities in China.

THE END OF THE STABILIZATION BOARD

Possible suspension of the Board's operations was considered early in 1942, after outbreak of the Pacific War practically halted foreign trade with China. But Adler telegraphed to Morgenthau on March 5 that such action would "emphasize China's isolation," and "further weaken American and British prestige and influence here." [17]

In the spring of 1943 the question arose whether to extend the American agreement, which was due to expire June 30. The British agreement had no definite limit, but of course could not continue if the American agreement ended. Kung did not like some of the terms of the American agreement, and at first wanted to wind up the Board. There was some nationalistic opposition in Chungking to this Sino-foreign agency, and some members of the Central Bank felt that the Bank could handle further problems of exchange control, according to the general practice elsewhere. Also there was the view that the American credit of US$50 million fell so short of China's postwar needs, that it would be well to let the agreement lapse and start afresh.

On the American side, the Treasury also inclined to terminate the agreements, influenced by the friction about the 20 to 1 rate and a feeling that membership on the Board associated the American government with rate policy. Britain, on the other hand, felt that the Board could be invaluable in postwar reconstruction, and that continuing contact between China and the American and British governments through the Board was desirable. Chairman K. P. Chen shared that view and on June 29 wrote to Kung that:

> . . . the closest collaboration and co-operation between our country and the United States and Great Britain is a desirable and important factor, particularly for the period of postwar reconstruction. Co-operation, not only between governments in general, but also between Treasuries and Central Banks in particular, was never more desired than it is today. The problems to be faced are so great and so interconnected that . . . a closer association in matters of policy cannot but be of the greatest value. It is also my belief that a Board such as we have today . . . could be developed into an instrument most effectively to further these ends.

I shared these views and urged keeping the Board, but seeking amendments to meet China's minimum objections; also keeping access to the American and British credits, of which only part of the British credit had been used.

The upshot was that Kung became convinced of the wisdom of trying to extend the work of the Board. He instructed his representatives at Washington to try to work out with the Treasury a revised arrangement. Britain supported extension of the Board. But White of the Treasury was opposed to extension, and did not present the issues fairly to the State Department, which Morgenthau directed him to consult. On November 10 the Chinese representatives reported that White had told them that the Treasury preferred to end the agreements because they wished no responsibility for the official rate, wanted to respect China's sovereignty, and felt that the Board was no longer useful. The Chinese representatives pointed out that Britain, as well as China, wanted the Board to remain. White said the United States knew that but that the agreement had expired, and indicated that the British view would not affect the American decision. Meanwhile the British Treasury representative in Washington, Sir David Waley, had presented the British view to White, but had not convinced him. A member of the British embassy took the matter to the State Department on November 25, but the presentation was ineffective and by then the decision had been taken.[18]

Kung decided to drop the matter after receiving the report of November 10 on the Treasury's views. He had really tried for an extension, with revision, even though only luke-warmly in favor of the action. With the ending of the Sino-American agreement, the Sino-British agreement also had to terminate. Britain proposed reconstituting the Hong Kong Committee, which conducted the 1939 stabilization operation, solely to liquidate the complex Sino-British transactions. But China objected, and I noted in my diary that the Generalissimo "hates the whole business." Eventually the Central Bank became the liquidator.

Winding up the American fund involved no problems, since no money was owing to the United States. But early in 1944 the Board held about £2.25 million advanced by the British banks, with Treasury guarantee, under the 1939 agreement; and about £2 million advanced by the British Treasury under the 1941 agreement. The Board drew up its final accounts as of March 31, 1944. China repaid with interest what was due to Britain under the 1941 agreement, mostly by using the afore-mentioned balances. Britain repaid the British banks' subscriptions under the 1939 agreement.[19] Final liquidation of the Board's transactions had to await the war's end, because of claims for the Board's currency which the Japanese seized at Shanghai and Hong Kong in December 1941.

It is unfortunate that the advantage of keeping a framework of international financial cooperation was not presented fully and in time to the highest officers of the American government. We can only speculate about how much the keeping of the Board might have helped to promote China's recovery after the war.

THE ISSUES AND THEIR CONSEQUENCES

The fear of China's leaders that to change to official rate would worsen inflation is understandable. An analysis of the interrelation of prices and exchange rates is contained in chapter XX, which concludes that China's stubborn stand had relatively little effect in checking inflation. But, regardless of the economic consequences, the consequences to American and other foreign opinion and good will were serious indeed. China could well argue that the aggravation of inflation in China resulting from American military activities created a measure of responsibility to help to build up reserves for postwar financial reform. That the United States did by paying US$392 million in connection with American military outlay in China, together with at least US$48 million to buy strategic goods from China — not to speak of the US$500 million credit of 1942. But China should not have thought of trying to cover the output of the printing presses at any fixed rate of exchange. In February 1944 General Stilwell said to me, as I noted in my diary of February 10, "If this keeps up, they will pay us all they owe with a basket of oranges."

In *China and the Helping Hand* I thus appraised the situation:

After China rejected the American proposal of a rate of 100–1, and insisted on not changing the 20–1 rate, the Americans were ready to provide dollars against local currency on terms very favorable to China, but without a rate protruding. China's leaders justified their stubborn position on rates of exchange by Roosevelt's undefined promise to pay the cost of the American military effort in China. They also were influenced strongly by the withdrawal of the promise of an amphibious operation to aid in recovering Burma and above all by the serious worsening of China's internal situation.

Whatever view be taken of China's justification, the long and sometimes bitter haggling left its mark, and a feeling that China was seeking to exploit the United States. China's cause suffered badly with high American officials, with the rank and file of military and civilian personnel in or connected with her war effort in 1943–1945, and with those who had dealings with China in philanthropic and business affairs. China indeed was able to build up large dollar reserves. But in parallel she built up much ill will . . .

Unhappily the split between the United States and China on these issues foreshadowed a breach which continued during the rest of the war and carried over into the postwar period.[20]

XIX. GOLD, GIVEN AND WITHHELD

To add to the war chest, the government collected gold and silver from the people until 1941. China's urgent need for more resources abroad outweighed the fact that payment for the metal added to inflation. There were patriotic drives, and about US$21.5 million of gold and US$9.5 million of silver were collected and exported in the first four years of fighting. Much came in the form of jewelry and ornaments, some of it donated. But in 1941 the need for foreign currencies eased, because of large credits and lend-lease. So the collection of precious metals was relaxed.

ORIGIN OF THE GOLD SALES PROGRAM

Gold sales were first seriously proposed in May 1942, by Hsi Te-mou of the Central Bank. He sought ways to reduce the dependence on printing-press money. Already it seemed that sale of the dollar-backed securities, under the plan adopted, would not bring in much revenue. Sales of gold, he thought, would attract broader buying than sales of securities, given the traditional fondness of China's people for gold. He proposed selling first about 44,000 ounces (US$1.5 million) held by the Bank, and importing more gold against the US$500 million credit.

In the previous year the rise of prices had quickened, and it was vital to make every effort to check inflation. I supported the proposal to sell gold. The government was favorably inclined, but did not act at once. On December 4, 1942, I pressed the matter, pointing out that people would regard import of gold as adding strength to the currency. Distribution of gold to the public was unorthodox. It would be better to sell goods, but their import was not then feasible. Hoarding of gold was less bad than hoarding of goods. Gold sales would promote speculation in gold — which in former days had been notorious at Shanghai. Some of the gold might get to the enemy and the puppets, but this I did not consider too serious since Free China would get value from it, largely goods. The government of course would need to have enough gold on hand or available to control the price. On balance I recommended proceeding with the scheme as a wartime expedient.

Late in 1942 Kung instructed the ambassador at Washington to begin

Note: This chapter is substantially the same as chapter XVII of *China and the Helping Hand, 1937–1945.*

negotiations to acquire gold for China. This led to an extensive program of domestic gold sales.[1]

THE TREASURY AGREES TO SUPPLY GOLD

In response to the Chinese ambassador's approach, the Treasury agreed in December 1942 to provide US$20 million of gold, to be charged against the US$500 million credit. This gold was earmarked in the Federal Reserve Bank of New York. Shipment to China, however, was delayed. There were difficult questions about transport and insurance. Kung had been doubtful about how much gold could be sold, and did not actively press the matter. The Treasury for its part doubted whether sale of the gold would help much.[2]

Early in July 1943, Kung advised Morgenthau that inflation was growing in China, and that American needs for airfields and other facilities added greatly to China's expenditures. Kung thought it desirable to sell gold actively, and asked that US$200 million of the credit be used for shipment of gold to China. He stated that Madame Chiang, at the time of her visit to Washington in June 1943, obtained the approval in principle of Roosevelt and Morgenthau for the use of US$200 million of the credit to supply gold.

Morgenthau replied that the Treasury agreed in principle, but had previously made it clear to China that it acquiesced because the Chinese government felt that the sale of gold to the public would help China to fight inflation and hoarding; and that such use of gold involved great costs and difficulties and the decision was primarily China's responsibility. Also, Morgenthau stated, China would be sacrificing assets which could be used for postwar reconstruction.

In response to a formal request by the ambassador, Morgenthau on July 27 agreed to provide US$200 million immediately for purchase of gold. The reply stated:

In order to avoid unnecessary raising of funds by the United States Treasury, it is suggested that transfers from the credit of the Chinese Government for the purchase of gold be made at such time and in such amounts as are allowed by existing facilities for the transportation to China of the equivalent amount of gold. Since it is intended that this gold will be sent to China for sale to the public, this procedure should not interfere with the program outlined in your message of July 23, 1943.

On receipt of requests from the Government of China that a specific amount should be transferred from the credit of the Government of China on the books of the Treasury and be used for the purchase of gold, the necessary action will be taken to consummate these requests.[3]

In reply Kung expressed appreciation and said he would "request transfers in specific amounts having regard to need for the gold." [4]

Adler telegraphed from Chungking July 17 that an effective scheme to sell gold in China with adequate controls "would undoubtedly have beneficial effects in checking inflation." He hoped it could be done through the Stabilization Board. But unfortunately nothing came of this idea.[5]

The Treasury clearly recognized the desirability in principle of using gold to raise funds for war purposes as a noninflationary expedient. A memorandum of September 22, from White to Morgenthau, stated that the Treasury expected to sell about US$20 million of gold in the next three months in the Middle East and India to cover local war costs of the United States, and that the amount of such sales was likely to grow. In the same memorandum White informed the Secretary: "China has asked us for $50 million worth of gold in accordance with your promise to make the gold available. I have taken the position that the gold is available as rapidly as they can ship it." [6]

A memorandum prepared by White recorded his conversation with Morgenthau on September 29, as follows:

> I said I thought that we ought to be tough with the Chinese on the question of earmarking $200 million of gold for gold sales which they could not make before the gold could be shipped to them. The Secretary agreed. He said he thinks that we should be tough in this matter and he told me to go ahead and let them have the gold only as rapidly as it could be shipped and sold in China.[7]

In the fall of 1943 there was discussion of possible sale of gold in China by the United States to meet American expenditures and thus overcome the disadvantages of the artificial official rate of exchange of C$20 for US$1. Kung had no objection in principle, but thought the plan inadvisable because other governments would be likely to claim the same privilege.

Negotiations with China's representatives in Washington, T. M. Hsi and T. L. Soong, went forward. There was no urgency about shipping gold against the US$200 million commitment. The above-mentioned US$20 million of gold earmarked in New York was available, and the Central Bank had a stock in Chungking from which sales could begin. On November 10 these representatives telegraphed to Kung:

> Dr. Harry White assured that Treasury feel duty bound by promise to supply China with gold according to original understanding but explained difficulty in making big transfer of gold because it might cause questioning in Congress and require borrowing from market. Dr. White also stated there is no difference whether our gold is on the book of the Treasury or earmark with Federal Reserve Bank and *assured whenever we need Treasury can make transfer at any time* (emphasis added). We expressed our appreciation of their position and asked whether transfer in four equal lots of 50 million will be feasible as 20 million being our reserve. However Dr. White suggested maintaining all the time a revolving amount of 10 million gold in account with Federal Reserve Bank available for shipment. This means if our gold in Federal Reserve Bank falls below 10 million Treasury would make up that amount.

I urged agreeing to the revolving fund of US$10 million of gold, and accommodating the Treasury by not asking them to provide gold "any more rapidly than it is actually needed for use in China" (memorandum of November 26). Otherwise they would have had to borrow the money and pay interest. But the proposal lapsed. Minister Kung hoped for larger transfers, because of his belief in the psychological value of holding larger reserves. In the light of later events it is unfortunate that China did not agree to the revolving fund, and take advantage of the fact that White was then ready to facilitate shipments *pari passu* with actual needs. Such a revolving fund would have provided the gold as fast as it could have been sold, and could have obviated later troubles if the gold had been transported to China as needed.

CHINA BEGINS TO SELL GOLD

Gold sales began in the fall of 1943, by the Farmers Bank on behalf of the Central Bank. These sales were from the Chungking stock of about US$1.5 million. In reserve was the US$20 million earmarked in New York nine months earlier, which was beginning to be forwarded to China, and the US$200 million which the Treasury promised to supply. The first US$1 million — a million dollars of gold weighs about a ton — left New York September 28. It went by rail to Miami and thence by air through South America, Africa, the Middle East, and India to Chungking. It arrived there November 19. By the end of 1943 arrivals totaled US$10.5 million. These shipments were from the US$20 million of earmarked gold.

The Farmers Bank managed its sales so as to avoid disrupting gold prices. Sometimes the bank bought to steady the market. Total sales through February 1944, after which the Central Bank took over the selling, were only a little over US$1 million. Some had the idea that mere presence of gold in China as reserve would be a major factor in checking inflation. On November 11, 1943, I wrote in my diary: "Fear China may not make enough use of the gold, but will sit with it instead — in which case effect will be small in checking inflation." But on February 24, 1944, I noted that instructions had been given "to sell gold more actively after having held back."

Public knowledge in China of the arrangements to get gold had a helpful effect. A telegram of Adler to the Treasury November 30 said the rate of price rise had slackened for various reasons including an adequate harvest, good war news from other theaters, and the psychological effect of announcing China's gold purchase.[8] Kung telegraphed to Morgenthau the following message of December 14:

You will be pleased to hear that the recent gold shipment is one of the outstanding factors contributing to the strengthening of *fapi*, because people believe that the arrival of gold has increased the much needed reserve of our currency, thereby influencing the stability of prices. The action of the United States Government re-affirms to the Chinese people that, despite difficulties arising from the blockade and the cumulative effects of over six years of war against the invasion, China has a powerful friend desirous of strengthening China's economy as conditions permit.[9]

The Treasury in this period was giving effect to Secretary Morgenthau's decision to "let them have the gold only as rapidly as it could be shipped and sold in China." Their reluctance about gold for China was shown by a statement by Morgenthau in a conference with his staff on December 17, 1943, at which he said: ". . . it was our fault or blame or responsibility that the gold left here so slowly. We thought that was the only way to make it last." [10] In a memorandum of December 18 Morgenthau reviewed the situation for Roosevelt. This was in relation to Chiang's request for the billion dollar loan. Morgenthau quoted Kung's message of December 14 about the good effects of gold shipments, and said it was too early to say definitely what effect they might have. In seeking alternatives to the loan, Morgenthau recommended:

Accelerate the shipment of gold purchased by China to twice the amount we have previously planned to send. It should be possible to raise gold shipments from $6 million a month to about $12 million. At the present price for gold in the open market this would be equal to the present 3.5 billion of yuan currency that is being issued.

The impact of this two-fold program should contribute to retarding inflation, always bearing in mind that the basic reason for inflation in China is shortage of goods.[11]

These proposals clearly show Morgenthau's desire to help China to check inflation, and his readiness to send to China such gold as she could really use. The "shortage of goods" argument, mentioned in the last-quoted sentence, cropped up frequently during the war on both the Chinese and the American side. In chapter XX there is a comment on the fallacy of treating the shortage as "the basic reason."

On January 19, the President in a telephone conversation with Morgenthau said he understood China was getting US$12.5 million of gold per month. Morgenthau checked with White, who was with him, and who said it was "less than that." (November and December shipments had been US$8 and 2 million, respectively). The President wanted to send US$25 million per month.[12] The Treasury went so far as to draft a message dated January 19 for the Generalissimo which included a statement that ". . . the Air Transport Command has agreed to make additional facilities available to the Treasury for shipment of gold to China so that we hope to be able to ship about 25 million dollars a month." [13] That statement was dropped from the message sent. Nevertheless it points up the insincerity of later Treasury arguments stressing lack of transport as an excuse for not sending gold.

At this stage China's gold-selling program was only beginning to get under way. Sales by the Farmers Bank were unaggressive, and totaled but US$329,300 to the end of 1943. But demand grew after the Central Bank took over gold-selling in March 1944. Sales were over US$2 million per month in May and June, and US$4.4 million in July. The proceeds began to cover a material part of the deficit of the budget. In July sales yielded about C$2.3 billion, compared with note issue growth of C$6.3 billion.

In the first half of 1944 the Treasury's operating officials, far from meeting Roosevelt's January wish to send monthly US$25 million, or even the US$12.5 million that Morgenthau thought China was getting, sent a total of only about US$2 million. Of that only half had arrived by June 30. Nevertheless, until then China's gold position was not so bad. At midyear about US$6 million of gold was on hand in Chungking. The Treasury's operators could claim that they were carrying out Morgenthau's decision to let China have the gold "only as rapidly as it could be shipped and sold."

THE TREASURY WITHHOLDS GOLD

In July 1944 the Treasury's foot-dragging began to be acutely felt. As gold sales mounted in the summer of 1944, the shortage in China became serious. On July 12 the Central Bank urgently telegraphed, asking immediate air shipments. That was the crucial moment, when the operating officials of the Treasury began to go back on Morgenthau's promises, and to depart from the intent of his instructions. The Treasury sent no gold until August 3, when US$3 million went forward. And that went *by sea*. It did not reach Chungking until September 23. Three further lots totaling US$4.3 million, however, went by air in August-September. By September 30 the Central Bank had only US$215,000 of gold on hand. The last of the three air shipments arrived October 3 and was quickly sold. Then China was out of gold.

China's representatives in Washington pressed for urgent shipments. On October 2 they conferred at the Treasury with White and others. They presented a telegram from the Central Bank at Chungking, stating that recent arrivals of gold were "far from being adequate to meet outstanding contracts." The original US$20 million was exhausted, and they asked for immediate transfer of US$20 million more, to be shipped "by plane." They pointed out that "the cessation of the sale of gold would have very serious effects at this time." But White questioned the merits of selling gold.[14] Despite China's urging there was no further shipment for a month. And that lot, about US$3 million sent on November 2, went by sea; whereas all previous shipments, except that sent on August 3 in response to China's urgent appeal of July 12, had gone by air. Apparently the chief effect of urgent appeals was to delay shipments, and then to have them go by sea.

Another lot of about US$3 million went forward on December 1, again by sea. *No more gold was sent until April 14, 1945, when about US$1.2 million went by sea.*

The fall of 1944, when the effects of the Treasury's action began to be felt, was a most difficult period for China. The Japanese drive to take the East China air bases was unchecked, and even threatened Chungking and Kunming. The fear that Japan would force evacuation of those cities greatly increased the demands for gold. In times of stress, gold, being of high value in small compass, is a wonderful asset to people who fear they may have to flee for their lives. Coupled with this, the rapid growth of inflation spurred flight from the currency into whatever purchases would be likely to hold their value, notably gold. For these reasons, in the autumn of 1944 the demand for gold was unprecedented.

Demand was increased also as doubt developed about arrival of Treasury shipments, because of the meager response to the Central Bank's appeal of July 12, and the fact that no shipments went forward until August 3. When the stock in China was exhausted early in October, the doubts mounted. The situation could not be kept from the public, since the Bank was out of gold for immediate delivery.

The Central Bank did not dare to stop sales, and depend only on actual arrivals to sell gold. The gold price in China had long been a major field of speculation; and a soaring free market for gold, with no demand met, would have added fuel to the fires of inflation. So the Bank, trusting in the Treasury's commitment and expecting deliveries even though delayed, turned to sales for future delivery. This was done partly by selling gold forward, but mainly by accepting deposits to be repaid later in gold. These sales of futures had to be made at unfavorable rates. Because of the rapid inflation, interest rates in China were then 8 per cent or more per month. Hence what the buyers would pay for the right to receive gold in six months was related to what they could make by putting out their money at interest for that period, in which the original sum would grow by something like 50 to 100 per cent.

A memorandum by White to Morgenthau dated December 9 said that the Chinese have been pressing to ship gold by commercial vessels, whereas the Treasury had insisted on military transport. "We have stalled as much as we have dared," said White, "and have succeeded in limiting gold shipments to $26 million during the past year. We think it would be a serious mistake to permit further large shipments at this time." White went on to say, however, that the Treasury was going ahead with its program to obtain in India "all our rupee needs through the sale of gold." [15] Some gold was available in India, and the Central Bank swapped 40,000 ounces (US$1.4 million) in New York for a like amount in Calcutta, under a deal which I negotiated with the Bank of England in the latter part of 1944.

China continued to press for shipments. O. K. Yui, who succeeded H. H. Kung as Finance Minister in December, telegraphed on December 30 that China urgently needed gold, and asked Kung, who was in the United States, to press Morgenthau to expedite shipments. On January 3 Kung wrote to the Secretary appealing to his friendship and asking his cooperation. The Secretary replied January 5, that he hoped to give a decision in the near future and was giving "fullest consideration to the best interests of China." [16] On January 18 Kung once more wrote to Morgenthau, expressing the "urgency of facilitating the shipment of gold to China and the minting of golden tokens for shipment to China." [17] The production of such tokens in 1-, ½-, and ¼-ounce sizes had been discussed for many months but nothing definite had been done. The Treasury took no action on this urging. Again in a letter of February 26, Kung reviewed the situation comprehensively. He pled for immediate shipments both by air and by sea. He again urged the early delivery of gold tokens. Finally, he said that the Chinese government fully realized that gold sales were justified only by the emergency, and that it was anxious to import and sell consumers goods instead.

In a memorandum of March 2 to Morgenthau, V. F. Coe said that the situation in China was unchanged. "Ambassador Hurley agreed with you on the desirability of holding down gold shipments to approximately the same magnitude as in the past"; that is, to ship about US$7 million over the next three months. Half of this should be earmarked for promoting the production of tin in West China under an arrangement made with the National Resources Commission of China. The Treasury's reply of March 3 was a gem of dissimulation. It said:

I am sure that you appreciate the many difficulties involved in making arrangements for the export of gold to China. As in every other phase of our activities these days, military necessity takes precedence over everything else.

I have, however, instructed my men to raise again with the military authorities the possibilities of shipping gold to China during the next few months. They will inform your representatives of their findings on this matter.[18]

On April 23 Minister Yui telegraphed that the delay in shipments reflected on China's credit, saying, "I feel much concerned and distressed." The Central Bank telegraphed April 28, "We cannot overemphasize the serious effect in consequence Doctor White's default in meeting its [sic] obligations."

Meanwhile, the deficiency of gold in China steadily grew. China's uncovered commitments to deliver gold were US$12 million at the end of 1944; US$50 million on March 31, 1945; and US$84 million three months later. By June 25, 1945, speculation in gold had become so panicky that the Central Bank suspended sales and sold practically no gold during the remaining weeks of the war.

Appendix E, Table 66, contains further particulars of the gold situation in China during this period.

THE CONTROVERSY: PRO'S AND CON'S

When China was pressing for urgent shipments of gold, White gave various arguments to justify his obstruction. At the conference on October 2, 1944, he pointed out that the gold would be a valuable asset postwar, and expressed the view that if sold in China, it "could not substantially retard rising prices or the basic economic situation which was due to the acute scarcity of goods," and also that much of the gold would disappear into hoards. He made the surprising statement that "it was cheaper for the Central Government to print *fapi* than to absorb *fapi* in exchange for gold at a time when the dent that was being made by the sale of gold was not significantly large." [19] China's representatives quickly challenged him on the size of the "dent," pointing out that in July gold sales had brought in C$2 billion against a note increase which Adler stated was C$9 billion (the actual figure was C$6.3 billion). In a situation where inflation was so grave, it is hard to see how anyone knowledgeable in economic matters could seriously argue that it was "cheaper" for China to print more notes than to sell gold! Also costs of printing paper money of low value are high.

In a memorandum of December 23, 1944, which he submitted to the Secretary for presentation to President Roosevelt, he amplified his arguments. The gold, he said, was being sold "in such a way as to be of benefit principally to hoarders and speculators" and much of it was finding its way to the occupied areas; it was having "practically no helpful effect on the inflationary situation"; and while it gave the Chungking government an additional source of revenue, this was "by the sacrifice of valuable national assets at inexcusably low prices." He went on to say that the Treasury had held back shipments despite pressure from China. The gold exports, he explained, clearly showed American support of Chungking. The memorandum suggested use of the shipments as a "bargaining weapon," to get Chungking to accept "your China program." The record indicates that the Secretary did not present this memorandum to the President.[20]

Let us look at the objections. There was no more reason to hold back gold for postwar use than to hold back troops because the men would be needed later. In war all kinds of assets must be sacrificed, even lives. White's objection on the ground of sacrifice of assets is without merit, if use of the assets yielded reasonable value in China and helped to check inflation. There is also the issue of what results China could have gotten with proper Treasury cooperation.

Gold was yielding good value in China. It is a striking fact that throughout the whole period of gold-selling, the value of gold in China at the official selling prices was well above the official American price of US$35 per fine ounce. It was as high as US$150 in the last part of 1943, but naturally fell as more and more gold was put on the market. Such premiums on gold were usual in many parts of the world in this period. Gold prices in China ruled above those in India. That tempted smuggling, for which a number of American and Chinese military and civilian personnel had to be punished. There were cases of hijacking gold smugglers at Chinese airfields. Compared with the American price of US$35, an ounce of gold brought in China in the first nine months of 1944 the equivalent of US$89 to 100 at official prices and a little more in the free market. Thereafter the equivalents were lower, because gold was sold almost wholly for future delivery. But even so the equivalents in the nine months to June 30, 1945, ranged between US$37 and US$51 per ounce at official gold prices, and US$66 to US$87 at free market prices. These equivalents are calculated at average quarterly rates for *fapi* in the free market for dollar notes. For example, in the third quarter of 1944 the average official and free market prices of gold were C$18,500 and C$20,070, respectively. The average value of dollar notes in the free market was C$209. At that rate the official and free market prices of gold in China were equivalent to US$89 and US$96, respectively. For further particulars see appendix E, Table 67.

After mid-1944 receipts from gold sales reduced materially the deficit met by the printing press. The swelling flood of paper money was the main cause of the price rise, and not scarcity of goods, as White suggested (see chap. XX). Gold sales in the third and fourth quarters of 1944 were 27 and 29 per cent, respectively, of the increase of note issue. In the first two quarters of 1945 the figures were 52 and 28 per cent. Figures of quarterly deficits are not available. But the proportion of deficit covered by gold sales was somewhat less than those percentages, since increase of note issue was then covering about 80 per cent of the cash deficit. A telegram from Adler at Chungking, March 11, 1945, reported that receipts from gold had become the chief source of revenue in January and February and were covering about one-fourth of the deficit.[21]

As to hoarding, the sale of gold was intended to attract the funds of those who otherwise would engage in hoarding rice or other important goods and speculate in them — in other words to divert them from that harmful activity, and thus add to the supply of goods available in the market. It was far better that people hoard gold, paid for by turning in money that could be reissued, than to have that money remain in circulation and be used in part to buy and hoard scarce goods. It was true that some of the gold found its way to occupied areas. But the buyers there were largely Chinese and in any event the government got value in local currency withdrawn from circulation for the gold that it sold, and probably Free China got goods from the occupied areas in exchange for the gold.

The Treasury made much of the argument that transport was scarce, though later Coe said, ". . . we all think that transportation is a thin excuse." [22] In January 1944 the Treasury was ready to arrange to transport about US$25 million of gold per month. The entire US$200 million weighed only about 200 tons. In 1944 the China National Aviation Commission flew nearly 2,000 tons of bank notes and bank note paper over the Hump. Sale of a million dollars of gold, at say C$20,000 per ounce, would have realized about C$560 million; whereas a ton of C$20 bank notes contained only about C$20 million.

The discrepancy between official and free gold prices became a bone of contention between the Treasury and China. Until the summer of 1944, when enough gold was on hand in China, official prices were kept closely in line with free prices. In the second quarter of 1944, the official price was C$18,500 and the free market price averaged C$18,803. But in the third quarter the free price began to fluctuate at levels considerably above the official price. On July 16 the Central Bank, in a surprise move, dropped the price from C$18,500 to C$17,500 to trap speculators and strengthen confidence. In September it raised the effective official price to C$19,250 and in October to C$21,000 by including a supplement, first of 10 per cent and then 20 per cent, for compulsory purchase of Chinese Government Treasury notes. In November the official price was raised to C$24,000.

At the conference of American and Chinese representatives at the Treasury on October 2, 1944, Adler stated that the spread had temporarily gone as high as 60 per cent early in September, but had dropped to C$1,500 (about 8 per cent) with the arrival of gold. This appears to refer to the shipment of about $1.5 million which arrived September 12, being the first arrival since July 12. The Chinese representatives went on to point out that if there were sufficient supplies of gold, the discrepancy could be obliterated. They stated correctly that "the market's lack of confidence in the Central Bank's ability to procure adequate supplies was apparently the main reason" for the discrepancy.[23] In a telegram of October 6 the Central Bank told its representatives in the United States:

Difference between official and black market prices entirely due to stock having been exhausted. As soon as we are selling cash again difference immediately disappears . . . Public got scared because we had no more gold. All rushed for what they could grab. This unfortunately happened not due to our fault here as we requested Federal Reserve Bank for shipment by air July 12. After awaiting 25 days no sight of new shipment while our stock giving out hence the black market.

Beginning in November 1944 the spread between official and free gold prices grew further. The Treasury continued to criticize China for not keeping the two sets of prices in line. But China argued quite correctly that it could not do that safely without spot gold to sell and thus control the spot price. The responsible officials in China feared that such raises would damage confidence and aggravate the inflation. At this stage, viewing the situation from Washington, I felt that the official price should have been raised more frequently and by smaller amounts, instead of waiting until March 30, 1945, to make a big increase. But the lack of spot gold, because of the Treasury's action, made any good handling of the situation impossible.

A background condition promoting a rise in the free gold market was the spiraling of inflation. The average monthly rise of general prices in the cities of Free China was 18 per cent in the nine months from November 1944 through July 1945. The deficit was worse because of the costs of reorganizing the Chinese armies with American aid, growing American operations in China, and the outlay for the new War Production Board which Donald M. Nelson helped to organize. Meanwhile, revenue suffered from enemy occupation of larger areas.

When no American gold arrived from January 26 to June 14, 1945, the free gold market became more and more panicky. Sales at official price for future delivery grew by leaps and bounds. Adler, in a memorandum of March 19, 1945, objected to China pegging the official price of gold so far below the free market price. He favored, however, "continuance of the sale of gold with a drastic revision of gold sales policy." He also favored issuing token gold coins of a quarter, half, and one ounce, also direct use of gold to meet expenditures. He said, "The effects of such a gold sales policy as an integral part of a broad anti-inflationary program might well be considerable and serve to keep the net monthly deficit within manageable proportions." [24] All along the Chinese government had wanted to do substantially what Adler now advocated. But withholding of gold had made it impossible to control the free gold market, and to keep free and official prices in line. Also the Treasury had delayed a decision about gold tokens.

With the gold market getting out of hand, the Chinese government was in a dilemma. On the one hand, gold was too cheap at the official price in the face of mounting inflation. On the other hand, raising the price was always a shock to confidence and was likely to be followed by a sharp jump in the free market so long as the government did not have a stock to sell in order to control the price. And such jumps in the free market price hurt confidence and tended to cause sharper increase of commodity prices in general. Because of this difficulty the government delayed too long in raising the official price. Effective March 30 the Central Bank raised to C$35,000 the price of C$24,000 set November 13, 1944. The new price was just under the current free market price. But because of the lack of spot gold to control the market, the free price at once became as much out of line as ever. As to the effects of raising the gold price, the Chungking edition of the *Shanghai Evening Post* on April 1 said:

The move promptly produced skyrocketing black market prices in gold, American currency and various commodities . . .

Within a few hours after sale of gold began at the new official price, the black market price of gold jumped to CN$60,000 per ounce, and American currency in large denominations increased on the black market from 525 to 660 to one.

Numerous commodities followed suit.

It was charged in some of the press in Chungking, and also reported in the American press, that insiders had advance knowledge of the rise and profited accordingly. But the Central Bank steadfastly denied this. They stated that the only large buyer immediately before the rise was a commercial company which had just received a down payment on a substantial order to be produced for the government, and was buying gold to hedge against the expected increase in its costs. However, some weeks later two minor officials of the Central Trust of China were arrested for alleged misuse of information on the gold price rise. I was in the United States during this period, and have no firsthand knowledge of what happened at that time in Chungking.

SETTLEMENT OF THE ISSUE

The question of gold deliveries to China came to a head in May 1945. Foreign Minister Soong came to Washington from the San Francisco Conference on organization of the United Nations. He presented to President Truman China's request for gold, and also asked for consumers goods to check the inflation. Truman asked the Treasury to consult the Departments of State and War. In a conference on the gold situation with these departments on May 1, Morgenthau said: "We've made it just as difficult for the Chinese to get it as possible, that being a sort of joint policy." [25] Representatives of those departments tended to agree with the Treasury view on gold, but undertook to give serious consideration to shipping consumers goods, especially textiles.

On May 8 Soong conferred with Treasury, State, and War Department officials. They presented to him a memorandum which recommended that China adopt an anti-inflation program comprising monetary, banking, fiscal, and administrative reforms and stabilization of foreign exchange. The memorandum proposed that China set up a "Currency Stabilization Fund" of US$500 million, to be used for purposes to be agreed with the Treasury. The memorandum further suggested that China stop forward sales of gold, a program about which the Treasury had not been consulted, but said that the Treasury would try to make available limited quantities of gold. This gold, however, ought to be financed from assets other than the proposed US$500 million stabilization fund. This fund should be constituted in part from what remained of the US$500 million loan, namely, US$240 million.

The memorandum went on to say, "China should investigate and cancel sales to speculators and illicit purchasers," and, "It is most unfortunate that the impression has arisen in the United States that the $200 million of U.S. dollar certificates and bonds and the gold sold in China have gone into relatively few hands with resultant large individual profits and have failed to be of real assistance to the Chinese economy." [26]

When the memorandum was read to Soong, he asked how he could combat the inflation with the US$500 million fund. He then said that he had come from the San Francisco Conference to settle matters in Washington. He read the communication of July 27, 1943, stating that the Treasury "agrees to the request . . . that $200 million be made available . . . for the purchase of gold," and that "the necessary action will be taken to consummate" China's requests for transfers of funds to buy gold. Morgenthau expressed surprise, thinking that this arrangement referred to only US$20 million, but was informed that it was US$200 million. He said that the Treasury had not envisaged sale of futures, but Soong pointed out that China made no commitment to consult when they sold gold. Soong said that he would raise the gold price and tax those who had bought for future delivery — a commitment which later was strictly carried out and a 40 per cent tax imposed in the fall of 1945. In response to the Secretary's statement that he (Morgenthau) had tried to keep quiet the abuses in China, Soong said that he had nothing to hide — if there had been anything wrong it should be investigated, and he had so told Chiang Kai-shek. Soong also discussed the proposed delivery of textiles and goods to China, remarking, "The country that first got beaten up by the aggressor will be the last to be rescued." [27]

The next day Morgenthau called in his staff. He was much upset by the position in which he found himself. He said that he did so many things he could not be expected to remember the terms of his letter of July 27, 1943, and that it was their responsibility to bring it to his attention.

I have given, in writing, the Chinese Government a firm commitment that they can have two hundred million dollars worth of gold . . . and you put me in an absolutely dishonorable position, and I think it's inexcusable . . .

. . . here I am acting like a huckster over something which has been settled . . .[28]

On May 10 at a further conference White told the Secretary:

. . . we had absolutely no legal grounds for withholding the gold . . . what we were doing was skating on thin ice and offering excuses and we were getting away with it as long as we could . . . We have been successful over two years in keeping them down to twenty-seven million.

Morgenthau said:

I think that the Army and State Department have advised me very badly on this thing last week and suddenly Will Clayton woke up to that fact himself, entirely on his own.[29]

Despite the Secretary's attitude, White and some of his associates prepared a draft memorandum for Morgenthau addressed to the President of which they had sent a copy to the State Department for clearance, suggesting an effort be made to get China to "withdraw for the time being her request for immediate heavy shipments of gold." The report of the discussion reads:

H. M. Jr.: The first thing I want, please call up whoever has a copy at the State Department. I want them immediately withdrawn, immediately. I'm not going to follow this position. It's ridiculous. Will you please, wherever they are, get them right back . . .

I mean, you just keep going over the same ground, the same ground, the whole time. This doesn't make it plain to the President of the United States that these people own this gold, that I, over my signature, told them they could have two hundred million dollars worth of gold.

Mr. White: That's where I disagree.

H. M. Jr.: I know you do.[30]

Morgenthau decided that in reversing the policy and sending to China large amounts of gold, he should have the backing of the State Department and the approval of the President. He obtained a memorandum of May 16, 1945, from Assistant Secretary Clayton, which was confirmed in a letter of the same date from Acting Secretary Grew. That letter, while expressing doubts as to the effectiveness of the sale of gold, recommended that "the Treasury, if transportation is available, deliver the gold to China in accordance with the time schedules put forward by Dr. Soong." [31]

After obtaining the approval of President Truman, Morgenthau on May 16 wrote to Soong that the Treasury would authorize shipment of the remaining gold in accordance with the schedule requested by Soong. The letter, however, went on to question the effectiveness of gold sales:

As you know, it is my opinion that the sale of gold by China has not proved effective in combatting inflation, and I am doubtful that it will prove effective. Also as I have told you, the manner in which the gold sales have been conducted and the consequent public criticism of them in China are not conducive to achievin the purposes for which our financial aid was granted.

The Secretary further urged constituting the US$500 million fund, stating, "the Chinese Government's response to our proposal to institute a $500 million fund and her conduct of the gold sales program will be important considerations in our financial relations with China." [32] In these discussions with Soong, no agreement was reached about the suggested new fund of US$500 million. But on February 26, 1946, the Chinese Supreme Defence Council ordered the setting aside of a fund of that size for eventual monetary stabilization, this being done as a part of the measures taken when China reopened the foreign exchange market at Shanghai.

RESUMPTION OF SHIPMENTS

Despite the promise to accelerate shipments the Treasury continued to send them by sea. Five shipments were made in May and ten shipments in June by sea, the first of which arrived July 17, 1945. Beginning June 16, however, some shipments were made by plane, the first two of which arrived June 26 and 28. During the rest of the year further large lots arrived — over US$100 million in July–October 1945.

But these massive shipments were too late to have the effect sought. Beginning in early June the gold market got completely out of hand. On June 8 the Central Bank raised the official price from C$35,000 to C$50,000. But even by that date none of the gold which Morgenthau promised on May 16 had arrived. None had even started on its way by air, though one lot sent by sea in April reached Chungking only on June 14, after the crisis. Indeed no American gold had arrived in China since January, until June 14. So in early June there was no spot gold in China to control the market, and no one could be sure when it would arrive. The free market price which on June 7 had been C$90,000 at once jumped to a range of C$105,000 to 128,000 in the next two days, and to C$185,000 later in June. On June 25 sales were suspended because of uncertainty how to deal with these extreme gyrations. During July the price range in the free market was C$167,000 to 225,000.

At the end of July the government announced a 40 per cent tax on settlement of forward commitments, and raised the official price to C$170,000. These measures practically put an end to the wartime sale of gold. With Japan's defeat approaching, a temporary deflation set in. During August the gold price slumped to C$75,000 and in September as low as C$50,000.

By September an ample supply of gold was on hand and the government began the liquidation of forward commitments, collecting the 40 per cent tax. On September 28 it set the official price at C$89,000. For the rest of the year the free market price range was C$82,500 to 100,000.

China's sales of gold were: C$114 million in 1943; C$20,940 million in 1944; and C$71,700 million in 1945. Details by quarters, compared with increase of note issue, are shown in appendix E, Table 68.

CONCLUSIONS

Secretary Morgenthau wanted to help China and was ready to send such gold as China could really use. His reluctance to earmark or ship gold beyond what China needed for her sales program was justifiable. The deliberate foot-dragging and obstruction of needed shipments, despite China's urgent pleas, was primarily the work of White and other subordinates. It was a clear and unjustifiable violation of Morgenthau's promise. He was quick to make amends as soon as the explicit nature of his commitment was brought to his personal attention.

The Treasury withheld gold when China's need to check inflation was greater than ever before. Besides, a major factor aggravating inflation was of American origin, the spending of C$6 billion in a short time in the first half of 1944 for new air bases desired by the United States. Late in 1944 began the sharpest inflation of the war, endangering the entire war effort in China and also China's future. Surely aid in holding back this inflation should have been a major American policy. And it was clear that gold sales helped, since they covered a material part of the deficit. In 1944, despite slow-down of gold shipments, the sales proceeds of about C$21 billion nearly offset American outlay in China of about C$23 billion. Most of the Treasury's arguments are answered by the mere fact that throughout the period they sent gold without hesitation to be sold in the Middle East and India to raise money by noninflationary means.

The withholding of gold, despite the Treasury's clear commitment upon which China had relied, suggested within China doubt of American support. It hurt confidence in the government. Thus the Treasury's action made it harder for China to hold out during the difficult last months after seven years of suffering, and made postwar reconstruction harder.

Why this unfriendly attitude toward China? Several factors played their part:

(1) China's overly hard bargaining and reluctance to make realistic arrangements to meet American army costs in China, as to which no settlement was reached until November 1944, was unjustifiable. The argument was acute in July 1944, when the Treasury began to embarrass China by delaying shipment. Certainly soreness about China's position on army costs influenced the American attitude on gold. It helped the Treasury to gain the general acquiescence of the State and War departments in the gold policy, though the record available does not show that they knew how definite had been the Treasury's commitment to send the gold.

(2) China's mishandling of the issue of US$200 million of dollar-backed securities did not encourage American officials to have confidence that the gold would be wisely used. But, as regards gold, it was American much more than Chinese action that prevented the sales operation from accomplishing what it could and should have accomplished. The Treasury people closed their eyes to the fact that China was getting good value from gold sales, and making a good record in keeping the official sales prices in line with the market prices of gold, until handicapped by the Treasury's foot-dragging. If the Treasury had loyally supplied enough gold, the Central Bank could have avoided sales for future delivery and gotten much better

prices for spot gold. Thus the excesses that developed in the futures market reflecting a shock to confidence, would not have occurred. And the inflation could have been somewhat slowed.

(3) Many American officials both in China and Washington felt that China had not fought as effectively as she should have after the spring of 1942. Many of them expected far too much from China. They did not sufficiently appreciate China's exhaustion; the suffering inflicted by the Japanese armies; the disorganization caused by fighting the enemy alone for seven years to mid-1944; the inability to do much against a modern mechanized army without adequate equipment and training; possible subconscious reaction in China that American oil and scrap-iron had previously helped Japan to fight China; the need to gird against a later communist threat; and the subtle but fundamental damage from inflation.

(4) Finally there is the question of communist influence. A report of the Internal Security Subcommittee to the Senate Committee on the Judiciary refers to "the Communist underground apparatus of Harry Dexter White," citing the testimony under oath of Whittaker Chambers and Elizabeth Bentley. The report states that FBI Director J. Edgar Hoover told the Subcommittee that White's involvement was "substantiated from more than 30 sources." On the other hand, members of White's family issued after his death a book fervently asserting his loyalty.[33]

The records available to me do not show specifically the motives of those concerned with gold shipments to China. In *China and the Helping Hand* I have indicated specifically the attitude and acts of White and his associates in the various dealings with China matters, so far as shown by available data. His is a mixed record. Part of the time, especially in the earlier war years, it was friendly to China; and part of the time unfriendly. I have no evidence whether there was a connection between changes in his attitude and changes in the communist attitude to China during the war. But in any event it is clear that White's efforts in 1944–1945, while blocking gold shipments to China, to promote a US$10 billion postwar loan to Russia,[34] show a strong anti-Chinese and pro-Russian bias. We felt this at the time on the Chinese side. Te-mou Hsi of the Central Bank wrote on March 2, 1945, from Washington to a colleague in Chungking that ". . . there is reason to believe that some elements in the Government here would like to 'wait and see' until such questions as the Kuomintang and the Communist Party are settled."

Certainly the withholding of gold from China aggravated the inflation, with all the grave consequences that followed during and after the war. To say how much that action aggravated inflation would be speculation. But those who held back gold, despite China's pleas and in violation of a clear American commitment, must bear part of the responsibility for later tragic events.

XX. ECONOMIC ANALYSIS

THE CAUSES OF THE INFLATION

China's wartime inflation was caused chiefly by monetary excesses, and to a much less extent by nonmonetary factors. In the first year of fighting the government made a good showing by limiting to 37 per cent the cash deficit covered by bank credit. But thereafter the figure ranged between 69 and 83 per cent. After the first 18 months, during which China lost control of the main areas where modern-style banking existed, approximately 80 to 90 per cent of this credit gave rise to expanded note issue. Thus the chief source of wartime receipts was the printing press. Expansion of credit to the government dwarfed expansion to the private sector, the latter being about 30 per cent of the total in the first 18 months and in the general range of 10 to 20 per cent thereafter (see Table 20). The shift of the government into the little developed western region inevitably added much to over-all buying power. The war occasioned increased demand for many goods.

During inflation, especially in wartime, both governments and the public commonly exaggerate the nonmonetary causes. Professor Cassel described this in detail in relation to World War I.[1] Economists have become hardened to expecting this attitude, though they do not find it easy to be tolerant of it and of the grave policy errors to which it gives rise. It is easier for governments to seek scapegoats for unpleasant phenomena than to face the facts, and to deal with symptoms rather than face up to the causes of the disease of inflation. It is painful for governments to admit that their own policies lie at the root of that evil, even when the policies may be basically inevitable as was the case in China. During this period China was no exception to this rule. A further factor is the real danger in such situations that too great frankness about inflation may make matters worse, by publicizing the inevitability of continuing price rises.

The nonmonetary causes of price rise in 1937–1945 included scarcity of many goods because of disruption of trade and communications and at times because of poor crops; destruction of goods and means of production; drastic reduction of the supply of imports in Free China; influx to Free China of tens of millions of refugees; and reduction of the number of productive workers by enlargement of the armies and by other wartime activities. Kia-ngau Chang has made a careful analysis of the factors of aggregate supply in China's inflation.[2] I shall not duplicate his detailed study, but only summarize the supply side.

China's chief railroads and readily navigable rivers were lost to the enemy early in the war. The lack of roads and modern-style transport handicapped distribution in the interior, although many existing roads were improved and a considerable mileage of roads was built. After the Burma Road was cut early in 1942, the supply of trucks and parts was curtailed, and toward the war's end only a few thousand trucks remained usable.

Fortunately the supply of agricultural goods could be fairly well maintained, in an economy in which about 80 per cent of the activity was agricultural. Figures of crop production must be taken with reserve because of the lack of an adequate statistical basis. Table 33 shows the available

TABLE 33. Agricultural production, indexes 1931–1945

Year	Rice	Wheat	Sweet Potatoes	Cotton	All crops, weighted average	Livestock
1931–1937	100	100	100	100	100	—
1937	—	—	—	—	—	100
1938	103	120	128	97	106	92
1939	105	117	115	121	110	98
1940	85	119	119	104	102	92
1941	89	98	128	93	96	87
1942	88	124	113	79	—	—
1943	84	118	135	98	—	—
1944	93	147	141	88	—	—
1945	81	130	144	147	—	—

SOURCE: National Agricultural Research Bureau, quoted in *China Handbook, 1943*, pp. 551–555. See also Kia-ngau Chang, *The Inflationary Spiral*, pp. 377–378.

official data. A study by an expert of the University of Nanking tends to corroborate these data for part of the period. This showed that in 15 provinces of Free China the total weight of crops in 1938–1942 averaged 1.5 per cent higher than in 1931–1937. Wheat crops were 15.5 per cent higher, sweet potatoes 20.5 per cent higher, but rice 6.1 per cent lower.[3] The drought of 1940 and 1941 was especially serious in Szechwan Province, the government's chief economic base, where in each year rice production was estimated at 37 per cent below the average of 1931–1937.[4] Until mid-1940, when rice crops were a little better than the prewar average, the price of rice rose less than general prices. But with the drought the scarcity factor became important Average rice prices in Free China increased about five-fold from mid-1940 to mid-1941, while average general prices a little more than doubled (see appendix B, Tables 48 and 56).

China made a brave effort to increase output of military and civilian items needed in the war Machinery and skilled personnel were transplanted to safer locations ahead of the retreating armies. The number of industrial plants in Free China grew strikingly. The official American historians of the war in China described the output of the arsenals in 1941–1945 as "a considerable national achievement in view of the difficulties." [5] The index of industrial production in Free China compiled by the Ministry of Economics, based upon prewar output as 100, was as follows:

Year	Including export goods	Excluding export goods
1939	133	133
1940	186	214
1941	243	276
1942	302	373
1943	376	520
1944	352	494
1944, January–June	372	—
July–December	333	—
1945, January–March	333	—

As the war dragged on, prices of imported goods rose on the average to more than three times the level of domestic goods, while average prices of exported goods were lower than the level of domestic goods by more than half (see appendix B, Table 54). The degrees of scarcity and of demand clearly showed in this situation.

Scarcity of desired items naturally led to hoarding by consumers as well as speculators. By leading people to spend money faster for goods they expected to become scarcer, the rate of turn-over of money quickened and inflation was stimulated. The drought of 1940–1941 promoted hoarding, both of foodstuffs and of other goods. The tightened blockade, especially after early Allied defeats and the loss of the Burma Road early in 1942, advertised the cutting off of imported goods and gave a further urge to hoarding. As prices rose more rapidly and the prospect of indefinite rise became clear, speculation and hoarding grew apace. I found various cases of merchants who all through the war had tried to preserve their capital by hoarding large stocks of goods, often cloth. Many were reluctant to sell, and when obliged to do so sold only the minimum. A supply officer of the American army at Kunming buying two desks had to pay more than twice the price of one. Also individual consumers tended to hold as large supplies as they could afford of items needed for family use. Farmers and other producers delayed as long as they could the marketing of their products. Analyzing the causes of the price rise, a Central Bank study in the fall of 1941 said:

Altogether, some thirty reasons were given by Chinese students of economics to explain the phenomenal price movement in China during the war. The most popular ones are the forestalling and engrossing by producers, merchants and speculators, the ever increased purchase of military supplies, the population growth in the interior, the disruption of transportation, the destruction of factories, the higher costs of production and transportation, the increase in note issues, the expansion of bank credit, the falling exchange rate of Chinese dollar, etc.[6]

The writer of this study went on to give his analysis, which generally agrees with mine, of the various forces at work and their interaction in 1938–1941. The supply situation worsened with the tightening blockade. Note issue grew, for military needs and to sustain industries in the interior. Credit often was provided too liberally. Hoarding and speculation flourished. These interacting forces constantly pushed prices higher. No way was found to break the vicious circle of price rises and larger note issue and bank credit. The analysis pointed to the eventual danger of complete breakdown of confidence in the currency. The analysis covered only the period before the Pacific War; but the situation described continued, aggravated by the still tighter blockade and by further damage to confidence as a result of early Allied defeats by Japan.

To conclude: It is clear that *over-all* scarcity did not account for any considerable proportion of the wartime price rise. When over a long period all prices in a country such as China rise together, even though unevenly, the root cause must be monetary. All China's various price indexes rose with hardly a break throughout the war period. Undoubtedly the non-monetary factors materially aggravated China's inflation. But they did not over-all become quantitatively worse at a rate that would cause a rise of 10 per cent or more monthly, which became the approximate rate of price rise after mid-1941 until it accelerated from late 1944 until just before the war's end.

NOTE ISSUE, RATE OF TURNOVER, AND PRICES

Although reliance on the printing press was throughout the main dynamic force back of China's inflation, the rate of price rise in Free China during the war became progressively greater than the rate of note increase. This accords with a classic principle of acute inflation. Table 34 compares increase of prices and of note issue in both Free and Occupied China, 1937–1945. The almost uninterruptedly increasing margin by which prices in Free China outran note issue shows that the note issue was turning over faster and faster, reflecting less and less confidence in the currency. The lessening of the ratio in the latter part of 1945 was caused by the very large increase of note issue needed to replace Japanese and puppet currencies in the recovered area, coupled with the price reaction at the war's end.

In Occupied China, for a time, note issue grew faster than prices rose, as shown by negative percentages in Table 34. Also for Shanghai and

TABLE 34. Comparison of increase of prices and of note issue in Free China
and in Occupied China, 1937–1945

	FREE CHINA Indexes		
Year	Retail prices (average) January–June 1937 = 1	Note issue June 30 1937 = 1	Percentage of excess of price index over note index
1937			
July	1.04	1.02	2
December	1.18	1.13	5
1938			
June	1.40	1.17	20
December	1.76	1.48	19
1939			
June	2.26	1.70	33
December	3.23	2.55	27
1940			
June	4.87	3.50	39
December	7.24	4.38	65
1941			
June	10.51	6.10	74
December	15.95	8.46	88
1942			
June	35.9	13.8	160
December	66.2	18.9	250
1943			
June	132	27.2	385
December	228	40.8	458
1944			
June	466	66.1	605
December	755	102	640
1945			
June	2167	214	912
December	2491	556	349

	OCCUPIED CHINA[a] North China			Central and South China		
	Indexes		Percentage of excess of price index over note index	Indexes		Percentage of excess of price index over note index
Year (end)	Wholesale prices at Peiping[b]	FRB note issue		Wholesale prices at Shanghai	CRB note issue	
1939	1.00	1.00	—			
1940	1.41	1.56	−9			
1941	2.36[c]	2.11	12			
1942	4.73	3.45	37	1.00	1.00	—
1943	13.6	8.22	65	4.76	5.18	−8
1944	142	34.6	310	55.3	37.8	46
1945 (August)	1535	183	740	1895	902	110

SOURCE: See appendixes B, Table 48, and D, Table 61; also Table 18.
  [a] The base used for North China is the end of 1939, by which time FRB notes had become established as the chief circulating medium of the enemy-controlled parts of North China. Similarly, the end of 1942 is used as the base for the CRB notes in Central and South China.
  [b] The figures for 1939 and 1940 are for Tientsin. No complete series is available for Tientsin or Peiping, but combining the two series appears to involve no substantial error.
  [c] January 1942.

Chungking, in the early part of the war, Shun-hsin Chou in a month-to-month study of link relatives found a similar situation — although this does not show in the averaged half-yearly data in Table 34.[7] At that stage confidence in *fapi* was widespread. These instances show that note issue is an effective fiscal device for a time, but becomes progressively less effective as people get the idea that larger issue is to come. In North China in 1938–1943 Japan was relatively conservative about note issue, as it had been for some time in neighboring "Manchukuo." In Central China that situation apparently suggested that Japan would also be conservative in issuing CRB notes. Besides, Japan's early successes in the Pacific War tended to sustain confidence in puppet money. But, as Japan's war prospects worsened, inflation in the occupied areas became faster than in Free China. Then growing distrust of puppet money led to an accelerating price rise involving faster velocity of circulation (see Table 34).

Chou also points out that the ratio between prices and note issue, as an indication of the pattern of inflation, is subject to qualifications because: (1) aggregate demand for money is not constant, and (2) the ratio omits the factor of velocity of bank credit, which may differ from that of notes. In this period in Free China, however, bank credit was much less important than notes. Data for measuring velocity of deposits are not available. I concur with the conclusions of Chou that bank credit was much less important than notes in promoting the wartime inflation.[8]

As issues of *fapi* grew, their total value shrank in terms of prewar prices, as shown in Table 35. This shrinkage reflects growing velocity of circulation,

TABLE 35. Value of note issue in terms of prewar prices, 1937–1945
(amount and value in millions of C$)

End of the period	Amount of note issue of government banks	Average price index[a]	Value of issue in terms of prewar notes
1937, July	1,445	1.04	1,390
1938	2,305	1.76	1,310
1939	4,287	3.23	1,325
1940	7,867	7.24	1,085
1941	15,133	19.77	765
1942	34,360	66.2	520
1943	75,379	228	330
1944	189,461	755	250
1945, August	556,907	2,647	210
1945, December	1,031,932	2,491	415

SOURCE: See appendixes B, Table 48, and D, Table 61.
 [a] For December of each year, except for the months specified for 1937 and 1945.

because money had to turn over faster to do the monetary work at the rapidly rising price levels. Of course the volume of transactions also shrank, as did the area of circulation. But the latter two factors could not have caused so great a progressive shrinkage of total value in real terms.

When growth of the rate of turn-over of money is not checked, it turns acute inflation into hyperinflation and collapse.[9] During an inflation such as China's, the rate of turn-over mirrors confidence or the lack of it, which affects propensity to spend. As the buying power of money falls, people are less willing to hold it, and they convert it into goods more and more quickly. The rise of general prices, first caused primarily by the increase of note issue, becomes itself a cause of further price rises by hurting confidence as the inflation progresses. This is the vicious circle of inflation.

So long as the rate of price rise in Free China remained moderate, accelerating turn-over did not reach the danger stage. The monetary reform of 1935 had succeeded beyond the expectations of most people, and in the early years of the fighting confidence in *fapi* remained impressive, despite military reverses and shocks to its foreign exchange value. But the accelerating turn-over during the war was an omen of eventual collapse — unless the deterioration of the total situation could be checked, which did not prove to be possible.

INTERACTION OF PRICES AND EXCHANGE: MARKET AND OFFICIAL RATES

Overvaluation of *fapi* in foreign exchange, which began to be significant in 1940–1941 and became a major issue during the Pacific War, is analyzed in chapter XVIII. Table 31 contains a calculation of the coefficient of overvaluation according to available data. The coefficient ruled above 3 much of the time during the Pacific War, reaching the remarkable figure of 7 at the end of 1943. This resulted primarily from the isolation of China's economy because of the enemy blockade, the lack of a broad foreign exchange market for transactions of the usual kinds, and the sale in a relatively narrow market of large amounts of American currency notes in connection with expansion of the American military effort in China.

Over-all, rates for notes, from the lowest to the highest, rose more than 100-fold in 1942–1945 — in about the same proportion as average prices (see appendix B, Table 48, and appendix C, Table 59). Since *fapi* were much overvalued in 1940–1942, the overvaluation at the war's end was roughly similar to that at the start of the Pacific War. But the rise in the intervening period was by no means uniform. In 1942–1943 the increase in rates for notes was relatively small, roughly doubling in each year while prices were rising at an average rate of around 10 per cent monthly, which involved a yearly rise of more than three-fold. Hence in that period overvaluation became extreme (see Table 31), although the smallness of the note market limited the significance. Early in 1944, however, rates for notes began to zoom upward, and grew about six-fold during that year, and again six-fold in the first seven months of 1945. The rise in these rates took place despite a considerable increase in the supply, as American military activities in China grew. Factors in the rise were, first, accelerating inflation accompanying the building of the B-29 airbases early in 1944 (see chap. XVIII, especially Table 32); then, in the second half of that year, the Japanese drive which for a time threatened to take Chungking and Kunming; and in 1945 a general weakening of confidence, despite the improving military situation, as China's political and economic troubles multiplied. Demand for dollar notes grew as people wanted to hold them for a possible emergency.

The relation between prices and both market and official exchange rates was a matter of major controversy during the war. The issues centered upon market rates in the period to August 1941, when operations were conducted to check undue fluctuations (see chaps. XV to XVII). China's business community was exchange-minded after years of fluctuations under the silver standard. Hence general prices during the war were sensitive to depreciation of *fapi* in the exchange market. Most noticeable was the effect on import prices, but increases radiated in the economy, abetted by impaired confidence and the growing purchasing power of the public as the money supply grew.

Until August 1941 the continuation of the prewar official rates had no discernible effect upon prices. People paid little attention to official rates, which were mainly for intragovernmental transactions, but watched rather the rates in the free market. Adoption of semiofficial foreign trade rates of 7d. and US$0.13⅝ in July 1939, and the change of these to 4½d. and US$0.07½ about a year later, likewise had no apparent effect upon prices, these changes being somewhat in line with market rates.

The official rates took on major importance from August 1941, when exchange control began on the basis of rates that were even then materially overvalued and that were only nominally changed in four and a half years while general prices rose nearly 200-fold.[10] Exchange control naturally gave rise to what was commonly called a black market but which became more or less tolerated. After outbreak of the Pacific War the main dealings were in dollar notes at Chungking and Kunming. Rising rates for notes reflected the depreciation of *fapi*, although not fully (see chap. XVIII).

During the Pacific War the issue in controversy, primarily with the American government (see chap. XVIII), concerned the possible effects if the official rate for the dollar were raised above 20 to 1. Minister Kung, as the chief protagonist of the policy of defending the rate of 20 to 1, was unwilling to engage in "chasing the black market." He feared that to raise official rates would touch off catastrophic inflation. This fear is understandable. Such a fear has existed, now exists, and will continue to exist during inflations anywhere when the question arises of changing fixed official rates of exchange. For a government to say that its own money has fallen in value is hard. Inevitably such an admission is a shock to confidence, although the shock is mitigated when incidental to a reform which the public believe can be maintained. In inflations that can be stopped, any large overvaluation is a serious and costly evil that should be remedied without needless delay. But in inflations that for the time being cannot be stopped, maintenance of some degree of currency overvaluation may tend to check the price rise. In the latter cases especially, finance ministers such as Kung in China bear a heavy and unenviable responsibility. Whatever they do is a choice of evils, and may seem wrong however carefully they weigh the consequences. But it is my considered opinion, after having been in or close to such situations, in a number of countries, that in principle the lesser evil, so long as inflation has to continue, is to find means to adjust periodically the rates at which major transactions in exchange take place, so that the internal and external values do not get too far out of line. Such adjustments should be carefully timed, and if possible coincide with good and not bad news.

Some conclusions may be summarized with respect to the experience with holding to fixed official rates after August 1941, in the face of rapidly rising general prices:

(1) Had large trade transactions in foreign currencies continued on a scale comparable to that in the fall of 1941 in the early period of the Stabilization Board, adjustments of the official rates would have been found unavoidable. But the coming of the Pacific War created a radically changed situation, with such transactions practically ended. The main sellers of exchange became the American government, individual Americans of the armed forces in China, and foreign philanthropic organizations. *Vis-à-vis* these and other sellers, the stubborn maintenance of the official rates led China into an indefensible position. Escape had to be found by indirection after much delay and friction. The main buyers, besides those seeking dollar notes for hoarding and later use, were the subscribers to the dollar-backed securities and those wanting exchange for personal requirements. For the latter buyers that could qualify, bargain rates remained the rule, at substantial cost to China.

(2) The mere maintenance of the official rate had little or no positive effect in checking inflation. The small change from 18.82 to 1 to 20 to 1 as of July 10, 1942, did not cause a ripple. The exchange supplements of 50 and 100 per cent from May 1943 and January 1944, respectively, were carefully stated to involve no change in the official rate. But, in substance, they did change the selling rate since hardly any exchange was offered in

the market at the 20 to 1 rate after the first of those changes. These supplements had no apparent effect upon confidence, nor did the government's acquiescence in June 1944 in use of the free market for sales of exchange for relief and philanthropic purposes. Exchange-minded opinion apparently paid little attention to the official rates, watching rather the free market.

(3) Had *fapi* been provided to the American military forces at rates that were reasonably realistic yet definitely less favorable to them than the free market rates, an arrangement that the American government was ready to accept, public knowledge of the arrangement would not in my opinion have had a serious or continuing effect in speeding the inflation.

(4) Rates for subscription to the dollar-backed securities issued in 1942–1943 should have been in effect only for relatively short periods of a few weeks, accompanied by pressure to subscribe, instead of being open for 15 to 18 months (see chap. VI). The rates should have been raised for subsequent *tranches*. These operations could have been handled, in my judgment, with a worth-while effect in checking inflation. If the authorities feared to risk raising the rates, the issues should have been withdrawn. The manner of handling these issues impaired confidence in the government.

(5) The granting of excessive bargains to private buyers of exchange at official rates could have been obviated by conserving official exchange and letting them use the free market.

(6) The economic results of the stubborn defense of the 20 to 1 rate in 1941–1945 despite inflation were bad, but less serious than otherwise they would have been because of China's isolation and the relatively small importance of foreign trade. More serious were the consequences to American and other foreign official and public goodwill, which are described in the final section of chapter XVIII.

In conditions such as existed in China during the war the root cause of rising prices both for (a) goods and services and (b) foreign currencies was the excessive creation of money. The rise of each contributed to the rise of the other, that is, the symptoms of acute inflation in turn operated as causes of further depreciation.[11]

COMPARISON WITH OTHER INFLATIONS

No inflation prior to World War I remotely approached the astronomical figures reached in 1914–1924 in Germany and Russia, or the lesser extremes in Austria, Hungary, and Poland. Such earlier inflations as the 18th century American continental currency and the French *assignats* collapsed after carrying prices to something like 100 or more times the earlier base. In these cases the hard money stayed in the hands of the people and the slump in terms of specie shocked confidence, so that collapse took place at a relatively early stage. In China the reform of 1935 introduced important elements of the modern systems of managed currency and credit, with notes convertible into foreign exchange and with little parallel circulation of hard money. That made possible an extended inflation of the World War I type.

In China in 1937–1945 these World War I inflations were the best available historical guide as to the sort of course inflation might follow. Of course each inflation is a separate case. Conditions in China were quite different from those in Europe a quarter of a century before. China had special ability to endure inflation because of being about 80 per cent agricultural, with subsistence farming usual, and with relatively small dependence upon money-using markets. Nevertheless, it was important to see what experience indicated about the "point of no return," when inflation would accelerate to eventual hyperinflation. The European experiences cited showed acute acceleration and a point of no return after prices reached about 75 to 100 times the prewar base. That level was reached in China in 1943. Fortunately, the improving outlook of the Allies in the War and the prospect of China's rescue helped to contain the price rise in 1942–1944 to an average of about 10 per cent per month, equivalent to a three- to four-fold increase in a year. The faster rise beginning late in 1944 was checked by the war's ending. But it seemed certain, in the light of Europe's earlier experience, that even greater danger would come after the war. In stressing this to the Chinese government, I urged careful financial planning for after the war supported by adequate foreign aid in financial and economic rehabilitation.[12]

The progress of inflation in China in 1937–1948 and in several European countries in 1914–1924 is shown in appendix B, Table 58. Although China's inflation did not become hyperinflation in 1937–1945, it is of interest to compare its progress in those years with that of the European inflations in periods of like length. It is outside the scope of this book to compare events in the respective periods of hyperinflation. Shun-hsin Chou, in *The Chinese Inflation, 1937–1949* (pages 259–271), has compared China's case with a number of cases of hyperinflation.

Several conclusions may be drawn from comparing China's wartime inflation with selected inflations of 1914–1924, for equal periods. Prices in China in the first four and a half years of the fighting, when China fought alone to December 7/8, 1941, rose less than in 1914–1918 in Austria-Hungary and much less than in Russia, though much more than in Germany with its effective controls. In China for about three years the rise was roughly similar to that in Russia in 1914–1917, that is, until the Bolshevik Revolution, after which faster deterioration and eventual hyperinflation took place in Russia. By the end of 1945 China, after eight and a half years, had less deterioration price-wise than Austria, and infinitely less than Russia, at the end of 1922; but it had more than Germany, although that country was then on the verge of hyperinflation.

In the first 18 months of fighting in 1937–1938, China covered by non-borrowed receipts a larger proportion of expenditures than did Britain, France, or Germany in a corresponding period of World War I (see Table 12). In the next two to three years of fighting, China's record in this regard was not so good as that of Britain, which was not the scene of battles, but was comparable to the record of France and Germany. Thereafter China's war went on for nearly four years, and the data are not comparable with the postwar data for the countries of Europe.

China, although engaged in a destructive war for over eight years, much longer than the war of 1914–1918, was able to use inflationary finance to meet a large part of the government's needs all through the war, and thereafter until 1947 before hyperinflation set in. It was only from about the beginning of 1947 that prices increased persistently at a rate more than four-fold yearly — a rate only met before in China for a few months in the first half of 1945, when China was at the verge of hyperinflation but was saved for the time being by the end of the war. Of the inflations in World Wars I and II that went on to collapse, China's lasted longest. The onset of rapid deterioration in China was delayed in 1937–1941 by the policy of exchange sales and operations to check undue fluctuations of rates in a free market. Foreign financial aid to China was a sustaining factor, despite its defects (see chapters VIII to X). On the other hand, delay of external military aid was very hurtful to confidence, and the cost of preparing the B-29 bomber operation from China speeded inflation, as did the American Treasury's withholding of gold in 1944–1945. Finally a comparison should recognize the appalling difficulties China faced, overrun by Japanese forces and split by the communists whose main aim was to take advantage of the confusion to expand. That China's inflation, in these wartime conditions, was definitely less bad than some other extreme inflations, and was able to provide fiscal resources longer than these, is to China's credit.

CHINA AND THE INTERNATIONAL MONETARY FUND AND BANK

Early in 1943 the White and Keynes plans for postwar monetary arrangements reached Chungking, with a request for China's views. Clearly the earliest practicable stabilization of currency values would be desirable. But it quickly appeared that neither plan sufficiently recognized the earlier need for rehabilitating the financial systems of countries suffering from the war. China could not for some time agree upon a gold parity for her currency, even under the best conceivable circumstances. The Chinese ambassador at Washington formally transmitted China's views on September 3, stressing these points. Since the stability of international exchange rates must rest upon a sound structure of individual monetary systems, a transitional period would be necessary during which these systems could be restored. Restoration would call for external aid, which could best be provided through the proposed new organization. Each nation whose monetary system was disrupted by the war would submit to the organization its program of financial rehabilitation, with a statement of its own resources available for the program and of the anticipated need for external assistance. China submitted a proposed redraft of the plan.[13] I sent informally to the State Department on July 20, 1943, a memorandum in support of the conclusions reached in China. "Repair of . . . injured monetary systems," I said, "is a need quite analogous to relief and repair of war devastation — though infinitely more difficult. It will require an all-out effort by the respective countries in a period of exhaustion," plus external aid. The text of this memorandum is contained in appendix G.

Unfortunately the Treasury did not seriously consider these views.[14] In extended discussions at Washington among experts of the various countries, the two Chinese experts, T. L. Soong and Te-mou Hsi, did not succeed in introducing flexibility about the setting of initial par values. White, in stressing immediate fixing of rates of exchange, was preparing to fight a currency battle like that of the 1930's and to combat competitive devaluation. My experience in China indicated that after the war a major problem would be just the opposite, namely, to attain rates that would avoid serious overvaluation. When I came to the United States in the summer of 1944 as a member of the Chinese delegation to the Bretton Woods Conference, I pressed for adoption of transitional arrangements that would permit China at once to become a member of the proposed new organization. Tsuyee Pei and I worked closely with Professor Dennis H. (later Sir Dennis) Robertson in drafting Article XX, Section 4, of the Bretton Woods agreement on "Initial determination of par values." The invaded countries were granted the necessary flexibility by this and other provisions. But there was no provision for international aid in their financial rehabilitation.

China's quota in the International Monetary Fund (IMF) was set at US$550 million — compared with US$2.75 billion for the United States, US$1.3 billion for Britain, and US$1.2 billion for Russia. Originally Russia's quota was proposed as US$1 billion, and Kung agreed to reducing China's quota from US$600 million to provide US$50 million to add to Russia's quota.[15] Russia's signature of the agreements suggested a cooperative attitude in postwar arrangements, but Russia did not ratify.[16]

China had hoped that the Monetary Fund's sister institution, the International Bank for Reconstruction and Development, would be in position to grant credit for postwar monetary rehabilitation. The instructions to China's delegates were that one or both institutions should be so empowered. The agreement for the Fund did not provide for such credits. The agreement for the Bank, Article I, stresses physical reconstruction but does not rule out aid in monetary rehabilitation. But the Bank has not granted such credits. China's quota for the Bank was set at US$600 million. Some quotas, including that of the United States, were larger than Fund quotas, and others were smaller.

THE PROBLEM OF POSTWAR MONETARY REFORM; SELF-HELP AND FOREIGN AID

As the war drew to a close discussion of monetary reform became active. But clearly it could not be considered apart from rehabilitation of expenditures, revenues, and debt. Also, there were the vast problems of recovering the occupied areas, where communism had spread insidiously. My recommendations concerning the many-sided postwar financial and economic problems are summed up in a memorandum of June 18, 1945, shown in appendix H.

How to deal with puppet money would become urgent immediately upon liberation. There were three main objectives, per my memorandum of November 27, 1944: "(1) All practicable regard to the welfare of bona fide Chinese holders, as contrasted with puppets and collaborationists; (2) promotion of economic recovery in the area; and (3) elimination of these currencies as soon as conditions permit." Since the chief holders were loyal Chinese, repudiation would be contrary to the first two objectives. Exchange rates for puppet money should take account of relative prices at the time in the respective currencies, but be "somewhat unfavorable to puppet currency." Procedure would involve seizure of unissued currency and plates; confiscation of notes held by puppet organs; refusal of exchange for collaborationists as far as possible, though with some leniency to minor employees; setting maximum amounts to be exchanged and blocking certain bank deposits, pending investigation; the supply of *fapi* and choice of denominations to be issued in exchange; destruction of exchanged puppet notes; and taking back control of seized banks. A special commission should be set up to prepare detailed plans. But there was little advance preparation. In chapter XIV I described how the exchange was handled, and the serious results of substantial repudiation of puppet money.

Attitudes in China toward prospective postwar financial problems were not encouraging. Many expected the end of the war would ease rather than intensify the problems. A high official told me that the currency would then revive "like a dry country after a rain," and that he expected exchange to revert to 20 to 30 per cent of the former level. Such ideas flowed in part from the widely held notion that shortage of goods and poor transport were the major causes of the inflation. While prices were bound to slump severely at the war's end, I pointed out repeatedly that improvement could be but temporary unless a solid program of financial rehabilitation were adopted and carried into effect; and that experience in Europe after World War I showed that the worst inflation was likely after the war.

Also, there was in China a strong urge to proceed at once after the war to new development, and seek huge loans abroad to that end, regardless of the effect upon inflation of the heavy *fapi* costs of the program. Many, too, exaggerated what external aid could do, and overlooked the need for self-help on the basis of a realistic plan to determine and allocate the internal resources likely to be available.

That China should scrap *fapi* and adopt a new currency was an idea that persisted almost from the start of the war. Several times I had to combat that notion and point out its extreme danger until conditions were ripe for success of a reform. China ordered a new set of notes before the end of the war, but there was no immediate effort to issue them. Eventual issuance of the "gold" *yuan* in 1948 was one of the causes of Nationalist downfall on the mainland.

In May 1945 I prepared an extensive report on currency reform, as "a tentative first approach." I stated that China eventually would need a new currency system, but that meanwhile China should do all possible to sustain the value of the old *fapi*, which should be stabilized substantially before being converted into a new currency. The prewar currency system, I stated, was "in truth a war casualty." Careful measures for transition to the eventual postwar system were necessary. When that system could be successfully put into operation, China should adopt a standard of gold or dollars as contemplated in the pending plan of the IMF. The eventual currency system should be free, without exchange control. The new level of exchange should not overvalue the currency, and in case of doubt a slight undervaluation would be preferable to overvaluation. Tentatively the eventual new unit might be given a value of US$0.25. That figure in 1945 was equivalent to about 14½d., the prewar sterling value of the Chinese unit. China's prewar exchange transactions were predominantly in sterling, and a return to the prewar dollar value around US$0.30 would mean a sterling equivalent of about 17¾d., that is, an appreciation in sterling of about 20 per cent because of the wartime drop in the dollar rate for sterling. The prewar nickel and copper coins, to the extent that they still existed, could be recognized as fractions of the new unit, and similar new coins issued after stabilization. The currency should be backed by reserves sufficient to meet exceptional postwar strains and tide over temporary imbalance in China's international payments. Reserves of US$1 billion, compared with total prewar external assets of US$379 million, would be desirable, but might be less if China's quota of US$550 million under the IMF were available. The Central Bank should be reorganized as the Central Reserve Bank, on the lines of the prewar project which was adopted but could not be put into effect because of the war. Banking reform was essential to cure defects of the prewar system. The government should sell to the public its shares in the Bank of China and other institutions engaged primarily in ordinary commercial activities. Unfortunately all such plans had to remain academic.

China accumulated large assets abroad during the Pacific War. The US$500 million credit was granted early in 1942; the American army paid US$392 million to acquire *fapi* at very favorable rates; and the Foreign Economic Administration paid at least US$48 million for strategic goods. Assets abroad in 1945 totaled nearly US$900 million, including the equivalent of about £15 million sterling and unsold gold in and enroute to China. Deducting funds earmarked to redeem the Dollar Savings Certificates and Bonds, about US$700 million remained. The position contrasted strongly with the low of about US$25 million in 1939, and the prewar total of US$379 million.

Besides, private Chinese holdings at the war's end were about US$300 million, including the Dollar Savings Certificates and Bonds. There was a movement in 1944–1945 to take over these private assets, and in May 1945 the Sixth Kuomintang Congress asked that the American government provide names and amounts. But that could not be done, and China would have had to act within her jurisdiction. I opposed the action under existing conditions, because of the difficulty of acting effectively; because China already was well supplied with foreign currencies; because payment in *fapi* would be inflationary; and because of damage to confidence, as shown by the effect of the discussion in raising prices of American currency and gold in the free market.

China's need for foreign funds for financial and economic rehabilitation I estimated at about US$1.5 billion for the first two postwar years, over and above what UNRRA might provide. Only US$100 to 200 million represented costs of new development. It was easy to exaggerate what foreign aid might do, compared with internal reform. In a memorandum of April 29, 1944, I pointed out that ". . . no amount of reserves can be a substitute for the necessary internal reforms."

Since China so badly needed guidance and stiffening in financial policy, it was unfortunate that external advice was uncoordinated and conflicting both during and after the war. Some influential Americans such as Donald M. Nelson wanted China to proceed at once after the war with big schemes of development, regardless of the galloping inflation. These spending ideas, which seemed to grow out of the policy followed in the depression of the 1930's, fitted only too well with ideas held in high circles in China. Strong American advice in favor of the priority of checking inflation before fresh spending schemes, could have stiffened in China what forces there were in favor of essential reforms.[17]

Throughout the war I hoped that China could have both technical and financial external help in stabilizing her finances, a precedent being the League of Nations aid to Austria and Hungary after World War I. Several possibilities of such help successively developed, as follows:

(1) In 1941 China proposed an Anglo-American economic mission to China, which might have developed into useful machinery for future use. This proposal was dropped when the United States indicated its reluctance.[18]

(2) The Chinese-American-British Stabilization Board, created in 1941, might have continued after the war. Britain wanted to keep the Board, especially for future aid in financial rehabilitation, but China was no more than lukewarm on the issue and the American Treasury was opposed to keeping the Board. The Board was abolished in the winter of 1943–1944 (see chap. XVIII).

(3) Late in 1943 the State Department proposed creating a joint Chinese-American commission for a broad discussion of China's problems, including the financing of postwar needs. The proposal, which was put forward as a means to smooth over acute friction over military aid and Chinese-American financial arrangements, was dropped when the American Treasury and War departments took the initiative in a sensitive issue of international relations, and the proposal was not adequately presented to China.[19]

(4) China sought to have the plans for the International Monetary Fund and Bank include provisions to help to restore the finances of invaded countries after the war. China formally proposed this to the American government in September 1943, when the White and Keynes plans were under discussion, in a memorandum which stressed the need for an all-out effort for financial reform by the invaded countries, plus external help. But, as explained earlier in this chapter, China's proposal did not receive serious consideration.

(5) The American Treasury in May 1945, during discussion of the controversy with China about deliveries of gold, proposed that China adopt a broad program of financial stabilization and checking inflation, and create a reserve fund of US$500 million out of the large balances which China then held abroad. In August, just after the end of the war, China proposed such a program, which I drafted. But no serious results followed. China, unfortunately, was more interested in grandiose plans for industrial development than in preventing her house from burning down. And, on the American side, the major effort came to be trying to bring together the National Government and the communists.

The severe wartime friction between China and the United States and Britain, with which I deal at length in *China and the Helping Hand*, interfered with any really serious American or international attempt to promote and support an effort by China for financial stabilization. The result was that postwar deterioration went on to eventual financial collapse, accompanied by the communist take-over.

XXI. THE EFFECTS OF THE INFLATION

During the war the government did not lack for money to spend, because the printing press was always at hand. The excesses resulting from this simple and easy means of finance had a profound effect upon China, both during the war and for the future.

GOVERNMENT FINANCE AND STABILITY

Inflation affords the means of raising adequate funds so long as the rate of price rise is moderate. But as time passes it gradually loses effectiveness, until governments find the greatest difficulty in raising enough from fresh issues. In China there was grave danger of the onset of this stage during the war, especially in 1945. But there was no breakdown and the end of fighting brought a respite. The government, however, failed to seize this opportunity to change the trend. The stage of collapse did not arrive until 1948–1949.

Inflation made budgeting most difficult. Needs were always outrunning estimates. Time after time the government had to issue revised and larger budgets for the various branches of its service. That involved delays, during which vital services often suffered from lack of funds. These increases in spending caused a vicious circle. Higher prices meant that appropriations had to be increased; more credit was granted and money printed; and this in turn added fuel to the flames. China's experience was one more illustration that acute inflation gets out of hand and inexorably leads to collapse unless drastic measures are taken to check the trend and then to stop it before it is too late.

One of the most serious effects of the inflation was to discourage efforts to develop the tax system. Raising money by note issue was, in the earlier stages, such an easy way to get revenue that it soothed the government into thinking that really effective wartime taxation was unnecessary. Efforts to adjust taxation to the war situation fell far short of what was needed. At best the increase of tax revenue is a difficult and unpopular problem. In 1937–1945 the government had so many problems it could not avoid that in taxation it took the easiest way. But, whatever the wartime errors, it was fatal not to plan during the war a postwar tax and fiscal system designed to stabilize the finances. The runaway inflation after the war and events related to it proved to be a major factor in Nationalist China's downfall on the mainland.

China's history shows that the strong governments were those that collected adequate taxes. In the 1920's the various Peking regimes were largely impotent because of lack of revenues. The Nationalists were able to stay in power and progress largely because they developed under Finance Minister Soong a system of revenues that was reasonably adequate. The communists, along with the government, relied heavily upon inflation to finance their needs during the Sino-Japanese fighting and later in the civil war, carrying inflation to quite an extreme. But when they came into power they found inflation utterly discredited. It has been said that a country cannot have more than one galloping inflation in a generation. Thus the communists, after their take-over, had to devise other means of raising money. Whatever may be thought of the burden and cruelty of their methods, which included confiscation of capital and other seizures, they at least found ways to meet fiscal needs without acute inflation. And that accomplishment was a factor in their fastening control on China's mainland.

DISTRIBUTION OF INCOME AND PROPERTY

The irregular rise of prices of goods and services drastically changed the distribution of income and property. Some people made excessive though often precarious gains. But most suffered severely and often tragically. Production and trade were hurt by rapid changes in costs, while hoarders and speculators gained.

Creditors and those whose savings were in terms of money suffered from the cheapening of money. In China the importance of longer-time obligations in local currency was less than in more developed countries. Yet these were important. The internal public debt in 1937 was about C$2 billion, equal to about US$600 million. The amount of corporate debt in local currency was much less than that figure, but still considerable. Of the order of C$1.3 billion (say US$400 million equivalent) was held in fixed and savings deposits, and about C$2 billion (say US$600 million) in current deposits. Banks held a great part of the internal debt, but were largely protected because the bonds backed deposits payable in local money. There was a growing amount of insurance in terms of Chinese currency. All holders of contractual debt in local currency stood to lose, for example, creditors for loans, interest, and rents.

Farmers maintained their position relatively well, as prices of crops rose. Inflation helped to solve a part of the land problem in a rough and ready way, because it reduced the burden of contractual money rentals and the debt of tenants. Also the right of redemption of land by tenants existed in parts of China and could be exercised in depreciated currency. As inflation went on, however, debts and rentals came more and more to be fixed in grain.

Holders of corporate stocks, real estate, and other property of course tended to be protected from shrinkage of value. On the Shanghai Stock Exchange prices soared along with the inflation.

Flight of capital abroad was stimulated. Realization on local currency assets and conversion into foreign currencies was a favorite means to beat the inflation throughout the war. Private assets abroad of Chinese nationals grew during the war to about US$300 million. It never was feasible to check this movement by exchange control, or to take over the assets abroad (see chap. XX).

Studies of the University of Nanking, located at Chengtu during the war, showed the varying impact of inflation on different classes in the community as the war dragged on. These figures were for only one city and sometimes for a limited sample, but they illustrate how capriciously inflation was working, as shown in Table 36.

TABLE 36. Impact of inflation upon classes in the community at Chengtu, 1942–1944

Items	Percentage of cost of living index represented by items listed[a]	
	December 1942	June 1944
Prices received by farmers	107	89
Purchasing power of farmers	96	102
Farm wages	96	71
City wages	87	88
Salaries, clerks	41[b]	31
Salaries, professors	15[b]	11
Soldiers' cash allowances	9	9

SOURCE: *Economic Facts* (monthly), University of Nanking, *passim*.

[a] The general cost of living indexes for Chengtu based upon January–June 1937 = 1 were 48.1 in December 1942, 49.5 in January 1943, and 546 in June 1944. The percentages shown are based upon the general indexes, for prices received by farmers; upon separate indexes for the laborer-peddler class, for wages and soldiers' allowances; upon separate indexes for the merchant-storekeeper class, for clerks' salaries; and upon separate indexes for the military-official-educational class, for professors' salaries.

[b] January 1943.

THE ARMY

The heaviest burden of inflationary finance fell upon those receiving salaries or payments that were more or less fixed; and first and foremost of these was the army. The highest officers could fare well because of their position and authority. They generally received lump sums in cash to disperse for their units, and this often tempted them to serious irregularities. But in the absence of irregularities the pay of officers, noncommissioned officers, and privates was meager and its real purchasing power was constantly shrinking. The commissary commonly supplied only rice. The pay of officers and men was supposed to enable them to buy vegetables and sometimes meat and other necessities for their life in the army. Though prices were constantly rising, the cash payments remained fixed for considerable periods of time. The University of Nanking calculated the purchasing power of soldiers' cash allowances at Chengtu based on six items commonly bought (as shown in Table 37).

TABLE 37. Comparison of indexes of soldiers' cash allowances and of cost of living at Chengtu, 1942–1944 (based on January–June 1937 = 1)

Period	Soldiers' cash allowances[a]	Cost of living, labor-peddler class	Column 2 as a multiple of column 1
December 1942	3.68	43.1	11.7
July 1943	6.99	158.1	22.6
December 1943	9.63	169.1	17.6
June 1944	44.4	514.1	11.6

SOURCE: *Economic Facts* (monthly), University of Nanking, *passim*.
[a] Purchasing power, based upon six items commonly bought.

The effect on the army's morale and value as a fighting force was grave. Two European Red Cross doctors who spent two years (1941–1942) with troops on the Ichang front, reached Chungking in January 1943, and told of their observations. About 20 officers monthly were deserting from one division for economic reasons. A surgeon-major thus told of his intention to leave:

I have no face any more. Although I may get leave to visit my wife in Wanhsien I cannot do so because I am not able to maintain her on my 175 dollars monthly salary. Even she herself earns $500 a month as a teacher. She will simply tell me: "What sort of a husband are you?".

Each soldier was supposed to get 24 ounces of rice daily. The doctors reported that officers, besides commonly registering more men than they actually had so as to get a surplus to sell, also squeezed rice to sell so that the men got only about 20 ounces. The troops were being issued pickled and salted vegetables as well as rice. But,

. . . for this badly insufficient food, 8 to 10 dollars per month are deducted from the soldiers' monthly pay of 16 to 18 dollars. The tragedy of the present food situation is mainly due to the fact that the soldiers' remaining cash wage, which used to make it possible for them to supplement the issued food with supplementary green vegetables (protein-rich) bean curd, oil or other fat, eggs and even with some meat and fruit, have become practically valueless on account of the rise of prices. In the Ichang sector at least, the year-long presence of large numbers of Chinese troops has cleared up livestock, etc. and generally upset the usual precarious equilibrium between supply and demand, more and more so every year, so that the factor of actual scarcity of food, from which the civilian population is also suffering, has combined with inflation in driving up prices even more than in Chungking. To give one example, carrots, which used to be a very valuable food supplement purchased by the soldiers last year, have risen in price from .30 per catty in January, 1942, to 3.00 or 4.00 dollars per catty in January, 1943. Even the officers who eat practically the same issued food as the men and have the same amounts deducted from their salaries, cannot buy adequate amounts of supplementary food any more from their gross salaries of 135 dollars and 175 dollars per month, respectively, for captains and majors; and malnutrition is increasing in the officers' ranks, too.

The doctors reported that in the military hospitals the management squeezed rice, usually giving only 16 ounces.

The hospital superintendent whom one of the doctors asked whether he could not give the sick soldiers the full 24 ounces of rice per capita instead of a mere 16, answered frankly that he had 7 children who could not live on his $240 salary per month (although he is entitled to buy military rice for all his family at $0.10 per catty, as against $5.00 in the free market), so that he cannot afford to give the soldiers more.

But these conditions were not universal. The doctors praised General Lo of the 18th Division:

In General Lo's division the soldiers are getting their full rations, and on the New Year he even pays every wounded man and officer a full month's extra wage, out of provision for office expenses which are never used but usually squeezed in all other divisions.

SALARIED PERSONNEL

The civil staff of the government and of salaried personnel in general suffered severely. By the end of 1943 at Chungking the money income of teachers, based upon the average of three groups, had risen only about a fifth as much as the cost of living, and of government officials only about a tenth, according to the following indexes prepared by Nankai University, as shown in Table 38. The continuation of the data is not available, as they did not appear in the new series of the publication which began in June 1944.

To mitigate hardship the government provided rice allowances in kind to the civil staff, especially after the adoption of collection of taxes in kind in 1940. Also during part of the time officials were allowed to buy rice at artificially low prices. But money income throughout the war was inadequate to maintain living standards of this group. Many good men left the service. Those who remained had to concentrate their family budgets more and more on food and absolutely vital necessities. Often they had to sell their furniture and other belongings. Many lost their lifetime savings. An extreme case was that of a Chinese family who had been saving a substantial amount each year for the education of their son. When toward the end of the war he had his 18th birthday, they took all the funds and bought him a cake.

TABLE 38. Impact of inflation upon salaried personnel, 1937–1943 (based upon 1936–1937 = 1)

	Index of income					Index of cost of living
Year[a]	College teachers	Middle school teachers	Primary school teachers	Government officials	All four groups	
1937	0.79	0.95	1.00	0.85	0.88	1.10
1938	0.88	1.08	1.03	0.85	0.96	1.42
1939	1.10	1.41	1.18	0.85	1.20	2.82
1940	2.24	2.02	2.04	1.69	2.13	11.8
1941	3.56	6.20	8.50	3.58	5.32	29.3
1942	5.29	11.31	15.54	5.91	9.42	62.9
1943	17.99	35.36	50.02	17.69	30.95	183

SOURCE: Nankai University Statistical Service, May 1944.
[a] Indexes are for December of each year.

During the war there was multiplication of concurrent jobs, so that often one man would hold several posts. Staff often skimped official work and were absent at length from office each day to engage in outside remunerative activities. There was constant stimulus to engage in irregularities and accept graft or squeeze. When an ordinary man is faced with a choice between irregular activities and seeing his family gradually starve, he is likely to consider that society owes him and his family a living and to feel that it is not wrong to supplement his income in devious ways.

In business the salaried classes did not fare so badly. Many businesses were family enterprises. Businesses commonly could afford to keep salaries somewhat in line with the price rise. They could act without awaiting a governmental decision. Many businesses provided for their staff food and lodging and other perquisites that eased the burdens of inflation. But many enterprises suffered so severely from the fighting, economic deterioration, uncertainty, and confusion, that this limited what they could do to meet the problems of inflation.

INFLATION AND CORRUPTION

Many of the thousands of foreigners, mostly Americans, who went to China after Pearl Harbor in the military or civil branches were shocked by the corruption. These, and members of the press, came back to tell about China's "corruption and inefficiency." The prevalence of this idea in governmental circles and among the public had much to do with the reluctance of the United States to follow a more positive policy as to China after the war ended.

Perspective on the situation would have shown several things. One was that in China there was a special situation. "Squeeze," nepotism, and official perquisites were for centuries viewed as wholly ethical, and squeeze, if not excessive, was part of the legitimate remuneration of officials. Before the war the government was combatting squeeze with growing effect, and trying hard to build a good public administration. I have utmost admiration for many Chinese officials with whom I worked before and during and after the war, who had a high conception of their responsibilities and strove for clean and efficient practices. But there were still far too many who viewed public position as giving them "face," an easy living, a chance for extra gains, and permitting them to disregard the rights and convenience of the public.

The Japanese attack forced the government westward into the most backward areas. Szechwan had to form the chief wartime base, and its rich agricultural and mineral resources fitted it well for this role. But this province had been brought into the government's fold only shortly before the war. Yunnan Province adjoining Indochina and Burma was even farther back in the middle ages. During much of the war relations with its corrupt regime, whose leader Lung Yun later joined the communists before their take-over and for some time was prominent in their activities, were a serious problem for Chungking.

The disruption of China's administrative organization, while it was still fragile and unfinished, was one of the great tragedies of the war. This disruption played a large part in China's eventual collapse. The number of trained government personnel who could leave the areas overrun by the enemy was limited. Many decided to stay to try to protect their families. Even if they could take their families there was the question of expense and transport and a place to live. There was risk often in leaving. On December 17, 1943, I wrote in my diary, "How can the government build an administration when inflation constantly takes away the buying power of salaries?"

Those who saw China at its worst should also have allowed for the fact that inflation anywhere breeds corruption and inefficiency. Americans and

Europeans can easily recall that their own lesser inflations led to black markets, evasions, speculative excesses, hoarding, bribery, and other abuses. Such happenings are "par for the course."

I have had contact over many years with many underdeveloped countries, where practices like those in China were common. The situation in China in 1937 was better than in many of these countries, and hardly any were improving at a better rate than China.

INFLATION AND THE INTELLECTUALS

In the educational system pressure of inflation was at its worst. Most of the personnel were state-paid and the buying power of their pay lagged like that of government staff generally. But less was done to help them because they were less directly related to the war effort. They had less means of supplementing income.

On intellectuals in the schools and universities and elsewhere the impact of inflation was far-reaching. In universities it bore upon faculty, administration, and students alike (except students from agricultural or business families). They saw individual speculators enriching themselves and living well, along with some military leaders and officials, while they were on the verge of starvation. As shown in Table 36 the purchasing power of salaries of professors at Chengtu, which became a chief educational center after 1937, came to be under 20 per cent of the prewar figure. It was no surprise that many leaders became disillusioned and antigovernment. Attempts from time to time to suppress criticism did not help their morale or gain their loyalty. Inflation softened up China's intellectuals for communism.

As showing the spirit of revolt that was brewing I quote part of a letter written on the eve of Pearl Harbor:[1]

Turning our thoughts to Chungking I have a feeling of complete fear. Fear not for myself but for my country.

With the present Sino-Japanese war now in its fifth year, millions of our countrymen have already lost their lives in the cause of national independence and freedom. While the sacrifice is noble and patriotic, it seems to me that the country as a whole is being duped for the sole benefit of those living off the land. This cannot be said to be an idle charge, for how else can one, whose chances of being killed in resisting the enemy is very high, and not getting the arms and ammunition to fight, view the selfish and extravagant mode of living of those in the war-time capital? Can anyone in Chungking deny that while the cost of daily necessities has increased several hundred per cent and is hurting those living from hand to mouth, the leading "officials" are importing fresh oranges, butter, and other foreign foodstuffs all by air? How can they waste so much to satisfy their craving for things foreign when the masses cannot buy food and shelter? The fact of the matter is the sufferers and the sacrificed are all of the poor masses who have to fight against the enemy in the front and to exert their utmost physical efforts in the constructive works in the rear, all on an empty or half-filled stomach.

Our people by nature is tame, submissive and above all loyal. But an empty stomach may change their nature, for hunger is real and cannot be satisfied by high-sounding words. Those sitting so smug in their homes, eating imported foods, remind us of the situation just before the French Revolution. It is indeed well for these leisure-loving folks to think of the fate of unhappy King Louis whose frivolous life and total disregard of the masses was his undoing.

Indeed it is the sacred duty of every person and the country to endure all sufferings for the nation's good. History is replete with examples of when a country is ruined no one can escape being enslaved, no matter whether he is a millionaire or a poor man. Of course the rich can afford to leave and live in foreign lands. And it is distressing to note that the "Government," that is, the officials, make profit from the muddled situation and thus further their private purses so as to live a comfortable life.

It is undeniable that the administrative system during the present hostilities has deteriorated and needs to be reformed thoroughly.

In order to save China and to give it real democratic government, the National Government must at once purge itself of all the elements obstructing this objective, and allow the representatives of the masses to have a say in their government. Our Government must be equally representative of the rich, the poor, the fairly well-to-do as well as the conservative, the radical and the dreamer.

I trust that China will be given this opportunity of demonstrating to the world what "democracy" is really like.

Regardless of whether that writer had communist connections — and some passages of the letter suggest that he did not — he reflected a viewpoint that became widespread and foreshadowed things to come.

Private universities suffered equally with public institutions. They were mostly mission institutions supported by gifts from abroad. Beginning in 1941 funds had to be brought in at official rates of exchange. These remained fixed for long periods, while prices marched ahead. The finance officers faced a grim problem in trying to make ends meet, and the personnel faced an impossible situation. When in Chengtu in January 1942 Professor Buck of the University of Nanking gave me a memorandum stating:

The present remuneration (salaries and all forms of subsidies) to teachers in educational institutions is so inadequate that the minimum needs of subsistence cannot be met. This situation is causing much instability. People are worrying how they are to maintain their living and for this reason many are leaving, or trying to leave for better positions in spite of the fact that they would prefer to remain with their own institutions.

It was not until June 1944 that the government sanctioned sales of exchange by philanthropic agencies in the free market by the United Clearing Board. The only relief to such agencies meanwhile had come from the exchange supplements which were far from adequate, and from occasional government subsidies. The effect on morale of personnel and their attitude toward the government was parallel to that in state educational institutions.

INFLATION AND THE MASSES

For the great mass of China's people inflation during the war caused less detriment than in more highly organized economies. Four fifths or more of the population were engaged in agriculture, and many families lived mainly on their own production. They did not primarily depend on money income. They could in effect barter their rice or other products for such things as salt and cloth which they themselves could not produce. Yet the tendency of money to shrink in value led farmers to be slow to part with their crops, thus aggravating the price rise.

Wage earners in both industry and agriculture fared much better than most classes. The call of the army lessened the supply of workers and in many places the demand increased, especially for those with special skills. A Central Bank study of October 1941 showed that at the end of 1940 the real wages of farm workers in Szechwan Province were 135 per cent of the 1938 level, of carpenters in Chengtu 99.5 per cent and of building workers in Chengtu 87 per cent. See also Table 36.

On the masses of the people in cities the effects varied greatly. In places where wartime activity centered conditions were often fairly good for them. But in other places there was widespread misery. Conditions in Nanking after the Japanese capture at the end of 1937 were particularly bad, and the situation there was thus described by M. S. Bates, of the University of Nanking, who stayed there, in a report of May 24, 1940, to the Church Committee for China Relief:

> The results of the increase in prices are also complex. But the greatest is misery. Employment is scant, and the iron law of wages is rigorously at work. Thousands of adult men and women who do find a place or way to toil are making scarcely enough to keep the individual worker alive. There has been no general increase in wages during the multiplication of prices by nearly three and one-half. The actual level of consumption has been drastically lowered, often among the common laborers and poorest groups who have never lived decently. Tens of thousands are weak and sick with hunger. The maximum wage for a vigorous man in unskilled labor is sixty-odd cents per day for employment dependent on weather and other uncertainties. Many laborers receive thirty and forty cents; while weavers, women on hand work, laundresses, fuel-gatherers, and adult peddlers often make ten to twenty cents — sometimes less. Perforce the children and the aged are driven wholesale into the competition, reducing further the meager possibilities for the men and women workers with dependents.

BUSINESS, HOARDING, AND SPECULATION

The trading classes could protect themselves fairly well by raising prices. A merchant, no matter how public spirited, had to raise his prices so that he could replace his goods in a constantly rising market. Both farmers and city producers were slow to part with valuable goods when the buying power of the money for which they could sell them was shrinking. This aggravated the scarcity and became a further cause of rising prices.

There was a clear stimulus to hoarding and speculation. The large and often quick gains so afforded diverted capital from useful production in agriculture and industry. Persons accumulating money inclined to buy goods rather than fixed property, because goods were subject to less risk of loss from invasion or air bombing and business was under public regulation. While traveling by road between Chungking and Chengtu early in 1942 I was told that a large supply of goods was being held outside of the cities along the route, so that hoarders could dodge the "economic police" and also have protection from air raids. There was said to be in the area a two years' supply of cloth, largely hoarded.

Most of the business of banks, other than the four government banks, consisted of financing and engaging in hoarding and speculation. In my report of February 5, 1942, on this visit to Chengtu I said:

In Chengtu, besides the Government banks, there are about 20 modern style banks and about the same number of native banks. Most of the business of these institutions in Chengtu (other than the government banks) now consists of buying or lending upon goods, and is thus largely hoarding and speculation. The government banks and commercial banks find that the public, instead of putting considerable funds with them on ordinary term deposit, are either directly buying goods or are putting out funds under the *pi-chi* system at high interest — perhaps 40% per annum. Outside Chengtu rates are even higher . . . As to Neikiang and other cities along the road, reports agreed that most of the operations of the native banks in particular, and to a large extent of the non-government commercial banks, were hoarding and speculation in goods. The commercial banks often get funds from their head offices because they can earn higher interest in these cities. Often commercial banks pay 30% *pi-chi* and re-lend the money to native banks at 50–60%. The native banks besides using their own capital, also get money from the public as deposits under a system of pass book deposit, not using the checking system.

It is obvious that the system of the modern (non-government) and native banks is almost entirely unregulated, and these banks are at liberty to determine their policies and activities almost wholly by motives of their immediate self-interest, without regard to the public welfare. Their operations not only contribute little to the war effort, but are often positively hurtful because the speculation and hoarding which they engage in and promote is so active and wide-spread. Remedies are to be found in action as follows:

(a) Require the commercial (non-government) and native banks to invest current funds in government bonds.[2] It is clear, according to all reports, that large amounts of free funds are available which otherwise will go into hoarding and speculation in goods.

(b) Press the public actively to subscribe to such bonds, thus drying up part of the source of free funds.

(c) Develop a plan for regulation of commercial and native banks through the Four Banks Joint Committee. One chief point would be to control the use of their funds, turning them toward investment in government bonds and in schemes to increase production of essential goods, rather than into commodity speculation which not only increases prices but which will eventually lead to an unsound position — overbought in goods — and a financial crash with huge loss. Maximum interest rates to be paid and charged could be standardized, and other matters could be regulated as the system develops.

(d) Stop the creation of more native banks throughout the country.

Interest rates rose during the inflation (see chap. XII). Before 1937 commercial rates had ruled from 15 to 30 per cent per annum, and in times of stringency were even higher. But as prices rose interest rates added an element of compensation for the smaller buying power of money at the time of payment of the loan. In many cases loans and interest on them were payable by farmers in grain rather than money. Rates of money interest working out at 100 to 200 per cent were common after 1942. Even so speculators could gain from borrowing at such rates, when the prices of goods rose even more. Loans were commonly made through the *pichi* system, renewable semimonthly at rates of interest figured at so much per day per C$1,000 and varying at times rather widely.

Kia-ngau Chang, in his analysis of China's inflation, describes the working of China's wartime banking system and the government's attempts to regulate it and check abuses. He states that in 1942–1945 the government was able to control fairly well the granting of private bank credit for speculation and other nonessential activities, but that the banks often shifted the use of their funds to their own speculations. He concluded that bank advances to the government rose at a rate of 3.4 times the growth of private credit in 1942, and 7.8 times in 1945, and that: "The restrictions on private credit, therefore, seem inconsequential when set against the fantastic increase in the money supply emanating from government deficit spending." [3]

THE AFTERMATH

When the war finally ended in August 1945, China faced an array of difficulties that would have taxed the capabilities of any government. Well over half of China's people were in areas under enemy occupation, where a Chinese administration had to be restored. Agriculture suffered from shortages of labor, animals, and fertilizers. There had been huge destruction of property. Industry was at a low ebb, working capital was decimated, stocks of goods were depleted, and foreign trade had practically ceased. Invasion had broken down much of the country's business organization. Communications except by air hardly functioned. The chaotic economic, financial, and political situation was unfavorable for support of measures that could promptly rehabilitate the currency and the national finances. [4]

With average prices at the war's end more than 2,500 times the prewar level, inflation paused for breath only briefly. It took a fresh start for an even faster advance. In three more years prices rose by the late summer of 1948 to about 2,500 times the level of August 1945. The new gold *yuan* issued in 1948 had a short and unhappy life. Starting with a nominal value of US$0.25, it fell to the vanishing point in about a year when the National Government withdrew to Formosa.

The government's inability to deal with the inflation, coming along with the disruption and suffering from enemy invasion, had a major part in making China ripe for revolution.

APPENDIXES
BIBLIOGRAPHIC NOTE
NOTES

APPENDIX A. RECEIPTS, EXPENDITURE, DEBT, FOREIGN AID

The tables in this appendix relate in particular to parts I and II of the text, chapters II to X. Those chapters contain further tables concerning receipts, expenditures, and debt; see Tables 1-15, 20, and 22.

RECEIPTS AND EXPENDITURE

The receipts and expenditures of the National Government from the time of its take-over in 1928 through 1945 are summarized in chapter II, Table 1. Details through the fiscal year ending June 30, 1935, are contained in the published reports of the Finance Ministry. For the two fiscal years from that date to June 30, 1937, detailed reports of the Ministry have not been published so far as I know. To fill this gap I present in Table 39 a statement for those two years in form comparable with the published statements for previous years. The data for those two years were furnished to me contemporaneously, and stated to be final accounts.

For the war period, from July 1, 1937, through 1945, the detailed figures are shown in Table 40. This is substantially a translation of statements in the *Public Finance Yearbook, 1948* (in Chinese), issued by the Finance Ministry, section III, pp. 98–101. The tabulation there for 1945 differs from that for 1937–1944, both in some headings and in order of presentation. Here I follow the order for 1937–1944, as far as practicable, to facilitate comparison, thus changing the order of the 1945 data. Items less than C$500,000 are here omitted. Tables 2 and 3 in chapter II contain summaries of the data in Table 40. The figures in Table 40 substantially agree with the figures which I received contemporaneously from the Ministry.

Other writers have used materially different figures for the two fiscal years 1936 and 1937 and for 1945, but for the intervening period there are no great differences. For fiscal 1937 Wei-ya Chang states receipts and expenditure as C$1,973 million and C$1,894 million, respectively, showing a surplus of C$79 million.* The surplus resulted from treating as a cash item the unissued part of the consolidation loan of 1936.† For 1945 he states expenditures of C$2,348 billion, nearly twice the C$1,215 billion (excluding the beginning cash balance) reported in the *Public Finance Yearbook* (Table 40 of this appendix). His much larger figures for 1945 result apparently

* Wei-ya Chang, *The Money and Finance of China*, pp. 138–145. Kia-ngau Chang, in *The Inflationary Spiral*, p. 124, uses these figures of Wei-ya Chang.
† See Kia-ngau Chang, *The Inflationary Spiral*, p. 124n.

TABLE 39. Receipts and expenditure, 1935–1937 (in millions of C$)

	1935–36[a]	1936–37[a]
RECEIPTS		
Revenue		
Customs	272	379
Salt	184	197
Consolidated taxes	135	159
Tobacco and wine	15	15
Stamp tax	10	9
Income tax	—	7
Mining tax	4	4
Government property receipts	9	3
Government enterprise receipts	67	13
Government administrative receipts	12	8
Profit on government business enterprises	10	9
Miscellaneous	82	68
	801	870
Proceeds from borrowing		
Domestic bonds and Treasury notes	148	223
Bank loans and overdrafts	128	113
	276	336
Recovery from suspense items of prior years	16	—
Unremitted balances of customs and salt revenue services at end of last fiscal year	67	—
Cash balance at beginning of the fiscal year	23	45
Total	1182	1251
EXPENDITURE		
Party	8	7
Civil expenses		
National Government Council and organs	15	18
Interior	13	13
Foreign affairs	11	10
Financial	67	64
Educational and cultural	37	42
Judicial	4	3
Industrial	7	3
Communications	6	5
Mongolian and Tibetan affairs	3	2
Reconstruction	88	54
Capital for government enterprises	33	—
Subsidies	99	86
Compensation and awards	2	3
	385	
Less refunds	7	—
	378	305
Military expenses	390	521
Capital for government enterprises	—	29
Loan service		
Domestic bonds	186	192
Foreign loans	62	63
Interest on bank loans and overdraft	5	7
Indemnity	36	38
Debt readjustment fund	5	5
	294	305
Net addition to reserves and suspense items	3	—
Unremitted balances of customs and salt revenue services at end of the fiscal year	65	—
Cash balance at end of the fiscal year	45	83[b]
Total	1182	1251

SOURCE: Office of the Accountant General, Finance Ministry. The figures were received contemporaneously and were stated to be final.

[a] Year ending June 30.

[b] In Table 40 the beginning balance for the next fiscal year is stated as C$93 million. I cannot explain the discrepancy.

TABLE 40. Receipts and expenditure, July 1, 1937, to December 31, 1945 (in millions of C$)

RECEIPTS

	1937–38[a]	1938[b]	1939	1940	1941	1942	1943[c]	1944	1945
Taxes									
Land	—	—	—	—	—	516	4,014	3,392	6,326
Income	19	8	27	44	80	197	751	1,145	2,009
Inheritance	—	—	—	—	—	1	15	49	111
Excess profits	—	—	—	25	70	291	884	1,189	1,833
Business	—	—	—	—	—	610	1,785	3,032	7,318
Stamp	5	3	5	7	16	26	355	1,063	3,140
Customs	239	128	346	38	15	160	377	494	3,321
Commodities	—	—	—	—	—	—	—	—	23,144
Factory	30	16	22	46	121	309	657	2,046	—
Wine and tobacco	14	9	20	24	63	273	1,278	2,929	—
Mining	2	1	2	2	5	24	66	186	740
Consumption	—	—	—	—	—	399	718	1,838	304
Salt	141	47	61	80	296	—	—	—	2,800
Salt surtax	—	—	—	—	—	—	1,202	13,439	48,925
Special business	—	—	—	—	—	—	57	45	11
Monopolies									
Salt	—	—	—	—	—	1,180	1,823	1,089	1,781
Matches	—	—	—	—	—	—	95	298	88
Tobacco	—	—	—	—	—	177	879	1,707	393
Sugar	—	—	—	—	—	—	359	470	7
Other									
Fines	—	—	—	—	—	—	—	—	229
Penalties	—	—	—	2	2	13	32	56	272
Fees	6	3	5	5	7	21	58	94	—
Estate tax	—	—	—	2	5	6	33	108	—
Property income	—	—	—	—	—	—	—	—	213
Public enterprises	2	—	—	27	20	101	95	201	5,003
Public property	2	—	1	—	—	—	—	—	1,031
Public business	6	4	5	2	2	1	3	1	—
Privilege taxes	—	—	—	2	3	78	4	5	—
Contributions	3	19	55	33	21	39	21	80	8,556
Sale of foreign loan purchases, commodities, gold	—	—	—	—	—	—	—	—	28,663
Interest on unissued bonds	—	—	—	—	270	675	635	606	2
Revenues of previous years	—	—	—	725	121	123	266	373	2,646
From previous periods, miscellaneous	—	—	—	—	—	—	—	141	1,065
Miscellaneous	90	60	165	253	65	31	22	187	63
Trusts	—	—	—	—	—	1	8	2	10
Refund of capital	—	—	—	—	—	—	—	4	31
Temporary receipts	—	—	—	—	—	—	14	5	28
Subsidies	—	—	—	—	1	13	—	—	—
Borrowing									
Domestic	256[d]	18[d]	25[d]	8	127	155	3,871	1,647	62,727
Foreign	—	—	—	—	—	208	15	342	92
Banks	1,195	853	2,311	3,834	9,443	20,082	40,857	140,091	1,043,257
Balance from previous year	93	12	12	266	137	889	2,091	4,536	10,298
Total	2,103	1,181	3,063	5,425	10,892	26,602	63,352	182,832	1,266,438

SOURCE: *Public Finance Yearbook, 1948* (in Chinese, here translated), issued by the Finance Ministry, Nanking, section III, pp 98–101.
[a] Year ending June 30, 1938.　　　　　　　[b] Second half year.
[c] One of the tax items for 1943 apparently should be C$10 million greater than here shown. See Table 2, note c.　　　　　　[d] Includes both domestic and foreign borrowing.
[e] In the original, expenditures for 1945 are classified differently than for 1937–1944. See the statement preceding this table.　　　　　　[f] Includes Economics Ministry from 1940 to 1945.
[g] Comprising (millions of C$): Administration 106; Food 53; Economic Affairs 1,686; Education 146; Communications 5,440; Agriculture and Forestry 44; Relief 9; Water Conservancy 144; Health 6; Land Administration 16; Social Welfare 40.

TABLE 40 (*continued*)

EXPENDITURE

	1937–38[a]	1938[b]	1939	1940	1941	1942	1943	1944	1945[e]
General									
Government, general	—	—	—	20	43	87	265	1,980	1,121
Party	7	4	10	—	—	—	—	—	13,549
Cabinet, general	12	5	12	8	9	13	34	165	—
Executive Yuan	—	—	—	9	33	64	100	595	1,901
Legislative Yuan	—	—	—	1	2	5	11	38	172
Judicial Yuan	2	1	3	12	42	74	162	1,320	225
Examination Yuan	—	—	—	1	3	9	20	99	486
Control Yuan	—	—	—	3	6	13	32	182	867
Education	36	20	43	116	176	505	1,178	3,790	22,181
Communications[f]	5	1	2	25	20	145	68	410	1,123
Health	—	—	—	6	24	34	46	168	1,079
Welfare	1	10	31	41	70	138	411	467	1,225
Defense	391	211	443	710	1,179	2,151	6,391	9,553	191,120
Defense Council	—	—	—	—	—	—	—	—	571
Foreign affairs	10	6	7	8	12	49	56	126	565
Overseas Chinese	—	—	—	—	1	2	2	16	99
Finance	47	26	79	57	102	680	756	5,681	24,759
Debt	374	242	546	346	480	1,587	3,493	5,220	7,017
Subsidies	24	14	54	115	234	51	73	137	461
Property expense	2	2	4	—	—	—	—	—	809
Capital investment	—	—	—	23	11	85	147	95	7,690[g]
Capital for enterprises	—	—	—	—	—	—	—	—	2,996[h]
Internal affairs	13	2	5	—	—	—	—	—	1,585
Agriculture and forestry	—	—	—	—	—	—	—	—	320
Food administration	—	—	—	—	—	—	—	—	14,970
Justice administration	—	—	—	—	—	—	—	—	5,985
Relief	—	—	—	—	—	—	—	—	850
Water conservancy	—	—	—	—	—	—	—	—	382
Land administration	—	—	—	—	—	—	—	—	1,440
Staff retirement	2	1	2	4	1	1	3	42	430
Mongolian and Tibetan affairs	1	1	2	—	—	—	—	—	316
Temporary payments	—	—	25	—	—	—	—	—	1,680
Expenditures of previous years	—	—	—	14	1	2	5	427	575
Miscellaneous	—	—	—	—	150	26	—	—	—
Provincial and city	—	—	—	—	—	1,832	3,394	6,302	30,021
Reconstruction[i]									
Defense	277	121	521	716	1,839	5,515	9,538	21,975	6,888
Economic affairs	104	71	122	96	213	492	523	1,643	602
Water conservancy	7	5	8	22	35	81	142	402	1,482
Agriculture and forestry	—	—	—	—	25	48	108	358	1,516
Communications	57	61	238	439	712	1,648	2,151	9,191	3,516
Northwest reconstruction	—	—	—	—	—	—	392	919	—
Miscellaneous[j]	—	—	—	—	—	—	—	—	478[j]
Extraordinary	720	367	572	—	—	—	—	—	862,389
Defense	—	—	—	2,347	1,862	3,482	7,033	12,478	—
Food for staff	—	—	—	—	1,458	3,040	8,590	13,869	—
Subsidies for staff	—	—	—	10	40	264	1,347	—	—
Commodity price control	—	—	—	—	—	—	954	836	—
Cost of bartered goods	—	—	—	—	906	983	—	—	—
Control of smuggling	—	—	—	—	—	44	—	—	—
Employees' rice subsidy	—	—	—	—	32	262	—	—	—
Loss on sale of rice	—	—	—	—	—	70	—	—	—
Emergency	—	—	64	139	279	1,028	11,392	73,205	—
Balance at end of year	12	12	266	137	889	2,091	4,536	11,142[k]	51,349
Total	2,103	1,181	3,063	5,425	10,892	26,602	63,352	182,832	1,266,438[l]

[h] Comprising (millions of C$): Administration 2,124; Education 106; Food 253; Communications 383; Justice 14; Water Conservancy 116.

[i] See notes g and h re analogous items listed under Capital investment and Capital for enterprises.

[j] Comprising (millions of C$): Administration 409; Finance 50; Education 6; Food 3; Relief 10.

[k] This item does not agree with the balance carried forward in the 1945 accounts.

[l] The total of all items listed for 1945 exceeds by C$200 million the total shown. See Table 3, note d.

from later inclusion of a big entry of about C$1 trillion, representing revaluation of dollars received from the American government in 1945 for army costs. Inclusion of this item puts current nonborrowed cash income at nearly half of expenditures;* whereas the realistic proportion as shown in Table 7 (chap. II) is about 17 per cent. Shun-hsin Chou states for fiscal 1937 expenditures of C$1,884 million, which is similar to Chang's figure; and for fiscal 1936, C$1,337 million.† I have not been able to obtain information as to the content of the larger figures for fiscal 1936 and 1937, which apparently were compiled other than by the Finance Ministry. They seem to include gross rather than net figures of borrowing and the repayment thereof; and perhaps also gross rather than net figures of the receipts and payments of some governmental organs. Whatever the figures are, they are misleading when compared with the official figures of the Finance Ministry for preceding and following periods.

The figures in Tables 39 and 40, which are summarized in Tables 1 to 7 in chapter II, seem to me to be the best available. For fiscal 1936, 1937, and 1945 where material differences appear as stated above, the figures I use seem to me to be the right figures for comparability with the rest of the series.

Table 41 presents a summary of advances through the Joint Committee of the Four Government Banks, with a breakdown of the objects for those advances.

Table 42 is a statement of the distribution by provinces of receipts in kind in 1943. A table of somewhat similar data for the year ending June 30, 1945, appears in *China Handbook, 1937–1945* (New York, 1947), p. 198. The total of 2,795,177 metric tons there shown for the year ending June 30, 1945, compares with 2,869,000 in the crop year ending three months later, as given in Table 8, chapter III, above. In Table 42, receipts converted to metric tons agree with the total in Table 8 for 1942–1943. The total value of receipts at the unit prices shown is C$27,860 million, which is 5 per cent greater than the figure of the Land Tax Administration quoted in chapter III.

DEBT

Tables 43–46 which follow show the position of the debt of the Finance Ministry, other than the Boxer Indemnity, as of July 1, 1937; the debt of the Railway Ministry, the Communications Ministry, and other governmental organs as of January 1, 1937; and the debt in arrears as of July 1, 1937.

* See Wei-ya Chang, *The Money and Finance of China*, pp. 140, 145; and Kia-ngau Chang, *The Inflationary Spiral*, pp. 124, 124n, 133–134.
† Shun-hsin Chou, *The Chinese Inflation*, 1937–1949, p. 72.

TABLE 41. Advances through the Joint Committee of the Four Government Banks, 1937–1945 (in millions of C$)

Period	Loans authorized	Renewals	Total	Balance at end of period	Increase
Sept. 1937 to Dec. 1939	636	—	636	—	[a]
1940	642	45	687	435	[a]
1941	1,551	247	1,798	1,227	792
1942	2,012	645	2,657	1,865	638
1943	9,512	1,589	11,101	10,282	8,418
1944	28,999	4,026	33,025	32,211	21,929
1945 (Jan. to Aug.)	42,358	6,840	49,198	[a]	16,200[b]
1945	63,115	12,553	75,668	74,855	42,644

Objects of advances

	Sept. 1937 to Dec. 1939	1940	1941	1942	1943	1944	1945
Food and agriculture	16	66	207	238	741	901	2,927
Salt	52	247	879	420	1,014	4,695	15,519
Communications	21	21	176	263	1,444	909	4,653
Industry and mining	30	147	158	918	6,639	23,822	37,436
Local reconstruction	163	67	22	11	—	—	—
Commodity purchase and price stabilization	17	137	155	434	767	1,970	5,707
Other	337	2	11	373	496	728	9,570
Totals	636	687	1,608[c]	2,657	11,101	33,025	75,812[c]

SOURCE: Joint Office of the Four Government Banks. The Central Bank of China's *Bulletin*, February 1946, p. 100, and *The Chinese Year Book, 1944–1945*, pp. 608–610, contain slightly different and less comprehensive figures.

[a] Not available.

[b] Estimated.

[c] The totals of the breakdown for 1941 and 1945 differ from the totals in the third column of the tabulation above, which are C$1,798 and C$75,668 million, respectively.

TABLE 42. Land tax and compulsory purchase: distribution by provinces of collections of rice and wheat in the year ended September 30, 1943 (in thousands of *piculs* of 50 kg)

Province	Tax in kind	Compulsory purchase	Total	Unit price C$ per picul
		Rice		
Szechwan	9,327	7,111	16,438	477
Hunan	4,875	5,799	10,674	223
Kiangsi	1,947	4,436	6,383	87
Yunnan	1,599	2,198	3,797	612
Kwangsi	1,555	1,445	3,000	413
Fukien	1,997	926	2,923	252
Anhwei	1,443	1,443[a]	2,886[a]	260
Kwangtung	1,505	1,219	2,724	269
Kweichow	1,301	1,154	2,455	230
Hupei	1,028	749	1,777	509
Chekiang	1,511	—	1,511	203
Hsikang	246	320	566	395
Kiangsu	291	—	291	233
Totals	28,626	26,801	55,427	
		Wheat		
Shensi	2,250	1,344	3,594	790
Honan	1,000	1,442	2,442	1,485
Kansu	806	799	1,605	450
Shantung	760	—	760	1,485
Shansi	354	250	604	648
Suiyuan	100	414	514	400
Ninghsia	502	—	502	367
Chinghai	39	160	199	396
Totals	5,810	4,409	10,219	

SOURCE: Land Tax Administration of the Finance Ministry.
[a] Including wheat.

Data showing the complete position of railway debt as of dates after January 1, 1937, are not available because of the confusion resulting from the hostilities. During 1937 the Ministry contracted some additional obligations to build new railways and improve existing lines, and after January 1, 1937, the Ministry paid off some principal, although most payments on railway debt ceased early in the hostilities because of enemy seizure of the lines. Early in 1938 the Railway Ministry was merged into the Communications Ministry. The total principal of the foreign debt here listed did not materially change because of repayment. Available information concerning changes after January 1, 1937, in the outstanding amounts of certain loans appears in note c to the first part of Table 44.

TABLE 43. Debt of the Finance Ministry receiving service as of July 1, 1937

FOREIGN LOANS[a]

Date of loan	Name of loan	Scheduled date of final redemption	Interest rate (per cent)	Security from which paid	Principal outstanding	
					July 1, 1937	August 15, 1945
1898	Anglo-German	1943	4½	Customs	£ 4,308,205	£ 2,996,425
1908	Anglo-French	1938	4½	Salt	£ 500,000	£ 250,000
1911	Hukuang Railway	1975	2½ to 5	Salt[b]	£ 5,656,000	£ 5,656,000
	Hukuang Railway, non-interest scrip	1961	—	Salt[b]	£ 441,667	£ 441,667
1912	Crisp	1952	5	Salt	£ 3,930,837	£ 3,666,971
1913	Reorganization	1960	5	Customs	£20,178,860	£19,691,880
1918	Marconi notes	1975	1½ to 3	Salt	£ 600,000	£ 600,000
1919	Vickers notes	1975	1½ to 3	Salt	£ 1,803,200	£ 1,803,200
1919	Chicago Bank	1954	2½ to 5	Salt	US$ 5,500,000	US$ 5,500,000
1919	Chicago Bank, non-interest scrip	1954	—	Salt	US$ 1,005,500	US$ 1,005,500
1919	Pacific Development	1954	2 to 4	Salt	US$ 4,900,000	US$ 4,900,000
1925	Gold Loan	1948	5	Customs	US$27,569,850	US$22,136,650
1928	Gold Loan	1941	6	Customs	US$ 1,420,300	US$ 828,900
1930	Sino-French Educational Fund advance	1948	6	Customs	US$ 265,000	US$ 265,000
1931–1933	U.S. Government Relief and Commodity Loans	1942	5	Customs surtax	US$14,700,000	nil
1934	Canton-Hankow Railway Loan	1947	6	Customs	£ 1,164,000	£ 972,000
	Miscellaneous				Y 3,022,000	[c]
	Totals				£38,582,769 US$55,460,650 Y 3,022,000	£36,078,143 US$34,736,050

Grand total, approximate equivalent at exchange of July 1, 1937: US$247,000,000;
August 15, 1945: US$180,000,000

INTERNAL LOANS

Date of loan	Name of loan	Scheduled date of final redemption	Interest rate (per cent)	Security from which paid	Principal outstanding July 1, 1937
1928	17th Year Long Term Currency Loan	1953	2½	Customs	C$ 37,125,000
1929	Hopei Conservancy Loan	1939	9.6	Tientsin customs surtax	800,000
1934	23d Year Yuping Railway Loan[d]	1943	6	Subsidy from salt revenue to provincial government	9,600,000
1935	24th Year Szechwan Rehabilitation Loan[d]	1944	6	Subsidy from salt revenue to provincial government	61,600,000
1936	25th Year Szechwan Rehabilitation Loan[d]	1951	6	Subsidy from salt revenue to provincial government. Also tobacco, wine and business taxes in Szechwan	14,400,000
1936	25th Year Kwangtung Currency Readjustment Loan[d]	1966	4	Consolidated taxes collected in Kwangtung	118,800,000
1936	25th Year Consolidation Loan		6	Customs	
	Class A	1948			148,350,000
	Class B	1951			148,500,000
	Class C	1954			346,500,000
	Class D	1957			544,500,000
	Class E	1960			257,400,000
1936	25th Year Recovery Loan	1960	6	Customs	336,600,000
	Miscellaneous				4,138,391
	Total				C$2,028,313,391
1937	Kwangtung Harbor Loan	1953	6	Canton customs surtax	US$ 2,000,000

Grand total, approximate equivalent at exchange of July 1, 1937: US$606,000,000

[a] Not including: (i) The Tientsin-Pukow Railway Loans of 1908–1910, which enjoyed certain customs security but were being paid from railway revenue by the Railway Ministry, and (ii) internal loans issued in terms of foreign currency.

[b] Interest was also guaranteed by revenue of the railway and from January 1, 1941, by customs revenue. Principal was guaranteed by revenue of the railway and by revenue under control of the Finance Ministry.

[c] The miscellaneous debts of Y3,022,000 as of July 1, 1937, are not included in the list as of the end of the war, because it was assumed that the peace settlements would require the enemy states to assume settlement of debts to their nationals.

[d] These loans were authorized by the National Government, for purposes primarily affecting the regions mentioned, and secured either upon subsidy from the government to provincial or local authorities or on specified revenues collected in the respective regions.

[337]

TABLE 44. Debt of the Railway Ministry receiving service as of January 1, 1937

FOREIGN DEBT: Loans and advances[a]

Date of loan	Name of loan	Interest rate (per cent)	Principal outstanding Jan. 1, 1937
1899	5% Loan (Peiping-Liaoning Railway)	5	£ 460,000[c]
1903	Shanghai-Nanking Railway Loan	5	£ 2,784,000
1903–1907	Kaifeng-Honan Railway Loan	5	F. fr. 23,500,000
1905	Honan Railway Loan (Taokow-Chinghua Railway)	2½ to 5	£ 485,700[c]
	Scrip for arrears of interest	0	£ 44,613
1907	Canton-Kowloon Railway Loan	2½ to 5	£ 1,111,500[c]
	Scrip for arrears of interest	0	£ 122,265
1908	Tientsin-Pukow Railway Loan	2½ to 5	£ 3,598,990
1910	Tientsin-Pukow Railway, Supplementary Loan[b]	2½ to 5	£ 2,550,780
	Scrip for arrears of interest on 1908 and 1910 loans	0	£ 843,663
1911	5% Railway Loan (Peiping-Hankow Railway)	5	Y 9,340,000
1912–1922	Nanchang-Kiukiang Railway Loans	5	Y 17,423,832
1913	Lung-Tsing-U-Hai Railway Loan	1½ to 4	£ 4,288,220[c]
1913	Pukow-Sinyang Railway Advance (railway unbuilt)	6 to 7	£ 207,256
1913	Tatung-Chengtu Railway Advances (railway unbuilt)	2	£ 588,480[c]
		2	F. fr. 4,334,888[c]
1914	Shanghai-Fengching Railway Loan (charged on Peiping-Liaoning Railway)	6	£ 262,500[c]
1916	Tientsin-Pukow Railway, Deutsch-Asiatische Bank Advance	0 to 3	£ 883,050
1919	Taokow-Chinghua Railway Loan	0	£ 53,367[c]
1920	Chinghua-Menghsien Loan (Honan Railway)	0	£ 110,681[c]
1920–1923	Lung-Tsing-U-Hai Railway 8% Treasury Bonds	1½ to 4	Fl. 31,483,000
1920–1923	Lung-Tsing-U-Hai Railway 8% Treasury Bonds	1½ to 4	B. fr. 137,743,000
1921	Peiping-Liaoning Railway Double Track Loan	5	£ 69,667
1922	Kiaochow-Tsinan Railway Loan	6	Y 40,000,000
1925	Lung-Tsing-U-Hai Railway 8% Treasury Bonds	1½ to 4	F. fr. 21,250,000
1936	Shanghai-Hangchow-Ningpo Railway Completion Loan	6	£ 1,100,000
	Totals		£ 19,564,732
			Y 66,763,832
			F. fr. 49,084,888
			B. fr. 137,743,000
			Fl. 31,483,000
	Approximate equivalent at exchange of July 1, 1937		US$140,000,000

[338]

TABLE 44 (*continued*). Debt of the Railway Ministry, etc.

FOREIGN DEBT: Debts for materials, etc.

		Principal outstanding Jan. 1, 1937
Peiping-Suiyuan Railway	£	144
	US$	7,579,071
	Y	17,648,675
Peiping-Hankow Railway	£	21,037
	US$	2,676,299
	Y	537,776
Tientsin-Pukow Railway	£	135,623
	Y	4,125,000
Canton-Kowloon Railway	£	10,397
Honan-Kaifeng Railway	B. fr.	4,302,057
Floating debt		
	£	22,005
	US$	1,547,171
	Y	271,420
	B. fr.	4,316,034
	F. fr.	226,805
Total	£	189,206
	US$	11,802,541
	Y	22,582,871
	B. fr.	8,618,091
	F. fr.	226,805
	Approximate equivalent	US$23,000,000
Grand total of external railway debt, approximate equivalent at exchange of July 1, 1937		US$163,000,000

ᵃ Not including two loans issued for railway purposes whose current service was being paid by the Finance Ministry, namely the Hukuang Loan of 1911 and the Canton-Hankow Railway Loan of 1934, which are listed in Table 43.

ᵇ In addition £678,000 of bonds of this loan, not theretofore issued, were validated pursuant to an agreement of 1936 with the Deutsch-Asiatische Bank, the said bonds being security for an advance made by the bank after issuance of the loan on the security of unissued bonds. The £678,000 of bonds were not to be marketed for the time being. Because the advance of larger amount for which these bonds were pledged is included in this table, the amount of these bonds is not here included.

ᶜ Partial data indicate that as of August 15, 1945, the outstanding principal of certain loans was as follows:

Peiping-Liaoning Railway (1899)	£ 172,500
Honan Railway Loan (1905)	£ 475,700
Canton-Kowloon Railway Loan (1907)	£1,101,500
Lung-Tsing-U-Hai Railway Loan (1913)	£4,580,380
Tatung-Chengtu Railway advance (1913)	£ 577,176
	Fr. fr.4,251,560
Shanghai-Fengching Railway Loan (1914)	£ 225,000
Taokow-Chinghua Railway Loan (1919)	£ 43,663
Chinghua-Menghsien Railway Loan (1920)	£ 90,553

The net decrease in principal of these loans outstanding at the end of the war, compared with the position as of January 1, 1937, was only about £100,000, because of a stated increase of £292,160 in the outstanding principal of the 1913 Lung-Tsing-U-Hai Railway Loan.

TABLE 44 (*continued*). Debt of the Railway Ministry, etc.

INTERNAL DEBT: Loans and Advances

Date of loan	Name of loan	Interest rate (per cent)	Principal outstanding Jan. 1, 1937
1914	Nanking-Hunan Railway Advance of 1913	0 to 1	C$ 6,100,000
1924	Lunghai Railway 8% Short Term Bonds	1½ to 4	895,600
1930	Canton-Hankow Railway (Southern Section) Redemption Bonds	2	20,000,000
	Railway Reconstruction Loan	6	
1934	1st Issue $ 9,000,000		
1936	2nd Issue 24,430,000		
1936–1938	3rd Issue, 1st instalment 40,000,000		73,430,000
	Advances from remitted British Boxer Indemnity funds		29,522,575
	Total		C$129,948,175

Debts for materials, etc.

Peiping-Suiyuan Railway			$ 6,020,889
Peiping-Hankow Railway			12,566,797
Tientsin-Pukow Railway			17,675,469
Canton-Hankow Railway			2,657,065
Shanghai-Hangchow-Ningpo Railway			40,000
Total			C$ 38,960,220
Floating debt			C$ 58,363,294
Grand total of internal debt			C$227,271,689
Approximate equivalent at exchange of July 1, 1937			US$ 68,000,000

TABLE 45. Debt of the Communications Ministry and of miscellaneous governmental organs, receiving service as of January 1, 1937

Communications obligations[a]

	Principal outstanding Jan. 1, 1937
External debt	
Telephone extension and materials loans	Y29,111,785
Telegraph extension loan	Y19,907,825
Wireless Station Loan	£ 153,339
China Electric Co. Loan	US$ 814,274
Miscellaneous	£ 9,614
	US$ 1,477,919
	Rmk. 33,260
Total approximate equivalent at exchange of Jan. 1, 1937	US$17,000,000
Internal debt	
24th Year Electric Power Administration Loan	C$ 5,996,550
Loan secured on international cable charges	4,738,572
Advances from remitted British Boxer Indemnity funds	1,379,495
Miscellaneous	4,875,133
Total	16,989,750
Total, approximate equivalent at exchange of Jan. 1, 1937	US$ 5,000,000

Obligations of other governmental organs

	Principal outstanding Jan. 1, 1937	
National Construction Commission		
19th Year Electrical Enterprises Long Term Loan	C$ 870,000	
19th Year Electrical Enterprises Short Term Loan	400,000	
22nd Year Loan for Extension of Electrical Enterprises	5,100,000	
Advances from remitted British Boxer Indemnity Funds	2,682,752	C$ 9,052,752
Advances to miscellaneous governmental organs from remitted British Boxer Indemnity funds		4,090,851
Total, other debts		C$13,143,603
Total, approximate equivalent at exchange of Jan. 1, 1937		US$ 4,000,000

[a] Not including debts of the China Merchants Steam Navigation Co. amounting to C$33,872,040 including advances of C$5,186,314 to that company by the Board of Trustees for the Administration of the Indemnity Funds Remitted by the British Government. This ministry did not have charge of railways until early in 1938; for the railway debt see Table 44.

TABLE 46. Debt in arrears: Original principal amounts as of July 1, 1937

FOREIGN DEBT

Date	Name	Foreign country chiefly interested	Original principal amount outstanding as of July 1, 1937
	Finance Ministry: Funded external loans		
1912–1914	"Skoda" or "Ex-Austrian" loans	Italy and other European countries	£ 3,500,000[a]
1913	Pechili Provincial loan, guaranteed by the Central Government	Belgium	£ 500,000
1914	Pukow Port Works loan	France	French francs 100,000,000
1922	Tsingtao Treasury Notes	Japan	Y13,300,000[b]
1922	96 Million, yen portion	Japan	Y32,479,200
	Unfunded external debt		
1918	Bank of Communications Japanese loan	Japan	Y20,000,000
1919	Kiousin debt	France	French francs. 4,473,210
1921	Marconi loan, coupon No. 5 advance	Great Britain	£ 24,000
	Miscellaneous, approximate equivalent	Various	US$ 6,000,000
	Total, approximate equivalent at exchange of July 1, 1937		US$49,000,000
	Railway Ministry		
1916–1920	Chuchow-Chingchow Railway Advances (Siems & Carey loan)	United States	US$ 1,150,000
1922	Railway Equipment Loan (Paotow-Ninghsia Railway)	Belgium	£ 800,000
	Total, approximate equivalent at exchange of July 1, 1937		US$ 5,000,000
	Grand total		US$54,000,000

INTERNAL DEBT

Date	Name	Amount
	Finance Ministry: Funded internal loans	
1920	Famine Relief Loan	C$ 1,610,220
1921	Consolidation bonds	
	1st Year National Loan	12,150,000
	8th Year National Loan	1,210,000
1922	96 Million, dollar portion	56,391,300
	Total	C$ 71,361,520

Unfunded internal loans

Name	Approximate number of items	Amount
Special Treasury notes	8 ⎫	C$ 52,140,873
Treasury notes	63 ⎭	
Other items		
Salt surplus loans	79 ⎫	
Short-term loans	140 ⎪	70,000,000
Bank advances	21 ⎪	
Debts of various government offices	41 ⎭	
Other loans in *fapi*, approximate		10,000,000
Total, approximate		C$132,000,000

Former Peking Communications Ministry

Date	Name	Amount
1921	Certificates of indebtedness	C$ 7,880,900
Various	Bank advances, etc.	4,339,412
	Total	C$ 12,220,312
	Grand total,	C$216,000,000
	approximately equivalent at exchange of July 1, 1937 to	US$ 64,000,000
	Grand total, foreign and internal debt in arrears, approximate equivalent at exchange of July 1, 1937	US$118,000,000

This tabulation does not include the Japanese "Nishihara Loans," which the National Government did not recognize. See the comment regarding them in chapter V.

[a] Approximate. Since this compilation deals with original principal amounts, the figure here used is based upon the amount of loans issued in 1912–1914, and not upon the amount of bonds issued under a 1925 arrangement which at once went into default.   [b] Approximate.

FOREIGN CREDITS AND LEND-LEASE TO CHINA, 1937–1945

The main particulars of the several credits which the Western powers and Russia granted to China in 1937–1941 are shown in Table 47A. These credits covered payments abroad for goods and services and for currency support as specified in the table. The amount of Lend-Lease aid granted by the United States before the end of 1941 is also shown. Table 47B presents a statement of the credits and Lend-Lease aid which the United States and Great Britain provided from 1942 to 1945, with an approximation of the amounts of the credits utilized by China.

The following comments concern the aid listed in Table 47B and its utilization:

Internal loans. The US$200 million was placed to China's credit in 1942, but not largely drawn upon until 1944 and thereafter.

Gold. China received only US$7 million in 1945 in time to be sold, that is, US$3 million in January and US$4 million in June. Sales in China were suspended June 25, 1945. US$37 million arrived in July. The rest of the US$111.3 million, that is, US$67.3 million, arrived after the end of hostilities. Also China received in 1946–1947 US$85.7 million of gold, that is, the remaining balance of the US$500 million loan.

Banknotes. The figures show the estimated division of purchases in 1944–1945, part being spent after the end of hostilities.

Textiles. All of this item was spent after the end of hostilities.

American Lend-Lease. About half of this aid was provided after V-J Day, including about US$300 million representing the cost of flying government troops to various places to receive the surrender of Japanese troops. In addition Lend-Lease aid of US$26 million was provided in 1941 and US$210 million in 1946.

British aid. In addition to £3 million of the £50 million credit charged by the end of 1945, £5.1 million (say US$20.5 million) was charged by July 1948. The total used from that credit was £8.1 million (say, US$32.5 million). Other British aid comprised official grants of £139,500 to the Chinese Red Cross Society, and £1,500 to the British fund for the relief of distress in China.

TABLE 47A. Credits and Lend-Lease to China, 1937–1941

Country granting	Date of agreement	Amount (millions)	Interest rate (per cent)	Final maturity	Security	Purpose
Russia	3/1/38	US$50	3	1943	Agricultural and mineral exports	Military supplies, etc.
France	4/22/38	Francs 150 £0.144	7	1953	Salt and mineral taxes; French Government Credit Insurance Department, 80 per cent guarantee	Nanning Railway construction
Russia	7/1/38	US$50	3	1945	Agricultural and mineral exports	Military supplies, etc.
United States	2/8/39	US$25	4½ later 4	1944	Wood oil exports; Bank of China guarantee	Nonmilitary purchases
Great Britain	3/10/39	£5	2¾	1945ᵃ	Principal guaranteed by British Treasury, interest by Bank of China and Bank of Communications	Currency stabilization
Great Britain	3/15/39	£0.5	5½	1943	Guarantee of Bank of China and of British Board of Trade	Motor truck purchase
Russia	6/13/39	US$150	3	1952	Agricultural and mineral exports	Military supplies, etc.
Great Britain	8/18/39	£2.859	5	1949	Guarantee of Bank of China and of British Board of Trade	Purchase of British goods
France	12/11/39	Francs 480	7	1954	Salt revenue surplus and the railway's revenue; French Government Credit Insurance Department, 80 per cent guarantee	Kunming-Suifu railway construction
United States	4/20/40	US$20	4	1947	Tin exports; Bank of China guarantee	Nonmilitary purchases
United States	10/22/40	US$25	4	1945	Tungsten exports; Central Bank of China obligation	Nonmilitary purchases
United States	2/4/41	US$50	4	1948	Tin and other exports; Central Bank of China obligation	Nonmilitary purchases
United States	4/1/41	US$50	1½	ᵇ	Chinese Government and Central Bank of China obligation	Currency stabilization
Great Britain	4/1/41	£5	1½	ᶜ	Chinese Government and Central Bank of China obligation	Currency stabilization
Great Britain	6/5/41	£5	3½	1951	Agricultural and mineral exports	Purchases in the sterling area
United States	1941	US$26			For later determination	Lend-Lease

Summary by countries, by years of announcement of credits or of conclusion if not announced, 1937–1941 (millions of US$ or equivalents)

	1938	1939	1940	Totals
United States: purchase credits	25		95	120
stabilization credits			50	50
Britain: purchase credits	2.3	13.2	20	35.5
stabilization credits		23	20	43
France: various credits	5	10		15
Total Western aid	32.3	46.2	185	263.5
Russia: credits for military aid, etc.	100	150		250

Amounts of pre-Pacific War credits utilized, partly estimated (millions of US$ or equivalents)

	Through 1941	In 1942–1945	Total
American purchase credits	95	10	105
American Lend-Lease	26		26
British purchase credits	20	8	28
British stabilization credits	27		27
French credits	12		12
Total, Western credits and aid	180	18	198
Russian credits for military aid, etc.	170	3	173
Grand totals	350	21	371

ᵃ The British government, pursuant to its guarantee, repaid in 1945 the British banks' subscription of £5 million.

ᵇ This credit was repayable on demand on 30 days' notice. But the question of repayment did not arise, because the Stabilization Board's dollar payments were covered from the Chinese banks' contribution of US$20 million and from the Board's dollar income. The credit was terminated in 1943.

ᶜ This credit was repayable on demand on a month's notice. China repaid it in 1944, mostly by applying the sterling balances then on hand of the 1939 and 1941 stabilization funds.

TABLE 47B. American and British credits and Lend-Lease aid to China, 1942–1945

AMERICAN
Credit of US$500 million

Year	Amount used	Purpose	Lend-Lease
1942	US$200.0 million	To guarantee internal loans	US$100 million
1943	10.5	Gold delivered	49
1944	20.0	Banknotes bought	53
	12.5	Gold delivered	
1945	111.3	Gold delivered	1107
	35.0	Banknotes bought	
	25.0	Textiles bought	
Totals	414.3		1309

BRITISH

By the end of 1945, the equivalent of US$12 million had been charged against the British credit of £50 million (US$201 million), for the purchase of goods and services in the sterling area for purposes arising out of the war. British Lend-Lease to China during the same period had amounted to the equivalent of US$44 million.

APPENDIX B. PRICES

This appendix contains tables of average retail prices in leading cities; wholesale prices in Chungking, Chengtu, and Shanghai; cost of living by social classes in Chengtu; prices of rice in ten cities; and a comparison of prices in China's inflation, 1937–1948, with prices in European inflations in 1914–1924. Further price data are contained in the text in Tables 17, 18, 26, 28 to 32, and 34 to 38.

The figures in Table 48 are averages of the monthly indexes compiled by the Farmers Bank of China for leading cities. Because of wide variations of price levels in the various cities, I have used simple geometric averages. The figures show market prices, rather than what were termed "composite prices" which included those prices that were officially fixed. The market prices are the more representative, because price controls were not effective. There are a few interpolations. Table 49 shows monthly rates of rise.

The number of cities for which indexes were compiled shrank as data became unavailable, mainly because of territory captured by Japan. From 1937 through February 1941, the 16 cities included were: Chungking, Chengtu, Kweiyang, Ya-an, Sian, Lanchow, Kweilin, Sining, Chukiang, Foochow, Kanchow, Shanghai, Yunyang, Loyang, Hengyang, and Kunming. Thereafter cities were dropped out as follows after the months stated: February 1941, Foochow; October 1941, Shanghai; May 1944, Kweilin, Hengyang, Loyang, Kanchow, and Chukiang; February 1945, Yunyang.

In each case when cities were dropped out, the average of the remaining cities became higher than it had been. The percentages by which the averages became higher, based upon comparing the averages in the preceding three months with the dropped cities included and excluded, are: from February 1941, 2.1 per cent; from October 1941, 3.4 per cent; from May 1944, 2.8 per cent; from February 1945, 1.2 per cent. Hence in comparing the averages for those months and the months immediately succeeding, it is necessary to allow for the increase caused by the drop-outs. The cumulative total of the increases is about 10 per cent. On the one hand, these increases distort, to the extent stated, the month-to-month guide to the progress of the inflation. On the other hand, despite the omissions, the averages afford what appears to be the best available indication of the wartime price level in the parts of China that remained free. Table 48 shows the averages immediately preceding the drop-outs both with and without the dropped cities, to facilitate comparisons. The base is January–June 1937 = 1.

TABLE 48. Averages of retail market prices in cities of Free China, 1937–1945

	Averages for 16 cities, July 1937, to February 1941				
Month	1937	1938	1939	1940	1941
January	—	1.24	1.90	3.47	7.58
February	—	1.28	1.95	3.76	8.18
March	—	1.29	2.02	3.99	—
April	—	1.31	2.09	4.24	—
May	—	1.37	2.17	4.58	—
June	—	1.40	2.26	4.87	—
July	1.04	1.42	2.36	5.23	—
August	1.08	1.50	2.46	5.61	—
September	1.11	1.55	2.76	6.04	—
October	1.13	1.60	2.88	6.61	—
November	1.15	1.67	3.03	7.03	—
December	1.18	1.76	3.23	7.24	—
Average	1.12	1.45	2.43	5.22	—

Averages for 15 cities, January–October 1941; and for 14 cities, September 1941, to May 1944

	1941					
Month	(Average including Foochow)	Average omitting Foochow and including Shanghai[a]	Average omitting Shanghai	1942	1943	1944
January	7.58	7.75	—	21.5	70.2	249
February	8.18	8.34	—	24.4	77.0	287
March	—	9.04	—	28.4	83.7	333
April	—	9.42	—	30.5	96.6	375
May	—	10.00	—	33.4	110	415
June	—	10.51	—	35.9	132	—
July	—	11.47	—	40.4	160	—
August	—	12.56	12.96	46.6	177	—
September	—	14.09	14.57	53.6	187	—
October	—	15.95	16.50	58.9	196	—
November	—	—	18.13	63.1	213	—
December	—	—	19.77	66.2	228	—
Average	—	12.23[b]	—	41.8	144	—

Averages for 14 cities, January–May 1944; for 9 cities, June 1944, to February 1945; and for 8 cities, March–December 1945

	1944		1945	
Month	Average, 14 cities	Average, 9 cities[e]	Average, 9 cities	Average, 8 cities omitting Yunyang[d]
January	249	—	881	889
February	287	—	1106	1133
March	333	339	—	1420
April	375	385	—	1637
May	415	430	—	1966
June	—	466	—	2167
July	—	498	—	2593
August	—	522	—	2647
September	—	562	—	1799
October	—	600	—	2010
November	—	669	—	2313
December	—	755	—	2491
Average	—	478[e]	—	1919[f]

SOURCE: See Table 50 re composite prices. (The base is January–June 1937 = 1). The data through June 1941 are from the publications of the Farmers Bank, *Index Numbers of Retail Prices in Leading Cities of China, July 1937–June 1941*, supplemented by data for Kunming which that bank supplied later. For succeeding months the data are from the bank's *Monthly Bulletin* and its unpublished data, confidential at the time, showing market prices as a supplement to data of composite prices.

[a] For December 1940 the figure was 7.40.
[b] Average of 16 cities, January–February; 15 cities, March–October; and 14 cities, November–December.
[e] The cities dropped were: Kweilin, Hengyang, Loyang, Kanchow, and Chukiang.
[d] For December 1944 the figure was 757.
[e] The average is for 14 cities, January–May, and 9 cities, June–December.
[f] The average is for 9 cities, January–February, and 8 cities, March–December.

TABLE 49. Monthly percentage rise of average retail market prices in Free China, 1937–1945

Months	1937	1938	1939	1940	1941	1942	1943	1944	1945
January	—	5	8	7	4	9	6	9	17
February	—	3	3	8	8	14	10	16	26
March	—	1	4	6	11[a]	16	9	13	28[b]
April	—	2	3	6	4	7	15	11	15
May	—	5	4	8	6	10	14	11	20
June	—	2	4	6	5	7	20	12[c]	10
July	—	1	4	7	9	13	20	7	20
August	4	6	4	7	10	15	11	5	2
September	3	3	12	8	12	15	6	8	−32
October	2	3	4	9	13	10	5	7	12
November	2	4	5	6	14[d]	7	9	12	15
December	3	5	7	3	9	5	7	13	8
Increase in the year	49%	83%	124%	173%	235%	245%	231%		230% (251% to August)

SOURCE: This table is based upon the figures in Table 48.

[a] The figure would be 9 per cent if based upon the average for the preceding month excluding Foochow, which dropped out in February 1941.

[b] The figure would be 25 per cent if based upon the average for the preceding month excluding Yunyang, which dropped out from February 1945.

[c] The figure would be 8 per cent if based upon the average for the preceding month, excluding Kweilin, Hengyang, Loyang, Kanchow, and Chukiang, which dropped out from May 1944.

[d] The figure would be 10 per cent if based upon the average for the preceding month excluding Shanghai, which dropped out from October 1941.

Table 50 compares "composite" prices with market prices, 1943–1945. In these years price controls were operative, but not effectively enforced. Hence the market prices are the more representative of actual conditions. The averages are simple geometric averages of the indexes of the several cities, except the "composite" data for June–December 1944, for which period I use simple arithmetic averages received in 1945 from the Farmers Bank. Indexes of composite prices for individual cities for those months are not available. The arithmetic averages appear to be of the order of 5 to 15 per cent higher than geometric averages would be in those seven months. The comments preceding Table 48 with regard to cities dropped out apply here also.

TABLE 50. Comparison of market prices and "composite" prices, 1943–1945

	1943		1944		1945	
Month	Composite[a]	Market	Composite[a]	Market	Composite[a]	Market
January	69.3	70.2	202	249	631	881
February	74.5	77.0	233	287	763	1106
March	78.6	83.7	265	332	902	1420
April	86.5	96.6	294	375	1025	1637
May	98.4	110	319	415	1177	1966
June	114	132	388	466	1255	2167
July	134	160	410	498	1414	2593
August	146	176	433	522	1455	2647
September	154	187	496	562	1127	1799
October	169	196	537	600	1222	2012
November	185	213	583	669	1352	2313
December	200	228	663	755	1415	2491
Arithmetic average	126	144	402	478	1145	1909
Excess of average of market over composite prices		14%		19%		67%

SOURCE: Farmers Bank of China (the base is January–June 1937 = 1).

[a] "Composite" prices include partly official and partly free prices. The market prices more nearly represent actual conditions.

Period	Chungking	Chengtu	Kweiyang	Ya-an	Sian	Lanchow	Kweilin	Sining
1937								
July	1.01	.97	1.08	1.08	1.05	1.06	1.00	1.00
December	1.14	1.01	1.14	1.39	1.14	1.28	1.19	1.08
1938								
June	1.23	1.07	1.62	1.96	1,32	1.51	1.21	1.36
December	1.57	1.36	2.17	2.53	1.60	1.79	1.64	1.75
1939								
June	1.91	1.55	2.97	3.22	2.19	2.07	2.04	2.40
December	2.82	2.82	4.12	4.20	3.00	2.70	3.47	3.84
1940								
June	5.33	5.22	5.94	7.15	4.46	3.39	4.40	5.51
December	11.12	10.49	7.78	11.07	7.75	5.68	5.68	6.69
1941								
June	14.97	15.02	10.21	16.53	10.95	9.35	8.58	9.93
December	26.79	22.68	21.26	29.02	21.88	14.61	17.78	14.61
1942								
June	48.3	36.2	39.6	45.6	37.7	24.8	34.6	20.3
December	69.5	68.4	61.8	89.3	71.8	40.6	61.0	36.7
1943								
June	105	127	116	147	206	84.8	133	62.8
December	199	246	238	302	301	136	213	134
1944								
June	422	543	469	812	468	253	409[a]	277
December	651	764	1533	1139	794	329	—	375
1945								
June	1763	1704	3601	2140	2671	1223	—	1079
December	2415	2509	3039	2995	2458	1615	—	1467

	Hengyang	Loyang	Yunyang	Shanghai	Kanchow	Foochow	Chukiang	Kunming
1937								
July	1.05	1.01	1.04	1.04	1.03	1.06	1.05	1.06
December	1.16	1.17	1.25	1.31	1.10	1.16	1.21	1.21
1938								
June	1.53	1.39	1.78	1.37	1.17	1.31	1.36	1.56
December	1.99	1.74	2.20	1.66	1.28	1.40	1.77	2.20
1939								
June	2.73	2.39	2.85	1.84	1.43	1.87	2.14	3.67
December	3.41	3.21	3.90	2.72	2.19	2.50	2.64	5.65
1940								
June	4.26	4.78	5.47	3.89	3.30	4.15	3.98	9.61
December	5.56	7.84	8.08	5.13	4.69	5.26	5.87	13.66
1941								
June	8.70	10.37	9.04	7.36	7.46	—	8.50	17.10
December	17.60	20.30	15.71		13.19	—	17.09	35.40
1942								
June	37.9	42.7	28.2	—	24.9	—	37.3	70.8
December	81.5	79.4	56.1	—	55.4	—	64.8	138.9
1943								
June	129	271	153	—	104	—	112	235
December	235	300	249	—	181	—	188	423
1944								
June	357[b]	427[b]	432	—	347[a]	—	351[a]	836
December	—	—	738	—	—	—	—	1273
1945								
June	—	—	—	—	—	—	—	5950
December	—	—	—	—	—	—	—	4620

SOURCE: Farmers Bank of China. Some series ended when the respective cities were evacuated or captured. Table 48 contains averages for all the cities by months (the base is January–June 1937 = 1).
[a] May 1944.
[b] April 1944.

TABLE 52. Wholesale prices and cost of living in Chungking, 1937–1945

The first column of each year gives indexes of wholesale prices (simple geometric average) and the second column indexes of cost of living (weighted aggregate average) excluding rent, which was regulated.

Month	1937		1938		1939		1940		1941	
January	1.02	1.00	1.16	1.10	1.66	1.42	3.31	3.20	11.7	13.2
February	1.07	1.06	1.22	1.14	1.70	1.48	3.53	3.26	12.3	14.4
March	1.07	1.06	1.25	1.14	1.74	1.55	3.90	3.46	12.6	14.5
April	1.08	1.04	1.25	1.10	1.78	1.62	4.46	3.95	13.1	15.4
May	1.10	1.08	1.25	1.13	1.87	1.75	4.99	4.34	14.3	19.9
June	1.11	1.08	1.30	1.21	1.97	1.87	5.61	4.92	15.7	22.1
July	1.07	1.03	1.30	1.20	2.00	1.90	6.42	5.94	17.2	23.1
August	1.07	1.05	1.31	1.21	2.25	2.02	6.98	6.75	18.4	22.9
September	1.11	1.07	1.40	1.23	2.55	2.23	7.88	7.56	20.0	23.1
October	1.14	1.11	1.46	1.20	2.72	2.28	8.62	8.61	22.1	24.9
November	1.16	1.12	1.55	1.30	3.00	2.72	9.92	11.30	25.3	30.3
December	1.15	1.10	1.60	1.41	3.16	2.82	11.30	12.70	26.7	31.8

Month	1942		1943		1944		1945	
January	30.1	31.9	85	73	242	215	762	711
February	33.0	32.9	92	86	273	250	963	977
March	36.7	35.8	95	86	337	328	1275	1261
April	41.0	41.6	100	89	377	380	1592	1457
May	44.4	46.7	112	103	425	461	1893	1620
June	48.1	46.0	127	119	468	505	2042	1679
July	51.7	50.0	145	129	493	520	2304	1851
August	60.6	52.9	164	151	494	487	2460	2074
September	67.3	56.2	179	160	526	497	2082	1927
October	73.7	60.0	189	172	557	503	2037	1873
November	77.6	66.2	208	192	584	548	2373	1980
December	80.1	68.2	228	205	648	588	2403	2033

SOURCE: Data of Nankai University, based upon July 1936 to June 1937 = 1.

TABLE 53. Wholesale prices of groups of commodities in Chungking, 1937–1945

	General index	Food	Clothing	Metals and products	Building materials	Fuel and light	Miscel-laneous
1937							
July	1.07	1.06	1.13	1.03	1.12	1.03	1.05
December	1.15	1.04	1.22	1.66	1.18	1.49	0.84
1938							
June	1.30	0.99	1.59	2.54	1.45	1.72	0.91
December	1.60	0.95	1.92	5.34	1.94	2.96	1.09
1939							
June	1.97	1.15	2.30	6.76	2.47	3.09	1.54
December	3.16	1.83	3.87	13.6	3.72	5.70	2.19
1940							
June	5.61	3.43	7.95	16.5	6.59	10.8	3.55
December	11.3	9.48	12.5	22.4	11.9	22.6	5.23
1941							
June	15.7	15.9	14.5	31.5	13.7	26.6	5.99
December	27.6	25.5	28.3	66.9	28.0	43.3	9.72
1942							
June	48.1	37.6	63.4	143	46.8	74.2	18.3
December	80.1	48.3	131	263	99.7	188	26.6
1943							
June	127	94.1	229	337	130	224	35.0
December	228	187	324	526	228	432	64.5
1944							
June	468	477	702	824	376	609	150
December	648	477	903	1283	695	1669	212
1945							
June	2042	1513	2889	3019	3385	4183	702
December	2403	1604	3759	4994	2933	5157	942

SOURCE: Weekly and monthly *Statistical Service* of the Nankai University Institute of Economics (simple geometric average based upon July 1936–June 1937 = 1).

TABLE 54. Domestic, import, and export wholesale prices in Chengtu, 1937–1945

	Domestic goods	Import goods	Export goods	General index
Number of items	38	9	10	57
1937				
January–June	1.00	1.00	1.00	1.00
December	1.01	1.43	0.67	1.00
1938				
June	1.02	1.98	0.75	1.08
December	1.29	2.89	1.22	1.45
1939				
June	1.75	3.75	1.40	1.83
December	3.03	7.52	2.29	3.33
1940				
June	5.47	11.58	3.83	5.75
December	10.22	22.22	5.39	10.33
1941				
June	15.68	26.03	5.89	13.76
December	26.76	85.78	13.37	28.48
1942				
June	38.47	112.7	18.29	40.01
December	64.83	157.4	35.50	67.10
1943				
June	129	415	62.37	137
December	220	882	89.00	234
1944				
June	540	1905	221	563
December	708	3078	355	791
1945				
June	1730	6258	1078	1951
July	2169	8372	1522	2523
August	2392	7339	1692	2685
September	1822	5028	987	1920
October	1942	5809	993	2052
November	2348	6958	1175	2469
December	2413	5790	1207	2459

SOURCE: *Economic Facts*, monthly publication of the University of Nanking, temporarily at Chengtu (simple geometric average based upon January–June 1937 = 1). A full set of this publication for the war period is in the Library of the Department of Agriculture, Washington, D.C.

TABLE 55. Cost of living by social classes in Chengtu, 1937–1945

Year	Laborer-peddler	Merchant-storekeeper	Military-official-educational	Three classes combined
1937				
June	0.98	0.99	1.00	0.99
December	0.93	0.98	1.00	0.96
1938				
June	0.95	0.99	1.02	0.98
December	1.01	1.13	1.17	1.09
1939				
June	1.05	1.25	1.32	1.18
December	1.85	2.18	2.30	2.06
1940				
June	3.22	3.51	3.57	3.40
December	8.00	7.69	7.55	7.79
1941				
June	20.8	15.6	14.2	17.2
December	20.9	20.6	20.4	20.7
1942				
June	31.7	31.5	32.3	31.8
December	43.1	49.5	55.9	48.1
1943				
June	110	106	111	109
December	169	193	204	185
1944				
June	514	572	566	546
December	598	749	836	699
1945				
June	1157	1685	1803	1463
August	1440	2024	2155	1781
December	1614	2382	2350	2022

SOURCE: *Economic Facts, passim* (weighted aggregative by individual classes, and weighted geometric average for the three classes combined, based upon February–June 1937 = 1).

TABLE 56. Average prices of rice in chief cities of Free China, 1937–1945
(in C$ per *shih tou*[a])

	1937	1938	1939	1940	1941	1942
January	0.90	0.93	1.27	2.23	8.06	24.82
February	0.94	0.93	1.33	3.06	9.37	28.76
March	0.96	0.97	1.33	3.20	10.19	33.65
April	1.04	0.96	1.44	3.39	12.92	36.39
May	0.98	1.00	1.51	3.72	16.02	38.72
June	0.96	1.02	1.49	3.97	20.16	40.31
July	0.93	1.05	1.50	4.67	21.70	42.58
August	0.91	1.02	1.55	5.05	19.50	43.21
September	0.89	1.00	1.62	5.64	18.32	45.30
October	0.87	1.00	1.79	6.43	19.30	49.31
November	0.87	1.08	2.17	7.14	23.45	52.84
December	0.91	1.17	2.25	7.59	23.15	56.22
Average	0.93	1.01	1.60	4.68	16.85	41.00

	1943[b]		1944[b]		1945[b]	
	Composite	Market	Composite	Market	Composite	Market
January	59.94	65.77	183	222	849	1028
February	60.07	71.83	216	267	1007	1298
March	59.73	75.88	259	315	1496	1894
April	71.32	101.31	305	381	1765	2184
May	84.79	141.88	336	435	2115	2657
June	105.49	150.90	382	497	2235	2946
July	108.86	174.15	419	511	2292	3128
August	107.15	170.89	418	496	1773	3238
September	108.63	170.63	470	578	1673	1969
October	124.58	162.00	472	567	1493	1712
November	138.79	178.87	569	667	1434	1711
December	147.58	197.16	536	699	1458	1789
Average	98.08	138.44	388	470	1633	2129

SOURCE: Data from the Farmers Bank of China, received January 14, 1946. They are averages of figures for 10 cities: Chungking, Chengtu, Kweiyang, Ya-an, Kweilin, Kunming, Hengyang, Yunyang, Kanchow, and Chukiang. Some of the cities were omitted as follows: Hengyang from June 1944; Kweilin from September 1944; Kanchow and Chukiang from January 1945; and Yunyang from March 1945. Data for the individual cities are not available for the full period.

The figures appear to be arithmetic averages. Because of considerable variations in prices in the several cities, especially in the later years of the war, these averages are higher than would have been geometric averages, such as I use in appendix B, Table 48, showing general prices. Available data indicate that the arithmetic averages are higher in the order of 5 to 15 per cent.

[a] One *shih tou* equals 0.2838 American bushel. One bushel of unhulled rice weighs about 45 pounds, hence one *shih tou* weighs about 12.8 pounds.

[b] Composite prices include officially fixed prices where they existed. The market prices better represent the actual situation.

TABLE 57. Wholesale prices in Shanghai, 1937–1945

	1937		1938		1939		1940		1941	
January	—	—	1.27	1.12	1.20	1.39	3.15	3.34	6.78	5.70
February	—	—	1.17	1.12	1.23	1.43	4.13	3.84	6.96	6.09
March	—	—	1.11	1.13	1.28	1.49	3.89	3.99	8.01	6.81
April	—	—	1.13	1.15	1.28	1.50	3.80	4.08	8.48	7.75
May	—	—	1.10	1.16	1.40	1.52	4.11	4.54	8.85	8.02
June	—	—	1.09	1.19	1.53	1.64	4.59	4.51	8.91	8.03
July	1.02	1.00	1.14	1.25	1.60	1.69	4.74	4.39	9.15	8.40
August	1.07	1.02	1.21	1.32	2.10	2.08	4.57	4.30	10.1	9.50
September	1.12	1.04	1.17	1.34	2.65	2.53	5.19	4.54	10.5	10.6
October	1.08	1.07	1.18	1.37	2.32	2.74	5.51	4.83	12.0	11.8
November	1.15	1.13	1.16	1.37	2.49	2.83	5.58	4.98	14.6	15.1
December	1.24	1.13	1.15	1.35	3.08	3.18	6.53	5.23	16.0	15.6

	1942		1943		1944		1945	
January	15.2	16.5	58.0	52.0	214	274	3128	3430
February	17.4	18.3	69.5	63.3	276	362	4237	4030
March	22.8	22.5	64.4	78.2	341	425	5809	4750
April	24.2[a]	24.9	57.9	87.9	329	421	6434	5500
May	26.8	27.9	64.3	94.0	383	457	8036	7610
June	26.8	29.4	73.7	104	576	560	32,301	21,300
July	29.7	31.6	115	139	634	628	41,886	42,800
August	30.7	32.8	140	156	618	712	86,400	85,200
September	30.7	33.9	126	152	742	942	—	54,200
October	32.5	35.8	133	158	1141	1360	—	—
November	42.1	39.2	144	172	1593	1770	—	—
December	49.3	44.7	176	214	2510	2490	—	—

SOURCES: The first column of each year gives figures of The Central Bank of China, based upon January–June 1937 = 1. The figures in the second column are from the China Institute of Economics. Their series was based upon 1936 = 1, but to make it comparable with the other series I have converted it to the basis of January–June 1937 = 1. The average of the latter period according to their index was 1.142.

[a] From April 1942 figures are in notes of the puppet Central Reserve Bank. That is also believed to be the approximate date of shift from C$ notes as regards the second column, though the data do not so state.

TABLE 58. Comparison of prices in China's inflation, 1937–1948, with prices in other inflations, 1914–1924

Period	Germany	Austria	Hungary	Poland	Russia	China	
1914						1937	
July	1 0	1.0	1.0	1.0	1.0	July	1.0
December	1.3	1.3				December	1.2
1915						1938	
June	1.4	1.8				June	1.4
December	1.5	2.5			1.4	December	1.8
1916						1939	
June	1.5	3.8			1.8	June	2.3
December	1.5	6.6			2.8	December	3.2
1917						1940	
June	1.7	6.2			4.5	June	4.9
December	2.0	8.3			15.4	December	7.2
1918						1941	
June	2.1	16			71	June	11
December	2.5	29			135	December	20
1919						1942	
June	3.1	30			516	June	36
December	8.0	46			1790	December	66
1920						1943	
June	14	56			6570	June	132
December	14	89			12,000	December	228
1921						1944	
June	14	136	42	364	62,000	June	466
December	35	850	83	570	138,000	December	755
1922						1945	
June	70	3090	129	877	5,087,000	June	2167
December	1475	15,670	334	3464	16,972,720	December	2491
1923						1946	
June	74,787	18,430	1445	18,814	79,930,000	June	5485[b]
December	1,261,600,000,000	19,660	7915	1,423,007	2,314,080,000	December	8613
1924						1947	
June		21,843	22,078	2,423,318	17,100,000,000[a]	June	36,872
December			23,466			December	129,384
						1948	
						June	1,335,303
						Sept. 20	8,740,600

SOURCES: Germany. Reichsamt indexes of wholesale prices. Data from John Parke Young, *European Currency and Finance*, Senate Commission of Gold and Silver Inquiry, Washington, 1925, vol. I, p. 530.

Austria. Data for 1914–1920 are from *Die Preizentwicklung Wichtiger Lebensmittel und Bedarfsartikel in Wien, 1914–1920*, by Klezl, and show cost of food necessities per family. No other series for this period is available. Data through July 1920 are for one month later than the month shown in the left hand column. Data for 1921–1924 are from the *Statistische Nachrichten* indexes of retail prices, adjusted to be comparable with the earlier series. The second series is based upon data from Young, *European Currency*, vol. II, p. 293.

Hungary. Pester Lloyd indexes of retail prices in December 1923, and thereafter indexes of wholesale prices of the Hungarian Central Statistical Office. Data are from Young, *European Currency*, vol. II, p. 322.

Poland. Wholesale prices, based upon January 1914 = 1. Data are from Young, *European Currency*, p. 349.

Russia. Retail prices, 1913 = 1. Data are from Young, *European Currency*, vol. II, p. 360.

China. For 1937–1945 the data are the average indexes of retail prices in cities of Free China, figures of the Farmers Bank (see appendix B, Table 48). Thereafter figures are indexes of wholesale prices in Nanking, University of Nanking index.

[a] Figure for February 1924.

[b] Figure for August 1946.

APPENDIX C. EXCHANGE RATES

Tables 59 and 60 show rates of foreign and domestic exchange, respectively. Related tables in the text are Tables 25 and 27, showing rates of exchange for puppet and Japanese military currency; Table 30, comparing indexes of foreign exchange rates and of prices; Table 31, presenting a calculation of purchasing power parities of *fapi* and dollars; and Table 32, showing the course of foreign exchange rates in 1943–1944 while the Changtu air bases were being built. Appendix F, Table 69, shows applications for foreign exchange and allotments under the allotment procedure in 1938–1939.

TABLE 59. Foreign exchange rates, 1935–1945

A. *1935–1941 (telegraphic transfers, cents and pence per C$, respectively)*

	U.S. dollars		Sterling			U.S. dollars		Sterling	
	1935					1939			
Month	High	Low	High	Low	Month	High	Low	High	Low
November	30.81	29.50	15.00	14.38	January	16.50	16.19	8.50	8.29
December	29.81	29.50	14.50	14.38	February	16.13	15.88	8.31	8.13
					March	16.38	15.81	8.34	8.09
					April	16.25	16.03	8.25	8.23
					May	16.06	15.94	8.24	8.19
					June	16.06	12.50	8.24	6.22
					July	12.63	7.94	6.41	4.06
		1936 range			August	8.81	6.25	4.50	3.22
	30.25	29.50	14.56	14.25	September	8.50	6.25	4.88	3.75
					October	8.88	7.31	5.31	4.38
					November	9.69	7.69	5.88	4.72
					December	7.94	7.00	4.81	4.34
						16.50	6.25	8.50	3.22
	1937					1940			
January	29.81	29.75	14.61	14.53	January	8.25	7.66	5.03	4.64
February	29.81	29.56	14.59	14.50	February	7.69	6.75	4.63	4.11
March	29.81	29.69	14.63	14.60	March	6.81	6.03	4.17	4.10
April	29.88	29.75	14.63	14.50	April	6.16	5.90	4.25	4.25
May	29.88	29.81	14.53	14.50	May	6.00	4.44	4.25	3.06
June	29.78	29.53	14.52	14.36	June	6.38	4.94	4.13	3.69
July	29.75	29.58	14.75	14.28	July	6.34	5.81	4.03	3.84
August	30.25	29.50	14.53	14.28	August	6.00	5.28	3.86	3.55
September	30.13	29.63	14.53	14.37	September	5.62	5.16	3.63	3.44
October	29.88	29.55	14.36	14.27	October	6.22	5.44	4.00	3.50
November	29.75	29.50	14.25	14.13	November	6.16	5.75	3.97	3.66
December	29.69	29.44	14.25	14.17	December	6.03	5.34	3.81	3.38
	30.25	29.44	14.75	14.13		8.25	4.44	5.03	3.06
	1938					1941			
January	29.75	29.63	14.25	14.20	January	5.56	5.31	3.52	3.36
February	29.90	29.69	14.25	14.20	February	5.75	5.31	3.61	3.33
March	29.91	24.37	14.25	11.75	March	5.59	5.22	3.42	3.20
April	27.81	25.69	13.31	12.44	April	5.34	5.25	3.28	3.16
May	26.56	21.43	12.78	10.37	May	5.43	5.22	3.34	3.19
June	21.19	16.75	10.25	8.10	June	5.46	5.34	3.33	3.28
July	18.50	17.12	9.02	8.37	July	5.43	5.00	3.27	3.03
August	17.31	16.16	8.53	7.97	August	5.25	4.66	3.13	2.80
September	17.75	17.06	8.88	8.50	September	5.13[a]	4.75[a]	2.91[a]	2.81[a]
October	16.56	15.69	8.29	8.00	October	4.75	3.63	2.81	2.19
November	16.10	15.65	8.25	8.00	November	3.63	3.25	2.19	2.00
December	16.69	16.00	8.58	8.22	December	[b]	[b]	[b]	[b]
	29.91	15.65	14.25	7.97		5.75	3.25	3.61	2.00

[a] The Shanghai free market closed September 7, 1941, official rates having been announced August 18, 1941, namely, $3\frac{5}{32}$d. and $0.05\frac{5}{16}$. From September 7, 1941, black market rates were not publicly quoted at Shanghai. Rates thereafter for 1941 are based on fragmentary quotations available from Shanghai and Tientsin.

[b] Rates for December 1941 are not available as Japan captured Shanghai on December 8.

TABLE 59 (*continued*). Foreign exchange rates, 1935–1945

B. *1942–1945 (C$ per US$1)*

After Pearl Harbor China was blockaded, and Shanghai and other cities where foreign exchange business centered were occupied completely by Japan. Hence there was no broad market for foreign exchange. At Chungking and Kunming relatively little foreign exchange business was done in 1942–1945, excepting (i) the market for U.S. dollar and rupee notes, and (ii) sales of drafts in 1944–1945 by the United Clearing Board for mission and other philanthropic agencies.

US$ Notes, 1942–1945[a]

Month	1942 (Kunming)	1943 (Kunming)	1944 (Chungking)	1945 (Chungking)
January	27	44 to 46	86 to 110	470 to 560
February	26	48 to 49.5	90 to 245	500 to 620
March	28	49 to 51	235 to 255	525 to 675
April	29	51 to 55	210 to 235	700 to 795
May	30	58.5 to 59.5	180 to 210	730 to 935
June	31	59 to 63.8	185 to 198	948 to 2,250
July	32	63.2 to 95	190 to 206	2,600 to 3,250
August	34 to 36	82 to 98	188 to 208	1,100 to 2,750
September	37	84 to 93	214 to 255	650 to 1,480
October	38 to 39	83 to 90	242 to 290	1,180 to 1,670
November	42 to 47	75 to 86	295 to 680	1,455 to 1,830
December	48 to 50	73 to 95	495 to 645	1,160 to 1,475

Dollar drafts sold by the United Clearing Board, average rates, 1944–1946

Month	1944	1945	1946
January	—	290	1,515
February	—	309	2,057
March	—	313	1,997
April	—	380	—
May	—	513	—
June	82	730	—
July	122	1,505	—
August	120	668	—
September	128	588	—
October	130	1,010	—
November	140	1,319	—
December	228	1,233	—

[a] Figures were collected by Arthur N. Young from sources believed to be the most reliable.

TABLE 60. Domestic exchange rates, 1938–1941

	1938 range	1939 range	1940 range	1941 range
		Chungking on Shanghai, 1938–1941		
January	—	1144 to 1160	1223 to 1247	1172 to 1188
February	—	1175 to 1190	1238 to 1248	1185 to 1242
March	—	1185 to 1200	1240 to 1420	1205 to 1258
April	—	1200 to 1210	1325 to 1390	1253 to 1290
May	—	1200 to 1225	1318 to 1380	1268 to 1335
June	1003 to 1005	1230 to 1255	1210 to 1358	1325 to 1387
July	1004 to 1005	1280 to 1345	1225 to 1255	—
August	1005 to 1006	1385 to 1442	1268 to 1312	1130[a]
September	1007 to 1025	1500 to 1570	1278 to 1305	1150[b]
October	1030 to 1075	1605 to 1665	1245 to 1260	1091[b]
November	1090 to 1155	1485 to 1540	1195 to 1235	1065 to 1099
December	1150 to 1165	1250 to 1375	1185 to 1196	1107 to 1122[c]
		Tientsin on Shanghai, 1939–1940[d]		
January		—	1010 to 1090	
February		—	1090 to 1160	
March		—	1030 to 1120	
April		980 to 1050[e]	1040 to 1130	
May		1010 to 1050	1020 to 1180	
June		1040 to 1160	1110 to 1160	
July		1170 to 1400	1070 to 1100	
August		1200 to 1280	1070 to 1110	
September		1160 to 1260	1030 to 1070	
October		1000 to 1250	1000 to 1060	
November		1000 to 1170	—	
December		1020 to 1170	—	

SOURCE: Central Bank of China.
[a] Rate on August 2, low of the day. Rates for July 1941 are not available.
[b] Rate at month-end.
[c] Rates December 1–6, 1941.
[d] Earlier and later data not available.
[e] For April 11–30.

[362]

APPENDIX D. NOTE ISSUES

TABLE 61. Note issues of the government banks, 1935–1945 (in millions of C$)

Period	Central Bank	Bank of China	Bank of Communications	Farmers Bank	Total, four government banks
1935					
November 2	136	187	105	30	458
Last Saturday of month					
December	176	286	180	30	673
1936					
December	326	459	295	162	1242
1937					
June	376	510	314	208	1407
July	383	518	336	208	1445
August	395	536	371	210	1512
September	417	544	372	214	1545
October	423	550	361	221	1556
November	429	573	371	230	1603
December	431	607	371	231	1639
1938					
January	432	623	373	249	1678
February	442	633	361	261	1697
March	444	654	319	262	1679
April	464	651	321	262	1698
May	473	648	322	262	1705
June	490	653	322	262	1727
July	516	652	322	264	1754
August	530	652	373	256	1820
September	566	662	430	267	1925
October	625	682	461	271	2039
November	682	696	507	273	2159
December	768	712	548	277	2305
1939					
January	778	712	547	277	2314
February	812	711	548	285	2356
March	853	710	548	299	2410
April	928	706	548	310	2492
May	1017	705	548	316	2587
June	768	991	603	339	2700
July	1147	1060	646	340	3193
August	1228	1090	666	357	3341

TABLE 61 (*continued*)

Period	Central Bank	Bank of China	Bank of Communications	Farmers Bank	Total, four government banks
1939 (*continued*)					
September	1388	1132	694	372	3587
October	1465	1170	708	375	3718
November	1586	1213	769	356	3924
December	1880	1227	814	365	4287
1940					
January	1940	1280	839	386	4445
February	2067	1348	858	395	4668
March	1982	1411	897	400	4690
April	2383	1486	931	414	5215
May	2565	1585	975	471	5596
June	2894	1650	1008	511	6063
July	2986	1670	1070	527	6250
August	3191	1728	1135	595	6654
September	3286	1777	1137	641	6842
October	3375	1831	1174	690	7071
November	3551	1965	1260	710	7486
December	3852	1947	1329	739	7867
1941					
January	3965	2152	1376	762	8255
February	4109	2369	1426	787	8692
March	4302	2540	1518	797	9156
April	4436	2691	1593	894	9614
May	4603	2852	1714	977	10,146
June	4808	3045	1784	1079	10,715
July	5011	3246	1845	1194	11,296
August	5137	3482	1965	1306	11,890
September	5487	3669	2126	1370	12,652
October	5754	3858	2294	1443	13,351
November	6105	4086	2540	1629	14,361
December	6341	4349	2631	1812	15,133
1942					
January	6601	4637	2749	2039	16,026
February	6909	4882	2876	2167	16,833
March	7167	5029	2906	2402	17,510
April	7555	5239	3013	2733	18,541
May	7943	5169	3055	3415	20,032
June	8278	7272	3295	4029	22,975
June 30[a]	8468	6848	4204	5425	24,945[a]

Issue of Central Bank of China from July 1942

End of Month	1942	1943	1944	1945
January		35,796	81,628	202,892
February		37,909	86,576	226,210
March		40,422	95,914	246,865
April		43,733	104,363	280,800

TABLE 61 (*continued*)

End of Month	1942	1943	1944	1945
May		46,486	113,789	336,485
June		49,873	122,779	397,773
July	25,308	52,505	129,057	462,327
August	26,401	56,258	137,640	556,907
September	27,852	60,460	150,175	674,233
October	29,903	64,377	161,236	805,923
November	31,833	68,912	170,319	901,024
December	34,360	75,379	189,461	1,031,932

SOURCE: Finance Ministry and Central Bank of China.
[a] Issue taken over by The Central Bank of China as of June 30, 1942.

TABLE 62. Note issue of provincial banks, 1937–1942 (in millions of C$)[a]

Bank	1937 June 30	1940 December 31	1942 December 31
Kwangtung Provincial Bank	235	193	198
Kwangsi Provincial Bank	35	40	52
New Futien Bank of Yunnan	20[b]	120	215
Kiangsi, Yu Min Bank	14	32	44
Shansi Provincial Bank	9[c]	55[c]	78
Fukien Provincial Bank	7	31	218
Hopei Provincial Bank	55[d]	[d]	[d]
Others[e]	43	94	152
Total	418	565	957

SOURCE: Wei-ya Chang, *The Money and Finance of China*, pp. 157–158, supplemented by contemporary data of the Finance Ministry and estimates.

[a] This issue consisted largely of one-dollar and fractional notes. As of December 31, 1942, the total of the provincial issues was less than three per cent of the total circulation of Free China, and as inflation progressed the notes of small denominations dropped out of circulation.

[b] Estimated.

[c] The first figure is as of the end of 1936, and the figure for 1940 is extrapolated.

[d] The figure for 1937 is from the *Peking Chronicle*, quoted in *Finance and Commerce*, Shanghai, February 23, 1938, p. 149. No figure for 1940 is available and the figure for the end of 1942 showed a negligible issue. Before the war the Japanese were pushing circulation of notes of the Hopei Provincial Bank, and these issues expanded many fold in 1935–1937. Apparently the shrinkage of circulation during the war is explained by the shift of the Japanese effort to the Federal Reserve Bank, whose issue began early in 1938 and by the end of 1941 was FRB$715 million.

[e] These included the issue of the provincial banks in Kiangsu, Chekiang, Anhwei, Hupei, Hunan, Szechwan, Sikong, Shantung, Honan, Shensi, Kansu, and Suiyuan.

TABLE 63. Japanese and puppet note issues in China, 1937–1945 (in millions)

Year (end)	Manchukuo Central Bank (yen)	Federal Reserve Bank (FRB$)	Central Reserve Bank (CRB$)[a]	China Incident Military Notes (MY)	Mengcheng Bank (yen)
1937	307			1.4	13
1938	426	162		36	36
1939	624	458		151	60
1940	947	715		248	63
1941	1201	964	237	244	114
1942	1670	1581	3477	381	143
1943	3011	3762	19,150	407	379
1944	5877	15,841	139,699	671	1058
1945	8085[b]	73,131[c]	1,847,374[d]	2299[e]	2799[f]
1945[g]	8158	83,506	2,697,231	1516	

SOURCE: Ministry of Finance, *Statistical Yearbook of Finance and Economy of Japan*, Tokyo, 1948, p. 823.

[a] Table 64 contains figures obtained from this bank at the end of the war, and shows different figures for some dates.

[b] August 8. [c] August 10. [d] August 20. [e] August 15. [f] July 31. [g] August 31.

TABLE 64. Note issue of the Central Reserve Bank, 1941–1945 (in millions of CRB$)

Year (end)	1941	1942	1943	1944	1945
January	19	326	3999	21,954	166,783
February	24	416	4122	22,228	200,374
March	30	636	4870	24,582	245,197
April	39	745	6206	27,317	320,688
May	49	774	7571	32,168	443,876
June	71	1278	9497	38,359	738,273
July	87	1485	10,450	42,894	1,487,394
August	105	1655	11,063	51,090	3,321,694[a]
September	120	1864	11,797	65,858	
October	151	2218	13,191	84,199	
November	181	2960	15,318	107,174	
December	258[a]	3696[a]	19,150	139,699	

SOURCE: Records of the bank, obtained after the war.

[a] Table 63 shows different figures for these dates.

APPENDIX E. TRANSACTIONS IN SILVER AND GOLD

Table 65 presents a summary of silver sales, 1935–1941, based on information derived from the records of the writer and from the Morgenthau Diaries.

A detailed statement of monthly official and free market prices of gold in China in 1943–1945 accompanies my testimony on page 1977 of the Hearings before the Subcommittee to Investigate the Administration of the Internal Security Act and Other Internal Security Laws of the Committee on the Judiciary, United States Senate, 84th Congress, Second Session, on Scope of Soviet Activity in the United States, July 13, 1956, Part 35. The Hearings on page 1970 contain data of monthly forward sales of gold and deposits redeemable in gold arriving in China.

Arrivals of gold in China in 1946 and 1947 were US$70.6 million and US$12.9 million, respectively. The total received in China in 1943–1947 was US$217.7 million. The balance of the US$220 million allocated for gold, out of the US$500 million loan, was delivered in New York.

Table 67 summarizes the main data of gold prices, retail prices, exchange rates, and the dollar equivalent of gold prices in China during the war period. Gold prices moved generally with average retail prices until 1943, but thereafter lagged far behind. Clearly this was due to sales of large quantities of gold. China's receipts from sales of gold are compared with the increase of note issue in Table 68.

TABLE 65. Silver sales, 1935–1941

Date of agreement	Amount Contracted (oz)	Delivered (oz)	Price U.S. cents (per oz)	Net proceeds
A. To July 10, 1937, Chinese data				
Nov. 15, 1935	50,000,000	50,208,396	65.17 and 65.03	US$32,256,865
May 18, 1936	75,000,000	75,629,077	45.0	34,033,085
July 10, 1937	62,000,000	62,514,710	45.0	28,131,620
Totals	187,000,000	188,352,183		US$94,421,570
B. After July 10, 1937, Chinese data				
				Gross proceeds, approximate
Nov. 3, 1937	50,000,000		45	US$22,500,000
Dec. 2, 1937	50,000,000		45	22,500,000
Feb. 25, 1938	{20,000,000		45	9,000,000
	{30,000,000		43	12,900,000
May 12, 1938	50,000,000		43	21,500,000
July, 1938	50,000,000		43	21,500,000
Sept. 29, 1938	19,500,000		43	8,400,000
Oct.–Dec. 1938	39,200,000		43	16,856,000
Jan. 1939	12,000,000		43	5,160,000
Jan. 17, 1939	14,000,000		43	6,020,000
Jan. 23, 1939	3,014,578		43	1,296,000
May 23, 1939	12,440,000		43	5,350,000
July 28, 1939	6,000,000		35	2,100,000
1940	5,142,000		35	1,800,000
1941	805,000		35	282,000
Totals	362,101,578			US$157,164,000
C. Summary, Chinese data				
To July 10, 1937	188,352,183			US$ 94,421,570
After July 10, 1937	362,101,578			157,164,000
Totals	550,453,761			US$251,585,570

D. *Silver Sales, 1934–1941, American data compared with Chinese data*

Year	American Treasury purchases of Chinese silver Ounces	Cost	Official Chinese sales Ounces	Receipts
1934	19,506,000	US$ 10,427,997	—	—
1935	50,115,000	32,166,303	50,208,396	US$ 32,256,865
1936	66,975,000	30,157,000	75,629,077	34,033,085
1937	130,026,000	58,512,000	162,514,710	73,131,620
1938	265,892,000	115,530,000	208,700,000	90,156,000
1939	33,341,000	13,787,000	47,454,578	19,926,000
1940	5,142,000	1,800,000	5,142,000	1,800,000
1941	805,000	282,000	805,000	282,000
Totals	571,802,000	US$262,662,300	550,453,761	US$251,585,570

SOURCES: The American data are from A. S. Everest's book, *Morgenthau, the New Deal, and Silver* (New York, 1950), page 178, and are derived from the Morgenthau Diaries. The Chinese data are from the records of the writer, who participated in the operations, except that Everest's data are incorporated for 1940–1941 because other records are incomplete. The number of ounces actually delivered varied slightly from the contractual amount because of varying outturn in refining, etc., and the available Chinese data show final figures only for 1935–1936 and for the first sale in 1937. Apparently the Treasury counted China's sales in the New York market in 1938–1939 as American government purchases.

The two sets of data cannot be reconciled by years because of different methods of reckoning. But the totals both by ounces and value correspond closely if the 1934 item is omitted, because China sold no silver officially in that year. The totals might be reconciled if data of actual outturn were fully available from the Chinese side.

Dickson H. Leavens, in *Silver Money* (Bloomington, Indiana, 1939), page 354, estimated sales of demonetized silver from China on the basis of the reports of Handy & Harman, as follows: in *1933*, 10.9 million fine ounces; *1934*, 200 million; *1935*, 190 million; *1936*, 302 million; *1937*, 177.9 million; and *1938*, 234.3 million — a total of 1115.1 million. Since perhaps 50 million ounces were sold after 1938, these figures indicate that the total of official and private sales was of the order of 1165 million ounces, and that private sales mainly smuggled were of the order of 600 million ounces.

TABLE 66. Gold sales, arrivals, and stocks in China, 1937–1945 (in thousands of US$)

	Sales		Arrivals, monthly amount	Cumulative supply or deficiency at month-end
	Monthly amount	Cumulative amount		
Farmers Bank sales				
1943				
September	6	6	—	1544[a]
October	14	20	—	1530
November	207	227	8417	9740
December	101	328	2070	11,709
1944				
January	218	546	—	11,491
February	605	1151	—	10,886
Central Bank sales[b]				
March	1088	2239	—	9798
April	613	2852	1077	10,262
May	2062	4914	—	8200
June	2118	7032	—	6082
July	4393	11,425	1093	2782
August	1800	13,225	—	982
September	5260	18,485	4493	215
October	7175	25,660	2849	−4111
November	7600	33,260	—	−11,711
December	3185	36,445	2949	−11,947
1945				
January	10,325	46,770	2927	−19,345
February	12,390	59,160	—	−31,733
March	17,815	76,975	—	−49,550
April	9240	86,215	—	−58,790
May	12,775	98,990	—	−71,565
June	16,345[c]	115,335	3979	−83,931
July			37,056	−46,875
August			36,836	−10,039
September			—	−10,039
October			30,489	20,450
Total			134,235	

[a] The Central Bank's stock of gold held in China prior to American shipments was US$1,550,000. Adding this stock to total arrivals, and subtracting total sales, the balance on hand at the end of the period was US$20,450,000.

[b] Includes forward sales and gold deposits from August 1944.

[c] Sales of gold were suspended on June 25, 1945, and practically ceased during the rest of the war.

TABLE 67. Gold prices, retail prices, exchange rates, and dollar equivalent of gold prices in China, 1937–1945

End of year	Retail[a] market prices (average)	Gold price (average per Chinese ounce)[b]	Free market exchange rate per US$	Equivalent value of gold per ounce (average)
1937	118	C$ 115	C$ 3.35	US$ 34.40
1938	176	210	6.10	34.50
1939	323	400	13.30	30.10
1940	724	750	18	41.70
1941	1977	2400	28	86.00
1942	6620	6150	49	125.00

End of quarter		Official price	Free price	(average)	Based on official prices	Based on free prices
1943 (4th)	22,800	12,500	12,977	83	150	157
1944 (1st)	33,300	17,000	17,895	170	100	105
(2nd)	46,600	18,500	18,803	203	91	93
(3rd)	56,200	18,500	20,070	209	89	96
(4th)	75,500	22,500	28,932	441	51	66
1945 (1st)	142,000	24,500	38,235	558	44	69
(2nd)	216,700	39,500	92,477	1060	37	87

[a] Retail prices are average free market prices in leading cities of Free China, based on data of the Farmers Bank of China, January–June 1937 = 100. Gold prices through 1942 are free prices at Chengtu as compiled by the University of Nanking; and thereafter are for Chungking as compiled by the Central Bank, average official prices being approximated for the quarters in which they were changed. Free market rates of exchange are T/T selling rates at Shanghai to 1942 and thereafter for US$ notes.

[b] The Chinese ounce or *tael* equals 1.00471 Troy ounces, and hence roughly comparable with the latter.

TABLE 68. China's receipts from sale of gold compared with increase of note issue, 1943–1945 (millions of C$)

Quarter	Receipts from gold sales	Increase of note issue	Ratio of receipts from gold to note increase[a] (per cent)
1943			
4th	C$ 114	C$ 14,900	0.8
1944			
1st	979	20,500	4.8
2d	2534	26,900	9.4
3d	6067	27,400	26.9
4th	11,360	39,300	28.9
1945			
1st	29,700	57,400	51.8
2d	42,000	150,900	28.0

[a] Note increase was equal to 86 per cent of the estimated cash deficit in 1944, and 81 per cent in 1945. Quarterly figures of cash deficit are not available.

APPENDIX F. MISCELLANEOUS

This appendix contains data regarding exchange rationing and Chinese and Japanese assets in the United States in 1941.

TABLE 69. Applications for foreign exchange and allotments, 1938–1939

	A. *DATA BY WEEKS* (in thousands of pounds sterling)			
Week ending	Applications	Allotments[a]	Ministry of Finance special authorizations	Total
1938				
March 17	1043	451		451
24	2192	593		593
31	2157	520		520
April 7	2209	450		450
14	2189	350		350
21[b]	1400	299		299
28	1448	228		228
May 5	1392	264		264
12	1413	236		236
19	1364	224		224
26	1572	200		200
June 2	1594	197		197
9[c]	1567	182	7	189
16	1571	121	26	147
23	1705	99	49	148
30	1614	104	46	150
July 7	1848	81	94	175
14	2130	81	94	175
21	2285	71	90	161
28	2069	60	100	160
August 4	1641	60	145	205
11[d]	856	60	95	155
18	918	50	47	97
25	963	50	54	104
September 1	994	38	77	115
8	945	39	67	106
15	999	35	41	76
22	886	30	79	109
29	619	24	61	85
October 6	601	24	103	127
13	553	19	94	113
20	514	20	340	360
27	467	15	95	110
November 3	469	15	101	116
10	476	15	111	126
17	502	9	107	116
24	520	10	70	80
December 1	475	10	145	155
8	497	10	104	114
15	502	10	133	143
22	539	10	71	81
29	535	7	52	59

[a] Allotments under this system ended June 30, 1939. The total does not include £160,000 (equivalent to about US$800,000) allotted in March-June 1938 through a "special account" in one of the foreign banks. See text, chapter XV.

[b] Beginning with this allotment, 100 per cent cash deposit was required with applications.

[c] Beginning with this allotment a preferred list for essential items was established.

[d] Beginning with this allotment applications were limited to goods "shipped" before January 1, 1938.

TABLE 69 (*continued*)

A. *DATA BY WEEKS* (in thousands of pounds sterling)

Week ending		Applications	Allotments[a]	Ministry of Finance special authorizations	Total
1939					
January	5	400	5	45	50
	12	378	5	79	84
	19	364	5	81	86
	26	327	6	146	152
February	2	304	5	263	268
	9	289	5	52	57
	16	261	4	48	52
March	2	231	4	49	53
	9	220	4	23	27
	16	214	3	51	54
	23	214	3	71	74
	30	205	3	86	89
April	6	207	3	158	161
	13	202	3	85	88
	20	203	3	48	51
	27	200	3	142	145
May	4	150	3	16	19
	11	153	3	159	162
	18	149	3	36	39
	25	152	3	48	51
June	1	149	3	97	100
	8	143	3	82	85
	15	125	3	65	68
	22	125	3	34	37
	29	107	3	72	75
Totals		£56,006	£5,462	£4,734	£10,196

B. *ALLOTMENTS*[a] *BY MONTHS, 1938–1939* (000 omitted from allotment figures.)

Year	Shanghai	Outports	Total		
	Pounds sterling		Pounds sterling	Average cross-rate	US$ equivalent approximate
1938					
March (13–31)	£1368	£196	£1564	US$4.98	US$ 7800
April	1192	135	1327	4.98	6600
May	814	110	924	4.97	4600
June	560	143	703	4.96	3500
July	207	86	293	4.93	1450
August	176	44	220	4.88	1175
September	113	53	166	4.80	800
October	44	34	78	4.77	370
November	34	15	49	4.71	230
December	37	10	47	4.67	220
1939					
January	21		21	4.67	100
February	14		14	4.69	65
March	17		17	4.69	78
April	12		12	4.68	55
May	12		12	4.68	55
June	15		15	4.68	70
Totals	£4636	£826	£5462		US$27,168

[a] Allotments under this system ended June 30, 1939. The total does not include £160,000 equivalent to about US$800,000 allotted in March–June, 1938, through a "special account" in one of the foreign banks. See text.

TABLE 70. Chinese and Japanese assets in the United States as of June 14, 1941 (values in millions of US$)

A. Amount of assets including official assets

Holdings of	China	Japan
Chinese	US$208	
Japanese		US$150
American citizens and American-controlled enterprises	64	6
Japan, Germany, Italy, and other European countries later becoming enemies	19	0.3[a]
Other countries	66	5
Totals	US$356	US$161

B. Private Chinese holdings including holdings by non-Chinese persons in China

Kind		Amount
Bank deposits		91.2
Securities		
Common stocks	27.6	
Preferred stocks	5.2	
Federal and other government obligations	9.3	
Corporate bonds and other	5.6	
Total securities		47.7
Interests in enterprises with 25 per cent or more control		13.3
Debts and claims		13.1
Checks and acceptances		10.4
Goods and merchandise		5.8
Insurance policies and annuities		5.1
Real estate, mortgages, estates, and trusts		2.2
Total		188.8

C. Holdings of Hong Kong assets

	Amount
Americans and American-controlled enterprises	20
Other, not specified	64
Total	84

D. Number and size of holdings

Size of holding	Number of persons and value in millions					
	China		Japan		Hong Kong	
Under US$10,000	3127	US$ 9.2	1527	US$ 5.5	446	US$ 1.5
US$10,000–99,999	933	26.2	512	15.4	176	5.4
Over US$100,000	205	321.0	93	139.6	70	77.4

E. Kind of holding (number reported with values)

	China	Japan	Hong Kong
Individual and sole proprietorship	3342	1566	483
Corporations and other profit organizations	771	508	187
Governmental	26	20	5
Other, including nonprofit	126	38	17

SOURCE: *Census of Foreign-Owned Assets in the United States*, Treasury Department, Washington, 1945, pp. 72, 74, 81, 83. The figures as of June 14, 1941, when the Treasury froze German and Italian assets, indicate in a general way the amounts and particulars of the Chinese and Japanese assets frozen six weeks later, pursuant to the President's Executive Order 8389 of July 26, 1941. The breakdown of private Chinese holdings is from the Morgenthau Diaries, vol. 861, pp. 94–95.

[a] This item apparently does not include Japanese assets.

APPENDIX G. MEMORANDUM OF ARTHUR N. YOUNG, JULY 20, 1943, ON THE INTERNATIONAL MONETARY PLANS

THE INTERNATIONAL MONETARY PLANS

I have very carefully studied the American and British international monetary plans, not only from China's standpoint but also in their broader aspects. In the light of such information as is available, my views are as follows:

1. Neither plan adequately recognizes the need for monetary rehabilitation as preliminary to longer-term stabilization. Many of the world's monetary systems have suffered grievous injury as a result of the war — some (such as China's) more so than others. I am of course sympathetic with the desire for the earliest possible exchange stabilization. But for many countries the establishment of more or less definitive exchange rates is not the beginning of the procedure. It is rather a chief aim of the first stage, namely, internal financial rehabilitation. It is not realistic to seek exchange stability by making an agreement fixing rates of exchange that purport to be definitive, without giving due regard to whether conditions will permit the rates to be maintained. The basic thing is the fundamental financial condition of the individual nations.

2. Repair of the serious intangible damage to injured monetary systems is a need quite analogous to relief and repair of war devastation — though infinitely more difficult. It will require an all-out effort by the respective countries in a period of exhaustion and psychological reaction. Most of these countries will have to draw upon external resources to bolster their public finances during a transitional period of monetary rehabilitation. In so far as they themselves do not have adequate external resources, the further provision they need is in theory essentially of the same kind as provision of relief. It is to be hoped that such further needed resources can be provided on lease-lend terms, as part of a comprehensive program of internal and external measures for each country that finds itself in this position.

3. Sound theory requires that the resources of any permanent international monetary organization be used as a regulator fund, to aid in maintaining longer-term stability. If the resources intended for this purpose have to be expended to aid in *achieving* stability, the fund is bound to be depleted and there will be disappointment and frustration. Countries will

be wrongly blamed for dissipating resources which, if no other provision exists, they are bound to use for the inescapable needs of monetary rehabilitation.

4. Clearly the solution in the case of many war-smitten countries is frankly to recognize a transitional period of monetary rehabilitation. But purely monetary measures are not enough. The program for this period must include relief, repair of devastation and restoration of productivity — as well as such financial measures as curtailment of military and civil expenditure, rebuilding of the revenue system, debt readjustment, price stabilization, reform of monetary and banking conditions, and improvement of the international balance of payments. For many countries, until these problems are more or less in hand, the fixing of definitive exchange rates is putting the cart before the horse. Rates are likely to be crystallized at which international balances of payments cannot attain equilibrium; and either external resources will be drained away or countries will be driven to protect these resources by measures of exchange control which will hamper economic recovery and retard the return of confidence.* After countries have restored a considerable degree of internal financial stability, there will be a chance to work a longer-term system on the lines of these two plans. The world badly needs such a system, but the difficulties are great and it would be a pity if the longer-time system were jeopardized by expecting it to start operating as a whole from scratch.

5. At an early date, perhaps very soon after end of the war, the United States and Great Britain and possibly some other countries may be ready to agree upon stable rates of exchange among themselves and thus to commence the operation of a longer-term system. It is very desirable that they do so, in order to provide a nucleus of stability. Thereafter other countries could move from the transitional arrangements into the longer-term system. This would be far better than to expect either the American or British plans as they stand to meet the demands of the transitional period. Of course in the long run, it may be that a large part of the world would become indebted through the proposed organization, to the United States and perhaps to some other countries. But this is less likely to develop suddenly, and might be avoided or corrected: (a) if a sound scheme is devised and carried out for the transitional period; (b) if proper arrangements can be made to promote greater freedom of trade, control of basic

---

* The idea in the British plan (paragraph 33) of controlling capital movements but giving "a general permission . . . to all remittances in respect of current trade," which also seems implicit in the American plan, is I believe impracticable for general application. China's experience shows that a half-way measure, short of general exchange control, will not work. The permission of current trade would give a loophole for flight of capital, e.g., through exporting goods and leaving the proceeds abroad. Also there could be a flight from the currency by overimporting staple goods for hoarding.

commodities and international capital investment; and (c) if proper international measures are adopted to maintain peace.

6. The procedure herein proposed would give opportunity and encouragement for stability. But in the long run the possibility of a properly working international monetary system depends largely upon the internal monetary policies of the various countries. Every country in the world now has a managed currency, and despite any nominal link with gold this condition is likely to continue. The stability of rates of foreign exchange will depend upon whether the various countries deliberately try to keep their policies of currency management moving substantially parallel. In other words, if one or more countries are following inflationary policies, or if most of the countries should have an inflationary tendency but some were inflating at a greater rate, balances of payment would soon get out of equilibrium. A great virtue in having an organization such as these plans contemplate is that it would help to bring about a common policy. There would be time and opportunity for individual countries to change policies that were putting them out of line with the rest of the world, that would adversely affect other countries, and that in the long run would not bring real benefit to the countries themselves.

7. As is clearly recognized by the authors of the two plans, the success of any scheme will be much affected by the degree of success in devising effective international arrangements for relief and economic rehabilitation, expansion of international trade, regulation of basic international commodities and international investment.

8. The existence of difficulties of course does not mean that creation of a comprehensive monetary scheme should not be tried. On the contrary, the need for it is very great, as the authors of the two plans have clearly proven. But it should be realistic, and should not expect too much in the early stages from a world that financially speaking will be very sick. The line of progress, I believe, is both to consolidate at the outset such exchange stability as can be soundly established, and gradually to enlarge the area of stability by measures that will promote the recovery of other countries to the point where they can take their places in a general system of stable exchanges.

APPENDIX H. MEMORANDUM OF ARTHUR N. YOUNG, JUNE 18, 1945, ON SOME TENTATIVE CONCLUSIONS AS TO CHINA'S PROSPECTIVE FINANCIAL AND ECONOMIC PROBLEMS

China's future is bound up with the wise handling of financial and economic problems. I summarize below some tentative conclusions of an analysis I am making of these problems as they will arise during the rest of the war and immediately thereafter. Where figures are given they are mostly tentative because of the great difficulty of making quantitative estimates while so many uncertainties exist. I have, however, ventured to make these estimates in order to give a starting point. They can be revised as more information becomes available. Even though some figures may be open to question, the general nature of the problem is clear.

The tentative conclusions stated below are given without much supporting analysis and argument, this being developed in separate memoranda.

1. Rehabilitation of China's currency and public finances after the war must take equal rank with repair of physical destruction. The financial plan, including the financing of relief and rehabilitation, must be a well-knit one, according to a time schedule, and in order to succeed must be carried out strictly without change of essential parts. The financial plan will involve drastic reduction and control of expenditures, rebuilding of revenues, organization of the Central Reserve Bank and banking reform as the major points which are related to and mostly preliminary to currency reform.

2. The first aim should be to get things back to where they were in 1937. This involves relief and repair of physical damage, and also, fully as important, restoration of a sound monetary and financial system. Until these aims are substantially accomplished, it is not practicable to think of relatively large expenditures for the program of development.

3. After the war China will need a new currency unit. Issuance of new currency, however, would be dangerous until conditions are ripe, namely: (a) that there is a prospect of balancing the budget and stopping inflationary note issue within a moderate time and a practicable program to those ends has been adopted; (b) that the principal shortages have been largely made good and a solid beginning made on repair of war damage; and (c) that there is reasonable prospect of stability in China's international and internal political affairs. The present currency, meanwhile, should be strongly sup-

ported until it can be converted at a fair value into the new. The rate of conversion of the old currency should depend fundamentally upon the general level of prices in the old currency at the time of conversion, and should aim neither to overvalue nor undervalue the old currency.

4. When exchange can be stabilized, the level should not over-value the Chinese currency. Without a sound level, and without a strict program of balancing the budget, the balance of payments will continue to be out of equilibrium. In case of doubt the new exchange level should slightly under-value rather than over-value China's currency.

5. If the International Monetary Fund is created, China would adopt a monetary standard based upon gold or the American dollar as provided in the agreement. Otherwise the logical standard would be based on the American dollar. Probably China will be wise to restore substantially the pre-war monetary unit. Its value, however, might be equivalent to US$0.25, equivalent to 14.88d. — since restoration of the old value of about US$0.30 would mean appreciation in terms of sterling from the pre-war level of 14.50d. to nearly 18d. But decision on this point and the exact method of determining the value of the postwar unit will have to be left open until nearer the time of action.

6. China should not rely upon its quota in the International Monetary Fund to cover the deficit during the currency reform. This cost should be financed out of foreign currency holdings as far as these suffice, over and above what should be held for longer-time currency reserves, and if neces-sary supplemented by a stabilization credit, e.g., from the International Bank for Reconstruction and Development.

7. Coins should not be issued except in connection with definitive stabilization of the currency. If the US$0.25 level is chosen the coins, subject to consideration by an expert committee, should be: a 50¢ silver coin of the "Quarternary" type with a security rim; pure nickel coins of 20, 10, and 5¢; and copper coins of 1¢ and ½¢. Probably C$1 "quarternary" coins with a security rim will be found desirable later after the currency reform is well established.

8. In dealing with enemy and puppet currencies in Occupied China the main objective should be: (1) all practicable regard for the welfare of *bona fide* Chinese holders; (2) avoidance of benefit to puppets and collaborators; (3) promotion of economic recovery in the area; and (4) elimination of these currencies as soon as conditions permit.

9. As soon as possible after the war Government expenditures should be drastically cut, particularly by demobilization of soldiers and stopping of war-time expenditures. Costs of the military establishment and the civil administration should be cut to the minimum needed. Debt payments should be definitely determined as soon as the necessary readjustments can be made. The amount of external and internal funds available for all other purposes

should be carefully rationed, after determining the external and internal costs of the various programs, i.e., for rehabilitation; development of transport and communications, industry and agriculture; public health; education, etc. That is, the coat should be cut according to the cloth. Priorities should be set up for the more urgent needs. Meanwhile, commitments now made for the respective programs should be kept within the limits of a fair proportion of what may be available.

10. Development of a strong tax system is fundamental, first, in order to balance the budget and check inflation, and second, because to a considerable extent China's program of development will have to be financed by the Government. But it will be hard to develop tax revenue rapidly after the war. For example, the total of non-borrowed revenue increased from C$498 million* in 1930–31 to C$870 million in 1936–37 (fiscal years ending June 30), due to great efforts by the government. It will not be easy to restore the yield of these revenues to the pre-war equivalent of C$870 million. The tax system should be as simple as possible. Careful attention will have to be given to the allocation of national, provincial and local sources of revenue. Development of a competent and adequately paid personnel to administer taxes will be of utmost importance. There should be a long-time program of reforming the land tax. This should be an important part of a program of agrarian reform.

11. Internal borrowing by the Government cannot be relied upon to finance the deficit during the early post-war period. First the public and the banks will have no considerable surplus out of which loans can be provided. They will need their resources to rehabilitate private production and trade, which is necessary before the Government can raise enough tax revenue. Second, interest rates will be prohibitively high until after the currency reform has been put into effect and confidence has been restored.

12. During the period of currency reform, and while the tax system is being strengthened, the deficit will have to be financed mainly by drawing on external funds. With energetic action, it should be possible to balance the ordinary budget within two to three years by expenditure of something like US$400 million, for import of goods and to stabilize exchange, provided that the Government adopts and adheres to a very strict program of restriction of expenditures and development of revenue. This figure includes emergency costs of demobilization of troops and restoration of governmental functions in liberated areas, but not costs of relief and rehabilitation and of the program of development.

13. Provision for the internal costs of relief and rehabilitation and of the program of development will be a serious problem for some time. Funds

* This is the figure after deducting costs of revenue collection, C$60 million, that being the basis used in 1930–1931. The figure comparable with that stated for 1936–1937 is C$558 million.

cannot be spared for this from the ordinary budget, because this would mean deficit financing and the currency reform cannot succeed so long as deficti financing is relatively great. Internal borrowing will not soon be feasible, as stated. Therefore these internal costs will have to be financed mainly: (a) from use in kind or sale of UNRRA supplies; (b) from use in kind or sale of imports for Government account; and (c) by sales of foreign currency to stabilize exchange, which may be necessary in the amount of something like US$100–150 million.

14. For the longer term, internal costs of the program of development will have to be met from China's economic surplus — whether mobilized through taxation or through private savings. The amount available out of the budget before the war for reconstruction and education was of the order of C$150 million yearly. But there was also a budget deficit of similar amount — largely offset however by retirement of debt. It may be some years before the budget can provide much more than C$150 million yearly for the program of development, without deficit financing which would threaten stability of the currency. As to private savings, it is difficult to measure the pre-war amount. Internal Government bond issues realized something like C$150 million yearly. In 1934–36 bank deposits in Shanghai increased by about C$400–600 million yearly. But not all such savings could be mobilized to finance the national program of development, since much of them are needed for private enterprise which adds to the national productivity. We can aim at internal savings of a few hundreds of millions of pre-war dollars available for the program in the first years after restoration of the economy and the financial system. But as productivity increases, the figure can become very large. Mobilization of labor when farmers have spare time is very important, both for public works and to increase productivity.

15. The burden of Chinese currency debt will be much reduced because of inflation. This does not mean, however, that the burden of the inflation has been small, as it has caused heavy loss to a large part of the community. The main item of debt will be owed to the Central Bank, and this will be largely nominal because it offsets war-time note issue.

16. Early readjustment of pre-war external debt will be important to restore credit and strengthen confidence. The principal amount of foreign currency loans outstanding before the war will be reduced, according to a preliminary calculation, from the equivalent of about US$500 million* to about US$300 million, (a) by debt retirement; (b) by cancellation of the Boxer Indemnity; (c) by anticipated cancellation of debt to Axis Governments and assumption by them of the debts to their nationals; and (d) because depreciation of sterling gives a lower United States dollar equivalent. Internal debt contracted during the war in terms of foreign currency,

* Excluding the "Nishihara loans," which the Chinese Government did not recognize.

however, is large and raises a special problem. Also inter-governmental commodity credits entail fairly heavy payments for several years. Whether these schedules will be revised, and also the position of the US$500 million and £50 million war credits, should be definitely determined as soon as practicable.

17. China's needs of foreign currency funds for relief and rehabilitation and for restoration of a sound financial system are likely to exceed available resources by something like US$1–2 billion. This deficit will have to be met, if it can be, out of grants and credits. This estimate includes only US$100–200 million for the beginning of the program of economic development.

18. An adequate currency reserve should be set aside with priority out of China's external assets. Foreign currency funds can be gotten much more easily for relief and rehabilitation and for new development than for currency reserves. China after the war ought to have currency reserves of the order of US$675 million, including China's subscription of the International Monetary Fund. If the Fund with its quota of US$550 million is not created, China's total currency reserves should be of the order of US$1 billion. These reserves do not include the cost of covering the post-war deficit and of achieving currency stability, as the cost of these measures should be regarded as a capital item along with repair of physical damage. Even after restoring China's financial system there will be economic and financial uncertainties, as to conditions both in China and throughout the world, which make it prudent for China to have total reserves of the order of size stated.

19. The Central Bank of China should be reorganized after the war into a Central Reserve Bank of China, on the lines of the plan adopted about July 1, 1937, but never promulgated. This is important in order to control the supply of money and as a means to aid in banking reform. The Government should sell 60% of its shares and reduce its holdings to 40%, the rest being divided between approved Chinese banks and the public. Government borrowing from the Central Reserve Bank should be limited to temporary advances up to one-fourth of the budget revenue of the previous year, repayable within four months after the close of the fiscal year.

20. Banking reform will be of urgent importance, especially since most of the banks in Occupied China and some of the banks in Free China will be completely insolvent. The fact that the banking situation will be in such a mess will give an opportunity to clean it up fundamentally. Banking reform is necessary to promote the development of trade and the formation of private capital, which will be essential to give a basis for China's program of economic development. The Government should sell all of its holdings of bank shares excepting 40% of the shares of the Central Reserve Bank and possibly the shares of the Central Trust of China and the Postal Remittances

and Savings Bank if the former limits its activities to Government service functions and the latter to operations indicated in its title.

21. After the war exchange control and control of exports and imports should be relaxed as rapidly as conditions permit. Particularly export control and official trading in exports (e.g., the National Resources Commission and the wood-oil and tea controls) should be abandoned so that normal export trade can develop.

22. United States Army expenditures after larger-scale war begins in China should be financed as far as possible in kind, because the landings will be in areas bare of essential supplies. An effort to finance these costs by any kind of currency will seriously aggravate inflation. But to the extent that currency must be used, it should be Chinese currency rather than United States dollars or an "invasion currency," use of either of which would tend to discredit the Chinese national currency.

23. In disposing of gold and goods it is very important to avoid the fixed-price situation which has caused so much difficulty in the case of the official rate of exchange, the sales of gold, and the sales of United States dollar savings certificates and bonds.

BIBLIOGRAPHIC NOTE

The papers which I collected in 1937–1945 while serving China as financial adviser, and to whose use the Chinese government has consented, are the chief source of information for this book. These papers, in English and Chinese, comprise letters and telegrams, memorandums, reports, statistics, periodicals, pamphlets, and books. Also I have drawn upon a partial diary, which I kept as time permitted.

Chinese official records published for this period are not extensive, other than press releases. The *Public Finance Yearbook*, 1948, in Chinese, issued by the Finance Ministry, contains extensive data. Many financial and economic data are contained in *The Money and Finance of China*, in Chinese, by Wei-ya Chang of the Central Bank of China (Taipeh, 1951). Information on a variety of subjects is contained in the *China Handbook, 1937–43*, . . . *1937–44* and . . . *1937–45*, issued by the Ministry of Information, and in *The Chinese Year Book, 1936–37* (2d issue) to . . . *1944–45* (7th issue), published by the Council of International Affairs in China making use of official sources. The long series of *The China Year Book*, dating from 1912 and published at Shanghai, contains issues for 1937–38 and 1939, edited by H. G. W. Woodhead.

American government records for this period are a mine of information. The Department of State's publication, *Foreign Relations of the United States* (herein referred to as FRUS), is a primary source, as are also the unpublished records of that Department, to which I had access. Also important are that Department's so-called White Paper of 1949, *United States Relations with China: With Special Reference to the Period 1944–1949* (Washington, 1949) herein referred to as *U.S. Relations with China, 1949*.

For Treasury records I was fortunate to have access to photostats of a considerable part of the Morgenthau Diaries. The Subcommittee to Investigate the Administration of the Internal Security and Other Internal Security Laws, of the Committee of the Judiciary, United States Senate, made available to me these records without restriction when I testified before them in 1956. The Subcommittee documented my testimony by publishing with it a number of extracts from the Diaries (see Hearings, *Scope of Soviet Activity in the United States*, part 35, July 13, 1956, Washington, 1957).* These Diaries, together with the publications and records of

---

* After this book was in type this Subcommittee published lengthy extracts from the Diaries, relating mostly to China and in particular to the activities of Harry Dexter White of the American Treasury (*Morgenthau Diaries (China)*, two volumes, 89th Congress,

the State and War departments, complement invaluably the story which the Chinese records reveal. Mr. Morgenthau is to be commended for preserving a record that shows so much of the process by which policy was made and carried into effect. The Diaries are closed except to Mr. Morgenthau or his agent, until opened to qualified scholars serially after 25 years have elapsed from the end of each Roosevelt term. John M. Blum, as an independent scholar working in close touch with Mr. Morgenthau, has published *From the Morgenthau Diaries, Years of Crisis, 1928–1938* (Boston, 1959), and *From the Morgenthau Diaries: Years of Urgency, 1938–1941* (Boston, 1965). These books contain some material on China. The study of A. S. Everest, *Morgenthau, the New Deal, and Silver* (New York, 1950), makes use of the Diaries. Also the papers of Norman H. Davis and Nelson T. Johnson in the Library of Congress, and of Harry D. White in the Princeton University Library, contain material relating to this period. In connection with charges that White was disloyal, Nathan I. White has published *Harry Dexter White, Loyal American* (Waban, Massachusetts, 1956).

British official records are not available for the whole period of study, but *Documents on British Foreign Policy, 1919–1939*, 3d series, vols. 8 and 9, contain data relating to some of the matters herein treated. British data on aid to China are summarized in the following documents: Chancellor of the Exchequer, *Mutual Aid, Second Report*, November 23, 1944, and *Mutual Aid, Third Report*, October, 1946 (CMD. 6931).

The Statistical Yearbook of Finance and Economy of Japan, issued by the Ministry of Finance, Tokyo, 1948, contains data on Japanese and puppet note issues in China in 1937–1946.

Works which deal wholly or in part with China's finances in the war period include: Kia-ngau Chang, *The Inflationary Spiral, The Experience in China, 1939–1950* (New York, 1958), and *China's Struggle for Railroad Development* (New York, 1943); Shun-hsin Chou, *The Chinese Inflation, 1937–1949* (New York, 1963); F. M. Tamagna, *Banking and Finance in China* (New York, 1942); and Arthur N. Young, *China's Economic and Financial Reconstruction*, Committee on International Economic Policy (New York, 1947), and *China and the Helping Hand, 1937–1945* (Cambridge, 1963).

Periodicals relating to the financial record in this period include the *Bulletin* of the Central Bank of China, in English, 1937–1940; the Bank of China's *Financial and Commercial Monthly Bulletin*, 1937–1939, partly in English and partly in Chinese, and *Fortnightly Letter on Economic Conditions in China*, 1943–1945; *Finance & Commerce*, Shanghai, 1937–1941; and, for the Japanese angle, the *Oriental Economist*, Tokyo, 1937–1945.

1st Session, February 5, 1965). These extracts contain much of the material which I saw in the Subcommittee's files in 1956, and more.

NOTES

I. Introduction: The Prewar Situation

1. In addition the Export-Import Bank authorized on May 4, 1937, before the hostilities, a credit of US$1,600,000 to buy locomotives, but the agreement was not signed until December 21, 1937. Only US$733,200 was utilized, and this was repaid by 1942.

2. I served first as Financial Adviser to the Ministry of Finance, and later also was appointed Financial Adviser to the Executive Yuan, or cabinet; concurrently as Adviser to the Central Bank; and, less formally, during part of the period, as adviser on communications and in particular aviation. I was a director of the civil air line, China National Aviation Corporation, from 1938 to 1945; adviser to the Chinese Commission on Relief and Rehabilitation in 1944-1945; and chairman or acting chairman during part of the period of the two committees handling distribution in China of American contributions for relief.

3. See Arthur N. Young, *China and the Helping Hand, 1937-1945* (Cambridge, 1963), hereinafter referred to as *China and the Helping Hand*, pp. 8-10, for a summary of the economic progress and the conditions and institutions that held it back. For criticism of Nationalist policy as to public finance and economic development, see D. S. Paauw, "The Kuomintang and Economic Stagnation" (*Journal of Asian Studies*, February 1957, pp. 213-220) and "Chinese National Expenditures during the Nanking Period" (*Far Eastern Quarterly*, November 1952, pp. 3-26). Paauw fails to give due weight to several factors hereinbefore set out in this chapter, including: (1) the importance of the government incurring the costs needed to restore order, establish nationwide authority, and eventually to resist Japan (see N. S. Buchanan's criticism of Paauw on this point following the second citation, pp. 45-46); (2) the disrupting effects of Japan's seizure of Manchuria and encroachments upon North China; (3) the crippling effects of the deflation of about 30 per cent in 1931-1935, largely caused by American silver-buying; (4) the fact that well over half of the borrowing to cover deficits in the prewar years was not for ordinary governmental operations but for payments to retire older debt; and (5) China's improving credit from 1928-1937 despite the difficulties, as shown by the great rise in prices of the chief external and internal bonds, selling respectively on about a 5 per cent and 8 per cent basis in mid-1937.

I know of no adequate analysis of China's economic progress in 1928-1937. The subject deserves further research.

4. *China and the Helping Hand*, pp. 10-11.

5. For analysis of the war-rooted causes of the downfall of the National Government on the mainland, see *China and the Helping Hand*, pp. 421-426.

II. Cash Receipts and Expenditure

1. Official data showing the proceeds of these sales of foreign currencies are not available, but the approximate proceeds by fiscal periods are shown in Table 4. Through March 12, 1938, the Central Bank supported the exchange rate, and the

sale of foreign currencies, which realized an estimated C$499 million, was an important offset to the budgetary deficit. After that date, the Central Bank rationed exchange to the market in 1938–1939 on a decreasing scale, realizing C$26 million in 1938 and C$3 million in 1939. From mid-1938 until April 1939 the Bank of China and the Hongkong and Shanghai Banking Corporation conducted stabilization operations. Then came the Anglo-Chinese stabilization operations, which realized about C$351 million from sales of foreign currency in the first seven months of 1939, including a small balance taken over from the preceding operation. After outbreak of World War II, the Fund spent about C$204 million in September-December 1939, to buy foreign currency. The result was a net withdrawal through stabilization operations in 1939 of about C$147 million of *fapi*, to which is added about $3 million received under the scheme of exchange rationing, total C$150 million. The Fund withdrew about C$132 million by exchange sales in 1940. In 1941 the Fund sold about £1.5 million, realizing an estimated C$108 million; and the Stabilization Board sold US$14.7 million and £1.92 million, while buying US$106,500 from exports and also some overseas remittances as to which figures are not available. For 1941 the net total realized in *fapi* was about C$525 million. After 1941 sales of foreign currencies were of only minor importance as a counterinflationary factor.

These various extrabudgetary and counterinflationary transactions are discussed at length in succeeding chapters.

2. The apparent failure to show these receipts in the accounts for those two years may be because part of the sales was from Central Bank reserves. Inasmuch as those sales in 1943–1944 were apparently treated as that bank's transactions, I include the proceeds here as extrabudgetary receipts of counterinflationary effect. For 1945, however, part of the receipts from gold is included in the item in Table 2, "Sales of foreign loan purchases, commodities, and gold," C$28,663 million. The rest apparently constitutes most of the item of C$62,727 million from "Sale of internal bonds." These obligations were largely certificates of deposit payable in gold when received, and were issued when the American Treasury delayed gold shipments (see chap. XIX and appendix A, Table 40).

In the spring of 1946 the Finance Ministry gave me an itemized statement of the fiscal results of 1945 which is generally similar to the closed accounts as per appendix A, Table 40. That statement listed under "Borrowing": "Gold deposits," C$60,335 million; "Internal borrowing," C$964 million; and "External borrowing," C$91 million. The total of the first two items is C$61,299 million, which as a preliminary figure is similar to the figure of C$62,727 million in the closed accounts. Also the item of C$91 million for external borrowing is similar to the item of C$92 million in the closed accounts. Thus the item of C$62,727 million is misleading if not explained. The difference between the C$71,700 million received from gold in 1945, as per Central Bank data, and receipts from certificates of deposit payable later in gold, C$60,335 million as per the preliminary figure of early 1946, is C$11,365 million. The latter amount represents the approximate receipts in 1945 from sales of gold that are included in the general item, "Sales of foreign loan purchases, commodities, and gold, C$28,663 million."

3. For further particulars concerning the Joint Committee see *The Chinese Year Book, 1944–1945*, pp. 594–595.

4. The *fapi* advances for expenditures made by the American forces in China do not show up in the Central Bank's statements for 1945. The statement of December 31, 1945, shows total "loans, discounts, and overdrafts" of C$1,370 billion, practically all of which were to the government. That figure checks roughly with the total of year-by-year advances to government by the Central Bank

and the other government banks (nearly 99 per cent by the Central Bank), amounting to C$1,262 billion (see chap. XIII), plus advances of C$75 billion through the four banks Joint Committee, a total of C$1,337 billion. There is no place in these accounts for advances of C$130 billion to the American government.

Moreover, the advances gave rise to large additional note issue. Had the advances not been taken into the general accounts, the ratio of increase of note issue to the cash deficit would have altered materially in 1944–1945. Instead it remained in the general range of 80 to 90 per cent which obtained in 1939–1945 (see chap. XIII).

I have not been able to clarify further, through inquiries in Taipei, the accounting for *fapi* expenditures by or for the American armed forces.

III. The Rice-Wheat Budget; Total Receipts and Expenditure in Cash and in Kind

1. Ta-chung Liu and Kung-chia Yeh, *The Economy of the Chinese Mainland: National Income and Economic Development, 1933–1959* (Princeton, 1965), pp. 27–32, 46–54, 132. This is a careful detailed analysis of communist output to 1959, and comparison with output in 1933, covering both agriculture and other sectors of the economy. Their estimates of crops are in *piculs* of 50 kg (0.05 metric ton). See also Chinese Ministry of Information, Chungking, *China Handbook, 1937–1943*, p. 550.

2. For an excellent study of communist China's statistical system, see Chohming Li, *The Statistical System of Communist China* (Berkeley and Los Angeles, 1962). Dr. Li explains the working of the system and its early relative success up to 1958; its breakdown at the time of the "great leap forward"; and its resurgence primarily as an instrument of policy and propaganda rather than as a factual instrument, and based largely upon data inflated at the source.

3. Letter of January 28, 1959, to Arthur N. Young.

4. Memorandum dated "1904" supplied by Inspectorate General of Customs, February 1946.

5. These quotations are from a photostat received by the State Department from the Franklin D. Roosevelt Library, Hyde Park, N.Y.

6. The initial rate per dollar of tax was two *shih tou* of grain (one *shih tou* equals 0.2838 American bushel). For Szechwan Province the rate was later set at *3.5 shih tou* of unhulled rice (paddy) per *shih mou* (0.1647 acre) of land. A bushel of unhulled rice weighs 45 pounds, and of hulled rice or wheat 60 pounds. Hence a *shih tou* of unhulled rice weighs 12.8 pounds (5.8 kg), and of hulled rice or wheat 17 pounds (7.7 kg).

7. *Economic Facts*, issued monthly by the Department of Agricultural Economics, University of Nanking, Chengtu, July 1943, p. 179.

8. Thus data of the Land Tax Administration as of November 15, 1943, showed that they had paid out C$1,617 million of Food Treasury Notes, C$283 million of Savings Certificates, and US$11.9 million of US$ Savings Certificates (the latter mostly in Yunnan). The total paid out in cash and obligations was C$3.3 billion. But the value bought, figured at official prices which were below free prices, was stated as C$12.5 billion. Even if the monetary obligations were valued at par, which they were not, the total value so figured was nearly four times what was paid.

9. The "new *picul*" or *shih tan* equals 50 kilograms or about 110 pounds. The old *picul* varied throughout China, and in Szechwan was about 133 pounds. A bag of wheat was considered to weigh 1.4 *piculs*, or 70 kilograms, or about 154

pounds. The figures of Food Treasury Notes are from the *Chinese Year Book, 1944–1945* (Shanghai, 1946), pp. 585, 593.

10. *Chinese News Service,* quoted in *New York Times,* September 4, 1945.

11. *The Chinese Yearbook, 1943,* pp. 559–563, gives details, including the amount supplied to the army by provinces.

12. The figures show the equivalent as calculated by the Land Tax Administration, after deducting the amounts actually paid in *fapi.* In the 1942–1943 data, I have corrected an obvious large arithmetic error in conversion of quantities to values.

13. The average increase of wheat prices is assumed to be similar. Total collections of rice were more than five times as large as collections of wheat.

14. These contemporary data for the first two crop years, and my estimates for the following two years, differ from Kia-ngau Chang's estimates (*The Inflationary Spiral,* p. 144), which are (millions of C$): 1941–1942, 2,731; 1942–1943, 19,712; 1943–1944, 46,446; and 1944–1945, 147,133. He also gives figures for calendar years, which are of the same order of size (*ibid.,* p. 374). The quantity data of the postwar compilation on which he bases his estimates are not very different from my contemporary data for the three years 1942–1943 to 1944–1945. Re the differences for 1941–1942, see the notes to Table 8. The difference in the increase in 1944–1945 over the previous year is affected by his using a price increase of about 3.6 times the previous year's level; whereas my contemporary price data stated above for the crop years ending September 30, show that the price of rice increased by over 5-fold. The difference in absolute amounts of estimated yield in the last three years largely results from my using as the base contemporary figures of free market prices in 1942–1943, which are a third larger than those which he uses.

15. *Economic Facts,* Chengtu, February 1943, p. 47 and *passim.*

16. Shun-hsin Chou, in *The Chinese Inflation,* pp. 61–62, 67–68, shows much smaller real equivalents of cash revenue and expenditure — in 1940–1945, only 10 to 20 per cent for expenditure and 3 to 5 per cent for revenue. His tables on pages 62 and 72 do not allow for the change of fiscal periods for July–June to the calendar year after 1938, and the fact that the fiscal period immediately after mid-1938 was for the rest of that year. His deflator is apparently not very different from mine. But he uses as a base for expenditure in 1936–1937 C$1,884 million; whereas my base of C$1,167 million is, I believe, the figure to use for comparison with the figures that precede and follow. In appendix A, I comment upon the sources of data of receipts and expenditure, and differences in figures used in analyzing the inflation. Chou does not state the figure used as a base for revenue, but it apparently is of the same relative order as that for expenditure. Also, he does not take account of the value of items in kind.

17. See chapters VIII and IX and appendix A, Table 47.

18. For a further discussion of China's war costs, see *China and the Helping Hand,* pp. 417–420.

IV. Fiscal Policy

1. For particulars supporting the above generalizations with regard to revenue in kind and nontax revenue, see chapters II and III.

2. Chang, in *The Inflationary Spiral,* pp. 114–117 and 137–140, describes these taxes and their working, and I shall not duplicate his account.

3. For American official views on the scheme, see *Foreign Relations of the United States, 1942, China,* pp. 495–498; 502–505. Hereinafter cited as *FRUS.*

4. For further discussion of the monopoly scheme, see Kia-ngau Chang, *The Inflationary Spiral*, pp. 135–137.

5. Re the Customs service see J. V. A. MacMurray, *Treaties and Agreements With and Concerning China, 1894–1919* (New York, 1921), vol. 1, pp. 105–107, 109; H. B. Morse, *The Trade and Administration of China* (London, 1920), pp. 385–410; S. F. Wright, *Hart and the Chinese Customs* (Belfast, 1950); and S. F. Wright and J. H. Cubbon, *China's Customs Revenue since the Revolution of 1911* (Shanghai, 1935).

6. For the agreement re the Salt administration see the Reorganization Loan agreement of 1913, in MacMurray, *Treaties and Agreements*, vol. 2, pp. 1009–1029. For President Wilson's statement criticizing the 1913 agreement, see p. 1025.

7. These seizures, in effect, were extensions of earlier Japanese acts. After the invasion of Manchuria in 1931, Japan took over the Customs there. Her puppets of "Manchukuo" offered to make some provision for foreign debt payments, but no way was found to obtain payments without prejudicing China's rights in Manchuria. In the fall of 1935 Japan set up a puppet regime in East Hopei Province on the coast south of Manchuria. This created a gap in China's tariff structure, depriving her of revenue and permitting smuggling of goods inward and of silver outward. See *The Chinese Year Book, 1936–1937*, pp. 891–945.

8. This and following statements on Customs matters are based primarily on papers in my files. Much of the record is contained in *FRUS, 1937*, vol. 3, pp. 858–915, and *1938*, vol. 3, pp. 626–752.

9. *Ibid.*, *1937*, vol. 3, pp. 859–868.

10. *Ibid.*, *1937*, vol. 3, p. 877. For the text of the commissioner's letter see *ibid.*, *1938*, vol. 3, pp. 654–655.

11. *Ibid.*, *1937*, vol. 3, pp. 886, 899–903; *1938*, vol. 3, pp. 626–627, 645–646; *1939*, vol. 3, p. 813.

12. *Ibid.*, *1938*, vol. 3, pp. 646–647.

13. *Reuter's News Service*, dispatch from Shanghai, February 1, 1938.

14. *FRUS, 1937*, vol. 3, pp. 904–905.

15. *Ibid.*, *1938*, vol. 3, pp. 627–630, 628n.

16. *Ibid.*, *1939*, vol. 3, pp. 818–820, 827–829, 861–862.

17. *Ibid.*, *1938*, vol. 3, pp. 634–642.

18. *Ibid.*, *1937*, vol. 3, pp. 904, 911–915.

19. *Ibid.*, *1938*, vol. 3, pp. 692, 701.

20. For the text of most of the documents, see *ibid.*, *1938*, vol. 3., pp. 678–681, 688–694.

21. *Ibid.*, vol. 3, pp. 684–698. For further details, especially on the international aspects of this situation, see *China and the Helping Hand*, pp. 90–96.

22. *FRUS, 1938*, vol. 3, pp. 704–705.

23. China's money was equivalent to between US$0.21 and US$0.26 in May 1938, but then slumped and in the rest of 1938 the rate was about US$0.16.

24. See *Documents on British Foreign Policy, 1919–1939*, 3d ser., vol. 8, pp. 231, 442, 451, 516, and vol. 9, pp. 150, 276.

25. Of this sum C$27 million was in the Hongkong and Shanghai Banking Corporation in Shanghai, and the remainder in the Yokohama Specie Bank there.

26. See *FRUS, 1939*, vol. 3, pp. 843–847, which contains my correspondence with the British ambassador.

27. By 1939 Japan was seizing about 90 per cent of the customs revenue, which was C$331 million in that year. During the whole war period, Japan provided less than C$4 million of the collections to meet debt payments, in January and June

1938. Collections in 1938–1941 were deposited in the Yokohama Specie Bank. The Inspector General of Customs could draw on them for expenses. But the rest presumably went to finance Japanese operations in China. Meanwhile, the Central Bank of China advanced to the Inspector General over C$175 million to meet debt payments up to suspension, and provided all the foreign currencies for these payments.

28. *FRUS, 1939*, vol. 3, p. 861.

29. *Ibid., 1939*, vol. 3, pp. 853–855, 865–866.

30. See the official American war history, in the three volumes of C. F. Romanus and Riley Sunderland: *Stilwell's Mission to China; Stilwell's Command Problems;* and *Time Runs Out in CBI*, Department of the Army, Washington, 1953–1959, *passim;* also *China and the Helping Hand*, pp. 269–276, 302, 356–362, 406–409.

31. F. F. Liu, *A Military History of Modern China, 1924–1949* (Princeton, 1956), pp. 94–95.

32. Morgenthau Diaries, February 18, 1942, vol. 485, p. 113.

33. See *China and the Helping Hand*, pp. 354–356, and "AZC's unofficial notebook on the second Nelson journey to China," in folder marked "China," Donald M. Nelson papers at the Huntington Memorial Library, San Marino, California.

34. Morgenthau Diaries, vol. 580, p. 109, September 5, 1942.

35. For an extract from this communication, see *China and the Helping Hand*, appendix 4.

36. For a further account of these matters, see chapter XX.

37. See *China and the Helping Hand*, chapter XIX, for a further discussion of planning.

38. For example, as to conditions in Lanchow, I noted in my diary April 6, 1944, that there was discontent, "most Central Government officials being from other provinces; too many brought in friends and relatives; and too much personnel. Said that many work only an hour a day, and have few important duties."

39. Department of State file 893.50/245 1/6.

V. The Debt Situation in Mid-1937

1. For a detailed account of China's railway development, and particulars of loans and settlements, see Kia-ngau Chang, *China's Struggle for Railroad Development* (New York, 1943). Dr. Chang was Minister of Railways from 1935 to 1937 and Minister of Communications from 1937–1943 and in the latter capacity handled railway matters. The fact that his list of foreign loans outstanding, published in 1943, was as of December 31, 1935, is indicative of the difficulty of presenting adequate up-to-date data.

2. The yields stated are figured on the basis of bonds held until final maturity. The bonds, however, were retired by yearly drawings which in 1937 would retire about 1 to 1½ per cent of the total issue. If yields are figured on an average basis, for example, assuming a maturity as of the date when half the issue was due to be retired, the yields would be increased slightly, that is, by about ½ per cent.

3. I omit particulars about arrears of interest. These old obligations generally bore high rates of interest, which sometimes was compounded. The government, if settlements had been made, would have insisted upon cancellation of back interest or at least figuring it at a nominal rate — partly to adjust to capacity to bear the burden of settlements, and partly in view of questions with regard to the dubious circumstances surrounding some of the early arrangements whereby the debt was contracted.

4. Particulars of the various obligations and the status of negotiations for

settlement involve too much detail to be stated here. Further data are included in documents which I have lodged with the Library of Congress and the Library of Harvard University.

VI. Internal Borrowing

1. The Central Bank *Bulletin* of February 1946 (in Chinese), p. 104, tabulates quotations in 1937–1945. The tabulation contains some apparent errors.

2. Data received from the Wartime Public Loans Commission give a breakdown for about half of the subscriptions in 1940–1941, and about 85 per cent of these subscriptions were for the dollar issues.

3. Bank of China, *Fortnightly Letter on Economic Conditions in China*, Chungking, January 1, 1945, p. 3.

4. See Table 2. For 1945 Wei-ya Chang states advances as C$1,058,641 million (*The Money and Finance of China* [in Chinese], Taipei, 1951), p. 145.

5. CGU signifies "customs gold unit," the money of account for collection of import duties. CGU 1 equaled US$0.40 in 1930. This unit was adopted early in 1930 following the recommendation of the Kemmerer Commission, primarily in order to stabilize customs revenue in terms of gold because (1) most of that revenue was needed for service of gold obligations, and (2) the silver price and the exchange value of China's currency were falling, thus reducing the gold equivalent of the revenue. This measure, which I suggested because of my knowledge of a similar expedient used in France during currency depreciation in the 1920's, benefited China by tens of millions of dollars in following years. Sir Robert Hart of the Chinese Customs service had proposed in 1901 that the Haikwan tael, which was the silver unit in which duties were collected before 1930, be given a fixed sterling value of 6s.8d. See Wright and Cubbon, *China's Customs Revenue*, p. 173.

After devaluation of the dollar in 1934, the customs gold unit equaled US$0.6773. By order of the Finance Ministry of March 31, 1942, the value was declared equivalent to C$20 and nominally to US$1.00. See chapter XVIII.

6. Cochran was visiting China to try to find means to deal with difficulties that arose concerning the Sino-American-British Stabilization Fund (see chap. XVII). Niemeyer's visit was apparently an outgrowth of a British-sponsored project for a joint Anglo-American official economic mission to China which did not materialize because of American coolness to the idea. The presence of these two men in China for several weeks at the same time was the closest that the project came to fruition.

7. See the letter of January 27, 1942, from Sir Frederick Phillips of the British Treasury to Secretary Morgenthau, *FRUS, 1942, China*, p. 447.

8. Morgenthau Diaries, vol. 521, p. 173, April 20, 1942.

9. *Ibid.*, vol. 515, pp. 269–287, April 11, 1942.

10. *FRUS, 1942, China*, pp. 516–517.

11. That this would happen was indicated by experience in the fall of 1939, when the government authorized the government banks to receive deposits payable in foreign currency and to pay 4 to 7 per cent interest. That was designed to attract funds being repatriated from Europe because of World War II, and to help the Chinese banks to compete with foreign banks, which paid no interest on such deposits. But the government banks obtained deposits of only about US$2 million up to the end of 1941, apparently because of fear of requisitioning by the government.

12. Besides sales to the public, some certificates were issued, especially in

Yunnan Province, against compulsory purchase of grains, instead of the Food Treasury Notes in *fapi*, which were generally used until compulsory borrowing of grains was introduced in the summer of 1943.

13. Bank of China, *Fortnightly Letter on Economic Conditions in China*, January 1, 1945, pp. 4–5.

14. Wei-ya Chang, *Money and Finance of China*, p. 202.

15. The only sizable monthly sales were US$14 million in December 1942, yielding C$280 million; US$56 million from July 1 to August 3, 1943, yielding C$1,120 million; and US$27 million (sold to the public) in October 1943, yielding C$540 million. Calculation of those yields assumes that buyers made full and prompt payment in cash, which probably was not wholly the case. In December 1942 growth of note issue was C$2.5 billion; in July 1943, C$2.6 billion, compared with C$3.4 and C$3.8 billion, respectively in June and August 1943, and C$3.9 billion in October. In 1942–1943 the growth of note issue was about 80 per cent of the cash deficit and thus we may approximate the cash deficit as C$3.1 billion in December 1942; C$4.5 billion for the month ended August 3, 1943 (based upon the average estimated deficits of June and July 1943); and C$5 billion in October 1943. Thus the proportion of cash deficits covered by the proceeds of sale of these securities was roughly a fourth in the period July 1 to August 3, 1943, and a tenth in the other two periods.

16. It is difficult to state what would have been a reasonable cost in dollars to obtain the sum in *fapi* (about C$3 billion) realized from sale to the public of these securities. For what it is worth, I have made the following comparisons on the basis of comparative prices in China and the United States, and of free market rates of exchange for the dollar:

1. From July 1 to August 3, 1943, when the largest amount of sales of certificates took place, China's average price level (in July) was 160 times the prewar level. The American price level rose by about 25 per cent in 1937–1943. If it is assumed, for our present purpose, that the 1937 exchange rate of about US$0.30 then represented comparative purchasing power, the comparable figure in July 1943 was US$0.0025. But the official exchange rate had fallen only from about US$0.30 to US$0.05. The latter figure was about 20 times the value based upon comparative price levels. On that basis, the US$56 million of certificates sold from July 1 to August 3, 1943, produced an equivalent of only about US$2.8 million.

2. In the free market a dollar cost C$48–50 in December 1942; C$63–95 and C$82–98 in July and August 1943, respectively; and C$83–90 in October, 1943. Those rates valued national currency at about 20 to 40 per cent of the official rates, 20–1. On the basis of the free rates the sale of one- to two-fifths of the amounts of dollar securities actually sold in those periods might have yielded the proceeds actually received in national currency.

Both methods of comparison are open to criticism, as indicated in the discussion of purchasing power parities in chapter XVIII. These parities have little meaning when a country is blockaded and the flow of goods and money is neither extensive nor reasonably free. In 1942–1943 the dollar had a low buying power in China. Partly that was a result of the condition just stated. Also, relatively large amounts of dollar currency were being offered for sale, for what they would bring, in the market of a poor country with low purchasing power.

17. *U.S. Relations with China, 1949*, p. 489.

18. These certificates, payable in gold upon arrival, were issued by the Central Bank when the American Treasury delayed gold shipments to China. The question of accounting for the proceeds, whether as receipts from internal borrowing or

from sale of gold, is discussed in note 2 of chapter II. The dealings in gold presented distinctive issues, discussed in chapter XIX, and I do not here treat the proceeds of these certificates as receipts from internal borrowing.

VII. The Prewar Foreign Debt

1. See *China and the Helping Hand*, pp. 99–105.

2. The government, however, on February 5 made a payment of about £70,000 on the 1898 Loan, the senior Customs issue, which with the five similar payments made in preceding months was enough to make possible the payment due March 1 to bondholders. And in March the government announced that funds already remitted would permit paying the interest due March 30 on the senior salt-secured loan of 1908. Those funds were guarantee deposits in Chinese currency, against which the Central Bank provided sterling at the official rate.

3. See *China and the Helping Hand*, chapter VI, for further background concerning these negotiations.

4. *Finance and Commerce*, Shanghai, August 11, p. 147, and September 1, p. 161, 1937.

5. These figures do not include two loans listed with the debt under charge of the Finance Ministry (see appendix A, Table 43), namely, (1) the Hukuang Railway Loan of 1911, and (2) the Canton-Hankow Railway Loan of 1934. Interest on the former was being paid from salt revenue, but retirement of principal, due to begin in 1941 under the 1937 settlement, was a charge upon the railway. The 1934 loan was charged upon a portion of the remitted British Boxer Indemnity, which the Finance Ministry was paying.

6. For a detailed account of the history of the Boxer Indemnity in the prewar period, see Wright and Cubbon, *China's Customs Revenue*, pp. 169–230, 442–591.

7. A credit of US$1.6 million, to buy locomotives, was pending at the Export-Import Bank of Washington, but the agreement was not signed until December 21, 1937. Of this US$733,200 was used, and the debt was repaid by 1942.

VIII. The Foreign Purchase Credits of 1937–1941

1. *FRUS, 1937*, vol. 3, p. 769. See also the Norman Davis papers in the Library of Congress, memorandum of November 27, 1937.

2. *FRUS, 1937*, vol. 3, pp. 565, 578, 606, 616, 780; and *1939*, vol. 3, pp. 136, 160, 261, 757, 764. See also *China and the Helping Hand*, chaps. II, IV, and VIII; and F. F. Liu, *A Military History of Modern China*, pp. 162–173.

3. *China and the Helping Hand*, chapters VIII and XVIII.

4. Chiang Kai-shek told Ambassador Nelson T. Johnson on January 30, 1941, that Russia had not been "giving the Communist armies any assistance whatsoever in the way of personnel, equipment or finances." See *FRUS, 1939*, vol. 3, pp. 208, 308, and State Department file 033.1193/9; also C. B. MacLane, *Soviet Policy and the Chinese Communists* (New York, 1958), chapters III and IV.

5. Official Chinese data indicate that there were no other credits by Russia to China in the war period, as suggested by unofficial sources mentioned by MacLane, *Soviet Policy and the Chinese Communists*, pp. 129–130.

6. Letter of Central Trust of China, June 5, 1946. The "new" *picul* equals 50 kilograms.

7. Letter of Finance Ministry, December 21, 1945.

8. Letter of Natural Resources Commission, June 15, 1946; International Monetary Fund, *Balance of Payments Yearbook, 1948–1949*, p. 115; *Statistical Abstract of the Republic of China, 1960*, pp. 210–211.

9. Letter from Finance Ministry, January 18, 1946.

10. For further discussion of the development of American policy and action see *China and the Helping Hand*, chapters II, V, and VIII.

11. *FRUS, 1937*, vol. 3, p. 514.

12. For an account of the background of the American purchase credits from the Treasury viewpoint see John Morton Blum, *From the Morgenthau Diaries: Years of Urgency, 1938–1941* (Boston, 1965), pp. 58–64, 123–125, 344–365.

13. *FRUS, 1938*, vol. 3, p. 586.

14. *Ibid.*, pp. 435, 586–590, and M. Shigemitsu, *Japan and Her Destiny* (New York, 1958), p. 190.

15. For a summary of this and other wartime credits to China see appendix A, Table 47.

16. Morgenthau Diaries, vol. 215, p. 282, October 4, 1939.

17. For more details see *China and the Helping Hand*, pp. 133–135, and Blum, *Morgenthau Diaries, 1938–1941*, pp. 347, 350–351, 356–365.

18. State Department file 893.51/7145, and *FRUS, 1940*, vol. 4, p. 430.

19. W. L. Langer and S. E. Gleason, *The Undeclared War, 1940–1941* (New York, 1953), pp. 238–239, 301–304.

20. For background from the viewpoint of the American Treasury see Blum, *Morgenthau Diaries, 1938–1941*, pp. 356–365. The statement on page 365 referring to "the $50 million credit for the purchase of military equipment" is in error. The agreement of February 4, 1941, forbade China to purchase under the credit "articles, except aircraft exclusively for commercial purposes, listed as arms, ammunition or implements of war by the President of the United States in accordance with the Neutrality Act of 1939." China paid from her own meager funds for the 100 P-40 planes procured early in 1941 for the Flying Tigers.

21. Letter from Department of State, January 10, 1958.

22. For further discussion of the development of British policy and action see *China and the Helping Hand*, chapters V and VIII.

23. *FRUS, 1938*, vol. 3, pp. 536–538, 540–542, 552, 559.

24. *Reuter's News Service*, December 20, 1938.

25. See *China and the Helping Hand*, chapter IX and *Documents on British Foreign Policy, 1919–1939*, 3d ser., vol. 9, p. 390.

26. *Statistical Abstract of the Republic of China*, 1960, pp. 210–211.

27. See Kia-ngau Chang, *Railroad Development*, pp. 243–250, for an account of the arrangements for building this railway.

28. *Domei News Service*, dispatches from Nanking and Tokyo, May 29 and 31, 1940.

29. See Kia-ngau Chang, *Railroad Development*, pp. 260–262, 274–284.

30. Kurt Bloch, *German Interests and Policies in the Far East* (Institute of Pacific Relations, New York, 1940), pp. xii, 24–36.

31. Statement of the Central Trust of China, received in the fall of 1938.

IX. Foreign Credits and Lend-Lease During the Pacific War

1. See *China and the Helping Hand*, Part Two, *passim*, for a full account of the international, internal, and military background of foreign financial aid to China during the Pacific War, and the use and results of the aid.

2. *FRUS, 1942, China*, p. 443.

3. Morgenthau Diaries, vol. 494, pp. 1–22, February 9, 1942.

4. *FRUS, 1942, China*, p. 487; Morgenthau Diaries, vol. 509, p. 113, March 19, 1942.

5. The text of the agreement is given in the *United States Relations with China*, Department of State, Washington, 1949, pp. 511–512. See also *FRUS, 1942, China*, pp. 419–495, for details of these developments.

6. *U.S. Relations with China*, 1949, p. 511.

7. See *China and the Helping Hand*, chapter XV.

8. Morgenthau Diaries, vol. 485, p. 113, February 18, 1942, and vol. 491, p. 94, February 2, 1942. See also *FRUS, 1942, China*, p. 447.

9. Chancellor of the Exchequer, *Third Report on Mutual Aid*, October 1946 (Cmd. 6931), pp. 7–8, supplemented by a letter of August 15, 1962, from the Chancellor's office.

10. See *China and the Helping Hand*, pp. 142–148, for further discussion of lend-lease aid in 1941.

11. *FRUS, 1942, China*, p. 33.

12. Letters from State Department, January 10 and March 26, 1958. Adjusted totals for lend-lease aid, involving reallocation of appropriations, corrections, etc., are US\$50,208 million and US\$1,602 million, respectively. These adjustments have not been allocated by years.

13. 21st, 22d, and 23d Reports to Congress on Lend-Lease Operations.

14. The figures are from the Chancellor of the Exchequer's *Third Report on Mutual Aid*, October 1946 (Cmd. 6931), supplemented by a letter of August 15, 1962, from the Chancellor's office. See also Romanus and Sunderland, *Stilwell's Command Problems*, pp. 279–280.

15. Morgenthau Diaries, vol. 712, p. 55, March 1944.

16. For a further account of these developments see *China and the Helping Hand*, pp. 289–290, 351–353.

17. *Ibid.*, pp. 362–364.

18. *Ibid.*, p. 366. For a further analysis of the shifting strategy during the Pacific War, see *ibid.*, Part Two *passim*, and Romanus and Sunderland, *Stilwell's Command Problems*, chapter II.

X. Summary and Appraisal, Debt and Foreign Aid; Planning for Postwar

1. *China and the Helping Hand*, p. 206.

2. *Ibid.*, pp. 280–286, 296–298.

3. *Ibid.*, p. 402; *FRUS, 1943, China*, p. 509, and *1942, China*, pp. 138–139.

4. Sets of these studies, which contain details concerning the position of the debt, are lodged in the Library of Congress and the Library of Harvard University. The quotations in this section are from a memorandum on China's Post-war Debt Policy, July 1945.

5. Harry B. Price, *UNRRA in China, 1945–1947*, published by UNRRA, Washington, 1948, pp. 11, 14, 32.

6. State Department file 893.51/6-745.

7. See *China and the Helping Hand*, pp. 385, 389–397.

XI. The Situation in Mid-1937

1. For details of American action concerning silver, its effects upon China, and the measures which China adopted, see Dickson H. Leavens, *Silver Money* (Cowles Commission for Research in Economics, Bloomington, Indiana, 1939); A. S. Everest, *Morgenthau, the New Deal, and Silver* (Columbia University, New York, 1950); and J. M. Blum, *From the Morgenthau Diaries* (Boston, 1959), chapters 5 and 10. For the texts of China's protests and the American replies, see Ministry

of Finance, *Report for the 21st and 22nd Fiscal Years, July 1932 to June 1934* (Nanking, 1935), pp. 21–23.

2. The plan was drawn by a Sino-foreign commission of which F. B. Lynch and I were members, the heaviest burden of the work having been borne by Cyril Rogers, who had been loaned to China by the Bank of England, and who was also a member of the commission.

3. For details of the Chinese banking system, see F. M. Tamagna, *Banking and Finance in China* (New York, 1942).

4. See G. H. Chang, *A Brief Survey of Chinese Native Banks*, Central Bank *Bulletin*, March 1938, pp. 25–32.

5. *Finance and Commerce*, February 23, 1938, p. 149, quoting the *Peking Chronicle*.

6. Re further data on these matters see note 1 of this chapter. American wartime buying of China's silver is discussed in chapter XV.

7. Wei-ya Chang, *Money and Finance of China*, p. 124.

XII. Prices, Exchange, Interest Rates

1. State Department file 124.936/2-2745.

2. Re the monthly rates of rise see appendix B, Table 49. Hyperinflation has been defined as beginning "in the month the rise in prices exceeds 50 per cent," and ending when the rate has been less than that for at least a year (see "The Monetary Dynamics of Hyperinflation," by Philip Cagan, in Milton Friedman, *Studies in the Quantity Theory of Money* (Chicago, 1956), p. 26. A 50 per cent monthly rise first appeared in China early in 1947.

3. Studies by the Research Department of the Central Bank of China and the University of Nanking showed that during the first years of the war there was high negative correlation (-0.739 and -0.696, respectively) between production and prices of rice. See *Price Movement in Wartime China*, memorandum, The Central Bank of China, October 1941; and J. L. Buck and K. H. Hu, The Price of Rice and its Determining Factors in Szechwan, *Economic Facts*, Chengtu, April 1941.

4. *Economic Facts*, and *Statistical Service*, issued weekly and monthly (in Chinese) by Nankai University Institute of Economics, Chungking, *passim*.

5. Weekly and monthly issues (in Chinese) of the *Statistical Service* of Nankai University Institute of Economics.

6. See Morgenthau Diaries, vol. 451, pp. 118–119.

7. *Kuo Min Kung Pao, Central Daily News*, December 1, 1942; *Hsin Hsu Pao*, December 10, 1942; *Central Daily News*, December 18, 1942; *Hsin Hua Jih Pao*, December 19, 1942.

8. State Department file 893.51/-1245.

9. See *China and the Helping Hand*, chapters XIV and XV.

10. Chou, *The Chinese Inflation*, pp. 250–253.

XIII. Credit, Note Issue, Deposits

1. Chang, *The Inflationary Spiral*, chapter 9; Chou, *The Chinese Inflation*, chaps. I and VI.

2. *Finance and Commerce*, January 1, 1941, p. 4, and January 15, 1941, p. 52.

3. Chou gives ratios for 1932–1948. Those for 1937–1945, while differing from those shown here, are of the same order of size. See Chou, *The Chinese Inflation*, p. 212.

4. Chang, *The Inflationary Spiral*, p. 187.

5. Chou, *The Chinese Inflation*, chap. VI, especially pp. 199–210.

XIV. Puppet, Japanese, and Communist Currencies

1. *Peking Chronicle*, quoted in *Finance and Commerce*, Shanghai, February 23, 1938, p. 149.

2. W. H. E. Thomas, *Vanished China* (London, 1952), p. 195.

3. G. E. Taylor, *The Struggle for North China* (New York, 1940), p. 84.

4. *South China Morning Post*, Hong Kong, September 9, 1938.

5. *FRUS, 1939*, vol. 3, pp. 375, 383.

6. *Ibid.*, pp. 376–381.

7. *Documents on British Foreign Policy, 1919–1939*, 3d ser., vol. 9, p. 224.

8. In *China and the Helping Hand*, pp. 154–158, I have described the pressure and blockade of the Concessions, the British resistance, and the compromise made.

9. *FRUS, 1939*, vol. 3, pp. 431, 440, 701.

10. Ministry of Finance, *Statistical Yearbook of Finance and Commerce of Japan*, Tokyo, 1948, p. 823. Especially in 1938–1939 much of the issue was held inactive by Japanese banks and by Japanese and puppet organs.

11. *Documents on British Foreign Policy, 1919–1939*, 3d ser., vol. 9, p. 463.

12. *FRUS, 1939*, vol. 4, pp. 243–255.

13. *Documents on British Foreign Policy, 1919–1939*, 3d ser., vol. 9, pp. 483–487.

14. *Manila Herald*, June 20, 1940.

15. *FRUS, 1939*, vol. 3, pp. 408–409.

16. *Ibid., 1940*, vol. 4, pp. 557, 564.

17. To help counteract the adverse effect of this move upon Free China, the American government announced immediately that it was making available a credit of US$100 million to China, of which half would be for currency support. The British also announced a currency credit of £5 million. See chapter XVI.

18. Report of A. B. Calder to the Secretary of State, November 16, 1942, pp. 1–3.

19. *Ibid.*, pp. 10–11.

20. *Ibid.*, pp. 7–10.

21. These practices are described at length in the report of September 12, 1938, The Currency Phase of Sino-Japanese Hostilities, by A. Bland Calder, Acting American Commercial Attaché in China.

22. *Far Eastern Financial Notes*, Department of Commerce, Washington, November 4, 1939, pp. 267–268.

23. Telegram from Bank of China, Hong Kong, to T. V. Soong, Washington, December 19, 1940; telegrams to Secretary of State from American embassy, Nanking, December 20, 1940, and from American consulate, Shanghai, January 10, 1941; *Finance and Commerce*, Shanghai, January 1, 1941.

24. *Foreign Commerce Weekly*, Washington, July 5, 1941, p. 19, report of Consul F. W. Hinke, based on statement by Chinese bankers.

25. Edgar Snow, *Red Star over China* (New York, 1938), see 1961 edition, pp. 222, 246; E. Kann, *Illustrated Catalog of Chinese Coins* (Hong Kong, 1954), pp. 278–284.

26. See the Report, *The Chinese Communist Movement, 5 July, 1945*, Military Intelligence Division, War Department, Washington, D.C., published in *Hearings, Institute of Pacific Relations*, before the Subcommittee to Investigate the Administration of the Internal Security Act . . . , of the Committee on the Judiciary, U.S. Senate, part 7 A, appendix II, 1952, pp. 2420–2422.

27. Cho-yuan Cheng, *Monetary Affairs of Communist China*, The Union Research Institute (Hong Kong, 1955), pp. 63–64.

28. *Hearings* (see note 26), p. 2421.

29. State Department file 893.00/15326.

XV. Monetary Management in the First Year

1. In *China and the Helping Hand*, pp. 30–34 and 61–62, I discuss the American wartime silver purchases from China from the standpoint of aid, and give a fuller account of the circumstances affecting the American policy and action. Regarding the American silver policy from 1933, and its effects on China, see Leavens, *Silver Money*, chaps. XXII, XXVIII–XXX, Blum, *From the Morgenthau Diaries*, chaps. V and X; and Everest, *Morgenthau, the New Deal, and Silver*.

2. Estimates of holdings in China at various times can be only guesses, based upon bank holdings, coinage effected, and recorded and smuggled imports and exports. Since the war, Nationalist China apparently has not exported silver, but communist China exported about 92 million ounces in 1959–1962. See Handy & Harman, *The Silver Market in 1963* (New York, 1964), p. 21. If we take the estimate cited in the text as the best available, the silver remaining in China as of 1964 would be of the order of 386 million ounces. Doubtless many people there still hold silver secreted as a personal reserve. The lack of recorded silver export in 1963, when communist China found difficulty in paying for imports of wheat and other goods, suggests either that (1) the regime has gathered already most of the silver on which it can lay hands; or (2) any remaining silver is being kept for an even greater emergency.

3. In the latter part of March 1938 a Treasury statement said that "the Treasury will defer continuation of the monthly silver purchase arrangements with Mexico until further notice." This caused weakness in the silver markets. For the Treasury view of this episode, see Blum, *From the Morgenthau Diaries*, pp. 493–497.

4. Everest, *Morgenthau and Silver*, p. 121.

5. The Treasury bought three million ounces of these coins that were at the San Francisco Mint.

6. Private sales of Chinese silver, mostly smuggled, are estimated at 600 million ounces, nearly all before the war. See appendix E, Table 65.

7. *China and the Helping Hand*, p. 34.

8. The customs gold unit (CGU) equaled US$0.6773. See note 5, chap. VI.

9. See the section on Prices in chap. XI.

10. Kia-ngau Chang, *The Inflationary Spiral*, pp. 213–214.

11. *Central News Agency*, April 29, 1938. Concerning this scheme see also Kia-ngau Chang, *The Inflationary Spiral*, pp. 186–188.

XVI. Stabilization Operations, June 1938 to August 1941

1. *Finance and Commerce*, Shanghai, October 26, p. 325; November 2, p. 345; and December 28, 1938, p. 513.

2. *FRUS, 1938*, vol. 3, pp. 582, 591; *1939*, vol. 3, pp. 639–648.

3. See chaps. IV and VII.

4. *Documents on British Foreign Policy, 1919–1939*, 3d ser., vol. 8, pp. 280, 295, 430–433.

5. The main provisions of the agreement are given in *ibid.*, vol. 8, pp. 486–487, and in *FRUS, 1939*, vol. 3, pp. 653–654.

6. *FRUS, 1939*, vol. 3, pp. 655–657.

7. There are no accurate figures of the wartime balance of payments. Trade data are of small value, because of large unrecorded Japanese imports and exports and varying bases of valuation of goods.

8. *FRUS, 1939*, vol. 3, pp. 396–401.

9. See chap. IV.

10. Periodic adjustments were contemplated but these rates stood until reduced to 4½d. and US$0.07½ in August 1940. There was no further change until the Stabilization Board, a year later, set rates of 3⁵⁄₃₂d. and US$0.05⁵⁄₁₆.

11. In 1939 France considered the possibility of joining with Britain in a credit for currency support, and was considering an advance of French francs 200 million, about US$5 million. But before anything could be consummated, the Anglo-Chinese fund had temporarily broken down. Then came World War II. See *FRUS, 1939*, vol. 3, pp. 674, 692.

12. *Central News Agency*, July 24, 1939.

13. I found no evidence, then or since, to support the charge that enemy operations in foreign exchange were an important factor in the exchange market in this period, or that the enemy obtained from the exchange support policy gains of sufficient substance to offset materially the clear advantages to China. See "The controversy: pro's and con's," later in this chapter.

14. *Central News Agency*, August 12, 1939.

15. *Documents on British Foreign Policy, 1919–1939*, 3d ser., vol. 9, pp. 341, 390, 490, 513.

16. *FRUS, 1939*, vol. 3, pp. 206–207, 854.

17. *China and the Helping Hand*, p. 164. Re the views of the American Commercial Attaché see *Far Eastern Financial Notes*, Department of Commerce, Washington, August 19, 1939.

18. See *FRUS, 1939*, vol. 3, pp. 677, 685.

19. For the text of the memorandum see *FRUS, 1939*, vol. 3, pp. 550–557.

20. *Ibid., 1940*, vol, 4, pp. 645–647.

21. *Ibid., 1940*, vol. 4, p. 651.

22. *Ibid., 1940*, vol. 4, p. 652, and *New York Times*, October 26, 1939.

23. Morgenthau Diaries, vol. 261, p. 199, May 10, 1940.

24. *FRUS, 1940*, vol. 4, pp. 656–657. Presentation of the first message, dated May 17, was delayed by exchanges between Ambassador Hu and Chungking about wording.

25. *Ibid., 1940*, vol. 4, pp. 654–656.

26. *Ibid., 1940*, vol. 4, pp. 658–659.

27. For an account from the Treasury's viewpoint of these matters and ensuing developments see Blum, *Morgenthau Diaries, 1938–1941*, pp. 345–348, 363–372, 376–381.

28. See *China and the Helping Hand*, pp. 170–171.

29. White's endorsement of July 2 on the memorandum said: "This is a copy of the preliminary draft which went to the Secretary and which I understand the Secretary took to the President." See Morgenthau Diaries, vol. 278, pp. 81–84, July 2, 1940.

30. See *China and the Helping Hand*, pp. 171–173.

31. For an example of this charge see the following statement by Richard A. Lester, *International Aspects of Wartime Monetary Experience*, Essays in International Finance, No. 3, August 1944, p. 5: "Until our Foreign Funds Control was extended to Japan and China in June [July], 1941, the Japanese were using their military currencies to acquire several hundred millions of American dollars, and British pounds sterling, with which they purchased scrap steel, oil, machine

tools, and other sinews of war. This they did either by obtaining Chinese national dollars in exchange for military currency or by using their military currency to obtain Chinese goods for export."

32. *Foreign Relations of the U.S., 1939*, vol. 3, pp. 402–403, contains Consul Smith's telegram. The information concerning the gold shipment was given me by a former officer of the Yokohama Specie Bank, from his records, in Tokyo in 1958.

33. *Far Eastern Financial Notes*, Department of Commerce, Washington, October 4, 1939, p. 240.

34. Repeatedly I argued the case both orally and in writing. A memorandum of July 4, 1939, is typical:

". . . the currency aspect of the war takes rank with the military as a major factor. Predominance of Chinese currency in the occupied areas shows to all that the Chinese Government remains a going concern despite military reverses. The strenuous efforts of the Japanese to substitute a currency under their own control, and their insistence that foreign governments should not help to sustain the Chinese currency, shows the importance they attach to the currency question. Maintenance of confidence in the currency of the people of these areas is highly important to sustain their loyalty and encourage resistance to the Japanese. Also guerrillas and Chinese organizations in the occupied areas can be financed in Chinese currency.

"On the other hand, if the Chinese currency should collapse it would open the way for the Japanese to introduce their own kind of currency. This would facilitate paying their military costs, financing of puppets, procurement of goods, labor, and property, and in general would aid in consolidation of their position which so far they have not been successful in doing.

"Moreover, . . . the Japanese would seize control of the financial system which would help them to dominate China's economy and exclude foreign interests. China has provided a free currency in which foreign exchange can be bought and sold; but the Japanese would introduce full exchange control and foreign firms could do only such business as the Japanese might permit.

". . . currency maintenance helps to hold back the inflationary forces that are inseparable from war. Should the rise of internal prices get out of hand, it would have serious internal repercussions economically, socially and perhaps politically. Sales of exchange in support of the market have very materially slowed down the inflationary forces by withdrawing from the markets a very large amount of Chinese currency.

". . . abandonment of the open market would be a serious defeat for China on the financial front."

35. Morgenthau Diaries, vol. 334, p. 13, December 1, 1940.

36. This memorandum said that holding behind the currency "adequate reserves . . . which will not be wasted" would sustain confidence. The new American and British funds should be used "entirely to strengthen the reserve of the national currency." The government was taking steps to develop the exchange market at Chungking, "which will be a free one provided purchasers have legitimate needs . . . It continues to be the Government's firm intention to maintain the value of the Chinese dollar both in terms of foreign exchange and in prices for domestic goods and services, but this policy is in respect to the value of the National Currency as a whole and not with reference to the black market in Shanghai or elsewhere."

37. *FRUS, 1941*, vol. 5, pp. 601–602.

38. *Ibid., 1941*, vol. 4, pp. 81–95, contains an extract from Currie's report of

March 15, 1941. The quotation above is from the full text, of which a photostatic copy was obtained by the State Department from the Franklin D. Roosevelt Library, Hyde Park, New York.

39. State Department file 893.51/7269.

40. Morgenthau Diaries, vol. 450, p. 365, October 14, 1941; vol. 496, p. 288, February 1, 1942.

41. The rise of average retail prices in the four half-yearly periods to mid-1941 was, respectively, 43, 51, 49, and 45 per cent. See appendix B, Table 48.

XVII. Freezing and Exchange Control, July to December 1941

1. Freezing was effected pursuant to the Trading with the Enemy Act of October 6, 1917, as amended. Under this authority the President issued Executive Order 8389 of April 10, 1940, which froze Norwegian and Danish assets after Hitler's invasion. Executive Order 8832 of July 26, 1941, froze the assets of China, Hong Kong, and Japan.

2. Morgenthau Diaries, vol. 238, p. 150, January 29, 1940, and vol. 263, p. 161, May 16, 1940; *FRUS, 1940*, vol. 4, p. 659; Herbert Feis, *The Road to Pearl Harbor* (Princeton, 1950), pp. 142–144; New York *Times*, January 19 and 20, 1941. For a further account from the Treasury viewpoint see Blum, *Morgenthau Diaries, 1938–1941*, pp. 326–343, 377–380.

3. In *China and the Helping Hand* I have discussed at length in chapter X the events leading to the freezing of Chinese and Japanese assets, and the consequences, from the viewpoint of aid to China and international relations. Here I discuss the events with special reference to currency and foreign exchange.

4. *FRUS, 1941*, vol. 5, p. 621.

5. See Currie's report, a photostatic copy of which the State Department later obtained from the Franklin D. Roosevelt Library, Hyde Park, N.Y.; the partial text of the report, *FRUS, 1941*, vol. 4, p. 93; and Morgenthau Diaries, vol. 390, pp. 4–7, April 19, 1941.

6. The editor of *Foreign Relations of the U.S.* told me in 1959 that no record of the Generalissimo's communication is in the Department's files.

7. *FRUS, 1941*, vol. 4, pp. 832–833, and vol. 5, p. 681.

8. See 40 Stat. 415, 55 Stat. 838, 840; *Documents Pertaining to Foreign Funds Control*, Treasury Department, Washington, June 15, 1945; and General License no. 58, U.S. Treasury Department, July 26, 1941.

9. *FRUS, 1941*, vol. 5, pp. 698–699.

10. Blum, *Morgenthau Diaries, 1938–1941*, p. 376.

11. Morgenthau Diaries, vol. 472, pp. 208–214, November 24, 1941.

12. *United Press* and *Reuter's News Agency* dispatches from Shanghai, October 14 and 15, 1941.

13. Morgenthau Diaries, vol. 472, pp. 208, 211, November 24, 1941, and vol. 496, pp. 285–288, February 1, 1942.

14. *Ibid.*, vol. 496, pp. 286–287, February 1, 1942.

15. *Ibid.*, vol. 485, p. 368, January 14, 1942, and vol. 496, p. 286, February 1, 1942.

16. *Ibid.*, vol. 463, p. 159, November 18, 1941.

17. State Department file 893.51/7259, 7311.

18. *Finance and Commerce*, April 16, 1941, p. 387.

19. *Ibid.*, July 9, 1941, p. 39.

20. *Ibid.*, July 16, 1941, p. 61.

21. The figures at the end of chapter II showing the estimated cash deficit

covered by credit inflation for 1939, 1940 and 1941 are, respectively, 79, 70, and 81 per cent. The 1940 figure, however, is derived after including as revenue C$725 million of receipts in respect of previous years. Deducting that item, the percentage for 1940 is 84 per cent, or larger than for 1941. Correspondingly, the percentages for 1939 and previous periods should be lower.

22. Morgenthau Diaries, vol. 472, pp. 208, 211, November 24, 1941; vol. 485, p. 368, January 14, 1942; vol. 496, pp. 285–288, February 1, 1942.

23. Letter of December 24, 1959, to Arthur N. Young.

24. The text of this letter of December 7, 1941, is in the record of the Hearings of the Subcommittee to Investigate the Administration of the Internal Security Act and Other Security Laws, of the Senate Committee on the Judiciary, July 13, 1956, part 35, pp. 1961–1964.

XVIII. Monetary Management during the Pacific War: Inflation, American Military Outlay, and the Rate of Exchange

1. See chapter XX and appendix B, Table 58 for comparison of the rate of rise of prices in China in 1937–1948 and in the most aggravated European inflations during and after World War I.

2. See chapter VI, note 5.

3. See also Romanus and Sunderland, *Stilwell's Command Problems*, pp. 288–293, regarding logistical problems of the American forces.

4. These figures are from a Treasury document prepared for the Bretton Woods financial negotiations of July 1944, on settlement of army costs (Morgenthau Diaries, vol. 754, pp. 52, 55). An earlier War Department resume dated May 19, 1944, puts the total at US$155.5 million (*U.S. Relations with China*, Washington, 1949, pp. 497, 501). I cannot explain the discrepancy, unless the latter is a preliminary figure that included the US$25 million paid in March 1944, in consideration of *fapi* advances for which no rate had been fixed.

5. Morgenthau Diaries, vol. 702, pp. 137–139, February 19, 1944.

6. Morgenthau Diaries, vol. 683, pp. 81, 94, December 10, 11, 1943; vol. 687, pp. 204–209, December 23, 1943.

7. Regarding the episode of the Chengtu bases, see State Department file 893.51/7750; and Morgenthau Diaries, vol. 702, pp. 137–139, February 19, 1944, vol. 705, pp. 160–165, March 1, 1944, vol. 714, pp. 215–216, March 27, 1944, and vol. 740, p. 337, April 13, 1944. See also *China and the Helping Hand*, pp. 299–306, for further discussion of this matter.

8. Morgenthau Diaries, vol. 798, pp. 203–248, November 25, 1944, and vol. 810, p. 171, January 17, 1945; *New York Times*, January 24, 1945.

9. Morgenthau Diaries, vol. 859, pp. 28–29, June 24, 1945. The New York *Times*, September 1, 1946, describes the surplus property deal.

10. See Executive Agreements, series no. 251, or 56 Stat. 1494.

11. Draft note of May 15 and memorandum of May 21, 1943, handed to Chinese representatives at Washington.

12. 21st Report to Congress on Lend-Lease Operations, September 30, 1945, p. 31, and 27th Report, March 31, 1948, p. 54.

For further information about provision by China of hostels and subsistence for American forces in China, see Romanus and Sunderland, *Stilwell's Command Problems*, pp. 290–291.

13. State Department files 893.51/5-2644 and 893.24/5-3045.

14. 27th Report to Congress on Lend-Lease Operations, March 31, 1948, p. 54.

15. New York *Times*, September 1, 1946.

16. *U.S. Relations with China, 1949*, p. 501.

17. *FRUS, 1942, China*, pp. 498–499.

In *China and the Helping Hand*, pp. 372–377, I present a fuller account of the negotiations bearing upon the end of the Board.

18. See Morgenthau Diaries, vol. 678, pp. 336–338, November 19, 1943, and *FRUS, 1942, China*, pp. 474–475. Re White's failure to present the matter fairly to the State Department, see *China and the Helping Hand*, pp. 374–375.

19. Finance Ministry announcement, April 13, 1945.

20. *China and the Helping Hand*, pp. 296, 298.

XIX. Gold, Given and Withheld

1. See my testimony before the Internal Security Subcommittee of the Senate Committee on the Judiciary, Hearings, July 13, 1956, re "Scope of Soviet Activity in the United States," Part 35, 84th Congress, Second Session, Washington, 1957. Hereinafter cited as Hearings, Part 35. Annexed to my testimony is the full text of many documents cited in this chapter.

2. *U.S. Relations with China, 1949*, p. 485.

3. For the texts of these communications, *ibid.*, pp. 485–488.

4. Message telegraphed July 31, 1943, through Chinese embassy, Washington.

5. *FRUS, 1943, China*, pp. 429, 431.

6. Morgenthau Diaries, vol. 666, p. 179, September 23, 1943; Hearings, Part 35, p. 1986.

7. Morgenthau Diaries, vol. 668, p. 68, September 29, 1943; Hearings, Part 35, p. 1987.

8. Morgenthau Diaries, vol. 682, p. 83, November 30, 1943; Hearings, Part 35, p. 1987.

9. *U.S. Relations with China, 1949*, p. 488.

10. Morgenthau Diaries, vol. 685, p. 26, December 17, 1943; Hearings, Part 35, p. 1990.

11. *U.S. Relations with China, 1949*, pp. 488–489.

12. Morgenthau Diaries, vol. 695, pp. 176 ff., January 19, 1944. See Report of the Subcommittee to Investigate the Administration of the Internal Security Act and Other Internal Security Laws, to the Committee on the Judiciary, U.S. Senate, 84th Congress, 2d session, December 31, 1956, section V, p. 72.

13. State Department file 893.51/7732.

14. For the minutes of this meeting, see *U.S. Relations with China, 1949*, pp. 502–504. For analysis of the arguments, see the following section of this chapter.

15. Morgenthau Diaries, vol. 802, pp. 1–3, December 9, 1944; Hearings, Part 35, pp. 1993–1994.

16. Morgenthau Diaries, vol. 807, pp. 257–259, January 3 and 5, 1945; Hearings, Part 35, p. 1994.

17. Morgenthau Diaries, vol. 814, p. 381, January 15, 1945.

18. *Ibid.*, vol. 824, pp. 230–236, March 2, 1945; vol. 825, p. 171, March 3, 1945; Hearings, Part 35, pp. 1999–2002.

19. *U.S. Relations with China, 1949*, p. 503.

20. From Harry D. White papers, lodged at the Princeton University Library, received by the Internal Security Subcommittee of the Senate Judiciary Committee, September 30, 1955. See Morgenthau Diaries, vol. 846, p. 35, where Morgenthau stated on May 10, 1945, in suggesting a letter to the President, that "there was a letter originally written on that to Mr. Roosevelt which I never took over."

21. Morgenthau Diaries, vol. 827, part I, pp. 53–55, March 11, 1945; Hearings,

Part 35, p. 1997. I was then in Washington and did not obtain detailed figures on the deficit by months.

22. Morgenthau Diaries, vol. 845, pp. 314–322, May 9, 1945; Hearings, Part 35, p. 2023.

23. *U.S. Relations with China, 1949*, p. 503.

24. State Department file 893.51/4-1245. Adler's memorandum outlined a policy of retarding inflation, in connection with Leon Henderson's visit to China.

25. Morgenthau Diaries, vol. 843, p. 106, May 1, 1945.

26. *Ibid.*, vol. 845, pp. 170–179, May 8, 1945. For the text of the memorandum see *U.S. Relations with China, 1949*, pp. 504–505.

27. Morgenthau Diaries, vol. 845, pp. 211 ff., 340, May 8, 1945.

28. *Ibid.*, vol. 845, p. 314, May 9, 1945; Hearings, Part 35, pp. 2022–2023.

29. Morgenthau Diaries, vol. 846, p. 32 ff., May 10, 1945; Hearings, Part 35, p. 2026.

30. Morgenthau Diaries, vol. 847, pp. 36–37, May 15, 1945; Hearings, Part 35, p. 2029.

31. Morgenthau Diaries, vol. 847, pp. 144–145, May 16, 1945; see also *U.S. Relations with China, 1949*, p. 507.

32. Morgenthau Diaries, vol. 847, pp. 149–150, May 16, 1945. For text of the letter see *U.S. Relations with China, 1949*, pp. 507–508.

33. See the Subcommittee's Report, section V, December 31, 1956, 84th Congress, 2d session, p. 71; and Nathan I. White, *Harry Dexter White, Loyal American* (Waban, Massachusetts, 1956).

34. Morgenthau Diaries, vol. 808, pp. 196–197, January 9, 1945; Hearings, Part 35, pp. 2035–2036.

XX. Economic Analysis

1. Gustav Cassel, *Money and Foreign Exchange after 1914* (New York, 1922).

2. Chang, *The Inflationary Spiral*, chap. 10.

3. Yin-Yuen Wang, "China's Agricultural Production in the War Period," in *Economic Facts*, September 1944, p. 539.

4. *China Handbook, 1943*, p. 567.

5. Romanus and Sunderland, *Stilwell's Command Problems*, pp. 413–414n. For figures of production of important commodities in the war period, see Chang, *The Inflationary Spiral*, pp. 379–381.

6. *Price Movement in Wartime China*, memorandum, Research Department, Central Bank, October 1941, pp. 14–15.

7. Chou, *The Chinese Inflation*, pp. 216–224.

8. *Ibid.*, pp. 217, 224.

9. For a definition of hyperinflation see chapter XII, note 2. In wartime China the rate of rise reached about 25 per cent monthly in 1945, but was checked by the war's ending (see appendix B, Table 49).

10. The rate for dollars announced by the Stabilization Board was C$18.82 to 1 as from August 18, 1941, and C$20 to 1 from July 10, 1942. The Central Bank announced a rate of 2,020 to 1 in February 1946.

11. For a discussion of the effects in the postwar period of fluctuating exchange rates that have a tendency to depreciate, see the *Annual Report, 1962* of the International Monetary Fund, Washington, 1963, pp. 62–67.

12. See *China and the Helping Hand*, chapter XIX.

13. An extract from the Chinese proposal is contained in appendix IV of *China and the Helping Hand*.

14. The Harry D. White papers in the Princeton University Library contain a copy of a letter of September 14, 1943, from Morgenthau to Kung, stating that the American experts would give special consideration to the needs of "China and countries in similar position." But the Treasury did not do so, and China had to press for changes at the Bretton Woods Conference, as explained on p. 311.

15. Morgenthau Diaries, vol. 756, pp. 184–191, July 20, 1944.

16. Inauguration of the Fund awaited ratification by countries with 65 per cent of the quotas. American approval under the Bretton Woods Act of July 31, 1945, practically assured that the Fund would come into being. It began operations in the spring of 1946.

17. See chapter X.

18. See *China and the Helping Hand*, pp. 229, 372.

19. *Ibid.*, pp. 282–285, 377.

XXI. The Effects of the Inflation

1. Letter from T. T. Chang in *China Weekly Review*, Shanghai, October 25, 1941.

2. At this time issuance of the dollar-backed bonds described in chapter VI was being considered.

3. See Chang, *The Inflationary Spiral*, p. 252.

4. For a further account of conditions at the war's end, see *China and the Helping Hand*, pp. 409–413, and Arthur N. Young, *China's Economic and Financial Reconstruction*, Committee on International Economic Policy (New York, 1947), pp. 12–13.

INDEX

HARVARD EAST ASIAN SERIES

1. China's Early Industrialization: Sheng Hsuan-huai (1844–1916) and Mandarin Enterprise. By Albert Feuerwerker.
2. Intellectual Trends in the Ch'ing Period. By Liang Ch'i-ch'ao. Translation by Immanuel C. Y. Hsü.
3. Reform in Sung China: Wang An-shih (1021–1086) and His New Policies. By James T. C. Liu.
4. Studies on the Population of China, 1368–1953. By Ping-ti Ho.
5. China's Entrance into the Family of Nations: The Diplomatic Phase, 1858–1880. By Immanuel C. Y. Hsü.
6. The May Fourth Movement: Intellectual Revolution in Modern China. By Chow Tse-tsung.
7. Ch'ing Administrative Terms: A Translation of the Terminology of the Six Boards with Explanatory Notes. Translated and edited by E-tu Zen Sun.
8. Anglo-American Steamship Rivalry in China, 1862–1874. By Kwang-Ching Liu.
9. Local Government in China under the Ch'ing. By T'ung-tsu Ch'ü.
10. Communist China 1955–1959: Policy Documents with Analysis. With a foreword by Robert R. Bowie and John K. Fairbank. (Prepared at Harvard University under the joint auspices of the Center for International Affairs and the East Asian Research Center.)
11. China and Christianity: The Missionary Movement and the Growth of Chinese Antiforeignism, 1860–1870. By Paul A. Cohen.
12. China and the Helping Hand, 1937–1945. By Arthur N. Young.
13. Research Guide to the May Fourth Movement: Intellectual Revolution in Modern China 1915–1924. By Chow Tse-tsung.
14. The United States and the Far Eastern Crises of 1933–1938: From the Manchurian Incident through the Initial Stage of the Undeclared Sino-Japanese War. By Dorothy Borg.
15. China and the West, 1858–1861: The Origins of the Tsungli Yamen. By Masataka Banno.
16. In Search of Wealth and Power: Yen Fu and the West. By Benjamin Schwartz.
17. The Origins of Entrepreneurship in Meiji Japan. By Johannes Hirschmeier, S.V.D.
18. Commissioner Lin and the Opium War. By Hsin-pao Chang.
19. Money and Monetary Policy in China, 1845–1895. By Frank H. H. King.
20. China's Wartime Finance and Inflation, 1937–1945. By Arthur N. Young.